The Art of Reverse Engineering

Unveiling the Secrets of Software Deconstruction
Introduction

Williams Moses

Copyright © 2025 Williams Moses

Table of Content

Preface

Welcome to *The Art of Reverse Engineering: Unveiling the Secrets of Software Deconstruction*. In an era where digital transformations are accelerating at an unprecedented pace, understanding the inner workings of software has never been more crucial. This book is born from the need to demystify the intricate process of reverse engineering a discipline that sits at the crossroads of innovation, cybersecurity, and creative problem-solving.

As you hold this book, you are about to embark on a journey that bridges theory and practice. My goal is to equip you whether you are an aspiring reverse engineer, a software developer looking to deepen your understanding, or a cybersecurity professional with the tools and insights required to navigate complex systems and uncover hidden design decisions. Every chapter is crafted to move from foundational concepts to advanced methodologies, ensuring that readers of all skill levels can find value and practical guidance.

The rapid evolution of technology brings challenges and opportunities alike. This book explores the latest trends, including the integration of artificial intelligence into reverse engineering processes, modern cybersecurity threats, and the emerging landscape of cloud-based and mobile environments. I have drawn upon a wealth of contemporary research, real-world examples, and hands-on case studies to ensure that the content is as current as it is robust.

Moreover, reverse engineering is not just a technical practice; it carries with it significant legal and ethical considerations. In these pages, you will find discussions that highlight the responsibilities and boundaries inherent in exploring and deconstructing software. It is my sincere hope that you will approach these insights with a thoughtful mindset, using your skills to innovate and protect in a rapidly changing world.

I extend my gratitude to the myriad experts, mentors, and communities who have contributed to my understanding of reverse engineering over the years. Their collective experience and shared knowledge have been invaluable in shaping this work.

Thank you for choosing this book as your guide. May it inspire you to look beyond the surface, challenge conventional boundaries, and unlock the secrets that lie within the very fabric of modern software systems.

Introduction

Welcome to an exploration of the fascinating world of reverse engineering! Whether you're a curious beginner, a seasoned developer, or a cybersecurity enthusiast, this chapter will serve as your friendly introduction and guide into the art and science of understanding software systems from the inside out.

What Is Reverse Engineering?

Imagine having a beautifully wrapped gift in front of you. You know there's something amazing inside, but the wrapping hides its secrets. Reverse engineering is a bit like carefully unwrapping that gift. It's the process of taking an existing piece of software—sometimes even without access to the original source code—and uncovering its design, functionality, and structure. This process can reveal vulnerabilities, unlock innovative ideas, and help build robust defenses against cyber threats.

In simple terms, reverse engineering allows you to "read" a program like a book, decrypt its logic, and see how each piece contributes to the overall functionality.

Why Reverse Engineering Matters

Today's digital landscape is full of complex, interconnected systems that power everything from our smartphones to critical infrastructure. Understanding these systems is essential for multiple reasons:

Innovation and Improvement: Reverse engineering can spark creativity, enabling engineers to learn from existing technologies and innovate new solutions.

Security Analysis: By breaking down code, security professionals can identify vulnerabilities and protect systems from malicious attacks.

Interoperability: It helps in understanding how disparate systems communicate, which is crucial for integrating new software with legacy systems.

Educational Value: For many, reverse engineering is an enlightening exercise that deepens one's understanding of how software truly works beneath the surface.

A Roadmap for This Journey

Before diving into the technical aspects, it's helpful to know how this book is organized. We'll move gradually from the basics to more advanced techniques:

Foundations: We start by establishing a clear understanding of software architecture, programming paradigms, and system operations.

Tools and Techniques: Next, you'll become acquainted with the essential toolkit of a reverse engineer—from disassemblers and debuggers to automated analysis tools.

Hands-On Analysis: Through step-by-step tutorials, you'll practice both static and dynamic analysis. We'll illustrate these techniques with real-world examples that you can try on your own.

Ethical and Legal Considerations: As we explore these powerful techniques, we'll also address the responsibilities that come with them. Ethical reverse engineering isn't just good practice—it's a critical part of maintaining trust and safety in the digital world.

Emerging Trends: Finally, we peer into the future, examining how advancements like artificial intelligence and machine learning are revolutionizing the field.

Getting the Most Out of This Book

This book isn't meant to be a one-way lecture. I invite you to actively engage with the content—experiment with the tools, try out the examples, and pose questions as you learn. Every chapter is designed to build not only your technical skills but also your critical thinking. Remember, the goal is not just to know how to take things apart, but to understand why things work the way they do and how you can reimagine them.

Throughout this journey, you might encounter concepts that feel challenging at first. That's completely normal! Reverse engineering, like any skill, takes time and practice to master. Embrace the challenge, and don't hesitate to revisit topics, experiment with your tools, and even explore additional resources offered in the appendices.

A Conversation on Ethics and Responsibility

Before we wrap up this introduction, it's vital to talk about the responsibility inherent in reverse engineering. With the ability to unlock the secrets of software comes the duty to use that knowledge wisely. In subsequent chapters, we delve into the legal frameworks and ethical standards that govern this field—ensuring that your newfound skills contribute positively to innovation and security rather than undermining intellectual property or privacy.

Let's Begin the Journey

Take a moment to reflect on what drew you here—whether it's a spark of curiosity, the desire to protect against cyber threats, or the pursuit of innovative software solutions. Now, let's embark on this journey together, unwrapping the layers of complexity one chapter at a time. I'm excited to guide you through the art of reverse engineering, and I hope that by the end of this book, you'll not only understand how to deconstruct software but also appreciate the intricate beauty of its design.

Chapter 1: Foundations of Reverse Engineering

welcome to the real starting line! In the Introduction, we peeked behind the curtain. Now, we're stepping through the door to properly explore this intriguing space called reverse engineering (RE). Think of this chapter as laying the groundwork – our foundation stones. Before we can build anything complex, we need to understand the terrain, where this field came from, and why it's so darn important today.

We'll break this down into three main parts:

What exactly *is* reverse engineering? We'll define it and figure out its boundaries.

Where did it come from? A little trip down memory lane to see how RE evolved.

1.1. Definition and Scope: Unpacking the Black Box

let's begin our exploration by establishing exactly what we mean by "reverse engineering," clarifying its fundamental definition and mapping out the vast territory it covers. It's more than just a technical term; it's a specific mindset, a methodical approach to uncovering the secrets hidden within complex systems when the original design documents, source code, or schematics are unavailable.

What Exactly is Reverse Engineering? Deconstructing the 'Black Box'

At its absolute core, reverse engineering is the **process of analyzing a subject system to identify its components, understand the relationships between those components, and determine precisely how the system functions and achieves its intended purpose.** This analysis is typically undertaken when we lack access to the original design specifications or source materials provided by the creator. Think of it as engineering in reverse gear: instead of starting with requirements and designing a solution, we start with the finished solution – the "black box" – and work backward to deduce the design, logic, and operational principles.

Imagine being presented with an intricate mechanical clockwork device encased in glass. You can observe its external behavior – the hands moving, perhaps chimes ringing – and maybe even provide inputs, like winding a spring. This is the "black box" perspective. A reverse engineer, however, isn't content with just observing the outside. They strive to understand the internal mechanism: What specific gears, levers, and springs constitute the device? How do these individual parts mesh and interact? What underlying principles govern their movement to produce the clock's behavior? They might carefully disassemble the device (conceptually or, in hardware cases, physically), study each component, trace the connections, and reconstruct the logic of its operation.

This process is fundamentally one of **deduction, inference, and structured analysis**. It often feels like solving an elaborate puzzle, where the available pieces are the observable behavior, the raw structure (like compiled machine code or physical circuitry), and the interactions with the environment (like network traffic or file I/O). The reverse engineer uses specialized tools and techniques – akin to a detective's magnifying glass, fingerprint kit, and forensic analysis methods – to gather clues, form hypotheses about the internal workings, test those hypotheses through further examination or controlled interaction, and gradually build a coherent model of the system's design and function.

That moment of breakthrough, when disparate clues suddenly connect and the underlying logic snaps into focus, is incredibly rewarding. It might be realizing how a complex algorithm is implemented from tangled assembly code, deciphering an unknown network protocol by analyzing packet captures, or understanding the purpose of an obscure hardware component. This intellectual challenge and the satisfaction derived from uncovering hidden mechanisms are significant driving forces for many who practice reverse engineering. It's a discipline that deeply engages analytical thinking and rewards persistent investigation.

Mapping the Terrain: The Broad Scope of Reverse Engineering

While this book will maintain a strong focus on **software** reverse engineering, it's crucial to appreciate that the principles and mindset extend far beyond executable files. The scope is remarkably broad, touching nearly every aspect of modern technology. Understanding these different facets helps appreciate the versatility and importance of the skill set.

Software Reverse Engineering: This is our primary domain. It involves analyzing software in its various forms, typically when source code is unavailable. Targets include:

Compiled Applications: Desktop programs (.exe on Windows, ELF binaries on Linux, Mach-O on macOS), command-line utilities, server-side applications.

Libraries: Shared libraries (.dll, .so, .dylib) that contain reusable code used by multiple applications. Understanding their internal functions or exported interfaces is often necessary.

Mobile Applications: Analyzing Android (.apk files containing DEX bytecode) and iOS (.ipa files containing compiled ARM native code) apps for security, functionality, or interoperability.

Firmware: The low-level software embedded directly within hardware devices (IoT gadgets, routers, controllers, BIOS/UEFI). Analyzing firmware often requires hardware interaction to extract it first.

Web Applications (Client-Side): Primarily involves analyzing the JavaScript, HTML, and CSS running in the user's browser to understand front-end logic, UI interactions, and especially how the client communicates with backend servers via APIs.

Malware: A critical security application involving the dissection of viruses, worms, trojans, ransomware, and spyware to understand their behavior, develop defenses, and attribute attacks.

Hardware Reverse Engineering (HRE): Venturing into the physical realm, HRE focuses on understanding the construction, components, and operation of electronic hardware. This might be done to:

Extract Firmware/Software: Directly accessing memory chips (like Flash or EEPROM) when software-based extraction fails.

Understand Interfaces: Figuring out undocumented communication protocols between chips on a board (e.g., SPI, I2C) or external connectors.

Analyze Security: Identifying hardware vulnerabilities, potential for side-channel attacks (gleaning information from power consumption or timing), or weaknesses against physical tampering.

Competitive Analysis: Understanding how a competitor's device achieves its performance or features (though this treads into complex legal and ethical territory).

HRE techniques range from non-invasive visual inspection and signal probing with multimeters/oscilloscopes/logic analyzers, to semi-invasive methods like accessing JTAG/SWD debug ports, up to highly invasive and often destructive techniques like chemical chip decapsulation and microscopic imaging of silicon layers.

Protocol Reverse Engineering: This focuses on deciphering the rules and formats governing communication between systems when documentation is lacking. It involves analyzing the actual data exchanged:

Network Protocols: Capturing and analyzing network traffic (using tools like Wireshark) between a client and server, or peer-to-peer, to understand custom TCP/UDP protocols, undocumented REST API structures, or proprietary application-layer communication.

Hardware Bus Protocols: Analyzing signals captured from hardware buses like USB, SPI, I2C, or CAN bus to understand how peripheral devices communicate with a main controller.

The goal is to reconstruct the message formats, understand the sequence of interactions, identify state machines, and determine the meaning of different commands or data fields.

File Format Reverse Engineering: Programs often read and write data to files using proprietary or undocumented formats. Analyzing these formats is necessary for:

Interoperability: Allowing different programs to read or write the same data.

Data Recovery: Extracting information from files created by obsolete or unavailable software.

Forensics: Understanding data storage structures relevant to an investigation.

Modding/Customization: Understanding save game formats or configuration files to allow modification.

This involves using tools like hex editors to examine the raw byte structure, identifying patterns (like headers, magic numbers, fixed-size fields, length prefixes, or chunk structures like Type-Length-Value), and often correlating file contents with the behavior of the program that uses them.

Conceptual Code Example: Basic File Type Identification

One of the simplest RE tasks is identifying a file type based on its "magic number" – a few specific bytes at the very beginning. We can simulate this deduction:

```
# Conceptual File Type ID using Python
import os
```

```python
def identify_file_type_from_header(filepath):
    """
    Attempts to identify a file type based on the first few
bytes (magic number).
    This is a simplified illustration of a common RE task.
    """
    try:
        # Open the file in binary read mode
        with open(filepath, 'rb') as f:
            # Read the first, say, 8 bytes - enough for many
common headers
            header_bytes = f.read(8)
    except FileNotFoundError:
        return f"Error: File '{os.path.basename(filepath)}'
not found."
    except PermissionError:
        return f"Error: Permission denied for file
'{os.path.basename(filepath)}'."
    except Exception as e:
        return f"Error reading file
'{os.path.basename(filepath)}': {e}"

    if not header_bytes:
        return f"File '{os.path.basename(filepath)}' is
empty."

    hex_representation = header_bytes.hex().upper()
    print(f"Read header from '{os.path.basename(filepath)}':
0x{hex_representation}")

    # Define known magic numbers (a small subset)
    # Format: magic_bytes: description
    known_signatures = {
        b'\x89PNG\x0D\x0A\x1A\x0A': "PNG Image File",
        b'\x47\x49\x46\x38\x37\x61': "GIF Image File
(GIF87a)",
        b'\x47\x49\x46\x38\x39\x61': "GIF Image File
(GIF89a)",
        b'\xFF\xD8\xFF':            "JPEG Image File (starts
with)", # Often need to check following bytes too
        b'\x25\x50\x44\x46':        "PDF Document (starts
with '%PDF')", # Check start
        b'\x50\x4B\x03\x04':        "ZIP Archive Entry
(PKZip)",
        b'\x7F\x45\x4C\x46':        "ELF Executable/Object
File (Linux/Unix)",
        b'\x4D\x5A':                "Windows PE Executable
(starts with 'MZ')" # Common 2-byte check
    }

    # Perform checks (more specific longer signatures first)
```

```python
    for sig, desc in known_signatures.items():
        if header_bytes.startswith(sig):
            # Special handling for MZ check (only need 2
bytes)
            if sig == b'\x4D\x5A' and len(header_bytes) >= 2
and header_bytes.startswith(sig):
                return f"Detected Type: {desc}"
            elif sig != b'\x4D\x5A' and
header_bytes.startswith(sig):
                return f"Detected Type: {desc}"


    return "File type unknown based on known headers."

# --- Demonstration ---
# Create dummy files with known headers for testing
try:
    files_info = {
        "document.pdf": b'\x25\x50\x44\x46\x2d\x31\x2e\x37',
# %PDF-1.7
        "archive.zip":  b'\x50\x4B\x03\x04\x14\x00\x00\x00',
# PK..
        "program.elf":  b'\x7F\x45\x4C\x46\x02\x01\x01\x00',
# .ELF..
        "image.png":    b'\x89PNG\x0D\x0A\x1A\x0A\x00\x00',
        "installer.exe":b'\x4D\x5A\x90\x00\x03\x00\x00\x00',
# MZ..
        "data.unknown": b'\x12\x34\x56\x78\x9A\xBC\xDE\xF0',
# Random bytes
        "empty.file":   b''
    }
    for fname, data in files_info.items():
        with open(fname, 'wb') as f:
            f.write(data)

    # Analyze the created files
    print("--- File Analysis ---")
    for filename in files_info.keys():
        result = identify_file_type_from_header(filename)
        print(f"-> {result}\n")

    # Clean up dummy files
    print("--- Cleaning up ---")
    for filename in files_info.keys():
        if os.path.exists(filename): os.remove(filename)
        print(f"Removed {filename}")

except Exception as e:
    print(f"An error occurred during file creation/deletion:
{e}")
```

Explanation: This script simulates the reverse engineer's initial step when faced with an unknown file. It reads the first few bytes and compares them against a dictionary of known "magic numbers." This simple act of examining the file's prefix, a core RE technique, often provides the first crucial clue about the file's nature and guides subsequent analysis using format-specific tools.

Cryptography Implementation Analysis: While breaking modern, well-established cryptographic algorithms (like AES, RSA, SHA-3) is generally considered computationally infeasible, reverse engineering often focuses on *how* these algorithms are *implemented* within software or hardware. The goal is usually to find weaknesses in the surrounding logic:

Are keys hardcoded directly in the binary? (A major vulnerability!)

Are keys generated using weak pseudo-random number generators?

Are keys stored insecurely in configuration files or memory?

Are standard algorithms used incorrectly (e.g., reusing nonces, using weak modes of operation)?

Does the implementation leak information through side channels (timing differences, power consumption variations)?

Finding such implementation flaws can completely undermine the security provided by an otherwise strong cryptographic algorithm.

Crucial Distinctions: What Reverse Engineering Is *Not*

To fully grasp the definition and scope, it's equally important to understand what reverse engineering *isn't*, clearing up common points of confusion. First, while debugging tools are absolutely essential for *dynamic* reverse engineering (as we'll see later), RE is **not simply debugging** in the traditional software development sense. Typical debugging involves finding and fixing flaws (bugs) in source code that you, the developer, wrote or have access to. You understand the intended logic and use the debugger to pinpoint deviations. Reverse engineering, however, frequently begins precisely *because* the source code is unavailable. The primary goal isn't necessarily fixing bugs (though identifying them is a common outcome), but rather achieving a fundamental *understanding* of the unknown code's structure, algorithms, and behavior. Debugging *without* source code is a core RE technique, used for exploration and verification rather than repair based on original blueprints.

Second, and this cannot be overstressed, reverse engineering is **not intrinsically malicious hacking**. The confusion arises because the technical *skills* and *tools* used can overlap significantly. Both a security researcher performing ethical vulnerability analysis and a malicious attacker seeking to exploit a system might use a disassembler and debugger to find weaknesses. However, the critical differentiator lies in **intent** and **authorization**. Ethical reverse engineering operates within legal frameworks and ethical guidelines, with objectives like enhancing security, achieving interoperability, conducting research, or learning. Malicious hacking uses these skills without authorization for illegal or harmful purposes, such as stealing data, disrupting services, or bypassing legitimate access controls. Throughout this guide, we emphasize the ethical and legal responsibilities inherent in wielding these powerful techniques.

Finally, reverse engineering goes far beyond simply **learning how to use** a piece of software. A regular user interacts with the application through its intended interface, understanding its features and menus. A reverse engineer seeks to peel back that interface and understand the complex machinery humming beneath the surface – the specific algorithms processing data, the logic handling user input, the way data is stored and transmitted, and the design decisions made by the original creators. It's the difference between knowing how to drive a car and understanding exactly how the engine, transmission, and electronic control unit work together to make it move.

In Essence: The Pursuit of Hidden Knowledge

Ultimately, reverse engineering is this dedicated, methodical pursuit of understanding the internal workings of man-made systems when direct access to the design information is unavailable. It combines elements of detective work, puzzle-solving, scientific investigation, and deep technical expertise. It requires patience, meticulous attention to detail, the ability to form and test hypotheses based on limited information, and proficiency with specialized analytical tools. It is a critical skill for anyone seeking to truly understand, secure, or interact with the complex technological systems that define our modern world, especially when those systems are presented as opaque "black boxes."

1.2. Historical Evolution: From Gears to Gigabytes

let's delve into the rich history of reverse engineering, tracing its lineage not just through the digital age but from its much deeper roots. Understanding this evolution isn't merely a historical curiosity; it provides crucial context for why reverse engineering is practiced today, reveals the origins of many fundamental techniques, and highlights how the discipline has constantly adapted in response to technological advancement and human motivations ranging from national security to commercial competition and sheer intellectual curiosity. It's a journey from analyzing physical mechanisms to deciphering the most complex digital creations.

Ancient Origins: Understanding the Physical World Through Deconstruction

The fundamental human desire to understand how things work by taking them apart predates electronics, software, and perhaps even recorded history itself. One can easily imagine an early human examining a captured, superior hunting tool or a more effective pottery technique developed by a neighboring tribe, trying to deduce the materials, design, and construction methods to replicate or improve upon it. This act of learning from a finished artifact, working backward from the product to the process, embodies the core spirit of reverse engineering.

Throughout history, this approach became more formalized, particularly in contexts of **craftsmanship, competition, and conflict**. Artisans seeking to master their trade would carefully study the works of renowned masters, deconstructing their techniques in ceramics, metallurgy, weaving, or construction. Trade guilds often guarded their methods fiercely, precisely because others could potentially reverse engineer their creations, diminishing their competitive advantage. This economic driver – the need to understand a competitor's product to either replicate its success, build a compatible alternative, or simply learn from its innovations – has been a constant theme. Early manufacturers of complex mechanical devices, from clocks to looms to firearms, undoubtedly engaged in dissecting competitors' products.

The stakes were raised considerably in **military applications**. Gaining an edge in warfare often depended on understanding and countering an adversary's technology. Analyzing captured weaponry, deciphering enemy communication systems, or understanding the capabilities of opposing vehicles became critical intelligence functions. The canonical example, often cited, is the monumental effort by Allied cryptanalysts, particularly at Bletchley Park during World War II, to understand the inner workings of the German **Enigma and Lorenz encryption machines**. This wasn't just theoretical cryptanalysis; it involved meticulous hardware reverse engineering based on captured machines, analyzing the rotors, wiring, plugboards, and operational procedures to uncover cryptographic weaknesses and build deciphering machines like the Bombe and Colossus. The success of this endeavor dramatically impacted the course of the war, demonstrating the profound strategic significance of reverse engineering even complex electro-mechanical systems. Similar efforts, though perhaps less famous, occurred throughout military history with captured artillery, aircraft, and communication equipment. The core activity remained the same: starting with a functional, often poorly understood system, and deducing its internal design and operational principles through careful examination and analysis.

The Electronic Age: Circuits, Signals, and Systems

With the advent of electronics in the early-to-mid 20th century, the targets of reverse engineering shifted from purely mechanical systems to increasingly complex arrangements of vacuum tubes, transistors, resistors, capacitors, and wiring. The fundamental motivations, however, persisted. The burgeoning electronics industry, encompassing radio, television, radar, and early computing, was fiercely competitive. Companies frequently engaged in analyzing competitors' circuits to understand design choices, identify key components (sometimes needing to figure out the properties of unlabeled or custom parts), learn new amplification or signal processing techniques, or simply check for patent infringement.

The methods evolved alongside the technology. While visual inspection remained crucial, understanding electronic circuits required new tools and techniques. Engineers used **multimeters** to measure voltages and resistances, **oscilloscopes** to visualize changing electrical signals over time, and eventually **logic analyzers** to capture and decode complex digital communication between components. Tracing intricate connections on printed circuit boards (PCBs) became a standard practice. Datasheets for standard components were invaluable, but analyzing systems often involved dealing with undocumented custom chips or obscured designs. This era solidified the link between reverse engineering and competitive intelligence in high-technology fields, laying the groundwork for analyzing the hardware

aspects of computing systems. Even early computing hardware, predating complex software, was subject to this form of analysis for understanding logic designs or peripheral interfaces.

The Software Dawn: Mainframes, Minicomputers, and the Documentation Void

The true genesis of what we now typically call *software* reverse engineering began as computers transitioned from specialized hardware calculators to programmable machines running complex instruction sequences. In the era of mainframes and minicomputers (roughly the 1950s through the 1970s), software was often bespoke, developed in-house by large organizations or bundled tightly with expensive hardware from vendors like IBM, DEC, or Sperry. This environment created unique pressures that necessitated understanding existing, often opaque, software systems.

One major driver was the lack of comprehensive **documentation**. Software development practices were still maturing, and thorough documentation explaining design choices, algorithms, file formats, and interfaces was often an afterthought or became outdated quickly. Personnel turnover added another layer of complexity; the original developers who held crucial knowledge in their heads might leave the organization, leaving behind critical software systems that nobody fully understood anymore. Yet, these systems often represented massive investments and performed vital business functions. The need to **maintain, update, or integrate** these aging behemoths became a powerful motivator for reverse engineering.

Imagine being tasked with fixing a bug in, or adding a feature to, a critical payroll system written a decade earlier in a specific vendor's assembly language, with minimal documentation and no access to the original developers. Your only resource would be the compiled object code or perhaps voluminous printouts of the assembly language itself. The process was incredibly **labor-intensive and painstaking**. Analysts would manually trace execution flow through listings, often using pencil and paper to track register values and memory changes. They might use rudimentary debugging tools provided by the vendor (often capable only of setting simple breakpoints and examining memory/registers), or even physically manipulate console switches to step through instructions. Deciphering non-obvious algorithms, understanding proprietary file structures stored on magnetic tape, or figuring out undocumented operating system interfaces required immense patience and deep expertise in the specific hardware architecture and assembly language. This wasn't recreational hacking; it was often a business necessity born from the challenges of managing complex, poorly documented software assets in the early days of computing.

The Microcomputer Revolution and the Rise of Software as a Product

The landscape transformed dramatically with the advent of microcomputers – the Apple II, Commodore PET, TRS-80, and crucially, the IBM PC – in the late 1970s and early 1980s. This era democratized computing, making it accessible to individuals and small businesses. Critically, it also decoupled software from hardware in a significant way. Software became a **mass-market commodity**, sold independently on floppy disks through retail channels. This created a huge economic incentive for developers but also introduced a massive new problem: **software piracy**.

Unlike mainframe software tightly controlled within organizations, PC software could be easily copied from one floppy disk to another. To protect their revenue streams, software companies began implementing various forms of **copy protection**. Early methods were often relatively simple: requiring users to type a specific word from the physical manual, using code wheels that needed to be aligned based on on-screen prompts, or performing basic checks to see if the software was running from the original distribution diskette.

However, disk-based protections quickly became more sophisticated. Techniques included:

Non-standard formatting: Writing data to floppy tracks or sectors in ways that standard operating system copying utilities couldn't replicate.

Intentional errors: Deliberately writing bad sectors or data with incorrect checksums to the disk, which the program would check for during startup. Copy programs would often try to "correct" these errors, revealing the copy.

Physical modifications: Some schemes involved minor physical alterations to the disk media itself (like small laser-drilled holes - "laser-locks"), requiring custom hardware in the drive to detect.

Dongles (early forms): Though more common later, some early protection involved hardware devices plugged into joystick or serial ports.

This widespread use of copy protection, often perceived by users as inconvenient or overly restrictive, inadvertently became the primary catalyst for the development and popularization of software reverse engineering techniques outside of corporate or military contexts.

The 'Cracking Scene': An Adversarial Crucible Forging Tools and Techniques

In direct response to copy protection, the **"software cracking scene"** emerged and flourished throughout the 1980s and early 1990s. This subculture consisted primarily of hobbyists, students, and technically skilled individuals motivated by a mixture of factors: the intellectual challenge of defeating complex protections, the desire for access to software without paying, a philosophical opposition to copy restrictions, or simply the pursuit of notoriety within their community. While their activities were often illegal and ethically questionable (primarily software piracy), the technical impact of this scene on the evolution of reverse engineering tools and methods is undeniable.

Early crackers operated with relatively primitive tools. Initial efforts involved manual tracing, much like the mainframe analysts, but often aided by simple **monitor programs** that allowed pausing execution, viewing memory, and changing bytes. The limitations of these tools spurred innovation. There was a strong need for tools that could:

Disassemble machine code back into readable assembly language, automatically identifying instructions and operands for the popular processors of the day (like the 6502, Z80, and especially the Intel 8088/8086). Early disassemblers were often basic, providing linear listings, but represented a huge leap over reading raw machine code.

Debug programs more effectively. This led to the development of increasingly sophisticated debuggers that could handle the complexities of segmented memory on early PCs, set various types of breakpoints, step through code gracefully, and present system state clearly. Tools that could operate underneath the operating system (like the famous SoftICE, which hooked into low-level system interrupts) became highly sought after because they were harder for protection schemes to detect.

Analyze Disk Structures: Tools specifically designed to read and analyze non-standard floppy disk formats, bypassing operating system limitations, were crucial for understanding and duplicating many disk-based protection schemes.

The *process* employed by these early crackers established many fundamental RE workflows still used today. They would meticulously:

Locate the Protection Code: Run the program under a debugger or tracer, deliberately triggering the copy protection check (e.g., by trying to run a copied version or failing a manual check). Observe where the program's execution path diverged or where failure messages originated.

Analyze the Check: Disassemble the relevant code sections. Understand the logic – what condition is being checked? Is it reading from a specific disk sector? Comparing a calculated value? Calling an external protection routine?

Identify the Bypass Point: Find the specific conditional jump instruction (JE, JNE, JZ, etc.) that determined whether the check passed or failed.

Patch the Code: The simplest bypass was often to directly modify the binary executable file. This usually involved changing the conditional jump to an unconditional jump (JMP) or replacing it with NOP (No Operation) instructions, effectively forcing the "success" path regardless of the check's outcome. Alternatively, sometimes changing a single byte in a comparison or zeroing out a specific check value was sufficient. This required basic hex editing skills.

Handle Anti-Tampering: Protectors quickly fought back. They introduced **checksums** (calculating a value based on the program's code and checking it at runtime to detect modifications) and **self-modifying code** (where the program altered its own instructions during execution, making static analysis harder and potentially breaking simple patches). Crackers then had to find and disable these secondary checks as well, sometimes involving complex tracing or recalculating checksums.

This intense back-and-forth between protection developers and crackers created a highly adversarial environment that rapidly accelerated the evolution of both offensive (cracking) and defensive (protection) techniques. While driven by often illicit motives, the cracking scene inadvertently served as a demanding crucible, forging many low-level analysis techniques and driving the demand for better disassemblers and debuggers, tools which later found widespread use in legitimate security research and software analysis.

Legitimate Needs Persist: Interoperability, Compatibility, and Competition

While the cracking scene garnered much attention, the legitimate needs for reverse engineering continued and arguably grew in importance, particularly concerning **Interoperability** and **Compatibility**. As the computer industry expanded, users and businesses increasingly needed different hardware and software components, often from competing vendors, to work together seamlessly. However, dominant players often had little incentive to fully document their interfaces, viewing proprietary control as a competitive advantage.

This created situations where competitors or third-party developers needed to understand undocumented aspects of widely used operating systems (like MS-DOS system calls and internal structures, early Windows messaging protocols, or file system layouts like FAT), hardware interfaces (like the PC BIOS or specific expansion card protocols), or application file formats to create compatible products. For example, developing a competing spreadsheet program might require understanding how Lotus 1-2-3 stored its files. Building a compatible graphics card required understanding how software interacted with the BIOS video routines and standard IBM cards. Performing reverse engineering for interoperability presented significant legal risks, primarily around copyright infringement. Simply copying disassembled code was clearly illegal. This led to the development of strategies like the **"Clean Room" design process**. In this approach, one team (the "dirty room") performs the necessary reverse engineering to understand the undocumented interface and produces a detailed specification document describing *only* the functional requirements and interface behavior, without including any of the original, copyrighted code implementation. A second, completely separate team (the "clean room"), having never seen the original product or its reversed code, then uses only this specification document to independently develop a new, compatible implementation. This painstaking process aimed to create a legal firewall, arguing that the final product was based only on the functional specification (which describes unprotected ideas and interfaces) and not derived directly from the copyrighted expression of the original code.

Several high-profile lawsuits tested the boundaries of reverse engineering for interoperability. The *Sega v. Accolade* case (1992) was particularly significant. Accolade had reverse engineered Sega Genesis console code to understand the mechanism required for third-party games to run on the console. The court ultimately ruled that Accolade's reverse engineering, undertaken solely to understand the functional requirements for compatibility and resulting in a non-infringing compatible product, constituted fair use under US copyright law. Similar cases, like *Atari v. Nintendo*, explored related issues. These legal battles didn't grant unlimited rights to reverse engineer, but they acknowledged that limited RE for the specific purpose of achieving interoperability with undocumented interfaces could, under certain circumstances, be permissible, recognizing its importance for competition and innovation in the software market.

The Networked Era and the Explosion of Malware

The popularization of the internet and networked computing in the 1990s and beyond marked another transformative phase. While networks enabled unprecedented communication and information sharing, they also created a highly efficient distribution channel for **malicious software (malware)**. Early viruses that spread via floppy disks were cumbersome; internet worms, email attachments carrying trojans, and malicious websites allowed malware to propagate globally with alarming speed.

This explosion of malware created an urgent, large-scale need for reverse engineering within the burgeoning **cybersecurity industry**. Antivirus companies, security researchers, and incident response teams needed to rapidly analyze the constant stream of new threats to:

Develop Detection Signatures: Early antivirus scanners relied heavily on finding unique byte sequences (signatures) within malware files. RE was essential to identify stable, unique patterns in the malware's code or data sections.

Understand Propagation: How did a worm spread? What vulnerabilities did it exploit (e.g., the famous Code Red and Nimda worms exploited flaws in Microsoft's IIS web server)? Analyzing the propagation mechanism was key to containment.

Identify Payloads: What did the malware *do* once it infected a system? Did it steal passwords (keyloggers, trojans like Zeus), provide remote access (backdoors, Remote Access Trojans - RATs), participate in Distributed Denial-of-Service (DDoS) attacks (botnets), or simply display annoying ads (adware)?

Attribute Attacks: Sometimes, code analysis revealed clues (unique coding styles, reused infrastructure, embedded comments in unexpected languages) that could help attribute attacks to specific criminal groups or nation-state actors.

The sheer volume and increasing sophistication of malware drove significant advancements in RE tools and techniques specifically tailored for this adversarial context. Malware authors began deliberately incorporating **anti-analysis** techniques learned from or parallel to software protection methods:

Packing/Encryption: Compressing or encrypting the main malicious payload so that simple static signature scanning of the initial file was ineffective. RE required dynamic analysis to unpack the code in memory first.

Polymorphism/Metamorphism: Automatically modifying the malware's code structure or encrypting it with different keys for each infection, making fixed byte signatures useless. Analysis shifted towards behavioral detection or needing to reverse engineer the mutation engine itself.

Anti-Debugging: Including code to detect if a debugger was attached (checking flags, using timing tricks) and altering behavior or exiting if found.

Anti-VM/Sandbox Evasion: Checking for artifacts indicating execution within a virtual machine or automated sandbox environment.

Defenders responded with more advanced disassemblers capable of handling obfuscated code, sophisticated debuggers with better anti-anti-debugging features, automated unpacking tools, behavioral analysis sandboxes designed to capture system interactions, and dynamic instrumentation frameworks. Reverse engineering became, and remains, the cornerstone of threat analysis and cybersecurity defense, a constant battle against adversaries actively trying to hinder understanding.

The Modern Era: Ubiquitous Computing, Cloud, IoT, and AI

Today, reverse engineering confronts a landscape defined by unparalleled technological diversity and complexity. The core principles remain, but their application spans numerous demanding domains:

Mobile Platforms: Analyzing Android (DEX bytecode) and iOS (compiled ARM native code) apps involves understanding platform-specific security models, framework APIs (Java/Kotlin for Android, Objective-C/Swift for iOS), inter-process communication, app store protection mechanisms (like FairPlay), and common obfuscation tools (ProGuard/R8).

Internet of Things (IoT): Analyzing firmware for resource-constrained embedded systems often requires hardware skills (firmware extraction via JTAG/SPI/UART), familiarity with diverse CPU architectures (ARM Cortex-M, MIPS, RISC-V), understanding Real-Time Operating Systems (RTOS) or bare-metal programming, and analyzing low-level hardware interactions (MMIO, interrupts). The sheer number of insecure devices makes this a critical area for vulnerability research.

Cloud Computing: As applications move to the cloud, RE often shifts from analyzing local executables to analyzing **APIs** exposed by backend services. This involves black-box network traffic analysis, understanding authentication protocols (OAuth, JWT), probing API endpoints, and inferring backend logic and potential vulnerabilities based on observed interactions, often without any access to the server-side code itself.

WebAssembly (Wasm): This relatively new binary instruction format allows near-native code execution in web browsers and other environments. Analyzing Wasm requires specialized tools and understanding its unique stack-machine architecture and interaction with the host environment (like JavaScript).

Advanced Software Protection: Modern software protection mechanisms (like Denuvo for games, sophisticated VM-based obfuscators like VMProtect/Themida) employ multiple layers of encryption, virtualization, anti-debugging, and code integrity checks, presenting formidable challenges that require deep expertise and often custom tool development to overcome.

Artificial Intelligence (AI): As AI/ML models become integrated into software, reverse engineering faces new challenges and opportunities. Analyzing compiled AI models to understand their structure, parameters, or vulnerabilities, and conversely, using AI/ML itself as a tool to *assist* in reverse engineering tasks (like function identification, vulnerability prediction, or de-obfuscation) are rapidly emerging fields.

The **tools** available to the modern reverse engineer are incredibly powerful compared to previous eras. Interactive disassemblers like IDA Pro and Ghidra offer integrated decompilers that can often translate complex assembly back into remarkably readable C-like pseudo-code. Dynamic instrumentation frameworks like Frida provide unprecedented flexibility for runtime analysis and manipulation across platforms. Sophisticated automated sandboxes handle initial malware triage at scale. Yet, despite these

advancements, the fundamental principles persist: meticulous static analysis to understand structure and potential, combined with careful dynamic analysis to observe actual runtime behavior and state.

An Ever-Adapting Discipline

Tracing this history reveals that reverse engineering is not a static discipline but one that has continuously evolved in direct response to technological progress and the changing motivations of those who practice it. From understanding mechanical contraptions and wartime ciphers, through deciphering mainframe assembly and battling floppy disk copy protections, to analyzing globally distributed malware and probing cloud APIs, the core goal remains unchanged: to unveil the inner workings of systems when the blueprints are unavailable. Its techniques have become vastly more sophisticated, its tools exponentially more powerful, and its applications more diverse and critical than ever before. It is a field perpetually adapting to the next wave of technology, ensuring its continued relevance in our complex digital age.

1.3. Applications and Significance: Why Does RE Matter?

We've established what it is and traced its evolution, but understanding its *applications* and *significance* is what truly anchors its importance in the modern technological landscape. Simply put, reverse engineering isn't just an academic curiosity; it's a fundamental capability that underpins vast swathes of the digital world, from securing critical infrastructure to enabling innovation and preserving our digital heritage. It's the key that unlocks understanding when the original blueprints are hidden, lost, or intentionally obscured.

1. Cybersecurity: The Bedrock of Digital Defense

Arguably the most visible and perhaps the most urgent driver for reverse engineering skills today lies within the vast field of cybersecurity. In the perpetual arms race between those who build defenses and those who seek to break them, reverse engineering is a primary weapon wielded by the defenders. Without it, much of modern cybersecurity would be functionally impossible.

Malware Analysis: Understanding the Enemy Within

When malicious software – be it ransomware demanding hefty payments, spyware silently stealing credentials, banking trojans looting accounts, worms spreading across networks, or sophisticated toolkits deployed by nation-states – strikes, the first critical step towards defense and remediation is understanding *exactly* what it does and *how* it does it. This is the core task of **Malware Analysis**, and it relies almost entirely on reverse engineering. Analysts receive a suspicious binary file, often packed or heavily obfuscated to hinder examination. Their job is to dissect this hostile code. Using static analysis tools like IDA Pro or Ghidra, they pore over the disassembly or decompiled pseudo-code, searching for clues. They look for suspicious API calls (like those related to file encryption, network communication, keylogging, process injection, or registry manipulation for persistence). They attempt to de-obfuscate encrypted strings that might reveal command-and-control (C&C) server addresses, target filenames, or ransom notes. They map out the malware's control flow, looking for logic designed to evade detection or achieve persistence after a system reboot (e.g., creating scheduled tasks, installing services, modifying startup registry keys).

Dynamic analysis is equally crucial. Analysts execute the malware within safe, isolated environments (sandboxes or dedicated virtual machines, often disconnected from critical networks or using network simulators like FakeNet-NG). Using debuggers (like x64dbg, WinDbg), they step through the code, observe its runtime behavior, watch as it unpacks itself in memory, see precisely what data it sends over the network, and monitor which system files or registry keys it modifies using tools like Process Monitor. They might use instrumentation frameworks like Frida to hook critical functions, intercept data before it's encrypted, or force the malware down specific execution paths.

The ultimate goals are multifaceted. First, **Develop Defenses:** By understanding the malware's unique code sequences, network traffic patterns, file system artifacts, or behavioral traits, analysts help create signatures for antivirus engines, rules for intrusion detection systems (IDS), and behavioral blockers for endpoint detection and response (EDR) tools. For example, identifying a specific sequence of bytes (a signature) unique to a malware family allows traditional AV scanners to detect it.

Code Example: Simple YARA Rule Conceptualization

Imagine during analysis, we discover a piece of ransomware consistently uses a specific, unusual mutex name (a synchronization object) to ensure only one instance runs, and it contains a unique debug string left by the author (perhaps after de-obfuscating it). We could create a YARA rule, a tool for pattern matching, like this:

```
    rule Ransomware_Example_Family_MutexAndString {
  meta:
      description = "Detects Example Ransomware Family
based on mutex and unique string"
      author = "Reverse Engineer"
      date = "2023-10-27"
      hash = "example_hash_of_analyzed_sample" // Link to
the sample
```

```
    strings:
      $mutex =
"\\Sessions\\BaseNamedObjects\\UniqueRansomMutex_XYZ123" wide
ascii // Looks for the specific mutex name
      $debug_string = "Krypt0rRoutine_v3_Final_DEBUG" ascii
// Looks for the accidentally left debug string
```

```
  condition:
      // The rule triggers if the specific mutex AND the
debug string are found in the file
      $mutex and $debug_string
}
```

Explanation: This YARA rule tells scanning tools to look for files containing both the specific mutex string (often checked using CreateMutex or OpenMutex APIs) and that unique debug string. Finding both is a strong indicator of this particular malware family. This rule is born directly from insights gained during RE.

Second, **Track Attackers and Campaigns:** By extracting C&C server domains/IPs, identifying unique code artifacts, or analyzing communication protocols, analysts contribute to broader threat intelligence. This helps track specific attacker groups, understand their Tactics, Techniques, and Procedures (TTPs), link different attacks into larger campaigns, and potentially identify infrastructure that can be taken down.

Third, **Enable Incident Response:** When a breach occurs, reverse engineering helps incident responders understand the scope of the compromise. What data did the malware steal? What systems did it spread to? How did it achieve persistence? Are there backdoors left behind? Answering these questions is crucial for effective containment, eradication, and recovery. Sometimes, analysis might even reveal flaws in the malware's encryption, potentially leading to the development of decryption tools for ransomware victims (though this is increasingly rare as attackers use strong crypto correctly).

Vulnerability Research: Finding Flaws Before the Attackers Do

Beyond reacting to malware, reverse engineering is proactive. **Vulnerability Researchers** use RE techniques to find security flaws in software and hardware *before* malicious actors exploit them. While open-source software can be audited directly, finding bugs in closed-source commercial products, operating systems, firmware, or even hardware often necessitates reverse engineering.

Researchers might statically analyze compiled code, looking for patterns indicative of common vulnerability classes. For example, they might scrutinize functions handling user input (like parsing network data or file formats) for potential **buffer overflows**, where providing more data than expected could overwrite adjacent memory, potentially allowing arbitrary code execution. They search for **integer overflow** issues, where mathematical operations result in unexpectedly small (or wrapped-around) values that might bypass size checks. They look for **use-after-free** vulnerabilities, where the program tries to use memory after it has been deallocated, potentially leading to crashes or exploitation. They analyze **format string vulnerabilities**, where improper use of functions like printf with user-controlled input can lead to information leaks or code execution. Logic flaws, race conditions, and insecure handling of cryptographic keys or protocols are also prime targets.

Code Example: Spotting a Simple Buffer Overflow Vulnerability

Consider this simplified vulnerable C function:

```
// vulnerable_func.c
#include <stdio.h>
#include <string.h>

void process_input(char* input) {
    char buffer[100]; // Fixed-size buffer on the stack
    // Vulnerability: strcpy does not check buffer bounds!
    strcpy(buffer, input);
    printf("You entered: %s\n", buffer);
```

```
}

int main(int argc, char* argv[]) {
    if (argc > 1) {
        process_input(argv[1]); // Pass command-line argument
directly
    }
    return 0;
}
```

Now, let's imagine a reverse engineer looking at the *disassembly* of process_input:

```
    ; Function: process_input(char*)
process_input proc near
    push    rbp
    mov     rbp, rsp
    sub     rsp, 70h            ; Allocate stack space (0x70 =
112 bytes, includes buffer[100] + overhead)
    mov     [rbp+arg_0], rdi ; Store 'input' pointer from RDI

    ; === The Vulnerable Call ===
    mov     rdx, [rbp+arg_0] ; RDX = source (input pointer)
    lea     rax, [rbp+buffer] ; RAX = destination (&buffer on
the stack)
    mov     rsi, rdx            ; RSI = source (input pointer)
- required for strcpy convention
    mov     rdi, rax            ; RDI = destination (&buffer) -
required for strcpy convention
    call    _strcpy             ; Call strcpy - *** The
dangerous part! ***
    ; === End Vulnerable Call ===

    lea     rax, [rbp+buffer] ; RAX = &buffer
    mov     rsi, rax            ; RSI = format string argument
2 (&buffer)
    lea     rdi, format_string ; RDI = format string argument
1 ("You entered: %s\n")
    mov     eax, 0              ; Required for printf varargs
    call    _printf

    ; ... function epilogue ...
    leave
    retn
process_input endp

buffer          db 100 dup(?) ; Shows buffer allocation
relative to RBP
arg_0           dq ?
format_string   db 'You entered: %s',0Ah,0
```

RE Interpretation: Even without the source, the analyst sees:

1. A buffer allocated on the stack (sub rsp, 70h and buffer db 100 dup(?)).

2. The input pointer is retrieved (mov rdx, [rbp+arg_0]).

3. The address of the stack buffer is loaded (lea rax, [rbp+buffer]).

4. A call is made to _strcpy. Crucially, the analyst knows (or quickly looks up) that strcpy copies bytes from source to destination *until it hits a null terminator*, with **no bounds checking**.

5. This immediately flags a potential stack buffer overflow. If the input string passed via argv[1] is longer than 99 characters (plus null terminator), strcpy will write past the end of buffer, overwriting other stack data, potentially including the saved base pointer (RBP) and the function's return address. An attacker could craft a long input string containing malicious code (shellcode) and overwrite the return address to point to that shellcode, gaining control of the program's execution.

Dynamic analysis, particularly **fuzzing** (feeding the program with large amounts of random or semi-random data) is another key technique. Fuzzers rapidly test edge cases and unusual inputs, often triggering crashes caused by vulnerabilities like buffer overflows or use-after-frees that might be hard to spot statically. When a crash occurs, the reverse engineer uses a debugger to analyze the crash state, examine memory and registers, and pinpoint the exact instruction and underlying flaw that caused it.

Ethical hackers performing **penetration testing** also rely heavily on RE. When testing a client's system or application (with explicit permission), they might reverse engineer components to understand internal logic, find non-obvious attack vectors, bypass security controls, or analyze proprietary network protocols to identify weaknesses. The goal here is explicitly defensive – finding and reporting flaws so they can be fixed *before* real attackers exploit them. This operates under strict rules of engagement and responsible disclosure protocols.

Digital Forensics and Incident Response (DFIR): Reconstructing Events

When a security breach or cybercrime occurs, DFIR professionals investigate to understand what happened, how the attackers got in, what they did, and what data was compromised. Reverse engineering is often a critical part of this process. Investigators might recover custom malware or hacking tools used by the attacker from compromised systems. Reversing these tools reveals their capabilities, indicators of compromise (IOCs) to search for on other systems, and potentially clues about the attacker's identity or origin. For example, analyzing a custom remote access trojan (RAT) might reveal its C&C infrastructure, communication methods, and data exfiltration capabilities, helping responders assess the extent of the breach and look for similar activity elsewhere in the network. RE can also help analyze file system artifacts, memory dumps, or log files where standard tools fall short, perhaps decoding custom log formats or reconstructing activity from damaged data structures.

Developing Better Security Tools: The knowledge gained from analyzing countless malware samples and identifying vulnerabilities feeds directly back into creating more effective security solutions. Understanding precisely how malware obfuscates itself, injects code, communicates covertly, or achieves persistence allows developers to design antivirus engines, EDR tools, firewalls, and IDS/IPS systems that can specifically detect and block these techniques, going beyond simple signature matching to incorporate behavioral analysis and heuristics informed by real-world attack methods. In summary, the cybersecurity landscape relies fundamentally on reverse engineering. It's the primary method for understanding threats, proactively discovering weaknesses, investigating incidents, and building smarter defenses. Without these skills, defenders would essentially be fighting blindfolded against increasingly sophisticated adversaries.

2. Interoperability: Making Systems Play Nicely Together

Beyond security, a major legitimate driver for reverse engineering is achieving **Interoperability** – enabling different software or hardware systems, often from different vendors, to communicate and work together. In an ideal world, manufacturers would publish open standards and detailed specifications for all their interfaces. In reality, interfaces are often undocumented, proprietary, or only partially specified.

Consider the challenge of writing an open-source driver for a piece of hardware (like a printer, network card, or graphics card) on an operating system the manufacturer doesn't officially support (e.g., Linux). Without official documentation for how the hardware expects to be controlled (which registers to write to, what command sequences to send), reverse engineering the existing driver (often the Windows driver) might be the only viable path.

Analysts would disassemble the driver, identify functions related to hardware initialization, data transfer, and control commands, trace interactions with the operating system's hardware abstraction layers, and potentially monitor communication on hardware buses (like USB or PCI Express) using logic analyzers. This painstakingly extracted information allows them to write a compatible open-source driver, benefiting users of the alternative OS.

Similarly, enabling two different software applications to exchange data might require reverse engineering a proprietary file format if no import/export option or documented API exists. Or consider needing to integrate a new system with a legacy application whose communication protocol is long forgotten and undocumented. Analyzing the legacy application's network traffic or its library functions responsible for communication might be necessary to build a compatible interface layer. This area is often fraught with legal complexities. As mentioned, EULAs frequently prohibit RE, and the DMCA restricts circumventing technological measures. However, specific legal exceptions sometimes exist *explicitly* for interoperability purposes, recognizing its value for competition and user choice. Landmark cases like *Sega v. Accolade* explored these boundaries, generally finding that reverse engineering necessary to understand undocumented interfaces for creating compatible, non-infringing software could be considered fair use under certain copyright doctrines (though specifics vary greatly by jurisdiction and the exact circumstances). Anyone undertaking RE for interoperability must tread very carefully, often requiring legal counsel, to ensure they stay within the narrow confines of permissible actions and do not infringe copyrights or patents beyond what is strictly necessary for compatibility.

Code Example: Conceptual Protocol Interaction

Imagine analyzing USB traffic (perhaps with Wireshark and USBPcap) for an undocumented device and discovering that sending the byte sequence \x01\xAB\x03\x00 makes its status LED turn green. You might write a simple Python script using a library like PyUSB to replicate this, representing the first step in building an interoperable tool:

```
# conceptual_usb_control.py
import usb.core
import usb.util
import sys
```

```python
# Vendor and Product ID (obtained from device manager or USB
analysis)
VENDOR_ID = 0xAAAA
PRODUCT_ID = 0xBBBB

# Find our device
dev = usb.core.find(idVendor=VENDOR_ID, idProduct=PRODUCT_ID)

if dev is None:
    raise ValueError('Device not found')

# Detach kernel driver if necessary (Linux specific)
needs_reattach = False
if sys.platform.startswith('linux'):
    try:
        if dev.is_kernel_driver_active(0):
            needs_reattach = True
            dev.detach_kernel_driver(0)
            print("Kernel driver detached")
    except usb.core.USBError as e:
        sys.exit(f"Could not detach kernel driver: {str(e)}")


# Claim the interface (usually interface 0)
# Note: Proper error handling and interface selection needed
in real code
try:
    usb.util.claim_interface(dev, 0)
    print("Interface claimed")

    # Find the OUT endpoint (Address usually identified
during traffic analysis)
    # Example: Endpoint address 0x01 (OUT)
    endpoint_out = dev[0][(0,0)][0] # Example indices,
depends on device config

    # The command sequence observed turning the LED green
    command_turn_led_green = b'\x01\xAB\x03\x00'

    print(f"Sending command: {command_turn_led_green.hex()}")

    # Send the command
    try:
        # Using control transfer OR write to bulk/interrupt
endpoint
        # The exact method (control_transfer, write) depends
on device & endpoint type
        # identified during RE of the protocol/driver. Using
write for illustration:
```

```
        bytes_written =
dev.write(endpoint_out.bEndpointAddress,
command_turn_led_green, 1000) # Timeout 1 sec
        print(f"Successfully sent {bytes_written} bytes.")

    except usb.core.USBError as e:
        print(f"Error sending command: {str(e)}")

finally:
    # Release the interface and reattach kernel driver
    usb.util.release_interface(dev, 0)
    print("Interface released")
    if needs_reattach:
        try:
            dev.attach_kernel_driver(0)
            print("Kernel driver reattached")
        except usb.core.USBError as e:
            print(f"Could not reattach kernel driver:
{str(e)}")

    # Recommended to reset the device after use
    # usb.util.dispose_resources(dev) # Might cause issues if
device needed later
    # dev.reset() # Potentially better
```

Explanation: This conceptual script demonstrates how observations from RE (the device IDs, the endpoint address, the specific byte command) could be translated into code using a standard library (PyUSB) to interact with the device, forming the basis for building an interoperable tool or driver.

3. Compatibility: Bridging Generations

Closely related to interoperability is **Compatibility**. As software and hardware evolve, developers often need to ensure that new versions work correctly with older systems, files, or plugins. Sometimes, the only way to understand the exact behavior or data format expected by an older, perhaps undocumented or unsupported, component is to reverse engineer it. For example, a new version of a word processor might need to perfectly load documents saved by a version from 10 years prior, whose exact file format details might be lost. Analyzing the older version's file parsing code might be necessary to replicate its behavior precisely. Similarly, an operating system update might need to maintain compatibility with existing device drivers, potentially requiring analysis of how those drivers interact with the previous OS version. RE acts as a bridge, ensuring smooth transitions and preventing obsolescence.

4. Software Development and Improvement: Learning and Debugging
Reverse engineering isn't just for analyzing *other* people's code; it has significant applications within the software development lifecycle itself.

Learning from Existing Solutions: Studying how well-designed existing software tackles certain problems can be incredibly educational (always respecting legal boundaries!). How does a particular graphics engine achieve its rendering performance? What algorithms does a successful data compression tool use? How does an operating system manage process scheduling? Analyzing compiled code (where legally permissible, e.g., examining interfaces, performance characteristics, or publicly documented aspects, rather than illicitly copying protected code) can reveal clever techniques, efficient algorithms, or effective design patterns that developers can learn from and adapt (not directly copy!) in their own work. It can spark innovation by providing insights into proven solutions. This must be done ethically and legally, focusing on understanding concepts rather than infringing IP. Competitive analysis often involves studying competitors' products' *behavior* and *public interfaces* rather than deep code RE, specifically to avoid IP issues.

Debugging Intractable Issues: This is perhaps one of the most immediately practical applications for developers. Sometimes bugs don't occur in your own well-documented source code, but deep within opaque third-party libraries, operating system components, or heavily optimized sections of your own codebase where the correspondence between source and assembly is unclear. Maybe your application crashes inside a graphics driver call, or hangs while waiting for a response from a closed-source network library, or behaves strangely due to an unexpected interaction with an OS feature. In these situations, standard source-level debugging hits a wall. Attaching a low-level debugger (like WinDbg or GDB) and stepping through the disassembly, examining memory, and tracing execution *into* the opaque code might be the *only* way to understand the state, sequence of events, and root cause of the problem. I've personally spent many hours stepping through Windows API internals or third-party library code in a debugger to solve bugs that were completely inexplicable from my own source code perspective.

5. Preservation and Documentation Recovery: Digital Archaeology

Technology moves fast, and sometimes knowledge gets left behind. Companies go out of business, source code repositories are lost in server failures or poorly managed acquisitions, documentation vanishes, and original developers move on. Yet, critical systems built years or decades ago might still be running in businesses or infrastructure. When these **legacy systems** need to be maintained, updated, migrated, or finally decommissioned, but the original blueprints are gone, reverse engineering becomes a form of **digital archaeology**. Analysts painstakingly reverse engineer the executables or libraries to reconstruct an understanding of the system's functionality, data formats, communication protocols, and dependencies. This knowledge is vital to keep the system running, interface it with modern systems, migrate its functionality to a new platform, or even just safely shut it down without disrupting other operations. It's often a last resort, incredibly labor-intensive, but sometimes the only way to recover lost knowledge embedded solely in the compiled artifacts.

6. Education and Curiosity: The Fundamental Drive to Understand

Finally, let's not underestimate the immense value of reverse engineering as an educational tool and a pursuit driven by pure intellectual curiosity. For many aspiring computer scientists, software engineers, and security professionals, taking software apart is the most tangible way to learn how computers *actually* work beneath the high-level abstractions of modern programming languages. Deconstructing executables forces you to understand CPU architecture, assembly language, memory management (stack, heap), operating system internals (system calls, process loading), file formats, and compilation/linking processes at a fundamental level. Engaging with **Capture The Flag (CTF)** competitions (which often feature RE challenges) or practicing on deliberately designed **CrackMes** (small programs designed to be reverse engineered) provides invaluable hands-on experience in a safe, legal environment. For many, including myself, the initial draw wasn't a specific application but the inherent puzzle-solving nature of RE – the challenge and satisfaction of deciphering complex, hidden mechanisms. This foundational understanding gained through RE makes one a better programmer, a better system designer, and a more insightful security professional.

The Inescapable Dual-Use Nature and Overarching Significance

It's impossible to discuss the applications of reverse engineering without acknowledging its **dual-use nature**. The same skills and tools used by a security researcher to find and report a vulnerability can be used by a malicious actor to develop an exploit. The techniques used to understand a file format for interoperability could be used to cheat in a game that uses that format. The methods used to analyze malware could theoretically be adapted to analyze and bypass legitimate software protections.

This duality underscores why **ethics and legality** are not optional footnotes but integral aspects of responsible reverse engineering practice, as we explored in detail in Chapter 11. The power of these skills necessitates a strong ethical compass and a thorough understanding of legal boundaries (copyright, DMCA, CFAA, EULAs). Responsible practitioners operate within these frameworks, using their abilities for defensive, constructive, or legitimate research purposes.

Despite the potential for misuse, the **significance of legitimate reverse engineering in today's world cannot be overstated**. It is absolutely fundamental to modern cybersecurity – we simply cannot defend effectively against threats we don't understand. It fosters innovation and competition by enabling interoperability and compatibility (within legal limits). It allows us to recover lost knowledge from legacy systems, debug the otherwise un-debuggable, and provide an unparalleled educational pathway to understanding the deep internals of computing systems.

In an era defined by increasingly complex technology, often delivered as opaque black boxes – from IoT devices and mobile apps to intricate cloud services and proprietary hardware – the ability to analyze and understand systems from the outside-in, to verify claims, uncover hidden behaviors, and ensure trustworthiness, is not just useful; it's essential. Reverse engineering provides the lens through which we can gain that crucial understanding, making it a vital and enduring skill for the foreseeable future.

Chapter 2: Essential Concepts

Imagine trying to understand how a car works without knowing anything about engines, transmissions, or electrical systems. You could maybe figure out how to turn the key and press the pedals, but you wouldn't grasp *why* it moves or how to diagnose a problem. It's the same with software! To effectively reverse engineer, we need a baseline understanding of a few key areas: how software is structured (its architecture), the different ways code is written (programming languages and paradigms), and the environment it runs in (the operating system).

2.1. Software Architecture Overview: The Blueprint of Code

When you first open a complex piece of software in a disassembler or decompiler, especially one that's been stripped of symbols and possibly obfuscated, it can feel overwhelming – a seemingly chaotic sea of instructions and data. Yet, beneath this apparent randomness, there's almost always an intended structure, an **architecture**. This isn't just about aesthetics; architecture is the high-level plan conceived by the developers to organize the different parts of the software, manage complexity, and define how those parts interact. Even convoluted malware often has an internal logic and structure, designed perhaps for modularity or evasion. Recognizing common architectural patterns, or even just developing a hypothesis about the likely structure, provides an invaluable navigational aid for the reverse engineer.

Think about the design of a physical building. It isn't just a random pile of bricks. It has a foundation, structural supports, distinct floors, specialized rooms serving different purposes (like kitchens handling food preparation or control rooms managing building systems), and interconnected systems like plumbing and electrical wiring that follow specific paths. Software architecture is analogous. Understanding the software's "floor plan" helps you predict where certain functions might reside and how information likely flows through the system.

Let's delve into some prevalent architectural styles and how recognizing them impacts the reverse engineering process.

The Monolithic Approach: Everything Under One Roof

Perhaps the simplest conceptual model is the **Monolithic Architecture**. Imagine a single, large building where all functions – living quarters, workshops, storage, administration – are contained within the same structure. In software terms, a monolith is typically a single, large executable program (possibly accompanied by some libraries) where all the application's features and functionalities are tightly coupled within one codebase and usually run within a single process space. Many traditional desktop applications, older web applications, or simpler utilities often follow this pattern.

Characteristics for RE: When analyzing a monolith, your primary target is often that single large executable. Component interactions usually happen through direct function calls within the same process's memory space. Data is often shared readily between different parts of the application, sometimes through global variables or well-defined internal data structures. While conceptually simple, monoliths can become incredibly complex as they grow over time ("The Big Ball of Mud" anti-pattern), making navigation difficult without a clear understanding of the internal modularity (or lack thereof). Debugging is often confined to this single process.

Analysis Strategy: Your approach often starts at recognizable entry points – the main function, event handlers for UI elements (like button clicks), or exported functions if it's a library component within the monolith. From there, you trace function calls inwards, mapping out the relationships between different modules or feature areas. Identifying key internal data structures and tracking how they are accessed and modified across different functions is crucial. Tools like function call graphs generated by IDA Pro or Ghidra become essential for visualizing the complex interdependencies within the single large codebase. Be prepared to spend significant time understanding how different, seemingly unrelated parts of the code might influence each other through shared state.

Layered Architecture (N-Tier): Separating Concerns into Floors

A very common approach to managing complexity, especially in business applications and web systems, is the **Layered Architecture**, sometimes referred to as N-Tier (where 'N' is the number of layers, typically 3). Think of this as designing a building with distinct floors, each dedicated to a specific purpose. For instance, the ground floor might be for public interaction (Presentation/UI), the middle floors for core business operations (Business Logic/Domain Layer), and the basement for utilities and storage (Data Access/Persistence Layer).

Characteristics for RE: The key principle is separation of concerns. The **Presentation Layer** handles user interaction and displays information. The **Business Logic Layer** contains the core rules, calculations, and processes that define the application's functionality. The **Data Access Layer** is responsible for retrieving data from and storing data into databases, files, or other persistent storage. Crucially, communication typically follows strict rules, often flowing downwards (e.g., UI calls business logic, business logic calls data access) or through well-defined interfaces. Direct calls from lower layers back up to higher layers are usually discouraged.

Analysis Strategy: Recognizing a layered structure is incredibly helpful for focusing your efforts. If your goal is to understand how user input is validated or displayed, you'd concentrate on the code modules associated with the UI framework (e.g., analyzing code related to Windows Forms, WPF, Cocoa, or web frontend JavaScript). If you need to understand the core algorithm for calculating an insurance premium or processing a transaction, you'd target the business logic layer, looking for functions that don't directly interact with UI elements or database APIs but perform calculations and enforce rules. If you're interested in how data is stored or retrieved, you'd focus on the data access layer, searching for calls to database APIs (like ODBC, JDBC, ADO.NET), file I/O functions (fopen, ReadFile, etc.), or Object-Relational Mapping (ORM) frameworks (like Hibernate, Entity Framework). Identifying the boundaries between these layers – perhaps represented by distinct DLLs, specific class namespaces, or characteristic function call patterns – becomes a primary objective. Data flow analysis focuses on tracking data as it passes through these layers. For example, how does a value entered in a UI text box get transformed by the business logic before being saved to the database via the data access layer?

Client-Server Model: The Front Office and the Back Room

Ubiquitous in modern computing is the **Client-Server Architecture**. Imagine a restaurant: the diners (clients) sit in the front and place orders (requests) with the waiter, who takes them to the kitchen (server) where the food is prepared (service provided) and then brought back out. The client initiates requests, and the server fulfills them. Your web browser is a client talking to web servers; your mobile game is a client talking to game servers; even database tools are often clients talking to a database server.

Characteristics for RE: This architecture involves at least two distinct pieces of software, often running on different machines, communicating over a **network**. The client typically handles the user interface and local processing, while the server manages shared resources, central logic, and data persistence. The communication protocol between them is paramount.

Analysis Strategy: The first crucial step is determining *which side* you are analyzing. Do you have the client application (like a mobile app or desktop executable)? Or, much less commonly for external analysts, do you somehow have access to the server-side code?

Client-Side Analysis: Your focus is on the code running locally. How does the client build requests to send to the server? What logic does it perform before sending data? How does it interpret and display the responses received? You'll analyze UI code, local data validation, and especially the code responsible for network communication. This invariably involves identifying calls to networking APIs (like socket, connect, send, recv in C/C++; HttpClient in C#; fetch or XMLHttpRequest in JavaScript). Often, the most valuable insight comes from intercepting and analyzing the actual network traffic between the client and server using tools like **Wireshark** (for general network traffic) or **Burp Suite/OWASP ZAP** (for web/HTTP traffic). By observing the requests and responses, you can reverse engineer the Application Programming Interface (API) or protocol the server exposes, even without seeing the server's code. This includes figuring out request formats (URLs, headers, message bodies, data encoding like JSON or XML), authentication mechanisms (cookies, tokens), and response structures.

Server-Side Analysis (Rare for external RE): If you *do* have server code (perhaps from a leak or authorized internal analysis), you focus on how it handles incoming requests, implements business logic, interacts with databases or other backend services, and formulates responses. You look for web framework code (like ASP.NET, Spring, Django, Express), database interaction logic, and security implementations.

Understanding the client-server division is fundamental. Trying to find the core data processing logic within a thin client application that merely sends data to a server for processing would be futile.

Microservices Architecture: A City of Specialized Shops

An evolution of distributed systems, particularly relevant for large-scale web platforms, is the **Microservices Architecture**. Instead of one large server application (a server-side monolith), the functionality is broken down into numerous small, independent, self-contained services. Each service focuses on a specific business capability (e.g., user authentication, product catalog, order processing, payment handling). These services run in their own processes, are often developed and deployed independently, and communicate with each other over a network, typically using lightweight protocols like REST APIs over HTTP or asynchronous messaging queues. Think of it less like one big restaurant kitchen and more like a food court with many specialized stalls, each handling one part of the meal, coordinating via runners.

Characteristics for RE: The application's logic is highly distributed. Communication between services is key. Services might be written in different languages or use different databases ("polyglot persistence"). Failure in one service should ideally not bring down the entire application.

Analysis Strategy: From an external reverse engineering perspective, analyzing a full microservices architecture is exceptionally complex. You typically don't have access to the code for all (or even most) of the individual services. The focus often shifts almost entirely to **API analysis**, similar to client-server but potentially much more involved. You might analyze the client application (web or mobile) to see which initial APIs it calls. From there, you might try to infer the downstream calls between microservices based on timing, correlation IDs in headers (used for distributed tracing), or error messages. Tools like Burp Suite or Postman are essential for mapping out the exposed API surface and probing individual endpoints. Dynamic analysis focuses heavily on tracing network calls. Static analysis might be feasible only if you can obtain the binary or container image for a *specific* microservice, allowing you to analyze that piece in isolation, focusing on its API handling and internal logic. Reverse engineering microservices often requires strong networking skills and an understanding of distributed system concepts like service discovery, load balancing, and inter-service communication patterns (e.g., API gateways, message queues).

Components and Libraries: Reusable Building Blocks

Regardless of the high-level architecture, almost all non-trivial software is built using reusable pieces of code known as **Components** or **Libraries**. These might be standard libraries provided by the operating system or programming language (like libc, Windows API DLLs, the .NET Framework Class Library, the Java Standard Library), third-party libraries (e.g., data compression libraries like zlib, GUI toolkits like Qt, JSON parsers), or internally developed modules shared across different parts of an application. How these libraries are integrated significantly impacts RE.

Dynamic Linking: This is very common. The main executable contains references to functions in external library files (like .dll files on Windows or .so files on Linux). When the program runs, the operating system's loader finds these libraries and maps them into the process's address space. The links between the executable and the library functions are resolved at runtime.

RE Implications: Dynamically linked libraries (DLLs/SOs) appear as separate files and are often easily identifiable. Tools like IDA Pro or Ghidra clearly show imported functions and which library they come from in the import table. This allows you to analyze the main executable and the library separately. You can focus on the unique code in the executable or dive into a specific library if you suspect the functionality resides there. Tracing calls *between* the executable and a DLL is a common RE task. Malware often uses DLLs to modularize its components.

Static Linking: In this case, the actual code from the library is copied directly into the final executable file by the linker during the build process. There's no separate library file needed at runtime.

RE Implications: Static linking makes the main executable much larger and blurs the boundaries between application code and library code. It's harder to immediately tell which functions originated from the application developer and which came from a standard library. However, static library code often has recognizable function signatures or patterns. Tools like **FLIRT (Fast Library Identification and Recognition Technology)** in IDA Pro or similar features in Ghidra analyze functions in the binary and compare them against databases of known library functions to automatically identify and label them. This "cleaning up" of statically linked library code is often a crucial first step in analyzing such binaries, allowing you to filter out the standard boilerplate and focus on the application's unique logic.

Understanding whether libraries are dynamically or statically linked helps you scope your analysis and choose appropriate techniques for identifying and potentially ignoring standard library code.

Why Does Architecture Matter So Much for Reverse Engineering?
Grasping the likely architecture of the software you're facing is more than just an academic exercise; it's a fundamental prerequisite for efficient and effective analysis. Having even a hypothetical architectural model in mind provides several key advantages:

Predicting Functionality Location: Architecture guides your search. If you suspect a layered architecture and need to understand data saving, you know to look for database or file APIs, likely within a specific layer or set of modules, rather than searching randomly through UI code. If it's client-server, you know core logic probably resides on the server, so client-side analysis focuses on UI and network request construction.

Understanding Data Flow: Architectural patterns dictate common data flow paths. In a layered system, data typically moves from UI to business logic to data access. In client-server, data flows from client request to server processing and back as a response. Visualizing these high-level flows helps you trace how specific pieces of information move through the application.

Focusing Your Efforts: Complex software can contain millions of lines of code or instructions. Trying to understand everything is usually impossible and unnecessary. Architecture helps you **prioritize**. Based on your analysis goals, you can concentrate on the specific components, layers, or communication points most likely to contain the relevant logic, significantly reducing the search space. You don't need to reverse engineer the entire graphics rendering engine if you only care about the license check mechanism.

Forming Hypotheses: As you analyze, you constantly form hypotheses ("I think this function handles user authentication," "This looks like the data serialization routine before sending to the server"). An understanding of architecture provides a framework for these hypotheses, making them more educated and testable.

Trying to reverse a large application without considering its structure often leads to feeling lost and overwhelmed. I distinctly remember early experiences analyzing medium-sized applications where the disassembly seemed like an impenetrable jungle. It wasn't until I stepped back, examined the imported libraries, observed network traffic, considered common patterns (like UI/Logic/Data separation), and started mentally sketching out a *potential* architecture that the different code sections began to fall into place. Suddenly, complex call graphs started making more sense because I could associate different clusters of functions with probable architectural roles.

Inferring Architecture During Analysis

Of course, developers don't usually ship architectural diagrams with their compiled software. As a reverse engineer, you often have to *infer* the architecture based on clues gathered during analysis:

File Structure: How is the application package organized? Are there multiple executables or DLLs/SOs with names suggesting different roles (e.g., AppCore.dll, AppUI.dll, AppData.dll)?

Imports/Dependencies: What libraries does the executable rely on? Imports from networking libraries suggest client-server communication. Imports from database libraries suggest a data access layer. Imports from UI framework libraries point to the presentation layer.

Network Behavior: Does the application make network connections on startup or during operation? Monitoring traffic with Wireshark or Burp Suite clearly indicates client-server or microservice interactions.

Framework Artifacts: Is the software built using a known framework (like .NET, Java Spring, Qt, Electron)? These frameworks often impose specific architectural patterns (e.g., Model-View-Controller - MVC) whose standard structures might be recognizable in the code.

Code Patterns: Even in compiled code, you might recognize patterns indicative of layers (e.g., distinct groups of functions handling UI events vs. complex calculations vs. data serialization) or component boundaries.

Naming Conventions (if available): If symbols haven't been completely stripped, function and class names can provide huge clues about architectural roles (UserService, DatabaseConnection, MainViewController).

Architecture analysis in RE is often an iterative process. You gather initial clues, form a hypothesis about the structure, use that hypothesis to guide further investigation, and refine your architectural understanding as you uncover more information. It provides the crucial context needed to make sense of the low-level details revealed by disassembly and debugging.

2.2. Programming Paradigms and Languages: The Echoes of Creation in Compiled Code

Software isn't just conjured from the ether; it's meticulously crafted using programming languages. Each language comes with its own syntax, features, and common idioms. Furthermore, developers don't just write code randomly; they typically adhere to established **programming paradigms** – fundamental styles or ways of thinking about structuring a program. The paradigm chosen influences how problems are broken down, how data is organized, and how different parts of the code interact. These choices, made by the original developers, leave distinct footprints in the compiled executable or script, directly impacting your reverse engineering efforts. Let's explore the major paradigms and language types and understand their implications for analysis.

The Procedural Approach: A Sequence of Steps

One of the most fundamental paradigms is **Procedural Programming**. Think of it like following a detailed recipe or a checklist. The core idea is to break down a task into a sequence of distinct steps, which are encapsulated into reusable procedures or functions (you'll hear both terms, often used interchangeably, though "function" usually implies returning a value). Languages like **C** are the quintessential examples of the procedural style, though languages like FORTRAN, Pascal, and even aspects of scripting languages often lean heavily on this approach.

In a procedural program, the focus is on these functions. Data is often passed between functions as arguments, and functions return results. You'll typically see a main execution flow that calls various functions to perform specific sub-tasks. When you, as a reverse engineer, encounter software primarily written in a procedural style (especially compiled from C), your analysis will heavily revolve around tracing these function calls.

What This Looks Like in Reverse Engineering:

Function Call Analysis: You'll spend significant time identifying function boundaries in the disassembly. Tools like IDA Pro or Ghidra are adept at this, showing you the call instructions and the start of the targeted functions (often marked with labels like sub_XXXXXXXX until you rename them). Understanding the **calling convention** becomes critical – this set of rules dictates how arguments are passed to functions (e.g., on the stack, in specific

CPU registers, or a combination) and how return values are provided. Recognizing patterns like the setup and teardown of stack frames (pushing the base pointer EBP, moving the stack pointer ESP) is fundamental.

Stack Analysis: Since arguments and local variables are often stored on the stack in procedural languages like C, understanding stack layouts is vital. You'll analyze offsets relative to the stack pointer (ESP) or base pointer (EBP) to identify local variables and parameters passed to the function. Tools often help by automatically identifying and labeling these var_XX stack variables.

Global Data: Procedural programs might also rely heavily on global variables accessible from multiple functions. Identifying accesses to fixed memory addresses can indicate the use of global state, which you need to track carefully.

Library Calls: Procedural code heavily relies on standard libraries (like libc on Linux/Unix or msvcrt.dll/kernel32.dll etc. on Windows) for common tasks like input/output, string manipulation, and memory allocation. Recognizing calls to functions like printf, strcpy, malloc, fopen provides immediate clues about the code's actions.

Example: Simple C Function and its Assembly Footprint

Let's consider a very simple C function:

```
// simple_proc.c
#include <stdio.h>

int add_numbers(int a, int b) {
    int result = a + b;
    return result;
}

int main() {
    int x = 5;
    int y = 10;
    int sum = add_numbers(x, y);
    printf("The sum is: %d\n", sum);
    return 0;
}
```

Now, let's imagine compiling this (using a typical compiler like GCC on Linux x86-64 architecture, perhaps without heavy optimizations for clarity) and looking at a snippet of the *disassembly* for the add_numbers function as a reverse engineer might see it in IDA Pro or Ghidra (syntax might vary slightly between tools):

```
; Function: add_numbers(int, int)
add_numbers proc near
    push    rbp             ; Standard function prologue: save
old base pointer
    mov     rbp, rsp        ; Set up new base pointer for this
frame
    mov     [rbp+var_4], edi ; Store the first argument (a,
passed in EDI) onto the stack
    mov     [rbp+var_8], esi ; Store the second argument (b,
passed in ESI) onto the stack

    mov     edx, [rbp+var_4] ; Load 'a' from stack into EDX
register
    mov     eax, [rbp+var_8] ; Load 'b' from stack into EAX
register
    add     eax, edx        ; Add EDX (a) to EAX (b), result in
EAX (sum)
    mov     [rbp+var_C], eax ; Store the result (sum) onto
the stack (local variable 'result')

    mov     eax, [rbp+var_C] ; Load the result from stack
into EAX (return value register)

    pop     rbp             ; Standard function epilogue:
restore old base pointer
    retn                    ; Return to the caller
add_numbers endp
```

RE Interpretation: Even without the source, we can deduce much from this assembly.

We see the standard prologue/epilogue (push rbp/mov rbp, rsp and pop rbp/retn), marking it as a typical function.

We see arguments being saved onto the stack relative to rbp (var_4, var_8). Based on the x86-64 calling convention, we know the first integer arguments arrive in EDI and ESI, confirming these stack locations hold a and b.

We see two values loaded from these stack locations into registers (EDX, EAX).

An add instruction performs addition, storing the result in EAX.

The result is temporarily stored back to the stack (var_C), likely corresponding to the result local variable.

Finally, the result is loaded into EAX again, which is the standard register for returning integer values in this convention.

By tracing the data flow and understanding the calling convention, we can reconstruct the function's purpose: it adds two integer arguments and returns the sum.

This procedural style, characterized by distinct functions, stack-based variables/arguments, and sequential execution flow, is common in systems programming (like operating system kernels), embedded firmware where resources are tight, and performance-sensitive applications where the overhead of other paradigms might be undesirable.

The Object-Oriented Paradigm: Bundling Data and Behavior

A major shift in thinking came with **Object-Oriented Programming (OOP)**. Instead of focusing solely on procedures, OOP revolves around the concept of **objects**. An object bundles together **data** (attributes or member variables) and the **operations** (methods or member functions) that can be performed on that data. Languages like **C++**, **Java**, **C#**, **Python**, and Swift are heavily influenced by OOP principles.

The core ideas include:

Encapsulation: Hiding the internal state (data) of an object and exposing functionality only through defined methods.

Inheritance: Allowing a new class (a blueprint for objects) to inherit properties and methods from an existing parent class, promoting code reuse.

Polymorphism: Allowing objects of different classes to respond to the same method call in their own specific ways. This often involves **virtual functions** (in C++) or similar mechanisms (in Java/C# interfaces).

When reverse engineering OOP code, you're no longer just tracing simple function calls. You need to identify object structures in memory, understand class relationships, and track method invocations, which can be more complex than straightforward procedural calls.

What This Looks Like in Reverse Engineering (Focusing on C++):

Identifying Objects: Objects usually reside on the stack (as local variables), in global memory, or most commonly, on the heap (dynamically allocated using new). You'll look for memory allocation functions (malloc, operator new) and track the pointers returned. Analyzing how these pointers are used helps identify member variable accesses relative to the start of the object's memory block.

The 'this' Pointer: Methods in OOP languages typically receive a hidden first argument, often called the this pointer (or self in Python). This pointer points to the specific object instance the method is being called on. In disassembly (e.g., for C++ compiled on x86), you'll often see this pointer passed in a register (like ECX in the thiscall convention common with Microsoft's C++ compiler, or the first argument register like RDI in x86-64 System V). Recognizing instructions that dereference this pointer (e.g., mov eax, [ecx+8]) are strong indicators of accessing an object's member variable (at offset 8 in this case).

Class Hierarchies and vtables: Inheritance and polymorphism, especially virtual functions in C++, introduce complexity. When a program calls a virtual method on an object pointer, the *actual* function executed depends on the object's *runtime type*. Compilers typically implement this using a **virtual table (vtable)**. Each class with virtual functions has a static vtable containing pointers to the actual implementations of its virtual methods. Each *object* instance then contains a hidden pointer (the **vptr**) to its class's vtable. A virtual method call in assembly usually looks like:

Load the object's vptr (e.g., mov eax, [ecx]).

Load the function pointer from the correct offset within the vtable (e.g., mov edx, [eax+12]).

Call the function pointed to by the register (call edx).

Recognizing this vtable lookup pattern is crucial for understanding polymorphic calls. Reverse engineering tools often have features to help identify vtables and reconstruct class hierarchies based on these patterns. Grappling with vtables and the this pointer was a significant step up in complexity for me when moving from reversing pure C to tackling large C++ applications.

Name Mangling: C++ supports function overloading (multiple functions with the same name but different parameters). To give each version a unique symbol name in the compiled code, compilers use **name mangling**, encoding parameter types and class information into the symbol name (e.g., add_numbers(int, int) might become _Z11add_numbersii). Reverse engineering tools often include "demanglers" to translate these cryptic names back into a human-readable form, which is essential for understanding C++ code.

Example: Simple C++ Class and its Assembly Implications

Consider a simple C++ class:

```
// simple_oop.cpp
#include <stdio.h>
```

```
class Calculator {
public:
    int last_result;

    Calculator() : last_result(0) {} // Constructor

    virtual int operate(int a, int b) { // Virtual method
        return 0; // Base implementation
    }
};

class Adder : public Calculator {
public:
    // Override the virtual method
    int operate(int a, int b) override {
        last_result = a + b; // Access member variable
        return last_result;
    }
};

int main() {
    Calculator* calc = new Adder(); // Create Adder object,
store pointer as Calculator*
    int x = 5;
    int y = 10;
    int sum = calc->operate(x, y); // Polymorphic call via
pointer
    printf("The sum is: %d\n", sum);
    delete calc; // Clean up
    return 0;
}
```

Without showing full disassembly, here's what a reverse engineer might focus on when analyzing the calc->operate(x, y) call:

    ; Hypothetical disassembly snippet for the virtual call site in main()
; Assuming 'calc' pointer is in RBX, 'x' in ESI, 'y' in EDX (arguments after 'this')

```
mov     rdi, rbx      ; Move 'calc' pointer (the 'this'
pointer for operate) into RDI (1st arg reg)
mov     rsi, 5        ; Move 'x' (5) into RSI (2nd arg reg) -
Simplified, would likely load from stack/reg
mov     rdx, 10       ; Move 'y' (10) into RDX (3rd arg reg) -
Simplified

; === Virtual Call Mechanism ===
```

```
mov     rax, [rbx]    ; Load the vptr from the object pointed
to by RBX (calc) into RAX
mov     rax, [rax+8] ; Load function address from vtable +
offset 8 (assuming operate is 2nd virtual func)
call    rax           ; Call the resolved virtual function
(will be Adder::operate)
; === End Virtual Call ===

mov     [rsp+var_sum], eax ; Store return value (the sum)
from EAX

; ... printf call ...
```

RE Interpretation:

We see the setup of arguments (RDI, RSI, RDX), including the object pointer RBX being placed in RDI as the implicit this pointer.

The crucial part is the sequence mov rax, [rbx], mov rax, [rax+8], call rax. This is the classic signature of a C++ virtual function call. We're dereferencing the object pointer to get the vptr, then dereferencing the vptr at a specific offset (here, +8, assuming it's the second virtual function defined) to get the actual function address, and finally calling it.

Even without knowing it's an Adder object at compile time, the *runtime* lookup via the vtable ensures the correct Adder::operate function is called.

The analyst needs to identify this pattern and likely examine the vtable structure associated with potential object types to fully understand the control flow.

Inside Adder::operate (if we analyzed that function), we would see instructions accessing memory relative to the this pointer (passed in RDI) to modify last_result.

OOP introduces abstractions that can make source code easier to manage but add layers (like vtables, implicit this pointers) that the reverse engineer must unravel in the compiled code.

Scripting Languages and Interpreted Execution: A Different Ballgame

A third category includes **Scripting or Interpreted Languages** like **Python**, **JavaScript**, **Perl**, **Ruby**, and many shell scripting languages. These languages often differ significantly from C/C++ in how they are executed, impacting the RE process.

Instead of being compiled *directly* to native machine code ahead of time, scripts are typically handled by an **interpreter** program. The interpreter reads the source code (or an intermediate representation) and executes the instructions one by one or "just-in-time" (JIT compilation).

What This Looks Like in Reverse Engineering:

Source Code Analysis (Sometimes): In many cases, especially with web applications (JavaScript) or simpler scripts, you might actually have access to the original, human-readable source code! Reverse engineering then becomes more like code review and understanding, although the code might be **minified** (whitespace removed, short variable names) or **obfuscated** (intentionally made hard to read) using specialized tools.

Bytecode Analysis: Some scripting languages, like Python, often compile source (.py) files into an intermediate **bytecode** format (.pyc files) for faster loading and execution. This bytecode is *not* native machine code but instructions for the Python Virtual Machine (PVM). Reversing might involve analyzing this bytecode directly using tools like dis (Python's built-in disassembler) or specialized Python bytecode analysis tools. Python bytecode is generally higher-level and easier to understand than native assembly.

Interpreter Interaction: Dynamic analysis often involves understanding how the script interacts with its interpreter or runtime environment. For JavaScript in a browser, you use the browser's developer tools to debug the script as it runs. For Python, you might analyze how the script uses standard libraries or interacts with the underlying operating system *through* the Python interpreter.

Native Extensions: Scripting languages often allow calling native code compiled from C/C++ (e.g., Python C extensions, Node.js addons). If significant logic resides in these native modules, your analysis shifts back towards traditional compiled code reversing for those parts.

Example: Python Script and its Bytecode

Consider a simple Python script:

```python
# simple_script.py

def greet(name):
    message = "Hello, " + name + "!"
    print(message)

user_name = "Alice"
greet(user_name)
```

If we look at the bytecode generated for the greet function (using python -m dis simple_script.py), we might see something like this (output details vary by Python version):

```
      Disassembly of greet:
2        0 LOAD_CONST            1 ('Hello, ')
         2 LOAD_FAST             0 (name)
         4 BINARY_ADD
         6 LOAD_CONST            2 ('!')
         8 BINARY_ADD
        10 STORE_FAST            1 (message)

3       12 LOAD_GLOBAL           0 (print)
        14 LOAD_FAST             1 (message)
        16 CALL_FUNCTION         1
        18 POP_TOP
        20 LOAD_CONST            0 (None)
        22 RETURN_VALUE
```

RE Interpretation:

This bytecode is much more abstract than native assembly. Instructions like LOAD_CONST (load a constant value), LOAD_FAST (load a local variable), BINARY_ADD (perform addition), STORE_FAST (store to a local variable), LOAD_GLOBAL (load a built-in or global function), and CALL_FUNCTION directly reflect Python operations.

We can clearly see the string concatenation (BINARY_ADD) and the call to the print function.

Analyzing this bytecode gives a direct view of the script's logic at a level much closer to the original source. Reverse engineering Python often involves analyzing .pyc files this way or directly analyzing the .py source if available.

Intermediate Bytecode Languages (Java, C#): The Virtual Machine Approach

Languages like **Java** and **C#** (part of the .NET framework) occupy a middle ground. Like Python, their source code is compiled into an intermediate **bytecode** (Java bytecode for the Java Virtual Machine - JVM, or Common Intermediate Language - CIL for the .NET Common Language Runtime - CLR). Like C++, they are strongly typed and heavily object-oriented.

What This Looks Like in Reverse Engineering:

Bytecode Focus: Analysis centers on the bytecode itself, contained within .class files (Java) or .dll/.exe assemblies (.NET). Numerous excellent decompilers exist (like **JD-GUI**, **Fernflower** for Java; **ILSpy**, **dnSpy**, **dotPeek** for .NET) that can often reconstruct surprisingly accurate Java or C# source code from the bytecode. This makes static analysis significantly easier than dealing with native code, assuming heavy obfuscation hasn't been applied.

VM Interaction: Dynamic analysis involves debugging the bytecode as it runs on the respective VM (JVM or CLR). Standard debuggers integrate with these VMs, allowing breakpoint setting, stepping, and variable inspection at the bytecode or even decompiled source level. Understanding how the code interacts with the extensive class libraries provided by the Java or .NET frameworks is key.

Obfuscation: Because decompilation is often very effective, developers concerned about protecting their IP frequently use sophisticated **obfuscators** specifically designed for Java or .NET. These tools aggressively rename symbols, encrypt strings, insert confusing control flow, and sometimes even embed sensitive logic in encrypted or dynamically generated code, making RE much harder despite the high-level nature of the bytecode.

The Critical Role of Compilation

Regardless of the language or paradigm (except for purely interpreted scripts), the **compiler** (or interpreter/JIT compiler) plays a huge role in shaping the final executable code you analyze. The compiler translates the human-readable source code into machine-understandable instructions.

Compiler Identity: Different compilers (GCC, Clang, MSVC, Intel C++ Compiler) often generate slightly different assembly code patterns even for identical source code. Experienced reverse engineers can sometimes identify the compiler used based on function prologues/epilogues, library functions linked, or specific instruction sequences, which might offer clues about the development environment.

Optimizations: Compilers perform numerous **optimizations** to make code run faster or use less memory. These optimizations can significantly transform the code's structure, making the resulting assembly harder to map back to the original source. Functions might be **inlined** (their code copied directly into the caller, eliminating the function call overhead but obscuring the original structure), loops might be **unrolled** or **vectorized** (using special

CPU instructions like SSE/AVX), and code might be heavily rearranged. Recognizing common optimization patterns is important for not getting lost in complex assembly. Sometimes, analyzing an unoptimized build (if available) is much easier initially.

Target Architecture: The compiler targets a specific CPU architecture (x86, x86-64, ARM, MIPS, etc.). The resulting machine code is entirely dependent on this choice, dictating the instruction set, register set, and calling conventions you'll encounter during analysis.

Why Understanding Languages and Paradigms is Foundational for RE
Having a solid grasp of these concepts is not just academic; it's intensely practical for reverse engineering:

Tool Selection: Knowing whether you're dealing with native x86 code, ARM firmware, Java bytecode, or a Python script dictates the primary tools you'll use (IDA Pro/Ghidra vs. JD-GUI vs. browser dev tools vs. Python bytecode disassemblers).

Pattern Recognition: Understanding the typical assembly patterns generated from C function calls versus C++ virtual method calls, or recognizing Python bytecode idioms, helps you make sense of the code much faster. You learn what structures to expect.

Interpreting Control Flow: The way you follow program execution differs. Tracing sequential function calls and stack usage in C is different from tracking this Pointers and vtable lookups in C++, which is again different from debugging JavaScript event handlers or analyzing Python bytecode instructions.

Anticipating Challenges: Knowing a program is written in C++ suggests you might encounter vtables and name mangling. Knowing it's .NET suggests potential ease of decompilation but also the likelihood of specific .NET obfuscators being used. This helps you prepare for the types of analysis hurdles you might face.

In essence, the programming language and paradigm are the "genetic code" of the software. While compilation obscures it, traces remain in the final executable. Learning to recognize these traces allows you to infer the original structure and intent, making the complex task of reverse engineering significantly more manageable. It transforms a seemingly random sea of instructions into a landscape with recognizable features derived from its creation process.

2.3. Operating System Fundamentals: The Stage for the Software

Let's transition from the software's internal structure and coding style to the environment where it actually executes – the **Operating System (OS)**. Software, even the most self-contained program, never truly runs in a vacuum. It lives and breathes within the context provided by an OS like Windows, macOS, Linux, Android, or iOS. The OS is the fundamental layer that manages the computer's hardware resources (CPU, memory, disks, network interfaces) and provides a vast array of essential services that applications rely on to function. Understanding these core OS concepts isn't just helpful for reverse engineering; it's absolutely non-negotiable, especially when you start watching the program run with dynamic analysis.

Think of the OS as the ultimate stage manager and technical crew for the performance that is your target application (the "play"). The OS allocates stage time (CPU scheduling), provides and manages the props and scenery (memory allocation and virtual memory), handles set changes and backstage access (file system operations and I/O), facilitates communication between actors and the outside world (networking APIs), and enforces the rules of the theater (permissions and security). Without understanding the stage manager's role and the rules of the stage, you can't possibly grasp the full context or meaning of the play itself. Trying to perform dynamic analysis without OS knowledge is like trying to understand a play by only watching one actor in isolation, oblivious to the lighting changes, sound cues, and interactions happening just offstage.

Let's break down some of the most critical OS fundamentals that every reverse engineer needs to internalize.

Processes and Threads: The Actors on Stage

At the most basic level, when you run a program, the OS creates a **process**. A process is essentially a running instance of that program, a container holding everything needed for its execution. Crucially, the OS typically provides each process with its own **private virtual memory space**. This isolation is a cornerstone of modern OS security and stability; one process generally cannot directly interfere with the memory of another (unless specific mechanisms for inter-process communication are used). Each process is managed by the OS and identified by a unique **Process ID (PID)**.

When you launch your disassembler or target application, you're creating one or more processes.

However, within a single process, there can be multiple independent flows of execution occurring seemingly simultaneously. These are called **threads**. Think of a process as the overall play, and threads as individual actors performing their parts concurrently. All threads within the same process share the same virtual memory space (meaning they can access the same global variables and heap memory), but each thread has its own execution state, including its own set of CPU registers and its own stack (for local variables and function calls). Having multiple threads allows a program to remain responsive while performing background tasks – for instance, one thread might handle the user interface, keeping it snappy, while another thread downloads a large file in the background, and perhaps a third performs complex calculations. The OS scheduler rapidly switches between active threads, giving each a slice of CPU time, creating the illusion of parallel execution even on a single-core processor (this is concurrency). On multi-core processors, threads can truly run in parallel on different cores. Threads within a process are often identified by a **Thread ID (TID)**.

Why Processes & Threads Matter for RE:

Understanding this distinction is fundamental for both static and dynamic analysis.

Targeting: When you attach a **debugger**, you typically attach it to a specific *process* (by its PID). Inside the debugger, you can then list and switch between the different *threads* running within that process. You need to know which process and potentially which specific thread is executing the code you're interested in. If you set a breakpoint, which thread will hit it first?

Malware Behavior: Malware often uses multiple threads for different tasks (e.g., one for network C&C, one for keylogging, one for spreading). More advanced malware might employ **process injection**, where it injects malicious code (often as a new thread) into the memory space of a *different*, legitimate process (like explorer.exe or svchost.exe on Windows) to hide its presence or gain elevated privileges. Recognizing thread creation (CreateThread, pthread_create APIs) or cross-process memory manipulation (WriteProcessMemory, CreateRemoteThread) is a huge red flag during analysis.

Concurrency Issues: In multithreaded applications, incorrect handling of shared resources (data accessed by multiple threads) can lead to **race conditions** or other synchronization bugs. While harder to spot statically, understanding thread interactions can reveal subtle vulnerabilities during dynamic analysis. Debugging multithreaded programs can be complex, as switching between threads might occur unpredictably.

Tools Interaction: Process identification tools like Task Manager (Windows), Activity Monitor (macOS), ps (Linux), or more advanced tools like Process Explorer (Windows) allow you to view running processes and their threads, see their resource usage, and find their PIDs for attaching debuggers.

Code Example: Basic Thread Creation (Conceptual Windows C++)

Let's illustrate the concept of creating a thread using the Windows API.

```cpp
// basic_thread_win.cpp
#include <windows.h>
#include <stdio.h>

// Function that will be executed by the new thread
DWORD WINAPI MyThreadFunction(LPVOID lpParam) {
    int threadId = GetCurrentThreadId();
    int processId = GetCurrentProcessId();
    printf("Hello from thread! PID: %d, TID: %d\n",
processId, threadId);
    Sleep(3000); // Simulate some work
    printf("Thread %d finishing.\n", threadId);
    return 0; // Thread exit code
}

int main() {
    HANDLE hThread;
    DWORD dwThreadId;

    printf("Main thread creating a worker thread...\n");

    // Create the worker thread
    hThread = CreateThread(
        NULL,                    // Default security
attributes
        0,                       // Default stack size
        MyThreadFunction,        // Thread function name
        NULL,                    // Argument to thread
function (none here)
        0,                       // Default creation flags
(run immediately)
        &dwThreadId);            // Variable to receive the
thread ID
```

```
    if (hThread == NULL) {
        printf("Error creating thread (%d)\n",
GetLastError());
        return 1;
    }

    printf("Worker thread created with TID: %d\n",
dwThreadId);
    printf("Main thread continues execution...\n");

    // Optionally wait for the worker thread to finish
    // WaitForSingleObject(hThread, INFINITE);
    // printf("Worker thread finished.\n");

    Sleep(5000); // Main thread waits a bit longer
    printf("Main thread finishing.\n");

    // Close the thread handle
    CloseHandle(hThread);

    return 0;
}
```

Compiling & Running: Compile using a C++ compiler targeting Windows (like MinGW g++ or MSVC cl). When you run the resulting .exe, you'll see output from both the main thread and the newly created worker thread, likely interleaved.

RE Perspective:

Static Analysis: Seeing the call to CreateThread in disassembly immediately tells the analyst that the program is multithreaded. They would then analyze MyThreadFunction (or whatever function pointer is passed) to understand what the new thread does.

Dynamic Analysis: Using Process Explorer while the program runs would show the main process with *two* threads. Attaching a debugger would allow setting breakpoints in MyThreadFunction and observing its execution independently of the main thread. Monitoring API calls might show thread creation events. Malware analysts look for CreateThread or especially CreateRemoteThread (to inject into another process) as key indicators. Understanding processes and threads is the first step in understanding the actors performing the software's logic on the OS stage.

Memory Management: Allocating the Stage and Props

Perhaps the most critical and intricate function of the OS relevant to RE is **Memory Management**. The OS acts as the ultimate arbiter of how the computer's physical RAM is divided and utilized by running processes. Mismanagement of memory by a program is the source of a vast number of security vulnerabilities. For a reverse engineer, understanding OS memory concepts is paramount for deciphering program state, identifying data structures, and finding bugs.

Virtual Memory: The Private Universe Illusion

Modern operating systems employ **Virtual Memory** management. Instead of programs directly accessing physical RAM addresses (which would be chaotic and insecure), the OS gives each process its *own* complete, private **virtual address space**. On a 64-bit system, this space is typically enormous (terabytes or even petabytes), far larger than the actual physical RAM available. The addresses you see in your disassembler, debugger, or within program pointers are *virtual addresses* within that process's private space. This abstraction provides several key benefits:

Isolation: One process cannot simply read or write to the memory of another process by using an address, because the same virtual address in two different processes maps to different physical locations (or is invalid).

Flexibility: The OS can map virtual addresses to physical RAM, to a swap file on disk (paging/swapping), or mark them as unused. It can rearrange physical memory usage without affecting the program's view of its virtual space.

Protection: The OS, aided by the hardware **Memory Management Unit (MMU)**, enforces access permissions (Read, Write, Execute) on *pages* (small, fixed-size blocks) of virtual memory. This allows the OS to prevent code execution from data areas (Data Execution Prevention - DEP/NX bit) or prevent writing to code areas.

RE Relevance: Understanding that you are always dealing with virtual addresses is fundamental. When malware uses **Address Space Layout Randomization (ASLR)**, the OS deliberately loads the program's components (the main executable, DLLs/SOs, stack, heap) at different, randomized virtual addresses each time it runs. This makes hardcoded addresses useless for attackers and complicates RE techniques that rely on fixed offsets. You need tools or techniques to determine the *base address* where modules are loaded in a particular run. Debuggers and tools like

Process Hacker can show you the memory map of a process, listing the virtual address ranges allocated, which modules (DLLs/SOs) are loaded where, and the protection flags (e.g., RW-, R-X, RWE) for each region. Analyzing these memory protection flags is crucial; for example, finding a memory region marked as both Writable and Executable (RWX) can be suspicious, as it might be used by self-modifying code or packed malware after unpacking.

The Stack: Managing the Function Call Drama

Within each thread's virtual memory space, a crucial region is reserved for **The Stack**. The stack operates on a Last-In, First-Out (LIFO) principle, like a stack of plates. Its primary purpose is to manage function calls dynamically.

When a function is called:

The **return address** (where execution should resume in the caller after the current function finishes) is typically pushed onto the stack.

Arguments passed to the function might be pushed onto the stack (depending on the calling convention).

Space is allocated on the stack for the function's **local variables**.

The old **frame pointer** (often EBP or RBP, pointing to a fixed location in the caller's stack frame) might be saved, and the current stack pointer (ESP or RSP) is saved into the frame pointer to mark the start of the new function's **stack frame**.

When the function finishes:

Local variable space is deallocated (usually by moving the stack pointer).

The saved frame pointer is restored.

The return address is popped off the stack, and execution jumps back to the caller.

RE Relevance: The stack is central to understanding program flow.

Function Analysis: Disassembly analysis relies heavily on identifying stack frame setup (prologue) and teardown (epilogue) to delineate functions. Analyzing offsets from the frame pointer (RBP) or stack pointer (RSP) is how you identify where local variables and passed arguments are stored.

Calling Conventions: Reverse engineering often requires figuring out the calling convention by observing how arguments are placed (stack vs. registers) before a call and how the stack is cleaned up afterwards.

Vulnerabilities: The stack is a primary target for exploitation. **Stack buffer overflows**, as discussed previously, occur when data written to a local buffer exceeds its allocated size, overwriting adjacent stack data, including the crucial return address. By carefully crafting oversized input containing malicious code (shellcode) and overwriting the return address to point to this shellcode, attackers can seize control of execution. Understanding stack layouts is essential for finding and exploiting (or defending against) these vulnerabilities. Protections like stack canaries (which place a random value before the return address and check it before returning) aim to detect such overflows.

The Heap: The Prop Room for Dynamic Needs

While the stack is perfect for data whose size and lifetime are known at compile time (local variables), programs often need memory whose size isn't known until runtime or whose lifetime extends beyond a single function call. This is where **The Heap** comes in. The heap is a generally larger region of a process's virtual memory reserved for **dynamic memory allocation**. Programs request chunks of memory from the heap using functions like: malloc(), calloc(), realloc(), free() (standard C library, often wrapping underlying OS calls).

new, delete (C++ operators, usually implemented on top of malloc/free). HeapAlloc(), HeapFree() (Windows specific Heap API).

The OS (or the C runtime library) manages the heap, keeping track of allocated and free blocks. This involves complex data structures (like linked lists of free chunks, bins for different sizes) maintained by the **heap manager** or **allocator**. Different allocators exist (e.g., ptmalloc on Linux, the Windows segment heap) with different performance and security characteristics.

RE Relevance: Analyzing heap operations is critical for understanding how a program manages complex data structures created at runtime.

Data Structure Analysis: Tracking calls to allocation functions (malloc, new) and observing how the returned pointers are used allows analysts to identify dynamically created objects or data buffers. Analyzing the code that accesses memory relative to these heap pointers helps reconstruct the layout of complex structures (like linked lists, trees, or custom class objects) stored on the heap.

Memory Leaks: Failing to free or delete allocated heap memory leads to memory leaks, which might be identified during long-running dynamic analysis.

Heap Vulnerabilities: The heap is another prime target for exploitation. **Heap overflows** are similar to stack overflows but involve writing past the boundaries of an allocated heap chunk, potentially corrupting the heap manager's internal metadata (like the size or free/in-use status of adjacent chunks). Corrupting this metadata can sometimes allow an attacker to gain control over the allocation process, leading to arbitrary writes or code execution. **Use-after-free** vulnerabilities occur when a program continues to use a pointer to heap memory *after* that memory has been freed. If the memory allocator reassigns that freed chunk to a new allocation, the old pointer might now point into unrelated or attacker-controlled data, leading to crashes or exploitation. **Double free** vulnerabilities (freeing the same chunk twice) can also corrupt heap metadata. Finding and exploiting heap vulnerabilities often requires a deep understanding of the specific heap allocator's internal mechanisms and is considered an advanced RE topic. Debugging tools and specialized heap analysis plugins can help visualize heap structures and track allocations. Malware frequently uses the heap to store downloaded payloads, decrypted configurations, or stolen data before exfiltration.

Understanding how the OS, in conjunction with runtime libraries, manages stack and heap memory is fundamental to analyzing program state, control flow, and security vulnerabilities.

File Systems: Organizing the Stage Scenery Persistently

Programs rarely operate solely in memory; they almost always need to interact with **persistent storage** – data that survives even when the program isn't running or the computer is turned off. This is managed by the OS through **File Systems**. A file system defines how data is organized into files and directories (folders) on storage devices like hard drives (HDDs), solid-state drives (SSDs), or USB drives. Common examples include NTFS (Windows), APFS/HFS+ (macOS), ext4/XFS/Btrfs (Linux), and FAT32 (older systems, removable media).

The OS provides APIs for programs to create, open, read, write, delete, and manage files and directories. Programs typically receive a **file handle** or **file descriptor** from the OS when they open a file, which they use in subsequent operations. The OS manages buffering (reading/writing data in larger chunks for efficiency) and translates logical file operations into low-level commands for the storage device controller.

RE Relevance: Analyzing file system interactions is a staple of reverse engineering, especially for malware analysis and understanding application behavior.

Identifying Program Actions: Monitoring calls to file system APIs is one of the clearest ways to see what a program is *doing*. Seeing CreateFile followed by WriteFile indicates data is being written. ReadFile shows data being loaded. DeleteFile shows removal. Specific filenames being accessed often reveal configuration files, log files, temporary data, input sources, or output destinations.

Malware Persistence and Artifacts: Malware often writes files to disk to store downloaded payloads, configuration data, stolen information, or copies of itself for persistence (e.g., dropping an executable in a startup folder). Identifying these file creations and locations is critical for detection and cleanup.

Configuration and Data Storage: Legitimate applications use files extensively for configuration (.ini, .xml, .json, registry on Windows), user data storage (documents, save games, databases), or temporary caches. Understanding which files an application uses helps analyze its configuration options or data formats (linking back to Chapter 6).

Vulnerabilities: File system operations can be vulnerable. **Path traversal** vulnerabilities occur if a program constructs filenames based on user input without properly sanitizing sequences like ../, potentially allowing an attacker to read or write files outside intended directories. **Time-of-check to time-of-use (TOCTOU)** race conditions can occur if a program checks file permissions or attributes but then operates on the file later, during which time an attacker might have changed the file or its properties.

Tools: Process Monitor (ProcMon) on Windows is invaluable for logging all file system activity in real-time, allowing you to filter by process and see exactly which files are accessed, read, written, or deleted. On Linux, strace can show file-related system calls like openat, read, write, unlink. Debuggers can also be used to set breakpoints on file I/O functions.

System Calls (APIs): The Request Line to the Stage Manager

As mentioned earlier, processes run in a restricted mode (user space) and cannot directly access hardware or perform certain critical operations that could destabilize the system. To perform these tasks – like accessing files, sending network packets, creating new processes, allocating large chunks of memory, or interacting directly with device drivers – the program must ask the **OS kernel** (running in a privileged mode, kernel space) to do it on their behalf. This request mechanism uses **System Calls** (often shortened to **syscalls**).

The exact mechanism for making a system call varies by OS and architecture but generally involves:

Placing the system call number (identifying the requested operation) into a specific CPU register (e.g., EAX on older Linux x86).

Placing the arguments for the system call into other specific registers.

Executing a special instruction (like syscall, sysenter on modern x86, or int 0x80/int 0x2E on older systems) that causes a trap into the kernel.

The kernel handles the trap, looks up the system call number, performs the requested operation (with necessary permission checks), and then returns control back to the user-space process, often placing a return value (like a success/error code or a file handle) in a specific register.

Most application developers don't make raw system calls directly. Instead, they use **Application Programming Interfaces (APIs)** provided by system libraries (like libc on Linux/Unix, or kernel32.dll, user32.dll, gdi32.dll, advapi32.dll, ws2_32.dll, etc., which collectively form the Windows API). These library functions provide a more stable, portable, and user-friendly wrapper around the underlying system calls. For example, when a C program calls printf(), the libc implementation might eventually make underlying write() system calls to send the formatted string to the standard output device. On Windows, calling CreateFileW() from kernel32.dll ultimately leads (often via the lower-level Native API in ntdll.dll) to a system call that asks the kernel to perform the file creation operation.

RE Relevance: Understanding and monitoring API calls or system calls is arguably the *single most powerful technique* for dynamic analysis.

Revealing Intent: Calls to specific APIs clearly signal the program's high-level intentions. Seeing socket(), connect(), send() reveals network communication. CreateFileW(), WriteFile() indicate file writing. RegCreateKeyExW(), RegSetValueExW() point to Windows registry manipulation. CreateProcessW(), CreateRemoteThread() signal process/thread creation or injection. CryptEncrypt() suggests encryption is happening. Malware analysis heavily relies on identifying these suspicious API sequences.

Static Analysis Clues: The **import table** of an executable lists the external DLLs and specific API functions it intends to call. Examining this table (using tools like PE-bear, CFF Explorer, or features within IDA/Ghidra) gives a quick overview of the program's potential capabilities even before looking at the code. Malware often tries to obscure its imports by resolving API addresses dynamically at runtime (e.g., using GetProcAddress) rather than listing them in the import table, so finding calls to LoadLibrary and GetProcAddress is itself an interesting clue.

Dynamic Monitoring/Hooking: Tools like Process Monitor (which primarily monitors specific types of APIs/syscalls), strace/dtruss (which trace system calls), and API hooking frameworks (like Frida, Detours, EasyHook) allow analysts to intercept calls to specific APIs or syscalls *as they happen*. They can log the arguments passed, the return values, and even modify them on the fly. This provides precise ground truth about what the program is actually doing and what data it's working with. For example, hooking CryptEncrypt could reveal the plaintext data *before* it gets encrypted by ransomware. Hooking network send functions can capture data being exfiltrated.

Finding Vulnerabilities: Incorrect usage of APIs (e.g., providing improperly validated arguments, misinterpreting return codes, using inherently unsafe functions like strcpy instead of safer alternatives like strncpy_s) is a common source of bugs and vulnerabilities.

Code Example: strace on Linux

Consider a simple C program making a file write call on Linux:

```c
// simple_write_linux.c
#include <stdio.h>
#include <fcntl.h>
#include <unistd.h>
#include <string.h>

int main() {
    int fd;
    char *message = "Hello from RE test!\n";
    ssize_t bytes_written;

    // Open (or create) a file for writing
```

```
    fd = open("output.txt", O_WRONLY | O_CREAT | O_TRUNC,
0644);
    if (fd == -1) {
        perror("open failed");
        return 1;
    }

    // Write the message to the file
    bytes_written = write(fd, message, strlen(message));
    if (bytes_written == -1) {
        perror("write failed");
        close(fd); // Close on error too
        return 1;
    }

    printf("Wrote %zd bytes to output.txt\n", bytes_written);

    // Close the file
    if (close(fd) == -1) {
        perror("close failed");
        return 1;
    }

    return 0;
}
```

Compiling & Running with strace: Compile (gcc
simple_write_linux.c -o simple_write) and then run it under
strace: strace ./simple_write. You'll see a lot of output
related to program startup, but interspersed (or at the end),
you'll find lines similar to these:

```
        ... (startup syscalls like execve, brk, access, openat
for libraries) ...
openat(AT_FDCWD, "output.txt", O_WRONLY|O_CREAT|O_TRUNC,
0644) = 3
write(3, "Hello from RE test!\n", 20)    = 20
fstat(1, {st_mode=S_IFCHR|0620, st_rdev=makedev(136,
0), ...}) = 0
ioctl(1, TCGETS, {B38400 opost isig icanon echo ...}) = 0
write(1, "Wrote 20 bytes to output.txt\n", 29Wrote 20 bytes
to output.txt
) = 29
close(3)                                 = 0
... (exit syscalls) ...
```

RE Interpretation: The strace output clearly shows the key system calls
being made:
1. openat (a modern variant of open) is called to open output.txt with
write/create/truncate flags, returning file descriptor 3.

2. write is called with file descriptor 3, the buffer containing "Hello from RE test!\n", and the length 20. The kernel returns 20, indicating success.

3. write calls with file descriptor 1 (standard output) are from the printf.

4. close is called on file descriptor 3.

This dynamic view instantly reveals the program's file writing behavior without even looking at the disassembly.

Permissions and Security: The Rules of Engagement

Finally, the OS acts as the ultimate security guard, enforcing rules about who can do what. This involves concepts like **user accounts**, **groups**, **permissions**, and **privilege levels**. The goal is to prevent users and programs from accessing resources they shouldn't or performing actions that could harm the system.

Modern OSes implement sophisticated security models:

Access Control: Discretionary Access Control (DAC) allows resource owners (like the user who created a file) to grant permissions to others. Mandatory Access Control (MAC) enforces system-wide policies (common in high-security environments). Filesystems have permissions (read/write/execute for owner/group/others on Unix-like systems; more complex Access Control Lists - ACLs on NTFS).

Privilege Levels (Rings): CPUs often enforce hardware privilege levels. The OS kernel runs at the most privileged level (Ring 0 on x86), having direct hardware access. User applications run at a less privileged level (Ring 3 on x86). System calls are the controlled mechanism for user code to request Ring 0 services.

User Accounts and Privileges: Standard users have limited permissions, while administrators (root/Administrator) have much broader control. Features like User Account Control (UAC) on Windows aim to limit applications from performing administrative actions without explicit user consent, even if run by an administrator account (running with medium integrity level by default). sudo on Linux allows specific users to run commands as root.

RE Relevance: Understanding the OS security model is vital for security-focused RE.

Malware Tactics: Malware constantly tries to bypass these protections. It might try to trick the user into granting elevated permissions (UAC prompts, phishing), exploit vulnerabilities in user-space applications to gain code execution, and then exploit separate **privilege escalation** vulnerabilities (often kernel bugs) to gain Ring 0 (kernel-level) access, which allows it to bypass most user-space security controls and install deep rootkits. Analyzing malware often involves identifying these privilege escalation attempts.

Vulnerability Analysis: Many security vulnerabilities involve bypassing permission checks or escalating privileges incorrectly. Understanding how the OS *intends* security to work is necessary to spot deviations or flaws in specific applications or drivers.

Testing Assumptions: Does the application correctly handle running as a non-privileged user? Does it request more permissions than it actually needs? Reverse engineering can help answer these questions during security audits.

Connecting the Dots: The Interplay of Concepts

It's crucial to see that these OS concepts – Processes/Threads, Memory Management, File Systems, System Calls/APIs, and Permissions – don't exist in isolation. They are deeply interconnected, and understanding their interplay is key for the reverse engineer.

The **Architecture** (Chapter 2.1) chosen by developers (monolith, layered, client-server) dictates *how* the application utilizes these OS services. A client-server application will heavily use networking APIs, while a data-processing monolith might focus more on file I/O and memory allocation APIs.

The **Programming Language and Paradigm** (Chapter 2.2) influence *which* specific OS APIs or wrappers are typically called. C programs will use libc wrappers around syscalls for file I/O and memory. C++ new/delete might call malloc/free which call OS memory functions. Java/.NET applications interact via the extensive libraries of their respective VMs, which in turn call the underlying OS APIs. Recognizing these different layers of interaction is important.

Having this foundational OS knowledge transforms your perspective during analysis. Instead of seeing a raw call to address 0x7C801AD4, you recognize it as kernel32!CreateFileW. Instead of just seeing data written relative to RBP, you understand it's a local variable on the current function's stack frame. Instead of seeing random bytes being sent over the network, you look for preceding socket and connect calls to understand the context. It provides the **mental framework** needed to interpret the low-level details uncovered by tools like disassemblers and debuggers. You simply cannot perform effective dynamic analysis, or fully understand the implications of many static analysis findings (especially related to vulnerabilities or malware behavior), without a solid grasp of how the software interacts with its operating system environment.

With this conceptual knowledge of software architecture, programming languages/paradigms, and operating system fundamentals now firmly established, we have the necessary background. We understand the "shape" of software and the "stage" it performs on. We're finally ready to get our hands truly dirty. In the next chapter, we'll delve into the specific tools and the core techniques that form the practical heart of the reverse engineering workflow. Let's open the toolbox.

Chapter 3: Tools and Techniques

We've talked theory and concepts (Chapter 2), and now it's time to open the toolbox. Reverse engineering isn't magic; it relies on specific tools that help us peek under the hood, understand the machinery, and sometimes even tinker with it. Think of yourself as a mechanic – you wouldn't try to fix an engine without wrenches, screwdrivers, and diagnostic equipment. This chapter introduces your digital toolkit.

Remember, though, tools are just enablers. A great mechanic understands *how* the engine works, not just how to turn a wrench. Similarly, the best reverse engineers understand the *concepts* (which we covered!) and use tools strategically to uncover insights.

3.1. Disassemblers and Debuggers: Seeing the Code and Watching It Run

let's delve into the absolute bedrock of the reverse engineer's toolkit: **disassemblers** and **debuggers**. These two categories of tools are utterly indispensable when tackling compiled software – the kind where you don't have the luxury of readable source code. They represent the two fundamental pillars of analysis: **static analysis**, where we examine the code's structure and potential behavior without executing it, and **dynamic analysis**, where we observe the program live, watching its actions and state changes as it runs. Mastering these tools, understanding their capabilities, limitations, and how they interact with the underlying system, is arguably the most crucial step in becoming proficient at reverse engineering. Think of them as your microscope and your probe, essential for revealing the intricate details hidden within the machine code.

Disassemblers: Translating the Native Tongue of the CPU

Imagine discovering an ancient artifact inscribed with symbols from a long-dead language. A **disassembler** acts as your expert linguist, translating the raw **machine code** – the fundamental sequence of binary instructions (opcodes and operands) that a specific Central Processing Unit (CPU) directly understands – into a more human-comprehensible form called **assembly language**. Assembly language uses mnemonics (like MOV for move, ADD for addition, JMP for jump, CALL for calling a function) to represent the machine instructions specific to a particular CPU architecture (e.g., x86, x86-64, ARM, MIPS, PowerPC).While assembly language is still extremely low-level, far more granular than high-level languages like Python, Java, or even C++, it possesses a defined structure based on the CPU's instruction set. It allows us, as analysts, to begin tracing the program's logic, understanding how data is moved between memory and registers, how arithmetic and logical operations are performed, and how the flow of execution branches and jumps. The disassembler's primary function is this crucial translation, turning opaque bytes like 89 D8 C3 (which on x86 means "move the value in EBX to EAX" followed by "return") into the readable line MOV EAX, EBX followed by RETN.

However, modern sophisticated disassemblers do far more than just a linear, instruction-by-instruction translation. They incorporate significant analytical intelligence to make the daunting task of understanding large programs more manageable.

Advanced Analysis Capabilities:

Function Identification: A key task is recognizing the boundaries of functions or procedures within the binary. Disassemblers use various heuristics, such as identifying standard function prologue and epilogue sequences (patterns of instructions commonly used by compilers to set up and tear down stack frames, like PUSH RBP; MOV RBP, RSP and LEAVE; RETN), locating CALL instructions and assuming their targets are function starts, or utilizing symbol information or metadata embedded within the executable file format (if present). Accurately identifying functions allows the disassembler to structure the code logically, presenting it as callable units rather than one continuous stream of instructions. This faces challenges in stripped binaries (where symbols are removed) or code using non-standard function call mechanisms or heavy optimization.

Cross-References (Xrefs): This is arguably one of the most powerful navigational features. Disassemblers meticulously track relationships within the code. **Code Xrefs** show every location within the program that calls a particular function or jumps to a specific code address. **Data Xrefs** show every instruction that reads from or writes to a particular memory address or variable. Need to know how a crucial data structure is used? Check its data xrefs. Want to understand the context in which a specific function is invoked? Follow its code xrefs backward. Navigating code by following xrefs is fundamental to tracing logic and understanding data dependencies across different parts of the application. It transforms the analysis from a linear reading task into an exploration of an interconnected graph of logic.

Control Flow Graphs (CFGs): While linear disassembly listing is essential, visualizing the *flow* of execution can be incredibly illuminating. Disassemblers can generate Control Flow Graphs, which represent a function's structure graphically. Each **basic block** (a sequence of instructions with no jumps in or out, except at the beginning and end) is typically shown as a node. Edges between these nodes represent possible transfers of control: unconditional jumps (JMP), conditional jumps (JE, JNE, JG, etc., often shown with different colored arrows for the 'taken' and 'not taken' paths), and function calls (CALL). Loops appear as cycles in the graph, while if-else structures show diverging and merging paths. Studying a CFG often provides a much more intuitive understanding of a function's complexity and decision-making logic than scrolling through pages of linear assembly. Complex, tangled CFGs can sometimes indicate compiler optimizations or deliberate obfuscation techniques like control flow flattening.

Stack Analysis and Calling Conventions: Based on the identified function prologues and the instructions used within a function, disassemblers attempt to analyze the **stack frame**. They identify where local variables are likely stored (relative to the stack or frame pointer, often assigning default names like var_4, var_8) and where passed arguments reside on the stack or are expected in registers according to standard **calling conventions** (like cdecl, stdcall, fastcall on x86; System V AMD64 ABI or Microsoft x64 calling convention on x86-64; AAPCS on ARM). This analysis significantly aids in understanding data movement during function calls.

Type Reconstruction and Propagation: Through sophisticated analysis of how data is used (e.g., passed to specific API functions, used in arithmetic vs. logical operations, accessed with certain offsets), advanced disassemblers and especially integrated decompilers attempt to infer the likely **data types** of variables and function arguments (e.g., guessing if var_8 is an integer, a pointer, or part of a larger structure). This type information can dramatically improve readability.

Library Code Identification (Signature Matching): When analyzing statically linked executables, where library code is copied directly into the binary, the analysis view can be cluttered with thousands of standard library functions. Tools like IDA Pro's **FLIRT (Fast Library Identification and**

Recognition Technology) or similar capabilities in Ghidra use databases of signatures (patterns of bytes or code characteristics) derived from common library builds. They scan the binary, match these signatures, and automatically label the identified library functions (e.g., recognizing and naming _printf, _malloc, _strcpy even when no symbols are present). This allows the analyst to quickly filter out the known boilerplate and focus on the application's unique, potentially interesting code.

Executable Format Parsing: Disassemblers understand standard executable file formats like **PE (Portable Executable)** on Windows, **ELF (Executable and Linkable Format)** on Linux, and **Mach-O** on macOS/iOS. They parse the file headers and section tables to correctly identify code vs. data sections, locate the program's entry point, extract the **import table** (listing DLLs/SOs and functions used), the **export table** (functions provided by a library), symbol tables (if present), and embedded resources. This structural information provides crucial context before even looking at the first instruction.

Popular Disassembler Choices:

IDA Pro: Often considered the industry standard for many years, IDA Pro (Interactive Disassembler) is renowned for its powerful analysis engine, extensive processor support, mature graphing capabilities, FLIRT signature matching, and its highly interactive nature allowing analysts to easily rename variables, define structures, add comments, and progressively refine the disassembly listing. Its killer feature for many is the optional **Hex-Rays Decompiler** addon, which attempts to translate assembly back into high-level C-like pseudo-code, dramatically accelerating analysis (though requiring careful verification). IDA also features powerful scripting capabilities via IDC and IDAPython. Its main drawback is its significant cost.

Ghidra: Developed by the NSA and released as free and open-source software, Ghidra has rapidly become a major contender. It offers features rivaling IDA Pro, including broad processor support, sophisticated graphing, excellent cross-referencing, and, crucially, a very capable **built-in decompiler** generating C-like pseudo-code. Ghidra is written in Java, making it cross-platform. It also includes features for collaborative reverse engineering projects. Its user interface and workflow differ from IDA's, representing perhaps a slightly steeper initial learning curve for some, but its power and accessibility make it an incredibly compelling choice.

radare2 (and its fork, rizin): For those who prefer the command line and seek ultimate flexibility, radare2 (r2) and rizin are powerful open-source reverse engineering frameworks. They offer a vast array of commands for disassembly, analysis, debugging, patching, hex editing, and much more. The learning curve is notably steep, as functionality is accessed primarily through terse commands (e.g., aa to analyze all, pdf to print disassembly function, ag to show graph). However, their scriptability, extensive feature set, and active development make them favorites among many advanced users and security researchers. Graphical interfaces like Cutter are available but the core power lies in the command line.

Hopper Disassembler: Particularly popular in the macOS and iOS RE communities, Hopper offers a clean graphical user interface, support for various architectures (x86, ARM), and integrated decompilation features. It strikes a balance between usability and power, though perhaps without the sheer depth of IDA or Ghidra for all scenarios.

The journey with a disassembler often starts with loading the target binary. You might begin at the main entry point or examine the import table for interesting API calls. From there, it becomes an exploratory process: follow code xrefs to see where a function is called, follow data xrefs to see how a variable is used, study the control flow graph to understand complex logic, rename functions and variables as you deduce their purpose (sub_4015A0 becomes validate_license_key, var_10 becomes user_input_buffer), add comments to document your findings, and use signature matching to filter out library code. It's an iterative process, gradually building a coherent understanding from the low-level details, like assembling a detailed blueprint from inspecting the finished building's components. Static analysis using a disassembler lays the essential groundwork, mapping out the possibilities before you ever run the code.

Debuggers: Controlling and Observing the Live Performance

If the disassembler provides the annotated script and stage layout for the play, the **debugger** is your director's chair combined with a universal remote control. It allows you to execute the software (the play) under tightly controlled conditions, pause the action at any moment, step through it instruction by instruction, examine the state of every actor (registers, variables in memory), and even change their lines or props on the fly. Debuggers are the primary tools for **dynamic analysis**, revealing how the software *actually* behaves with specific inputs and runtime conditions. Debuggers work by leveraging specific Operating System APIs (ptrace on Linux, the Windows Debug API) or hardware features to control another process (the "debuggee"). You can either launch the target program under the debugger's control or attach the debugger to an already running process (identified by its PID). Once attached, the debugger can exert fine-grained control over the debuggee's execution.

Essential Debugging Capabilities:

Breakpoints: Setting Strategic Pauses: The most fundamental debugging feature is the ability to set **breakpoints**. These are instructions to the debugger to halt the execution of the target program whenever it reaches a specific point.

Software Breakpoints: The most common type. The debugger overwrites the instruction byte at the target address with a special trap instruction (e.g., INT 3, opcode 0xCC on x86). When the CPU executes this instruction, it generates an exception that the OS intercepts and forwards to the debugger. The debugger then halts the program and replaces the original instruction byte before the user continues execution. They are easy to set but detectable (the code modification can be checked).

Hardware Breakpoints: These use dedicated debug registers built into the CPU. You can typically set a small number (often 4) of hardware breakpoints based on instruction execution address, memory write address, or memory read/write address. Since they don't modify the code, they are stealthier than software breakpoints but limited in number. They are invaluable for setting breakpoints on data access (e.g., "stop when this variable is written to") or in self-modifying code where software breakpoints would be overwritten.

Memory Breakpoints: Functionally similar to hardware breakpoints targeting memory access, these halt execution when a specific range of memory is read from or written to. Crucial for tracking data changes.

Conditional Breakpoints: Advanced debuggers allow setting breakpoints that only trigger if a certain condition is met (e.g., "stop at this instruction only if the EAX register equals 0" or "stop here only on the 10th time it's hit"). This helps filter out noise when a location is executed frequently.

Setting breakpoints effectively is key – you might set them at the start of functions identified during static analysis, before critical API calls, after loops, or just before conditional jumps to inspect the state leading to a decision.

Stepping Through Code: The Fine-Grained View: Once paused at a breakpoint (or the program's entry point), you need to control execution flow precisely.

Step Into (F7 in many debuggers): Executes the single next instruction. If that instruction is a CALL, execution will pause at the very first instruction *inside* the called function. Use this to dive deep into function logic.

Step Over (F8): Executes the single next instruction. If that instruction is a CALL, the debugger executes the *entire* called function and pauses only *after* it returns, on the instruction following the CALL. Use this to execute library functions or functions you've already analyzed or aren't interested in without stepping through their internals.

Step Out (Shift+F8): Continues execution until the current function returns to its caller, then pauses. Useful if you accidentally stepped into a long or uninteresting function and want to get back out quickly.

Run to Cursor: Allows you to place the cursor on a future instruction and tell the debugger to run until it reaches that point.

Meticulously stepping through code, observing the state changes after each instruction, is how you unravel complex algorithms or pinpoint the exact moment things go wrong.

Inspecting State: Understanding "What Is Happening": While stepping or paused at a breakpoint, the debugger provides windows into the program's internal state:

CPU Registers: View the current values of general-purpose registers (EAX, EBX, RDI, RSI, R0-R12, etc.), the instruction pointer (EIP/RIP/PC indicating the next instruction to execute), the stack pointer (ESP/RSP), the base/frame pointer (EBP/RBP), and the flags register (showing results of comparisons like Zero Flag, Carry Flag). Register values are critical for understanding calculations and control flow decisions.

Memory View: Examine the contents of memory at any virtual address within the process's space. Debuggers offer various views: raw hexadecimal bytes, corresponding ASCII characters, disassembled instructions, interpretations based on data types (integers, floats, pointers), or even structure-aware views if you define data structures. You can watch how buffers are filled, how heap metadata changes, or how objects are laid out.

Stack View: Visualize the current call stack, showing the sequence of nested function calls. You can often see return addresses, saved registers, and parameters/local variables for each stack frame, providing vital context for where you are and how you got there.

Variables (Watch): If debugging with symbols or after identifying variables, you can add them to a watch window to monitor their values continuously. Inspecting state is crucial for understanding *why* the program takes certain paths (e.g., checking the flags after a CMP instruction before a conditional jump) and *what* data is being processed.

Modifying State: Most debuggers allow you to change register values or memory contents while the program is paused. This is incredibly useful for testing hypotheses. For instance, you could change the value of a flag just before a conditional jump to force execution down a different path, or modify a return value from a function call to see how the caller reacts. This requires caution, as arbitrarily changing state can easily lead to crashes or unpredictable behavior, but it's a powerful way to probe program logic.

Popular Debugger Choices:

x64dbg / OllyDbg: These are graphical debuggers primarily for user-mode Windows applications (OllyDbg for 32-bit, x64dbg for both 32-bit and 64-bit). They are immensely popular in the RE community, especially for malware analysis and software cracking, due to their intuitive multi-pane layout (CPU/Disassembly, Registers, Stack, Memory Dump), extensive plugin support (adding features like advanced unpacking, scripting, and anti-anti-debugging), and focus on presenting information clearly for assembly-level analysis. Their user-friendly nature makes them a good starting point for Windows RE.

WinDbg: Part of the Debugging Tools for Windows package from Microsoft, WinDbg is an extremely powerful, if somewhat intimidating, debugger. Its main strength lies in its versatility – it can debug both user-mode applications and, crucially, the Windows kernel itself (requiring a two-machine setup, often using VMs connected via serial or network). It's indispensable for analyzing device drivers, diagnosing system crashes (via memory dump analysis), and performing deep OS-level investigation. While it has a GUI (WinDbg Preview offers a more modern interface), much of its power is accessed through a rich command language. Learning commands like bp (set breakpoint), bl (list breakpoints), g (go/continue), p (step over), t (step into), k (display stack trace), d* (display memory commands like db, dw, dd, dq, da, du), and extension commands (!process, !thread, !heap) is essential for effective use. The learning curve is steep, but the capabilities are unmatched for Windows debugging.

GDB (GNU Debugger): The standard debugger across the Linux, macOS (historically), and general Unix-like ecosystem. It's primarily a command-line tool, known for its robustness and integration with the GCC compiler toolchain. While the base GDB interface is spartan, it's often used with powerful enhancement frontends like **GEF (GDB Enhanced Features)**, **PEDA (Python Exploit Development Assistance for GDB)**, or **Pwndbg**, which add colorized, contextual displays of disassembly, registers, stack, memory, backtrace, and other useful information directly in the terminal, making it much more user-friendly for RE tasks. GDB commands like b (breakpoint), r (run), n (next/step over), s (step into), c (continue), info registers, x/<format> (examine memory), and bt (backtrace) are fundamental. It's the go-to tool for compiled code RE on Linux.

LLDB: Originating from the LLVM compiler infrastructure project, LLDB is the default debugger in Apple's Xcode environment and commonly used for macOS and iOS development and reverse engineering. It shares many concepts with GDB but uses a different command syntax (e.g., breakpoint set, run, next/n, step/s, continue/c, register read, memory read, thread backtrace). Like GDB, it's often enhanced by external scripts or plugins for RE work.

The Debugging Workflow: A typical dynamic analysis session often mirrors detective work. You might start with a hypothesis from static analysis ("I think this function decrypts the config data"). You set a breakpoint at the start of that function. Run the program under the debugger. When it hits the breakpoint, you inspect the input arguments (registers, stack, memory pointers). Are they what you expected? Then you meticulously step through the function's instructions (step into or step over), watching how register values change, examining memory where results are stored. Does the output look like decrypted data? Perhaps you set another breakpoint later, after the function returns, to see how the caller uses the decrypted data. You might set memory breakpoints on the input buffer to see where it was populated, or on the output buffer to see when it's used. This cycle of hypothesis -> breakpoint -> run -> inspect -> step -> observe -> refine hypothesis -> repeat is the essence of debugging for reverse engineering. It's often the only reliable way to understand runtime behavior determined by user input, network data, complex state interactions, or obfuscated code whose static representation is misleading.

The Critical Synergy: Static Mapping Meets Dynamic Validation

It's crucial to understand that disassemblers and debuggers are not mutually exclusive tools; they are profoundly complementary. The most effective reverse engineering workflow almost always involves a constant interplay between static and dynamic analysis.

Static analysis with a disassembler gives you the **overview**, the **map** of the software's structure and potential paths. You can explore the entire codebase, identify key functions, understand data structures (as defined), trace potential control flows, and filter out irrelevant library code. It lets you see *what the code could possibly do*.

Dynamic analysis with a debugger provides the **ground truth**, the **validation** of specific execution paths under real conditions. You can confirm hypotheses formed during static analysis, observe actual runtime data values (crucial for understanding encryption keys, network packets, or user input processing), resolve dynamically calculated addresses or function pointers, and navigate the complex state changes that are difficult or impossible to predict statically. It lets you see *what the code actually does* in a specific scenario.

Imagine trying to navigate a city. Static analysis is like studying the map beforehand – you learn the street layout, identify major landmarks, and plan potential routes. Dynamic analysis is like actually driving through the city – you see the traffic conditions, confirm your route is viable, observe temporary events, and discover details not shown on the static map. You wouldn't rely solely on the map (you might hit unexpected road closures), nor would you drive aimlessly without consulting it.

The typical workflow involves bouncing back and forth:

Static Exploration (Disassembler): Identify a function or area of interest (e.g., potential license check, network sending routine, encryption function). Understand its basic structure, inputs, and outputs based on the disassembly/decompilation. Formulate a hypothesis about its behavior.

Targeted Dynamic Setup (Debugger): Set breakpoints at strategic locations identified statically (e.g., function entry, specific instruction, before a critical comparison, after a suspected decryption loop).

Execution and Observation (Debugger): Run the program, let it hit a breakpoint. Inspect registers, memory, and the stack to see the actual runtime values. Verify or refute your initial hypothesis based on the observed state.

Detailed Tracing (Debugger): Step through the code, instruction by instruction if necessary, carefully watching how data is transformed and control flow decisions are made. Maybe set additional breakpoints based on what you're seeing.

New Insights: The dynamic analysis might reveal unexpected behavior, the actual value of an important variable, or confirm the purpose of a code section.

Return to Static Analysis (Disassembler): Armed with new runtime knowledge (e.g., "variable var_24 actually holds the decrypted network key," "this function is only called if the license file is missing"), go back to the disassembler. Rename variables/functions accordingly, add comments reflecting the observed behavior, and explore xrefs related to the newly understood data or functions. This refines your overall map.

Repeat: Continue this cycle, progressively deepening your understanding of the software piece by piece.

This synergy is essential for tackling complex targets, especially those employing obfuscation or anti-analysis techniques designed to thwart either static or dynamic analysis alone.

In conclusion, disassemblers and debuggers are the foundational instruments for any serious reverse engineering effort involving compiled code. The disassembler acts as your translator and cartographer, revealing the static structure and potential pathways within the code. The debugger serves as your interactive probe and observation platform, allowing you to control execution and witness the software's actual runtime behavior and state.

While each is powerful on its own, their true potential is unlocked when used together in a complementary, iterative workflow. Mastering their features, understanding how they interact with the underlying CPU architecture and operating system, and developing strategic analysis approaches based on their combined strengths is the key to successfully unveiling the secrets hidden within the binary code.

3.2. Decompilers and Hex Editors: Higher-Level Views and Raw Data

Okay, let's build upon our understanding of the reverse engineer's core toolkit. We've discussed disassemblers and debuggers – the essential instruments for deciphering the language of machines and observing software in motion. However, sometimes we need a higher level of abstraction to grasp complex logic more quickly, or conversely, we need to strip away all interpretation and interact directly with the raw, fundamental bytes of data. This is where **decompilers** and **hex editors** come into play, offering powerful alternative perspectives that complement the insights gained from disassembly and debugging. They represent two ends of a spectrum: decompilers strive for human-like abstraction, while hex editors provide unvarnished, low-level truth.

Decompilers: Striving for Human-Readable Logic

We established that disassemblers act as translators, converting raw machine code into assembly language – a symbolic representation of CPU instructions. While invaluable, wading through thousands of lines of assembly (MOV, ADD, JMP, CALL) can still be a slow and mentally demanding process to understand the overall algorithm or logic of a complex function. A **decompiler** attempts to take this process one giant leap further. Its ambitious goal is to translate low-level assembly language (or sometimes intermediate bytecode, like that used by Java or .NET) *back* into a high-level programming language, most commonly resembling C or C++.

The output produced by a decompiler is often referred to as **pseudo-code**. It's crucial to understand that this is almost never the original source code written by the developer. The compilation process is inherently "lossy" – information like original variable names, comments, precise source code formatting, and some high-level structural information is typically discarded by the compiler during optimization and translation to machine code. A decompiler attempts to reconstruct a *functionally equivalent* high-level representation based purely on the surviving machine code instructions and the results of prior analysis stages (like control flow analysis).

Think of it like translating an ancient text written only in consonants back into a modern language with vowels and sentence structure. The decompiler has to infer the missing vowels (variable types, high-level structures) based on context and known rules (CPU architecture, common compiler patterns).

The Decompilation Process (Conceptual):

Decompilation is a complex analytical process, typically involving several stages, often building directly on the results of thorough disassembly:

Lifting to Intermediate Representation (IR): The process usually starts by taking the assembly language (already derived by the disassembler) and lifting it into a more abstract, machine-independent **Intermediate Representation**. This IR simplifies the code, making platform-specific instructions more generic and easier to analyze consistently. Many different IRs exist (e.g., Ghidra's P-code, IDA's microcode).

Control Flow Structuring: This is a critical stage where the decompiler analyzes the Control Flow Graph (CFG) derived from the assembly's jumps and branches. It identifies basic blocks and uses sophisticated graph analysis algorithms (like structure analysis or dominator tree analysis) to recognize and reconstruct high-level control flow constructs. Sequences of conditional jumps and backward edges are transformed into if/else statements, while loops, for loops, and switch (or goto, if necessary) statements in the pseudo-code. This transformation from explicit jumps to structured control flow is a major contributor to readability.

Data Flow Analysis and Type Recovery: The decompiler performs extensive data flow analysis on the IR to understand how data moves between registers and memory locations. It tracks variable lifetimes and dependencies to reconstruct expressions. It attempts to infer the **data types** of variables and function parameters based on how they are used (e.g., passed to specific APIs, used in floating-point vs. integer instructions, accessed with certain offsets suggesting structures). Type information recovered here allows the decompiler to generate more meaningful pseudo-code, showing int x, char *buffer, or struct MyData *ptr instead of just raw memory accesses.

Expression Propagation and Simplification: The analysis tries to combine multiple simple IR instructions back into more complex high-level expressions (e.g., turning several MOV and ADD instructions into y = x + 5;). It also applies simplification rules to make the expressions more concise.

Pseudo-code Generation: Finally, the decompiler translates the analyzed and structured IR into the target high-level language syntax (usually C-like), applying the inferred types, variable names (often still generic initially), and control structures.

The Benefits: Why Decompile?

The primary advantage of decompilation is **speed of understanding**. Reading well-structured, C-like pseudo-code is almost always significantly faster and more intuitive for understanding the *overall algorithm* and logic of a function than reading the equivalent assembly language. Complex loops, nested conditionals, and intricate calculations become much clearer when presented in a familiar high-level format. This abstraction hides many of the low-level implementation details related to register allocation, specific instruction choices made by the compiler, or stack management minutiae, allowing the analyst to focus on the *what* rather than the intricate *how*. It also makes it easier to spot familiar programming **patterns** or **algorithms** that might be obscured in the assembly. For example, recognizing a standard sorting algorithm or a common data structure manipulation is much simpler in pseudo-code.

The Challenges and Caveats: Decompilation Isn't Magic

While incredibly powerful, it's absolutely vital to approach decompiler output with healthy skepticism. Decompilers are sophisticated tools, but they make assumptions and use heuristics, and the process is fundamentally attempting to reverse an information-losing transformation (compilation). Consequently, the generated pseudo-code is often imperfect and can sometimes be actively misleading:

Not Original Source: It will almost never perfectly match the original source code. Variable names will be generic unless manually renamed. Comments are gone. Source formatting is lost. Some elegant high-level constructs might be represented in a clunkier but functionally equivalent way.

Impact of Optimizations: Compilers employ aggressive optimizations to improve performance or reduce code size. These optimizations (like function inlining, loop unrolling, strength reduction, code hoisting, heavy use of SIMD instructions like SSE/AVX) can drastically restructure the code in ways that fundamentally confuse current decompilation algorithms, leading to very complex, convoluted, or even incorrect pseudo-code. Analyzing heavily optimized code often still requires significant reliance on the disassembly view.

Compiler Idioms and Quirks: Different compilers might generate specific assembly patterns (idioms) for certain high-level constructs. The decompiler needs to recognize these idioms. If it encounters an unusual pattern or code generated by an unsupported compiler, the output might be awkward or fail entirely.

Architecture-Specific Code: Code that directly interacts with hardware registers (common in embedded systems or drivers) or uses highly architecture-specific assembly tricks may not have a clean high-level representation and can result in pseudo-code containing strange "intrinsic" functions or casts that only hint at the underlying assembly operation.

Ambiguity: Sometimes, a given sequence of assembly instructions *could* have originated from slightly different high-level constructs. The decompiler makes a statistically likely or structurally simple guess, which might not always be the *intended* original logic.

Vulnerability to Obfuscation: Code obfuscation techniques, particularly virtualization-based obfuscation (like VMProtect or Themida) which translate native code to a custom bytecode, are often specifically designed to break or severely hinder decompilers, potentially producing pages of meaningless or nonsensical pseudo-code focused on the VM interpreter rather than the original logic.

Language Nuances: Decompiling C++ introduces challenges like reconstructing class hierarchies, identifying template instantiations, handling exceptions correctly, and dealing with complex name mangling, which can sometimes lead to less accurate or harder-to-read pseudo-code compared to decompiling simpler C code. Conversely, decompiling bytecode languages like Java or .NET often yields much higher fidelity results because the bytecode itself retains more high-level type information and structure compared to native machine code.

Prominent Decompilers and Integration:

The landscape of decompilers has evolved significantly.

Hex-Rays Decompiler (IDA Pro Add-on): For a long time, this was widely considered the gold standard for native code decompilation, particularly for C/C++. Its maturity, sophisticated analysis engine, tight integration with IDA Pro's interactive database (changes in one view reflect in the other), and generally high quality of pseudo-code output made it indispensable for serious analysts, despite its considerable cost. It supports numerous processor architectures.

Ghidra's Decompiler: The release of Ghidra by the NSA revolutionized the field by providing a highly capable, integrated native code decompiler completely free of charge. Based on the P-code intermediate representation, it supports a wide range of architectures and produces pseudo-code often comparable in quality to Hex-Rays. Its integration within the Ghidra framework allows seamless navigation between disassembly, decompilation, and other analysis views. Being open-source also allows for community contributions and extensibility. It has rapidly become a primary tool for many reverse engineers.

Java Decompilers (JD-GUI, Procyon, Fernflower/Quiltflower, CFR): Several excellent decompilers focus specifically on Java bytecode (.class files). Tools like JD-GUI provide a simple graphical interface for browsing JAR files and viewing decompiled source. Others like Procyon or Quiltflower are often used as libraries within other tools or from the command line and are known for their accuracy in handling modern Java language features.

.NET Decompilers (ILSpy, dnSpy, dotPeek): The .NET ecosystem also benefits from superb decompilers. ILSpy is a widely used open-source option. dnSpy (now often maintained as forks) gained popularity for its powerful features combining decompilation with integrated debugging and memory editing capabilities, making it very popular for .NET RE and modification (though use requires ethical considerations). JetBrains' dotPeek is another polished commercial-grade decompiler. These tools can often reconstruct C# (or VB.NET/F#) code from .NET assemblies (DLLs/EXEs) with remarkable fidelity, unless heavy obfuscation has been applied.

Other Native Decompilers (RetDec, Snowman): Several other projects aim to provide native code decompilation, often open-source. RetDec (initially developed by AVG, now open-source) is a notable example that uses sophisticated techniques like static single assignment (SSA) form. Snowman is another open-source effort. While perhaps not always as mature or polished as Hex-Rays or Ghidra for all cases, these provide valuable alternatives.

Using Decompilers Effectively:

To leverage the power of decompilers without being misled by their limitations, adopt these practices:

Verify, Verify, Verify: This is the golden rule. **Never** trust the decompiler output blindly, especially for critical sections of code or parts that look confusing. *Always* switch back to the disassembly view to confirm that the pseudo-code accurately represents the underlying assembly instructions. Understand how the high-level construct maps to the low-level code. If there's a discrepancy, trust the disassembly – it's closer to the machine's actual execution.

Interactive Refinement: Treat the pseudo-code view as another interactive analysis layer. As you understand variables, rename them in the decompiler view. Correct inferred data types if they are wrong. Add comments explaining the logic directly in the pseudo-code. Good tools like IDA/Hex-Rays and Ghidra synchronize these annotations between the disassembly and decompilation views, allowing insights gained in one view to enhance the other. Iteratively improving the decompiler output significantly aids long-term understanding.

Know the Limits: Recognize situations where decompilers typically struggle – heavily optimized code (especially complex loops or vectorization), manually written assembly, self-modifying code, heavily obfuscated code (especially virtualization), or low-level hardware interactions. In these cases, lean more heavily on analyzing the disassembly directly.

Focus on the Big Picture: Use the pseudo-code primarily to grasp the function's overall *purpose*, the *algorithm* being implemented, and the high-level *control flow* (loops, conditionals). Once you understand the "what," you can dive back into the disassembly for the precise "how" if needed (e.g., to check specific flag handling, exact memory access sizes, or instruction timings).

Decompilation feels almost magical when it works well, transforming dense assembly into something immediately recognizable and saving immense amounts of analysis time. But always remember it's an interpretation, a reconstruction based on incomplete information. Use it as a powerful guide, but always keep your hand on the rudder of the underlying disassembly to ensure you're not sailing into misconception.

Code Example: Assembly vs. Decompiled Pseudo-code

Let's revisit the if/else assembly from before:

```
        ; Function: check_value(int)
check_value proc near
    ; ... prologue ...
    mov     [rbp+arg_0], edi ; Store input argument 'input'
    cmp     dword ptr [rbp+arg_0], 10 ; Compare input with 10
    jnz     short loc_Failure       ; Jump if Not Equal
; 'Then' Block
    mov     eax, 1
    jmp     short loc_End
; 'Else' Block
loc_Failure:
    mov     eax, 0
loc_End:
    ; ... epilogue ...
    retn
check_value endp
arg_0               dd ?


A capable decompiler (like Ghidra or Hex-Rays) analyzing this
assembly would likely produce pseudo-code closely resembling
this:
        // Decompiled pseudo-code for check_value
int check_value(int input_arg) { // Renamed arg_0 based on
type/usage
  int return_value; // Inferred local variable for EAX result

  if (input_arg == 10) { // Reconstructed if condition from
CMP and JNZ
    return_value = 1;
  } else {
    return_value = 0; // Reconstructed else block
  }
  return return_value; // Single return point reconstructed
}

// Could even be simplified further by some decompilers to:
int check_value_simplified(int input_arg) {
  return (input_arg == 10) ? 1 : 0;
}
```

Analysis: Comparing the assembly and pseudo-code highlights the decompiler's power. It correctly interpreted the CMP and JNZ instructions to form an if (input_arg == 10) condition. It correctly identified the two distinct code paths leading to setting the return value (EAX) to either 1 or 0 and reconstructed the else clause. It consolidated the flow to a single return statement. The result is instantly understandable C code that accurately

91

reflects the assembly's logic, saving the analyst the mental effort of manually tracing the jumps and flags. This amplification of understanding is the core value proposition of decompilers.

Hex Editors: Interacting with Raw Binary Data

Now, let's swing the pendulum to the other extreme. While decompilers strive for high-level abstraction, **Hex Editors** provide the absolute ground-level view, stripping away *all* interpretation imposed by disassemblers or compilers. A hex editor presents the raw **binary data** of a file or a process's memory region simply as a sequence of bytes.

The Hex Editor Interface:

The typical display consists of three main columns:

Offset: This column shows the address or offset (usually in hexadecimal) of the first byte on each line relative to the beginning of the file or memory region. This allows you to precisely locate data.

Hexadecimal View: The main area displays the data itself, byte by byte, represented as two-digit **hexadecimal** (base-16) numbers (00-FF). Hexadecimal is convenient because a single byte (8 bits) can be represented perfectly by two hex digits (each hex digit represents 4 bits, nibble). This is more compact than binary and easier to align than decimal for raw byte manipulation. Data is usually shown in rows of 8, 16, or 32 bytes for readability.

Character View: Alongside the hex values, most editors show the corresponding **ASCII** (or sometimes another character encoding like EBCDIC, configurable) representation for each byte. Printable characters (letters, numbers, punctuation) appear as expected, while non-printable control characters or bytes outside the standard ASCII range are often represented by a dot (.) or similar placeholder. This view is invaluable for quickly spotting embedded text strings within the binary data.

Why Drop Down to the Bytes? Core Use Cases:

Working at the byte level might seem primitive, but it's essential for numerous RE tasks where higher-level interpretations can be insufficient or misleading.

File Format Analysis: This is a prime application. When trying to understand an unknown or undocumented file format (as detailed in Chapter 6), you often *start* with a hex editor.

Finding Headers and Magic Numbers: You load the file and examine the very first few bytes, looking for recognizable sequences (like ‰PNG, GIF89a, %PDF, PK.., MZ, ELF) that identify the file type, regardless of its extension.

Identifying Structure: You visually scan for patterns: repeating byte sequences (padding or backgrounds), fixed-size fields (often aligned), ASCII strings (potential labels or metadata), blocks of zeros or FFs (unused space or delimiters). You look for values that might represent lengths or offsets pointing to other parts of the file.

Diffing/Comparison: When you have two versions of a file (e.g., a game save before and after picking up an item), opening them side-by-side in a hex editor or using its built-in diffing tool highlights the exact bytes that changed. Correlating the change in the application (getting an item) with the specific changed bytes helps you map the file structure (e.g., "these 4 bytes at offset 0x1A4 represent the player's gold count"). This is a fundamental technique for undocumented formats.

Examining Memory: While debuggers provide sophisticated views of memory, sometimes you need the raw hex perspective:

Verifying Data Structures: You might have a pointer to a structure in a register. Dumping the memory region pointed to by that register in the debugger's hex view lets you manually examine the raw byte layout and verify if it matches the structure definition you hypothesized during static analysis, paying close attention to **endianness** (byte order) and field alignment.

Analyzing Raw Buffers: Before data read from a network socket or a file is parsed into meaningful structures by the program, examining the raw buffer contents in a hex dump can reveal protocol details or encoding issues.

Searching for Secrets/Signatures: You can search a process's entire memory space (or a dumped portion) for specific hex sequences – perhaps known shellcode patterns, parts of hardcoded encryption keys (a severe vulnerability), or other forensic artifacts that higher-level views might miss.

Binary Patching: This involves directly modifying the bytes of an executable file or library on disk to change its behavior. A hex editor is the most direct tool for this (though specialized patching tools exist). *Use with extreme caution and full awareness of legal/ethical implications.*

Changing Instructions: You can overwrite the bytes corresponding to specific assembly instructions. For instance, to change a JNE (Jump if Not Equal, typically opcode 75 followed by a relative offset byte on x86) to an unconditional JMP (Short JMP, opcode EB), you would find the 75 byte and overwrite it with EB, leaving the offset byte unchanged (assuming the target is close enough for a short jump). Or, to disable an instruction entirely, you might overwrite its bytes with the NOP (No Operation, opcode 90 on x86) instruction. This requires knowing the exact byte encoding of the instructions for your target architecture. *Mistakes here can easily corrupt the executable.* *Modifying Data:* You can directly change embedded strings (e.g., altering a message, making sure to handle null termination and buffer sizes) or overwrite configuration flags stored as immediate data within the binary. *Checksum/Integrity Alert:* As strongly emphasized before, patching often breaks internal checksums or external digital signatures designed to detect tampering. A successful patch often requires *also* finding and disabling these integrity checks, which usually necessitates more advanced RE using disassemblers and debuggers. Simply hex-editing a modern protected binary will likely cause it to crash or refuse to run.

Finding Hidden Data/Forensics: Sometimes data is concealed in ways that structured analysis might miss. A hex editor allows examining file slack space (unused space within the last cluster allocated to a file), alternative data streams (on NTFS), or looking for data deliberately hidden using steganography within seemingly innocuous files (like images). Forensics analysts frequently use hex editors to examine raw disk images, searching for deleted files or fragments by recognizing their header patterns in unallocated space.

Advanced Hex Editor Capabilities:

Modern hex editors often go beyond simple byte viewing and editing:

Data Interpretation: Select a range of bytes (e.g., 2, 4, or 8 bytes) and have the editor display their interpretation as various numerical types (8/16/32/64-bit signed/unsigned integers, float, double) automatically handling the correct **endianness** (Little Endian vs. Big Endian). This avoids manual byte-swapping calculations. Some can even interpret timestamps or GUIDs.

Templating/Parsing: This is a killer feature in tools like **010 Editor** and increasingly **ImHex**. You can write a script or "template" (often in a C-like syntax) that describes the structure of a specific file format (e.g., "struct

Header { uint32 magic; uint16 version; ... }"). The editor then uses this template to parse the binary file, overlaying the structure definition onto the raw data. Instead of just seeing hex, you see a tree view of named fields with their correctly interpreted values. This makes navigating and understanding complex formats vastly easier than manual hex analysis and serves as excellent self-documentation of the reverse engineered format.

Code Example: Conceptual 010 Editor Template for a Simple Structure
Suppose you reverse engineered a simple record structure saved in a file:

```
// Original C structure (for reference)
struct SimpleRecord {
    uint32_t recordID;      // 4 bytes
    char     name[16];      // 16 bytes (null-padded
potentially)
    uint16_t value;         // 2 bytes
    uint8_t  flags;         // 1 byte
    uint8_t  _padding;      // 1 byte padding for alignment
}; // Total size = 24 bytes
```

A conceptual 010 Editor template for a file containing an array of these records might look like this (syntax simplified for illustration):

```
    // Conceptual 010 Editor Template: SimpleRecord.bt
LittleEndian(); // Assume little-endian byte order

struct SimpleRecord {
    uint32 recordID;
    char   name[16];
    uint16 value;
    uint8  flags;
    byte   _padding <hidden=true>; // Define but hide the
padding byte
};

// Assume the file is just a sequence of these records
// Loop until the end of the file is reached
while (!FEof()) {
    SimpleRecord record; // Declare and parse one record
structure
}
```

Usage: When you open a data file containing these records in 010 Editor and apply this template, the editor wouldn't just show raw hex. It would display a "Template Results" panel showing each record as a structure, with fields like recordID, name, value, and flags clearly labeled with their parsed values, dramatically improving readability and understanding compared to raw hex.

Diffing: Many hex editors include sophisticated side-by-side file comparison (diffing) features, highlighting byte differences, which is invaluable for the comparison technique in file format RE.

Scripting: Programmable hex editors (often using Python, Lua, or custom languages) allow automating repetitive tasks, complex searches, data extraction, or custom transformations directly on the binary data.

Large File Handling: Efficiently opening and navigating multi-gigabyte files without consuming excessive RAM is a crucial feature for dealing with disk images or large data logs.

Popular Hex Editors:

HxD: A free, lightweight, and widely used hex editor for Windows. It covers the basics very well (viewing, editing, searching, large file support, checksums) and is an excellent starting point.

010 Editor: A commercial, cross-platform editor renowned for its powerful binary templating engine. If you frequently work with complex or custom binary formats, the ability to write and apply templates makes it incredibly efficient, despite the cost. It also has scripting and many other advanced features.

ImHex: A modern, open-source, cross-platform hex editor with a node-based graphical pattern language for defining formats (an alternative to text templates), data analysis features (entropy graphs, histograms), and a rich feature set. Its popularity is growing rapidly.

Built-in Views: Don't forget that many disassemblers (IDA Pro, Ghidra) and debuggers include integrated hex dump views for examining memory or file segments directly within the main tool, often sufficient for quick checks.

The Indispensable Foundation:

In an age of sophisticated decompilers and high-level analysis tools, it might seem archaic to focus on raw hexadecimal bytes. However, the hex editor remains an absolutely indispensable tool in the reverse engineer's arsenal. It provides the **ground truth** – the actual sequence of bytes that constitutes the file or memory region, free from any interpretation or potential misrepresentation by higher-level tools. For tasks involving low-level file format analysis, precise binary patching, specific memory inspection, or forensic data carving, the hex editor is often the primary and most reliable tool. It represents the foundation upon which all other interpretations (disassembly, decompilation) are built, and the ability to comfortably navigate and understand data at this fundamental level is a non-negotiable skill for any serious reverse engineer.

Complementary Perspectives for Deeper Understanding

Decompilers and hex editors offer vastly different but equally valuable perspectives that complement the core views provided by disassemblers and debuggers. Decompilers accelerate understanding of algorithmic logic by translating complex assembly into more familiar high-level pseudo-code, albeit with inherent limitations and the critical need for verification against the disassembly. Hex editors provide the ultimate low-level view, allowing direct interaction with the raw bytes essential for file format analysis, binary patching, and certain memory forensics tasks. Mastering when and how to leverage each of these tools – switching seamlessly between the high-level abstraction of pseudo-code, the structured representation of assembly, the live execution view of the debugger, and the raw byte truth of the hex editor – allows the reverse engineer to build the most complete and accurate understanding of the target software.

3.3. Automated Analysis Tools: Handling Scale and Speed

let's broaden our discussion of the reverse engineer's toolkit. While the meticulous, manual examination of code using disassemblers and debuggers, complemented by the raw byte-level perspective of hex editors, forms the absolute core of deep understanding, it's undeniable that this approach can be incredibly time-consuming and mentally taxing. Imagine analyzing dozens of similar malware samples per day or trying to grasp the structure of a multi-million-line commercial application purely through manual stepping and static reading. The sheer scale can be overwhelming. This is precisely where **automated analysis tools** step into the spotlight. They aren't designed to replace the human analyst's intuition or deep understanding, but rather to act as powerful assistants, handling repetitive tasks, providing quick initial assessments, filtering massive datasets, and enabling analysis at a scale simply impossible through purely manual means.

Think of it like building a house. Manual tools like hammers, saws, and measuring tapes are essential for precision work and understanding the fine details of construction. But for tasks like digging the foundation or lifting heavy beams, automated tools like excavators and cranes are indispensable for efficiency and handling scale. Automated RE tools serve a similar purpose – they handle the heavy lifting and provide broad overviews, allowing the human analyst to focus their expertise on the critical, complex, or novel aspects.

Sandboxes: Observing Behavior in a Controlled Detonation Chamber

One of the most widely used and invaluable forms of automated analysis, especially in the realm of malware investigation, is the **sandbox**. Picture receiving an email attachment you *know* is suspicious, or downloading a program from an untrusted source. Running it directly on your work machine or personal computer is out of the question – the risk of infection, data theft, or system damage is far too high. A sandbox provides the solution: a secure, isolated environment, specifically designed to execute potentially malicious or unknown software while meticulously observing and recording its every action, all without endangering the host system or connected networks.

How Sandboxes Work: Isolation and Monitoring

The core principle behind most sandboxes is **isolation**, typically achieved using **virtualization** technology (like VMware, VirtualBox, KVM/QEMU) or sometimes containerization. The sandbox runs a guest operating system (usually Windows, sometimes Linux or Android) within a Virtual Machine (VM). This VM is deliberately walled off from the host operating system and, often, from the real network. Any changes the executed program makes – file creations, registry modifications, process launches – are contained entirely within the disposable VM environment. After the analysis run, the VM can often be instantly reverted to a clean, pre-analysis state (a "snapshot"), effectively erasing any trace of the executed software and ensuring the environment is ready for the next sample.

While the suspect program runs inside this isolated guest OS, the sandbox environment employs sophisticated **monitoring** techniques. This isn't just passive observation; the sandbox actively intercepts and records interactions between the analyzed program and the operating system. It achieves this primarily through **API Hooking**. The sandbox injects special monitoring code into the guest OS or modifies system libraries (like kernel32.dll, ntdll.dll on Windows) in memory. This allows it to intercept calls made by the target program to critical OS functions. Common categories of monitored APIs include:

File System Operations: CreateFile, WriteFile, ReadFile, DeleteFile, MoveFile, etc. The sandbox records filenames, paths, data written (sometimes), and success/failure status.

Registry Operations (Windows): RegCreateKeyEx, RegSetValueEx, RegDeleteKey, RegQueryValueEx, etc. It logs keys and values accessed, created, modified, or deleted.

Process Operations: CreateProcess, OpenProcess, WriteProcessMemory, CreateRemoteThread, TerminateProcess, etc. This reveals if the program launches other processes or attempts to manipulate them (common malware behavior).

Network Operations: socket, connect, send, recv, InternetOpen, HttpSendRequest, etc. The sandbox logs attempted connections (IP addresses, ports, domains), protocols used, and often captures the transmitted data. Some sandboxes include built-in network simulators (like INetSim or FakeNet-NG) to respond to common network requests (DNS lookups, HTTP requests) even when disconnected from the real internet, potentially tricking the malware into revealing more of its C&C communication behavior.

Other System Interactions: Calls related to service creation, COM object interaction, scheduling tasks, loading drivers, system information queries, and more can be monitored depending on the sandbox's capabilities.

The Output: A Behavioral Summary

After the program finishes executing (or after a predefined timeout), the sandbox aggregates all the recorded events and generates a detailed report. This report provides a comprehensive summary of the program's observed behavior, often including:

Static Information: File hashes (MD5, SHA1, SHA256), detected file type, embedded strings, packer identification.

Behavioral Summary: A high-level overview of key actions (e.g., "modified registry for persistence," "connected to suspicious domain," "dropped executable file").

Detailed Event Logs: Timestamped lists of specific API calls, file system changes, registry modifications, network connections (with resolved domains/IPs), and created processes.

Extracted Artifacts: Copies of files created or dropped by the program, memory dumps of the process at various stages (useful for analyzing unpacked code), captured network traffic (PCAP files), and potentially screenshots of any windows the program displayed.

Signatures/Scores: Many sandboxes apply heuristics or signature sets (like YARA rules run against memory dumps or network traffic) to classify the behavior, often providing a "maliciousness score" or identifying known malware families.

Popular Sandboxes and Their Roles:

Cuckoo Sandbox: A widely used, highly customizable, open-source, self-hosted sandbox framework. It requires significant setup and maintenance (configuring VMs, installing guest agents, managing dependencies) but offers immense flexibility. Analysts can tailor the guest environments, add custom analysis modules (e.g., specific decryption routines), and integrate it with other security tools. It's excellent for organizations needing a dedicated, private sandbox infrastructure.

Online/Interactive Sandboxes (Any.Run, Hybrid Analysis, Joe Sandbox Cloud, etc.): These platforms provide sandboxing as a service. Users upload suspicious files or URLs via a web interface.

Any.Run is particularly notable for its *interactive* nature. Instead of just getting a static report, the analyst can interact with the desktop of the sandboxed VM in real-time during the analysis, clicking buttons, opening documents, or providing input, potentially coaxing malware into revealing behavior it might hide during a purely automated run. You can watch processes being created and network requests happening live.

Other cloud platforms offer sophisticated analysis, often correlating results with vast threat intelligence databases and providing detailed reports accessible via the web or APIs. They remove the burden of maintaining local infrastructure but involve submitting samples to a third party (which might have privacy implications or risk tipping off attackers if the service is monitored).

Commercial Sandboxes (VMRay Analyzer, CrowdStrike Falcon Sandbox, FireEye AX, etc.): These enterprise-grade solutions often boast advanced features, superior evasion resistance, deeper kernel-level monitoring, integration with broader security platforms, dedicated support, and extensive threat intelligence feeds. They represent a significant investment but are crucial for many security operations centers (SOCs).

The Value Proposition: Sandboxes provide immense value, especially for **malware triage**. Faced with hundreds or thousands of suspicious files daily, analysts can quickly submit them to a sandbox and get a behavioral summary within minutes. This allows them to rapidly identify known threats, prioritize potentially novel or highly dangerous samples for deeper manual investigation, and immediately extract actionable IOCs (IPs, domains, file hashes) to update firewall rules or blocklists. It acts as a powerful filter, allowing human experts to focus their time where it's needed most. For a reverse engineer investigating an unknown program, a sandbox report provides that initial "summary from the detective" – highlighting key behaviors like network activity or file modifications – which can guide where to start looking during manual static or dynamic analysis.

Limitations and Evasion: Despite their power, sandboxes are not foolproof. Malware authors are acutely aware they are primary analysis tools and actively develop **anti-sandbox** and **anti-VM** techniques (as discussed in Chapter 7). These include:

VM Artifact Checks: Looking for specific files, drivers, registry keys, MAC address prefixes, CPU instructions, or BIOS strings associated with common virtualization platforms (VMware, VirtualBox, KVM).

Tool Detection: Checking for the presence of sandbox agent processes, known analysis tools, or debugger hooks.

Timing Attacks: Measuring the time taken for certain CPU instructions or API calls, which can differ significantly between native hardware and emulated/virtualized environments.

Human Interaction Requirements: Waiting for specific mouse clicks, scrolling activity, or complex user input before executing malicious payloads, hoping to defeat non-interactive automated sandboxes.

Delayed Execution: Simply sleeping for an extended period (minutes or even hours) or waiting for a specific date/time before activating, aiming to exceed the typical sandbox execution timeout.

Environment Keying: Checking for specific language settings, keyboard layouts, usernames, domain memberships, or installed software that indicate a generic analysis environment rather than a real user machine.

If a sandbox environment is detected, the malware might simply refuse to run its core payload, exit silently, or even present fake, benign behavior to mislead the analysis report. Therefore, while sandbox reports are invaluable starting points, they cannot always be trusted as the complete picture, especially for sophisticated threats. Sometimes, "no malicious behavior detected" simply means the evasion worked.

Beyond Sandboxes: Other Forms of Automated Analysis

While sandboxes excel at automated behavioral analysis, other tools automate different aspects of the RE process, primarily focusing on static characteristics or providing more targeted dynamic analysis capabilities.

Static Scanners: Pattern Matching Without Execution

These tools analyze executable files or memory dumps *without actually running* the code. Their strength lies in rapidly identifying known patterns, signatures, or characteristics associated with malware, packers, or potentially vulnerable code constructs.

YARA Rules: This is the undisputed champion of static pattern matching in the RE and malware analysis world. YARA provides a simple yet powerful rule-based language for creating descriptions of malware families or other file characteristics based on textual or binary patterns. Analysts write rules specifying strings (text, hexadecimal sequences, regular expressions) and conditions under which these strings must appear (e.g., $string_a at entry_point, all of ($string_b, $hex_pattern), pe.imphash() == "..."). YARA engines can then scan vast numbers of files very quickly, flagging any that match the defined rules. Security teams maintain huge collections of YARA rules to detect known threats. Reverse engineers write custom YARA rules during analysis to capture unique features of a specific sample, helping to find related files or track campaigns.

Code Example: More Detailed YARA Rule

```
import "pe" // Import the PE module to access PE-specific
features

rule Packed_Or_Encrypted_UPX_Variant {
    meta:
        description = "Detects a likely UPX variant often
used in malware - checks sections and entry point"
        author = "Analyst X"
        date = "2023-10-27"

    strings:
        // Standard UPX section names (but check presence,
not exact content)
        $upx0 = "UPX0" ascii
        $upx1 = "UPX1" ascii
        // Sometimes .rsrc section is kept or renamed
```

```
        $rsrc = ".rsrc" ascii

        // Look for common byte sequence near entry point in
packed code
        // (Example only - real patterns are more complex)
        $entry_pattern = { E8 00 00 00 00 5? 81
C? ?? ?? ?? ?? C3 } // CALL $+5 ; POP reg ; ADD reg, offset ;
RET

    condition:
        // Must be a PE file
        uint16(0) == 0x5A4D and // Check MZ header
        pe.number_of_sections >= 2 and
        // Require either UPX0 or UPX1 section name AND .rsrc
        // (or just UPX0 and UPX1 maybe)
        ( ($upx0 or $upx1) and $rsrc ) and
        // The entry point pattern must exist within the
first 256 bytes
        // of the section marked as executable containing the
entry point
        $entry_pattern in (pe.entry_point..pe.entry_point +
256) and
        // Often packed files have high entropy in the code
section

pe.sections[pe.section_index(pe.entry_point)].entropy > 7.5
}
```

Explanation: This more complex YARA rule tries to identify a packed UPX
variant. It checks for the standard "MZ" header, ensures there are at least two
sections, looks for the common UPX section names (UPX0, UPX1)
potentially alongside a resource section (.rsrc), checks for a specific byte
pattern often seen near the entry point of packed code (a CALL-POP
sequence for getting the instruction pointer), *and* leverages the PE module to
check that the entry point code section has high entropy (entropy measures
randomness; highly compressed or encrypted data tends to have high
entropy). Combining these conditions makes the rule more specific and less
prone to false positives than just checking for section names alone. This
demonstrates how RE insights (common packing techniques, typical section
names, entry point behavior, entropy characteristics) are codified into
automated detection rules.

Other Static Techniques: Beyond YARA, automated static tools can
perform:

Packer/Protector Detection: Identifying the specific tools (like UPX, Themida, VMProtect, Aspack) used to pack or obfuscate the binary using known signatures or structural heuristics.

Import Hashing (Imphash): Calculating a hash based on the names and order of imported API functions. Malware families often use similar sets of APIs, resulting in the same imphash, which can be a quick way to link related samples even if their file hashes differ.

String Analysis: Automatically extracting all printable strings from a binary, which can quickly reveal URLs, filenames, error messages, or other clues (though often obfuscated in malware).

Entropy Analysis: Calculating the entropy (randomness) of different file sections. Sections with very high entropy often indicate compressed or encrypted data (like packed code or embedded resources).

Basic Vulnerability Scanning: Some tools scan code for potentially unsafe function calls (like strcpy, sprintf without proper bounds checking) or known vulnerable library versions, though this is generally less reliable without deeper semantic analysis.

Static scanners are excellent for quick filtering, identifying known patterns, and extracting easily accessible information without the risks or overhead of execution. Their main limitation is that they are easily defeated by polymorphism (malware constantly changing its code structure while retaining functionality), sophisticated obfuscation, or novel threats that don't match existing signatures.

Dynamic Analysis Frameworks (Instrumentation): Targeted Runtime Control

Falling somewhere between passive sandbox monitoring and manual debugging are powerful **Dynamic Instrumentation Frameworks**. These tools allow you to inject code into a running process and programmatically **instrument** its execution – meaning you can intercept function calls, examine or modify arguments and return values, log specific events, trace execution flow, and essentially automate complex dynamic analysis tasks with far more flexibility than a standard debugger script allows.

Frida: This is currently the dominant framework in this space. Frida is a dynamic instrumentation toolkit that works across multiple platforms (Windows, macOS, Linux, iOS, Android, QNX). It allows you to inject a JavaScript engine (or use Python, Swift, C bindings) into a target process.

You then write scripts (most commonly in JavaScript) to interact with the process's memory and execution flow.

Key Frida Capabilities:

Function Hooking/Tracing: Easily intercept calls to *any* function within the process (exported APIs, internal functions, methods in object-oriented languages) using its address or name. You can define onEnter callbacks (triggered just before the function executes, allowing you to inspect/modify arguments) and onLeave callbacks (triggered just after the function returns, allowing you to inspect/modify the return value).

Memory Access: Read and write arbitrary process memory.

Code Injection: Inject and execute your own code within the target process.

Class/Object Interaction: Inspect and manipulate objects and classes in languages like Java/Objective-C.

Thread Management: Create new threads or enumerate existing ones.

RPC (Remote Procedure Call): Expose functions within your Frida script that can be called from an external control script (e.g., written in Python).

Code Example: Frida Script to Log File Creation (Windows)

```
// frida_createfile_log.js
// Target: Windows processes calling CreateFileW

// Get the address of the CreateFileW function in
kernel32.dll
const createFileWPtr = Module.getExportByName('kernel32.dll',
'CreateFileW');

// Attach an interceptor to this address
Interceptor.attach(createFileWPtr, {
    // Code to run when the function is entered
    onEnter: function (args) {
        // args[0] is the first argument (lpFileName)
        // We read it as a wide string (UTF-16)
        let filePath = args[0].readUtf16String();
        console.log("[CreateFileW] Attempting to open/create:
" + filePath);

        // We can store arguments for use in onLeave if
needed
        // this.filePath = filePath;

        // Example: We could even modify the filename here if
desired
        //
args[0].writeUtf16String("C:\\Totally\\Different\\Path.txt");
    },
```

```
    // Code to run when the function returns
    onLeave: function (retval) {
        // retval is the return value (HANDLE in this case)
        console.log("[CreateFileW] Returned handle: " +
retval);
        // We could check if retval is INVALID_HANDLE_VALUE
(0xffffffff) to detect failure
        if (retval.toInt32() == -1) {
            // Could call GetLastError() here using
NativeFunction, but omitted for simplicity
            console.log("  -> CreateFileW failed!");
        } else {
            console.log("  -> CreateFileW succeeded.");
        }
        // console.log("  -> Filename was: " +
this.filePath); // Using stored value
    }
});

console.log("Interceptor attached to CreateFileW. Waiting for
calls...");
```

Running this with Frida:

Save the code as frida_createfile_log.js.

Choose a target process, e.g., Notepad (notepad.exe). Find its PID or just use its name.

Run Frida from your command line: frida -l frida_createfile_log.js -f notepad.exe

-l script.js: Loads the JavaScript script.

-f process_name: Launches the process and immediately attaches Frida. (Use -p PID to attach to an existing process).

Frida will inject its agent, execute the script, and print the "Interceptor attached..." message.

Now, interact with Notepad. For instance, go to File -> Save As.... As soon as the Save As dialog appears or you interact with it, you will likely see [CreateFileW] messages logged in your Frida console as Notepad probes the file system. Saving a file will definitely trigger it.

RE Interpretation: This Frida script provides real-time visibility into every attempt the target process makes to open or create a file using the primary CreateFileW API. For malware analysis, this could reveal exactly which files it tries to infect, delete, or use for persistence. For application analysis, it helps understand configuration loading or data saving behavior. It's far more targeted and flexible than simply running Process Monitor, as you can add arbitrary logic (like modification) directly within the hooks.

Intel Pin / DynamoRIO: These are lower-level **Dynamic Binary Instrumentation (DBI)** frameworks. Instead of scripting with JavaScript, you typically write "Pintools" (for Pin) or "Clients" (for DynamoRIO) in C or C++. These frameworks operate closer to the instruction level, recompiling or modifying code dynamically as it executes. They offer extremely fine-grained control and potentially better performance than Frida for complex analysis tasks, but come with a significantly steeper learning curve and are often used more in academic research or for building highly specialized analysis tools (like dynamic taint tracking systems or advanced obfuscation analysis).

Dynamic instrumentation frameworks bridge the gap between passive monitoring and manual debugging. They allow analysts to automate targeted observations and manipulations at runtime, essential for tasks like bypassing SSL pinning, defeating simple anti-debugging checks, extracting dynamically decrypted data, or tracing complex interactions without needing to manually step through thousands of instructions.

The Crucial Role of Human Interpretation

While automation brings immense power and scale, it's critical to remember its limitations. Automated tools operate based on predefined rules, signatures, heuristics, or trained models. They lack true understanding and contextual awareness.

Clever malware can often **evade sandbox detection** or fool automated signature matching. Complex legitimate software might exhibit behavior that triggers naive behavioral rules, leading to **false positives**. Obfuscation techniques can be specifically designed to confuse static scanners or even instrumentation tools. AI-based analysis can be misled by adversarial examples or struggle with novel code constructs.

Therefore, automation should be seen as a powerful *assistant*, not a replacement for skilled human analysis. The output from automated tools – sandbox reports, YARA hits, Frida logs – provides crucial clues, data points, and starting points. But it's the human reverse engineer who must critically evaluate these results, correlate findings from different tools, understand the *context* behind observed behaviors, form hypotheses about the underlying logic, and ultimately perform the deep-dive manual analysis (using disassemblers and debuggers) needed to unravel complex, novel, or heavily obfuscated code. The real skill lies not just in running the tools, but in knowing *which* tools to use, *how* to configure them effectively, *how* to interpret their output critically, and *when* to transition to manual techniques for deeper understanding.

Putting It All Together: An Integrated Toolkit

In practice, effective reverse engineering rarely relies on a single tool. It involves skillfully orchestrating a combination of manual and automated techniques tailored to the specific target and analysis goals.

A common workflow, especially for malware analysis, might look like this:

Initial Triage (Automated): Run the sample through a sandbox. Scan it with YARA using a comprehensive rule set. Check static properties like packers, entropy, and imports.

Prioritization: Based on the automated reports (e.g., high sandbox score, detection by specific YARA rules, presence of known packing), prioritize the sample for deeper analysis or potentially discard it if it's clearly known/benign.

Guided Static Analysis (Manual + Automated): Load the (potentially unpacked) sample into IDA Pro or Ghidra. Leverage automated library function identification (FLIRT/etc.). Use the sandbox report to identify key functions related to observed behaviors (e.g., find the code responsible for the network connections seen in the sandbox report). Begin mapping control flow, analyzing interesting functions, renaming variables/functions, and documenting findings.

Targeted Dynamic Analysis (Manual/Frida): If specific runtime values are needed (e.g., decryption keys, C&C communication content) or if anti-debugging checks interfere, use Frida to hook relevant functions and extract the data, or use a debugger carefully (perhaps in a VM configured to minimize detection) to step through critical sections identified statically.

Deep Dive (Manual): Use the debugger (x64dbg, WinDbg, GDB) to meticulously step through complex algorithms, unpack intricate logic, or analyze specific interactions that remain unclear after initial steps. Use the disassembler concurrently to understand the broader context of the code being debugged.

Iteration: Continuously feed insights from dynamic analysis back into the static analysis view (renaming, commenting) and use the improved static understanding to guide further dynamic investigation.

This integrated approach leverages the speed and scale of automation for initial assessment and handling volume, while reserving the irreplaceable depth and critical thinking of manual analysis for understanding the core logic, tackling obfuscation, and verifying automated findings. Mastering this entire toolkit – knowing when and how to employ disassemblers, debuggers, hex editors, sandboxes, static scanners, and instrumentation frameworks – is the hallmark of a proficient reverse engineer.

Now that we have a firm grasp on the essential tools and techniques, both manual and automated, we'll move on in the following chapters (Chapters 4 and 5, as originally intended in your book structure) to formalize the *methodologies* of Static and Dynamic Analysis, detailing systematic approaches for applying these tools to effectively deconstruct software.

We're fully equipped – let's start putting these tools into structured practice!

Chapter 4: Static Analysis

We've got our tools laid out (Chapter 3), and now it's time to learn the first major approach to using them: **Static Analysis**. If dynamic analysis (which we'll cover next) is like watching a car drive around a track, static analysis is like meticulously examining the car's engine, wiring, and blueprints while it's sitting still in the garage. You're looking at the code and structure without actually running the program.

Why start here? Because static analysis lets you explore *every* potential path the code *could* take, not just the one path it happens to follow when you run it under specific conditions. It's your chance to build a mental map of the software's landscape before you start driving through it. This chapter focuses on the core methods: basic code inspection, understanding the program's logical paths (control flow), and tracking how information moves around (data flow).

4.1. Code Inspection Methods: Reading Between the Lines (of Assembly)

let's truly immerse ourselves in the foundational practice of **Static Analysis**, starting with the essential art of **Code Inspection**. This is where the journey into the heart of an unknown program begins. Forget about running the code for now; we're putting on our archaeologist hats, grabbing our magnifying glasses (in this case, our disassemblers and decompilers), and preparing to meticulously examine the digital artifact before us, byte by byte, instruction by instruction.

At its very essence, the initial phase of static analysis revolves around disciplined **code inspection**. You begin by loading your target program – perhaps a Windows executable (.exe), a Linux shared object (.so), firmware extracted from a device, or an Android application package – into your chosen analysis platform. Tools like **IDA Pro**, **Ghidra**, **radare2/rizin**, or **Hopper** become your workbench. And then, quite simply, you start... reading. Now, let's be clear: reading machine code or the assembly language produced by a disassembler isn't like curling up with a good novel, particularly when you're first starting. It's far more akin to deciphering a highly technical, incredibly dense manual written in a cryptic language you're only just beginning to learn. The syntax is sparse, the logic can be

convoluted by compiler optimizations, and the sheer volume of instructions can feel overwhelming. Patience and a systematic approach are your most valuable allies here.

Your immediate goal is usually **orientation**. Before you can understand the intricate plot, you need to get a feel for the setting and the main characters. In software terms, this means identifying the basic structural building blocks. Your analysis tool will parse the executable file format (like PE for Windows, ELF for Linux, Mach-O for macOS/iOS), identifying different sections – typically distinguishing code sections (like .text) from data sections (.data, .rodata, .bss). Find the program's **entry point**, the very first instruction executed when the program is loaded. From there, begin looking for the boundaries that delineate **functions** or procedures. As we discussed, disassemblers use heuristics like standard function prologues/epilogues (common instruction sequences used to manage the stack frame) and the targets of CALL instructions to make educated guesses about where functions begin and end. Spend some time navigating the list of identified functions provided by your tool – how many are there? Do any names seem interesting (if symbols are present)?

Within the boundaries of these identified functions, start looking for familiar patterns – echoes of the high-level programming structures you already understand. Even in raw assembly, you can often spot the tell-tale signs of control flow constructs. Look for instruction sequences implementing **loops**: perhaps a counter being initialized, incremented within a block of code, compared against a limit (CMP), and then a conditional jump (JL, JNE, etc.) branching back to the beginning of the block. Or maybe you'll see the simpler LOOP instruction on x86. Recognizing these recurring patterns signifies iterative processing. Similarly, **conditional logic** (if-then-else statements) manifests as comparison instructions (CMP, TEST) followed immediately by conditional jumps (JE - Jump if Equal, JNE - Jump if Not Equal, JG - Jump if Greater, JZ - Jump if Zero, etc.). Following the 'taken' and 'not-taken' paths of these jumps in the disassembly listing or, more intuitively, on a control flow graph, helps you reconstruct the decision-making logic of the function. Sometimes you might encounter patterns suggesting a switch statement, often implemented using a **jump table** – an array of code addresses where the program calculates an index based on an input value and then jumps indirectly to the corresponding address in the table. Identifying these fundamental structures provides the initial scaffolding for understanding a function's purpose.

Code Example: Recognizing an If/Else in x86 Assembly

Let's imagine a simple C snippet:

```c
    // simple_if.c
int check_value(int input) {
    if (input == 10) {
        return 1; // Success code
    } else {
        return 0; // Failure code
    }
}
```

A reverse engineer looking at the compiled x86-64 assembly (System V ABI convention, common on Linux) might see something like this:

```asm
        ; Function: check_value(int)
check_value proc near
    push    rbp
    mov     rbp, rsp
    mov     [rbp+arg_0], edi ; Store input argument 'input'
(passed in EDI) on stack

    ; === The Conditional Logic ===
    cmp     dword ptr [rbp+arg_0], 10 ; Compare the stored
input value with 10
    jnz     short loc_Failure       ; Jump Not Zero (i.e., not
equal) to the 'else' block

; --- 'Then' Block ---
loc_Success:
    mov     eax, 1              ; If equal, set return value
(EAX) to 1
    jmp     short loc_End    ; Jump to the end of the function

; --- 'Else' Block ---
loc_Failure:
    mov     eax, 0              ; If not equal, set return value
(EAX) to 0

loc_End:
    ; --- Function Epilogue ---
    pop     rbp
    retn
check_value endp

arg_0           dd ?            ; Stack variable for input
```

RE Interpretation: The core logic is revealed by the cmp instruction followed by the jnz (Jump if Not Zero flag set, meaning the comparison was *not* equal).

The value passed into the function (edi, stored at [rbp+arg_0]) is compared with the immediate value 10.

The cmp instruction sets the CPU's internal Zero Flag (ZF) if the values are equal, and clears it otherwise.

The jnz instruction checks the Zero Flag. If ZF is clear (values were not equal), it jumps to the label loc_Failure.

If ZF is set (values were equal), the jump is *not* taken, and execution proceeds to the instruction sequence under loc_Success (conceptually, the then block), which sets the return value eax to 1 and then jumps unconditionally (jmp) to the end.

The code at loc_Failure (the else block) sets the return value eax to 0.

The loc_End label marks where both paths converge before the function returns.

This CMP followed by Jcc (any conditional jump) pattern is the fundamental building block of conditional execution in assembly, and recognizing it allows the analyst to reconstruct the if-else structure of the original code.

Decoding Meaning through Known Functions: Your Vocabulary Anchors

One of the most significant breakthroughs in making sense of raw disassembly comes when you start recognizing **calls to known functions**. Very few programs are built entirely from scratch; developers rely heavily on standard libraries provided by the operating system or programming language runtime to perform common tasks. These library functions, often residing in external dynamically linked libraries (DLLs on Windows, SOs on Linux) or sometimes statically linked into the executable, provide standardized ways to interact with the OS, manipulate data, and perform complex operations. Think of these API calls as the key nouns and verbs in the assembly language "sentence" – they provide crucial context and meaning.

Learning to identify these common calls is essential. When you see a call instruction targeting an address that your disassembler identifies (via the import table or internal signatures) as, say, printf (from the C standard library) or sprintf, you immediately know the program is involved in formatting text, likely for display or logging. Spotting calls to memory allocation functions like malloc, calloc, realloc, free (or their OS-level equivalents like HeapAlloc, VirtualAlloc) tells you the program is managing memory dynamically on the heap – a critical area to watch for vulnerabilities and data structures.

On Windows, the **Windows API** provides a vast collection of functions exported by core system DLLs. Recognizing calls into these DLLs is fundamental to understanding program behavior:

File I/O (kernel32.dll): CreateFileW, ReadFile, WriteFile, SetFilePointer, DeleteFileW, MoveFileW, FindFirstFileW/FindNextFileW. Seeing these indicates direct interaction with the file system.

Registry Access (advapi32.dll): RegOpenKeyExW, RegCreateKeyExW, RegQueryValueExW, RegSetValueExW, RegDeleteValueW, RegEnumKeyExW. Calls here signal manipulation of the Windows Registry, often used for configuration or malware persistence.

Networking (ws2_32.dll, wininet.dll): socket, bind, listen, accept, connect, send, recv (Winsock API) or InternetOpenW, InternetConnectW, HttpOpenRequestW, HttpSendRequestW (WinINet higher-level API). These are unmistakable signs of network communication.

Process and Thread Management (kernel32.dll): CreateProcessW, OpenProcess, TerminateProcess, CreateThread, CreateRemoteThread, WriteProcessMemory, ReadProcessMemory, VirtualAllocEx. Essential for understanding process creation, inter-process communication, and common malware techniques like process injection.

Memory Management (kernel32.dll): VirtualAlloc, VirtualFree, VirtualProtect, HeapCreate, HeapAlloc, HeapFree. Indicate dynamic memory management beyond standard C library calls.

User Interface (user32.dll, gdi32.dll): CreateWindowExW, GetMessageW, DispatchMessageW, SendMessageW, RegisterClassExW (basic windowing); GetDC, CreateFontIndirectW, TextOutW (drawing). While complex UI code can be hard to reverse, recognizing these core calls confirms UI activity.

Cryptography (crypt32.dll, bcrypt.dll, ncrypt.dll, advapi32.dll CryptoAPI): CryptAcquireContext, CryptGenKey, CryptEncrypt, CryptDecrypt, BCryptEncrypt, etc. Calls here strongly suggest encryption or decryption operations are being performed.

Similarly, on Linux and other Unix-like systems, recognizing calls to standard **libc functions** (often wrappers around direct system calls) provides equivalent insight:

File I/O: open/openat, read, write, close, lseek, stat, unlink, rename, opendir/readdir.

Process Management: fork, execve (and variants like execlp), waitpid, kill, getpid, pthread_create.

Networking: socket, bind, listen, accept, connect, send/sendto, recv/recvfrom.

Memory Management: malloc, free, mmap, munmap, brk/sbrk.

Initially, you might need to frequently look up these function names (your RE tool often provides links to online documentation, or you can search MSDN/POSIX manuals). However, as you gain experience, recognizing the purpose of these common calls becomes second nature. They act as invaluable signposts, quickly revealing the high-level intent of a code section even when the surrounding logic is complex or unfamiliar. Identifying a call to connect followed by send within a loop tells a much clearer story than just seeing dozens of unrelated assembly instructions.

Annotation and Renaming: Transforming Code into Knowledge

This leads directly to what I personally consider one of the most impactful techniques during static code inspection: diligent **annotation and renaming**. When you first load a stripped binary into a disassembler, it does its best but often presents you with generic, automatically generated names. Functions are typically labeled sub_ADDRESS (e.g., sub_4015A0), code locations are loc_ADDRESS, jump targets are loc_NNN, stack variables are var_XX (relative to the frame pointer) or arg_XX, and global data might be dword_ADDRESS. While technically accurate based on location, these names convey absolutely zero semantic meaning about the *purpose* of the code or data.

The process of reverse engineering is largely about *building* that semantic understanding. As you analyze a function or a piece of data and deduce its role, you *must* capture that understanding directly within your analysis tool by **renaming** the generic labels and adding descriptive **comments**. This is not just about neatness; it's fundamental to managing complexity and building a reusable knowledge base about the target.

Renaming Functions: If, after analyzing sub_4015A0, you determine its purpose is to verify a license key against data loaded from a file, rename it! Change sub_4015A0 to something meaningful like VerifyLicenseKeyFromFile or CheckRegistrationStatus. Now, every time you see a call VerifyLicenseKeyFromFile instruction elsewhere in the code, its purpose is immediately obvious without needing to re-analyze the function.

Renaming Variables: If you figure out that the stack variable var_10 (perhaps located at [rbp-10h]) is used as a loop counter, rename it to loop_counter. If arg_8 (passed in the ESI register) is clearly a pointer to a buffer containing user input, rename it pUserInputBuffer. If dword_458A00 holds the network port number, rename it g_NetworkPort. This makes data flow analysis immensely easier to follow.

Renaming Locations: Giving meaningful labels to important code locations, especially the targets of conditional jumps within complex logic or states in a state machine, can clarify control flow. loc_Failure in the earlier if/else example is much clearer than loc_40105F.

Adding Comments: Use comments liberally to explain your reasoning, document complex algorithms, note unresolved questions, reference external documentation (like API descriptions or protocol specs), or describe the overall purpose of a code block. Why did you rename this function? What assumptions are you making about this data structure? What does this obscure sequence of bitwise operations actually achieve? Your future self (or colleagues) will thank you.

This systematic process of annotation transforms the disassembler from a mere code viewer into your interactive **reverse engineering notebook**. The cryptic assembly listing gradually evolves into a narrative that tells the story of the program's logic, written in a language you are actively defining through your renaming and commenting efforts. It requires discipline – pausing to rename and comment as soon as you understand something – but the payoff in clarity and efficiency is enormous, especially on large projects. Without it, you'll find yourself constantly re-analyzing the same code sections, unable to retain the understanding you previously gained.

Searching for Embedded Clues: Strings and Constants as Breadcrumbs

Beyond analyzing the structure of executable code itself, significant clues are often hidden within the program's **data sections** or embedded directly within the code as immediate operands. Two particularly fruitful areas to search are **strings** and **numerical constants**.

Strings: Programs often contain human-readable text strings used for various purposes. Disassemblers typically include a "Strings Window" that automatically extracts sequences of printable characters (often identifying both standard null-terminated ASCII strings and UTF-16 "wide" strings common on Windows) from the entire binary file. Browsing this list can provide instant insights:

Error Messages: "Error: File not found.", "Invalid license key.", "Connection timed out." These directly point to error handling logic and potential failure points.

Filenames and Paths:
"C:\\Users\\Admin\\AppData\\Local\\MyApp\\config.dat", /etc/myapp.conf, \\.\PHYSICALDRIVE0. Reveal files the application interacts with.

URLs and Hostnames: "https://updates.example.com/check", "api.internal.service:8080". Indicate network communication targets.

Registry Keys (Windows):
"SOFTWARE\\VendorName\\AppName\\Settings". Show registry locations used for configuration or persistence.

User Prompts: "Enter your password:", "Save changes before closing?". Point to user interaction logic.

Debug Messages: Sometimes developers accidentally leave behind debug print statements ("Entering function X...", "Decryption key: %s"). These can be goldmines!

Commands: "cmd.exe /c copy %s %s", "DROP TABLE Users;". Reveal commands executed or potential vulnerabilities (like SQL injection if concatenated unsafely).

Unique Identifiers: Mutex names, named pipes, GUIDs, protocol identifiers.

Once you find an interesting string, your RE tool allows you to find **xrefs** to it – that is, locate the code that actually *uses* this string (e.g., passes it to printf, uses it in a file open call, sends it over the network). This provides immediate context and directs your analysis towards the relevant code sections. Of course, be aware that strings are easily obfuscated. Malware and protected software often encrypt or encode critical strings, decrypting them only at runtime. Seeing large blobs of seemingly random data being passed to functions named something like decrypt_string or decode_resource is a strong indicator of this technique. Analyzing the decryption routine then becomes necessary to reveal the hidden strings.

Numerical Constants and Magic Numbers: Specific numbers embedded in the code (as immediate operands to instructions) or stored in data sections can also be highly revealing:

Magic Numbers: Specific byte sequences used to identify file formats or protocol types. If code reads the first few bytes of a file and compares them to 0x504B0304 (the magic number for a ZIP file entry), you know it's dealing with ZIP archives. Seeing a comparison against 0xFEEDFACE might indicate Mach-O binary handling. You can often look up encountered constants in online databases of magic numbers.

Cryptographic Constants: Standard cryptographic algorithms often involve specific initialization vectors (IVs), fixed constants used in rounds (like in SHA variants), or default table values. Recognizing these constants can help identify the specific algorithm being used. (Note: Hardcoding actual secret keys as constants is a terrible security practice, but sadly still occurs sometimes!)

Protocol Identifiers: Network protocols often use specific port numbers (e.g., 80 for HTTP, 443 for HTTPS), fixed message type identifiers, or command codes.

Error Codes: Comparisons against specific numbers before jumping to error handling routines often correspond to defined error codes (e.g., Windows GetLastError() codes, standard errno values on Linux). Looking these up clarifies the nature of the failure.

Sizes and Offsets: Constants used in memory calculations (ADD EAX, 100h) or loop bounds might represent fixed buffer sizes, structure offsets, or iteration counts.

Bit Flags: Constants used with bitwise operations (AND, OR, TEST) often represent flags controlling behavior. Understanding which bit corresponds to which option requires careful analysis of the surrounding code.

Finding where these constants are used (via data xrefs) helps understand their purpose and the logic they influence.

Examining the Overall Structure: Imports, Exports, and Dependencies

Before diving too deep into individual functions, it's often helpful to step back and examine the program's high-level structure and its dependencies on external code, primarily through the **import** and **export tables** embedded within the executable file format.

Import Table Analysis: This table lists all the functions that the executable intends to use from external shared libraries (DLLs/SOs). Your RE tool will parse this and display it clearly, often grouping imports by library. Quickly scanning the list of imported DLLs/SOs (e.g., kernel32.dll, ws2_32.dll, user32.dll, libc.so.6, libcrypto.so) and the specific functions imported from each gives you a powerful, high-level summary of the program's capabilities *before* you analyze a single line of its own code. A program importing heavily from ws2_32.dll is definitely doing networking. One importing from crypt32.dll is likely doing cryptography. One that imports only basic kernel32 and libc functions might be a simple console utility or potentially malware trying to minimize its footprint and dependency footprint. Malware often tries to hide its intentions by *not* importing suspicious APIs directly, instead loading libraries manually (LoadLibrary/dlopen) and resolving function addresses at runtime (GetProcAddress/dlsym). Finding *these* import resolution functions being used is therefore a significant indicator itself. Analyzing the import table helps scope the application's functionality and potential areas of interest.

Export Table Analysis: If the file you are analyzing is itself a shared library (DLL/SO) designed to be used by other programs, it will likely have an **export table**. This table lists the functions (and sometimes global data) that the library makes available for others to call. Examining the export table reveals the library's intended public interface. The names of exported functions (if present) often clearly indicate their purpose (e.g., EncryptData, ConnectToService, ParseConfiguration). Analyzing these exported functions is key to understanding the library's capabilities and how other modules might interact with it.

Understanding these structural elements – how the program is linked to the outside world via imports and how it exposes itself via exports – provides crucial architectural context that frames your subsequent detailed code inspection.

The Iterative Cycle of Discovery

It's crucial to reiterate that code inspection, and indeed all static analysis, is rarely a linear process from start to finish. It's inherently **iterative and exploratory**. You don't just read the disassembly from the entry point downwards like a book. Instead, you jump around, following clues and forming hypotheses:

Initial Scan: Load the binary, let the tool perform auto-analysis, examine imports/exports, browse strings. Identify potentially interesting areas (e.g., network-related imports, suspicious strings).

Dive In: Choose a starting point (e.g., a function called just before the interesting network API, or the code using a suspicious string).

Analyze Function: Understand its purpose, inputs, outputs, and logic using disassembly/decompilation, CFG analysis, stack/data flow tracing. **Rename and comment immediately.**

Follow Xrefs: See where this function is called from, or how the data it produces/consumes is used elsewhere. This leads you to new functions or data structures.

Analyze Related Code: Repeat the analysis process for these newly discovered related areas, renaming and commenting as you go.

Hit a Wall?: If you get stuck or the code is confusing (maybe obfuscated), step back. Look for other clues – search for related strings or constants, examine other imported functions, perhaps revisit the overall architecture. Or maybe this is a point where dynamic analysis (Chapter 5) is needed to resolve ambiguity.

Refine Understanding: As you uncover more pieces of the puzzle, your overall understanding of the program's architecture and functionality grows. Go back and refine earlier renaming or comments based on new insights. This cycle of reading, hypothesizing, testing hypotheses (statically via xrefs and pattern recognition), documenting findings through renaming and commenting, searching for new clues, and iterating continues until you achieve your analysis objectives or decide a different approach (like dynamic analysis) is required. Code inspection isn't about understanding every single instruction; it's about strategically exploring the code, identifying key landmarks (APIs, important functions, data structures), understanding their relationships, and building a semantic map of the software's logic from the ground up. It requires patience, meticulousness, and the willingness to constantly refine your understanding as new evidence emerges.

4.2. Control Flow Analysis: Mapping the Program's Roads

Okay, let's move beyond inspecting individual instructions or data points and focus on understanding the program's dynamics, specifically how it *navigates* through its own code. After performing initial code inspection (Chapter 4.1), you quickly realize that programs rarely execute instructions in a simple, linear sequence from the first instruction to the last. Instead, they exhibit complex behaviors: making decisions based on data, repeating sections of code, jumping to different routines, and calling upon other functions. This order of execution, the path that the program's instruction pointer carves through the code, is known as **Control Flow**. Mastering **Control Flow Analysis** is absolutely fundamental to reverse engineering, as it's the key to deciphering the program's underlying logic, decision-making processes, and overall algorithmic structure. It's about mapping the intricate network of roads and intersections within the software's landscape.

The Foundation: Basic Blocks and Control Transfers

The core concept in understanding control flow is the **Basic Block**. Think of a basic block as a straight stretch of road in our city map analogy. It's a sequence of consecutive instructions where:

Control flow enters *only* at the very beginning of the sequence (no jumps into the middle).

Control flow leaves *only* at the very end of the sequence (no jumps out from the middle).

The end of a basic block is always marked by a **control transfer instruction** – an instruction that potentially changes the program counter (instruction pointer) to something other than the immediately following instruction. These include:

Unconditional Jumps (JMP on x86, B on ARM): Like a mandatory turn sign, forcing execution to continue at a different specified address.

Conditional Jumps (JE, JNE, JG, JL, JZ, JNZ, etc. on x86; BEQ, BNE, BGT, etc. on ARM): These are the decision points, the forks in the road. Based on the current state of the CPU's **flags register** (which is set by preceding comparison (CMP, TEST) or arithmetic instructions), execution either continues to the next sequential instruction (the "fall-through" or "not taken" path) or jumps to a different target address (the "taken" path).

Function Calls (CALL on x86, BL/BLX on ARM): These instructions push the address of the next instruction (the return address) onto the stack and then jump to the beginning of the called function (subroutine). They transfer control *out* of the current function temporarily.

Returns (RETN, RET on x86; BX LR, POP {PC} on ARM): These instructions retrieve the return address (usually saved on the stack by the corresponding CALL) and jump back to that address in the caller function, transferring control *back*.

Indirect Jumps/Calls: Jumps or calls where the target address isn't fixed in the instruction itself but is loaded from a register or memory location (e.g., JMP EAX, CALL DWORD PTR [EBX+4], BX R0). These are often used for implementing switch statements (via jump tables) or virtual function calls (via vtables), making static analysis more challenging as the exact target might only be known at runtime.

System Calls/Interrupts (SYSCALL, INT, SVC): These transfer control to the operating system kernel to request services. While control eventually returns, they represent a significant departure from the program's user-mode flow.

Understanding these control transfer instructions and how they define the boundaries of basic blocks is the first step in control flow analysis. Disassemblers automatically identify basic blocks by analyzing these instructions.

Visualizing the Flow: Control Flow Graphs (CFGs)

While you can trace control flow by manually following jump targets in a linear disassembly listing, this quickly becomes unmanageable for functions of even moderate complexity. This is where **Control Flow Graphs (CFGs)** become an indispensable visualization tool. Nearly all modern disassemblers (IDA Pro, Ghidra, radare2/rizin with graph view, Hopper) can automatically generate CFGs for each identified function.

Imagine the CFG as that city map we discussed.

Nodes (Vertices): Each **basic block** of code is represented as a node or vertex in the graph, typically drawn as a box containing the assembly instructions of that block.

Edges (Arcs): Directed lines or arrows connect these nodes, representing the possible **control flow transfers** between basic blocks.

An unconditional jump (JMP) or sequential execution ("fall-through") from the end of one block to the beginning of another is shown as a single edge. A conditional jump (JE, JNE, etc.) results in *two* outgoing edges from the node: one leading to the target address if the condition is met (the "taken" edge, often colored green or marked 'T'), and one leading to the next sequential instruction if the condition is not met (the "not taken" edge, often colored red or marked 'F').

A function call (CALL) might be represented as an edge leading out of the function's graph, often labeled with the name of the called function. Sometimes, graphs might represent calls differently, perhaps focusing only on intra-function control flow.

Return instructions (RETN) typically mark exit nodes from the function's graph.

Visualizing the code this way offers immediate structural insights that are hard to grasp from linear text:

If-Else Statements: Appear as a diamond shape – a node with two outgoing conditional edges that diverge and later converge back at a common successor node.

Loops (while, for, do-while): Are easily identifiable as **cycles** in the graph – a path of edges that leads from a node back to itself or an earlier node in the sequence. The conditional jump that exits the loop is clearly visible as an edge leading *out* of the cycle.

Switch Statements (using Jump Tables): Often appear as a node with an indirect jump (JMP EAX, etc.) having multiple outgoing edges pointing to different subsequent blocks (the case handlers), deduced by the disassembler analyzing the potential values loaded into the jump register.

Function Complexity: The overall shape and density of the graph give an immediate impression of the function's complexity. A long, mostly linear graph indicates simple sequential logic. A graph with many nodes, dense interconnections, and numerous conditional branches suggests complex logic.

Studying the CFG is often the most efficient way to get an initial understanding of a function's structure before diving into the specifics of each instruction. You can quickly identify the main decision points, locate loops, and trace the high-level flow through different execution paths.

Code Example: CFG Visualization (Conceptual)

Let's revisit the if/else example:

```
        ; Function: check_value(int)
; Basic Block 1 (Entry, Prologue, Store Arg)
push    rbp
mov     rbp, rsp
mov     [rbp+arg_0], edi

; Basic Block 2 (Comparison & Conditional Jump)
cmp     dword ptr [rbp+arg_0], 10
jnz     short loc_Failure

; Basic Block 3 ('Then' path) - Falls through if JNZ not
taken
mov     eax, 1
jmp     short loc_End  ; End of Basic Block 3 (Unconditional
Jump)

; Basic Block 4 ('Else' path) - Target of JNZ
loc_Failure:
mov     eax, 0
; End of Basic Block 4 (Falls through to Loc_End)

; Basic Block 5 (Merge point, Epilogue, Return)
loc_End:
pop     rbp
retn
```

A CFG tool would visualize this something like this:

    graph TD
    BB1[BB1: Prologue, Store Arg] --> BB2{BB2: CMP input, 10};
    BB2 -- JNZ (Not Equal) --> BB4[BB4: EAX = 0];
    BB2 -- Fallthrough (Equal) --> BB3[BB3: EAX = 1];
    BB3 --> BB5[BB5: Epilogue, RETN];
    BB4 --> BB5;

Explanation:
The graph starts at BB1.
Execution flows to BB2, the decision point based on the CMP and JNZ.
If the condition (input != 10) is true, flow goes to BB4 (Else).
If the condition is false (input == 10), flow falls through to BB3 (Then).
Both BB3 (after an unconditional JMP) and BB4 (via fall-through)
eventually converge at the exit block BB5.
This graphical representation makes the branching if-else structure
immediately apparent.

124

Core Techniques in Control Flow Analysis

Analyzing control flow isn't just about looking at the pretty graphs; it involves specific techniques to extract meaning:

Identifying Decision Points: Locate every conditional jump instruction (Jcc). This is where the program's behavior diverges. The crucial task is then to look at the instructions *immediately preceding* the conditional jump, typically a CMP or TEST instruction, to understand *what condition* is being checked. Is it comparing user input against a stored password hash? Checking if a file operation returned an error code? Testing a flag set earlier? Understanding the condition is paramount to understanding the logic. Analyze both the "taken" and "not taken" paths originating from the conditional jump to see the consequences of the decision.

Tracing Execution Paths: Systematically follow the possible paths of execution through the function, either mentally using the CFG or by stepping through linear disassembly. When you encounter a conditional branch, mentally bookmark it and explore one path first (e.g., the "taken" path), then backtrack and explore the other ("not taken") path. This helps understand all possible behaviors. When you hit a CALL instruction, note the target function. You might need to pause your analysis of the current function, jump into the called function's CFG, understand its purpose and return value, and then resume analysis back in the caller, incorporating the knowledge of what the call achieved. Leveraging **cross-references (xrefs)** provided by your tool is essential here. Seeing all the locations (xrefs) that *call* the function you're currently analyzing provides context about how it's used.

Detecting and Analyzing Loops: Loops are fundamental for repetitive processing. Visually, they are cycles in the CFG. Analytically, you need to identify:

The Loop Body: The sequence of basic blocks forming the cycle. What operations are being repeated?

The Loop Condition/Exit: The conditional jump *within* the cycle that eventually allows execution to *leave* the loop. What condition is checked to terminate the repetition (e.g., counter reaching a limit, end-of-file reached, specific flag being set)?

Initialization: How are loop counters or state variables set up *before* the loop begins?

Iteration Logic: How are loop counters or state variables updated *within* the loop body to eventually meet the exit condition?

Understanding these components reveals the purpose of the loop – is it iterating over elements in an array (often using an index register incremented each time), processing data from a buffer until a null terminator is found, waiting for a specific network event, etc.? Recognizing loop patterns is key to understanding many algorithms.

Function Call Analysis (Intra- and Inter-procedural):

Intra-procedural analysis focuses on the control flow *within* a single function, as described above.

Inter-procedural analysis considers how control flows *between* different functions via CALL and RET instructions. Building a **call graph** (different from a CFG – this graph shows which functions call which other functions) for the entire program provides a high-level view of module dependencies and overall program structure. Following execution flow across function call boundaries is crucial for understanding how different parts of the application collaborate. Again, xrefs are indispensable for navigating these calls efficiently.

Challenges in Control Flow Analysis

While CFGs and analysis techniques help immensely, certain factors can complicate understanding control flow:

Indirect Control Transfers: Jumps or calls where the target address is determined at runtime (loaded from a register or memory) are harder to resolve statically. Jump tables (for switch statements) can often be partially reconstructed by analyzing the code that calculates the index and accesses the table. Virtual function calls (via vtables in C++) require identifying the vtable structures and potentially analyzing object creation logic to determine possible runtime targets. Function pointers passed as arguments or stored in data structures pose similar challenges. Static analysis tools might present multiple possible targets or indicate an unresolved indirect call, sometimes requiring dynamic analysis for definitive resolution.

Compiler Optimizations: Optimizations like function inlining (where the compiler replaces a CALL with the entire body of the called function) can eliminate function boundaries and create larger, more complex CFGs. Loop optimizations (unrolling, vectorization) can drastically change the apparent structure of loops in the assembly compared to the source. Recognizing the effects of optimization is important to avoid misinterpreting the underlying logic.

Exception Handling: Structured Exception Handling (SEH on Windows) or similar mechanisms in other languages/platforms introduce non-obvious control flow paths. When an exception occurs (e.g., division by zero, accessing invalid memory), the normal execution flow is interrupted, and control is transferred to a registered exception handler, potentially bypassing large sections of code, including normal function returns. Analyzing exception handler registration and the logic within the handlers themselves is necessary to understand these alternative control paths.

Obfuscation: This is a major challenge, particularly in malware analysis or when analyzing protected software. **Control Flow Flattening** is a common obfuscation technique specifically designed to destroy the readability of CFGs. It breaks a function into many tiny basic blocks and uses a central "dispatcher" block. Each real block ends by setting a state variable and jumping back to the dispatcher. The dispatcher then uses complex conditional logic (often involving opaque predicates – conditions that always evaluate to the same outcome but are hard for static analysis to prove) based on the state variable to determine the *next* real block to jump to. The resulting CFG looks like a tangled mess of blocks all connecting back to the central dispatcher, obscuring the original loops and conditionals. Analyzing flattened control flow often requires significant manual effort, dynamic analysis, or specialized de-obfuscation tools/scripts to reconstruct the original logic. Other techniques include inserting dead code paths that are never actually taken or using convoluted indirect jumps.

Why Control Flow Analysis is Essential for RE

Understanding the flow of control is not merely an academic exercise; it's absolutely critical for achieving most reverse engineering goals:

Grasping Logic: You cannot understand *what* a program or function does without knowing the *order* in which it performs its actions and the *conditions* under which different actions are taken. Control flow analysis reveals the algorithmic structure.

Finding Vulnerabilities: Many security vulnerabilities depend on specific control flow paths being taken. For example, a use-after-free vulnerability requires that control flows first through the code that frees memory and *then* through code that attempts to use the dangling pointer. A logic bug might only manifest if a specific sequence of conditional branches is followed. Analyzing control flow is essential for identifying potentially vulnerable execution paths.

Locating Specific Functionality: By tracing control flow forwards from input points (like user interface interactions or network packet reception) or backwards from output points (like file writes, network sends, or displaying results), you can pinpoint the code responsible for specific features.

Bypassing Protections/Checks: Software protections or license checks often boil down to a critical conditional jump that determines success or failure. Identifying this jump and the preceding comparison through control flow analysis is the first step towards potentially patching or bypassing the check.

Understanding Malware Behavior: Analyzing the control flow of malware reveals its execution stages: initial infection, persistence mechanisms, C&C communication loops, payload activation conditions, and evasion routines. Mapping this flow is key to understanding the threat.

In essence, mapping out the program's roads through control flow analysis provides the fundamental structure upon which you layer understanding of data manipulation (data flow analysis, Chapter 4.3) and overall program purpose. It turns the static collection of instructions revealed by code inspection into a dynamic, logical sequence, allowing you to follow the program's decision-making process and ultimately comprehend its behavior. While initially challenging, particularly when faced with optimized or obfuscated code, mastering control flow analysis using tools like CFGs and systematic path tracing is a cornerstone skill for every reverse engineer.

4.3. Data Flow Analysis: Following the Information Trail

we've meticulously mapped the roads and pathways within our target program through Control Flow Analysis (Chapter 4.2). We understand how the program *can* navigate from one instruction block to another, making decisions and repeating tasks. But just knowing the road network isn't enough to understand the city's commerce or social life. We also need to know what's being transported along those roads – the goods, the messages, the people. In software terms, this cargo is the **data**. **Data Flow Analysis**

(DFA), in the context of static reverse engineering, is the critical practice of tracking how information – represented by values in registers, memory locations on the stack or heap, or global variables – originates, moves through the program, gets transformed by instructions, and is ultimately used.

Where did the value currently sitting in the EAX register actually come from? What specific piece of information is stored at the memory address pointed to by the stack offset [rbp-20h]? How is the block of data just read from a configuration file subsequently processed before influencing a critical decision? Answering these types of questions is the core purpose of static data flow analysis. It moves beyond the structure of execution (control flow) to focus on the substance being manipulated (data). The ultimate goal here is often to deduce the **purpose** and **meaning** of the variables and data structures the program operates on, even when the original variable names and type information are lost.

Tracing the Currents: Register Usage

One of the most immediate and fundamental levels of data flow analysis happens within the CPU's **registers**. Registers are small, extremely fast storage locations directly within the CPU core, used as scratchpads for calculations, temporary storage for intermediate values, and often for passing arguments to functions and receiving return values according to specific **calling conventions**. Common general-purpose registers on x86/x86-64 architectures include EAX/RAX, EBX/RBX, ECX/RCX, EDX/RDX, ESI/RSI, EDI/RDI, along with stack pointers (ESP/RSP), base pointers (EBP/RBP), and the instruction pointer (EIP/RIP). ARM architectures have a similar concept with registers like R0-R12, SP, LR (Link Register), and PC (Program Counter).

Tracking register usage involves carefully observing the sequence of instructions within a basic block or across a function to understand how values are loaded into, manipulated within, and stored from registers.

Data Movement: Instructions like MOV (move data), LEA (Load Effective Address – calculates an address but often used for arithmetic too), PUSH (store on stack), and POP (retrieve from stack) are key indicators of data entering or leaving registers. You trace where the source operand for a MOV into a register comes from – is it an immediate constant value, another register, or a memory location? Where does the value *in* a register get moved or stored *to*?

Data Transformation: Arithmetic and logical instructions (ADD, SUB, MUL, DIV, AND, OR, XOR, SHL, SHR, ROL, ROR, NEG) modify the values held within registers. By observing the operands (which registers or immediate values are involved) and the destination register, you can understand how computations are performed. For example, seeing MOV EAX, [input_var], followed by ADD EAX, 5, then SHL EAX, 1 tells you the input variable was loaded, incremented by 5, and then multiplied by 2 (left shift by 1).

Argument Passing and Return Values: Understanding the architecture's calling convention is crucial. For instance, in the common x86-64 System V ABI (used on Linux/macOS), the first six integer/pointer arguments are passed in registers RDI, RSI, RDX, RCX, R8, R9, respectively. Floating-point arguments use XMM0-XMM7. The integer/pointer return value is placed in RAX. Tracking how these specific registers are loaded *before* a CALL instruction and how RAX is used *after* a CALL returns helps identify function parameters and results. Seeing MOV RDI, [some_buffer_ptr], MOV ESI, 100h followed by CALL read_data strongly suggests read_data takes a buffer pointer and a size as its first two arguments. Seeing the code immediately after the CALL use the value in RAX suggests RAX holds the function's return value (perhaps the number of bytes read).

Tool Assistance: Modern disassemblers significantly aid register tracking. They often allow you to **highlight** all uses of a specific register within the current view. Selecting a register in one instruction might automatically highlight every other instruction within that function that reads from or writes to the same register. Cross-references (xrefs) can also sometimes be applied to register usage within a function, although this is less common than xrefs for memory addresses or function calls. Decompilers implicitly perform extensive register tracking to reconstruct high-level variables and expressions.

Code Example: Simple Register Tracing

Let's extend the add_numbers C example and look at its assembly again, focusing purely on register data flow for the core addition:

```
// From simple_proc.c
int add_numbers(int a, int b) {
    int result = a + b;
```

```
      return result;
}

      ; Function: add_numbers(int, int)
add_numbers proc near
      ; ... prologue ...
      mov     [rbp+var_4], edi ; Store arg 'a' (from EDI) to
stack
      mov     [rbp+var_8], esi ; Store arg 'b' (from ESI) to
stack

      ; === Data Flow Focus ===
      mov     edx, [rbp+var_4] ; 1. Load 'a' from stack into
EDX
      mov     eax, [rbp+var_8] ; 2. Load 'b' from stack into
EAX
      add     eax, edx         ; 3. EAX = EAX + EDX (EAX now
holds sum)
      mov     [rbp+var_C], eax ; 4. Store sum (from EAX) to
stack (local 'result')

      mov     eax, [rbp+var_C] ; 5. Load sum from stack back
into EAX (for return)
      ; === End Data Flow Focus ===

      ; ... epilogue ...
      retn
add_numbers endp
```

RE Interpretation (Focusing on Data Flow):

Instruction 1: edx receives its value directly from the memory location [rbp+var_4], which we know holds the first argument a. So, edx now contains a.

Instruction 2: eax receives its value directly from [rbp+var_8], which holds the second argument b. So, eax now contains b.

Instruction 3: The add instruction reads the current values of eax (b) and edx (a), performs the addition, and writes the result (a + b) back into the destination register eax. edx's value is only read here, not changed. After this instruction, eax holds the sum.

Instruction 4: The value currently in eax (the sum) is written to the stack location [rbp+var_C]. This identifies the purpose of this stack location as storing the intermediate result.

Instruction 5: The value is read *back* from [rbp+var_C] into eax. Since eax is the return value register according to the calling convention, this confirms that the value calculated and stored in var_C is indeed the intended return value of the function.

By tracing the source and destination operands for each instruction involving registers eax and edx, we meticulously follow the flow of the input arguments (a and b) through the computation (add) to produce the final result delivered in the return register eax.

Tracking the Flow Through Memory: Stack, Heap, and Globals

While registers are crucial for intermediate calculations, programs need memory to store data that doesn't fit in registers, data that needs to persist across function calls (local variables on the stack), data whose lifetime is dynamic (heap), or data shared across the entire program (globals). Data flow analysis must therefore extend beyond registers to track how information moves into and out of memory.

Stack Memory Flow: As discussed regarding OS fundamentals and procedural programming, the **stack** is heavily used for local variables and function parameters. Data flow analysis involves identifying instructions that **read from (MOV reg, [RBP+offset])** or **write to (MOV [RBP+offset], reg)** specific stack locations.

Variable Initialization: Where does a local variable get its initial value? Is it loaded from a register (passed as an argument)? Copied from another stack location? The result of a function call (MOV [rbp+var_X], EAX after a CALL)? Assigned a constant (MOV DWORD PTR [rbp+var_Y], 1)?

Variable Usage: Where is the value stored in a specific stack location subsequently *read* and used? Is it loaded into a register for calculation? Passed as an argument to another function (MOV EDI, [rbp+var_Z]; CALL some_func)? Used in a comparison (CMP DWORD PTR [rbp+var_W], 0)?

Pointer Issues: Stack variables can also hold pointers. Tracking where a pointer stored on the stack is loaded (MOV RAX, [rbp+ptr_var]) and then dereferenced (MOV ECX, [RAX]) is crucial for understanding indirect data access.

Structure Layout: Observing accesses at different fixed offsets relative to a base stack location (e.g., MOV EAX, [RBP+var_S], MOV EBX, [RBP+var_S+4], MOV ECX, [RBP+var_S+8]) strongly suggests var_S might be the start of a struct with multiple members. This helps in defining data structures within your RE tool.

Heap Memory Flow (Static Perspective): The **heap** is used for dynamic allocation. While static analysis can't know the *exact addresses* returned by malloc or new (these are determined at runtime), it can still reveal much about how heap memory is *intended* to be used.

Allocation Points: Identify calls to heap allocation functions (malloc, calloc, new, HeapAlloc, VirtualAlloc). Note the requested size if it's obvious (constant or derived from a tracked variable).

Pointer Storage: Trace where the pointer returned by the allocation function (usually in EAX/RAX) is stored – often in a local stack variable, a global variable, or within another data structure on the heap itself (forming linked lists or trees).

Heap Data Access: Find instructions that load this stored heap pointer into a register (MOV RBX, [stack_var_holding_heap_ptr]) and then use it as a base address for memory accesses (MOV DWORD PTR [RBX+10h], EAX, CMP BYTE PTR [RBX+4], 0). These accesses reveal how the dynamically allocated memory is structured and used. Consistent offsets relative to the heap pointer suggest member variables of a struct or class allocated on the heap.

Deallocation Points: Locate calls to deallocation functions (free, delete, HeapFree, VirtualFree) and trace which pointer is being passed as an argument. Does it correspond to a pointer returned by an earlier allocation call? This helps understand object lifetimes. Mismatches (double frees, freeing invalid pointers) or missing frees (leaks) are potential bugs, though often hard to definitively prove statically.

Challenges: **Pointer aliasing** is a major challenge for static heap analysis. The analysis might see two different pointer variables, but it's hard to know statically if they might, at runtime, end up pointing to the *same* heap block, making it difficult to be certain about the effects of modifications through one pointer on reads through the other.

Global/Static Memory Flow: Programs often use fixed memory addresses for **global variables** (accessible from any function) or **static variables** (persistent within a function or file scope). These typically reside in data sections like .data (initialized data) or .bss (uninitialized data, zeroed out by the loader).

Identifying Accesses: Look for instructions that use hardcoded, absolute memory addresses as operands (e.g., MOV EAX, ds:dword_40A010, ADD byte_40A014, 1). Disassemblers usually label these locations based on their address.

Tracking Across Functions: The key challenge is that global variables can be read or modified by *any* function in the program. To understand the full lifecycle and purpose of a global variable, you need to use your RE tool's **cross-reference (xref)** features extensively. Find *all* locations in the entire program that read from (xref -> Read) or write to (xref -> Write) that specific global address. Examining the context of each access across different functions helps piece together its role (e.g., a global configuration flag, a shared counter, a pointer to a central data structure).

Tracking data flow through memory – understanding where variables reside (stack, heap, global), how they are initialized, accessed, modified, and potentially deallocated – is crucial for reconstructing data structures and understanding how different parts of the program share and manipulate information.

Connecting the Dots: Following Data Dependencies

Individual register and memory tracking operations are building blocks. The real power comes from connecting them to understand **data dependencies** – how the result produced by one instruction is used as input for subsequent instructions, potentially cascading through a complex series of calculations and memory accesses. The goal is often to trace a piece of data from its origin (e.g., input parameter, file read, constant value) to its final use (e.g., output, conditional check, argument to another function), understanding all the transformations it undergoes along the way.

This often involves conceptually performing **program slicing**:

Backward Slicing: You identify a point of interest – perhaps a variable used in a critical CMP instruction just before a conditional jump determining success/failure, or the value being returned from a function. You then trace *backward* through the code, instruction by instruction. For each instruction encountered, you ask: "Did this instruction contribute to the value I'm interested in?" You recursively trace the source operands of contributing instructions, effectively identifying the "slice" of the program that could influence the value at your point of interest. This helps answer the question, "Where did this value *come from* and what calculations produced it?"

Forward Slicing: Conversely, you start at a source of data – perhaps an input parameter to a function, a value read using ReadFile, or a global configuration setting. You then trace *forward*, identifying all instructions that *use* this data directly or indirectly. This helps answer the question, "Where does this data *go* and what parts of the program does it affect?"

While manual slicing can be tedious, modern RE tools offer significant assistance:

Operand Highlighting: Selecting a register or memory operand in one instruction might automatically highlight other instructions in the same function that use the same operand, visually showing direct dependencies.

Variable Cross-References: In decompiled views, tools often allow you to find all references (reads and writes) to a specific reconstructed high-level variable within the current function, simplifying the tracking of its usage.

Taint Analysis (More Advanced/Dynamic): Though primarily a dynamic analysis technique, some advanced static analysis tools or plugins attempt **static taint analysis**. They conceptually "taint" data coming from untrusted sources (like user input or network sockets) and track how this taint propagates through the program. If tainted data reaches a "sensitive sink" (like a function executing system commands or indexing into memory without proper validation), it indicates a potential vulnerability like command injection or buffer overflow. Static taint analysis faces significant challenges with complex control flow and aliasing but represents an attempt to automate aspects of data flow security analysis.

Code Example: Tracing Dependency Backward

Let's look at a slightly more complex sequence:

```
        ; ... previous code sets up input_val in [rbp-8] ...

loc_Start_Calc:
   mov    eax, [rbp-8]       ; 1. Load input_val into EAX
   add    eax, 5             ; 2. EAX = input_val + 5
   imul   eax, 3             ; 3. EAX = (input_val + 5) * 3
   mov    [rbp-0Ch], eax     ; 4. Store result temporarily on
stack (temp_var)
   mov    ecx, [rbp-0Ch]     ; 5. Load temp_var into ECX
   shr    ecx, 1             ; 6. ECX = temp_var / 2 (integer
division)
   mov    edx, [rbp-8]       ; 7. Load input_val again into EDX
   sub    edx, ecx           ; 8. EDX = input_val - (temp_var / 2)
   cmp    edx, 100           ; 9. Compare EDX with 100 <<< Point
of Interest
   jl     loc_Handle_Less_Than_100
```

RE Backward Slice from Instruction 9 (cmp edx, 100):

Target: We want to know how the value in edx at instruction 9 was calculated.

Instruction 9: Reads edx. Where did edx get its value?

Instruction 8: Writes to edx. It reads edx (previous value) and ecx.

Trace previous edx: comes from instruction 7.

Trace ecx: comes from instruction 6.

Instruction 7: Writes to edx. It reads from memory [rbp-8] (our original input_val).

Instruction 6: Writes to ecx. It reads ecx (previous value) and shifts.

Trace previous ecx: comes from instruction 5.

Instruction 5: Writes to ecx. It reads from memory [rbp-0Ch] (our temp_var).

Instruction 4: Writes to [rbp-0Ch]. It reads eax.

Trace eax: comes from instruction 3.

Instruction 3: Writes to eax. It reads eax.

Trace previous eax: comes from instruction 2.

Instruction 2: Writes to eax. It reads eax.

Trace previous eax: comes from instruction 1.

Instruction 1: Writes to eax. It reads from memory [rbp-8] (input_val).

Result: By tracing backward, we discover that the value compared against 100 in edx is derived from the formula: input_val - (((input_val + 5) * 3) / 2). Data flow analysis, through dependency tracing, allowed us to reconstruct the calculation affecting the critical comparison.

The Transformative Power of Renaming Fueled by Data Flow

This ability to trace data dependencies directly underscores the immense power of **annotation and renaming**, which we discussed under Code Inspection. It is *precisely because* you can follow the data flow that you gain the confidence to apply meaningful names. You don't just guess; you deduce based on evidence.

When you successfully trace a value from where it enters a function (e.g., as parameter arg_0 in RDI), see it passed through several intermediate registers, perhaps stored temporarily on the stack (var_10), then loaded again and finally passed as the first argument to a call _decrypt_block, you have strong evidence to rename arg_0 to pEncryptedDataIn, var_10 to intermediate_decryption_state, and the result potentially returned in EAX to pDecryptedDataOut. These meaningful names, born from data flow analysis, make the code surrounding the decryption call instantly comprehensible. Every subsequent time you encounter pEncryptedDataIn or pDecryptedDataOut in that function's analysis (or potentially elsewhere, if you propagate the understanding), the code's purpose becomes clearer. Consider the scenario mentioned in the prompt: analyzing a network protocol handler. By tracing a specific field read from an incoming network packet buffer (perhaps at [packet_buffer + 0x8]), watching it get loaded into ECX, then used as an index into a memory table (mov eax, [command_table + ecx * 4]), and finally seeing the value loaded from the table (eax) being used in an indirect call eax instruction, you deduce the field's purpose. The data flow reveals it's not just random data; it's a **command code** used as an index to dispatch handling routines. Renaming the field variable to command_code, the table to g_CommandDispatchTable, and the called function pointer to pCommandHandlerFunc transforms obscure memory accesses and indirect calls into a clear description of a command dispatch mechanism. This realization, directly driven by meticulous data flow tracking, can unlock the understanding of an entire protocol or module. Without DFA, assigning such meaningful names would be guesswork; with DFA, it becomes evidence-based documentation embedded directly in your analysis.

Static Data Flow Analysis: Recognizing the Boundaries

Despite its power, static data flow analysis has fundamental limitations that stem from its inability to know the actual **runtime values** of data. It analyzes the structure of the code and can tell you how data *could potentially* flow based on all possible control paths, but it cannot predict the concrete values that will exist during a real execution, especially when those values depend on external factors.

Input Dependency: If a program's behavior depends on user input, data read from a file, or messages received from the network, static analysis alone cannot know what that input will be. Consider a password check: read_user_input(buffer); result = check_password(buffer); if (result == TRUE) .... Static analysis can show you the check_password function is called and its result influences the if statement, but it cannot tell you whether the if condition will be true or false because it doesn't know what the user will type. Dynamic analysis (entering a password and observing the result) is required.

Pointer Ambiguity (Aliasing): As mentioned, static analysis often struggles to determine if two different pointer variables might point to the same memory location at runtime. If code modifies memory through ptr_a and later reads from ptr_b, static analysis might not be able to definitively say if the read value reflects the modification or not, hindering precise data tracking.

Indirect Calls/Jumps: When control flow depends on a function pointer or jump target stored in memory or calculated dynamically (common with C++ virtual functions, jump tables, or callbacks), static analysis may not be able to determine the exact function(s) that will be called or the exact location(s) that will be jumped to. It might list several possibilities or simply mark the target as unresolved. Dynamic analysis, by observing the actual value loaded into the register/memory location at runtime just before the indirect call/jump, can resolve this ambiguity.

Environment Dependency: Program behavior can depend on environment variables, system configuration, the presence or absence of certain files, or even the current date/time. Static analysis typically cannot model these external factors.

Complex Interprocedural Flows: Accurately tracking data flow across complex chains of function calls, especially involving pointers passed through multiple functions or modifications to global variables, can be computationally expensive and sometimes intractable for static analysis tools, leading to approximations or incomplete results.

These limitations mean that static data flow analysis provides a picture of *potential* data movement and transformation based on the code's structure, but it cannot give you the ground truth of a specific execution. This is precisely why **Dynamic Analysis (Chapter 5)** is the essential counterpart. By running the program and observing its state with a debugger or instrumentation tools, we can capture the actual runtime values, resolve indirect calls, and see which control flow paths are actually taken, confirming or refuting the hypotheses generated during static analysis and filling in the gaps where static analysis inherently falls short.

Concluding Thoughts on Static Analysis Pillars

In this chapter, we've explored the three essential pillars of static analysis:

Code Inspection: The foundational process of reading disassembly/decompilation, identifying basic structures, recognizing known

API calls, searching for clues like strings and constants, and most importantly, annotating the code through renaming and commenting to build semantic understanding.

Control Flow Analysis: Mapping the program's execution paths by analyzing basic blocks and control transfer instructions, often aided immensely by visualizing Control Flow Graphs, allowing us to understand loops, conditionals, and the overall logical structure.

Data Flow Analysis: Following the information trail by tracking register usage, memory accesses (stack, heap, globals), and data dependencies to understand how values originate, transform, and are used, ultimately revealing the purpose of variables and data structures.

These techniques, primarily employed using disassemblers and decompilers, work in synergy. You inspect code to find starting points, analyze control flow to understand the context, and trace data flow to understand the operations being performed on the data within that context. The findings constantly feed back into renaming and commenting, refining your overall model of the software.

The immense strength of static analysis lies in its **completeness** regarding potential execution paths. It allows you to examine every single instruction, every possible branch, every function, including obscure error handling routines or hidden functionalities that might never be triggered during normal dynamic testing. This makes it indispensable for comprehensive vulnerability research (finding bugs in edge cases), thorough malware analysis (understanding all capabilities, not just those seen in one sandbox run), and achieving a deep, foundational understanding of the software's design.

Its weaknesses, however, are significant. It struggles fundamentally with values and targets determined only at **runtime**. It can be incredibly **time-consuming** for large, complex applications. And it is highly vulnerable to **obfuscation techniques** specifically designed to confuse disassemblers, break control flow graph reconstruction, or obscure data dependencies.

Despite these weaknesses, static analysis is almost invariably the **first and foundational step** in any serious reverse engineering endeavor. It provides the initial map, the structural understanding, and the context necessary to guide more targeted and effective dynamic analysis. It lays the groundwork, identifies the questions, and points towards the areas where runtime observation is most needed. With this solid static foundation built through code inspection, control flow mapping, and data flow tracing, we are now perfectly poised to start the engine, engage the debugger, and explore the vibrant, dynamic world of watching software run.

Chapter 5: Dynamic Analysis

Dynamic analysis is crucial because static analysis, while powerful, has its limits. It can't always predict runtime values, resolve indirect function calls determined on the fly, or fully understand how a program interacts with changing external factors like network responses or user input. Dynamic analysis fills these gaps by observing the program *in action*. Think of it as reality-checking the hypotheses you formed during your static exploration. We'll explore this through three interconnected themes: directly observing and controlling behavior with debuggers, monitoring the program's broader interactions with the system, and using safe environments like sandboxes for initial assessment.

5.1. Behavioral Analysis Techniques: Watching the Code Live

let's roll up our sleeves and get hands-on with the execution. We've diligently examined the static blueprints using disassemblers, perhaps even glimpsed higher-level logic with decompilers, and poked at raw bytes with hex editors. We have formed hypotheses, mapped potential roads, and identified points of interest. Now, it's time to witness the program in its natural habitat – running, interacting, *living*. This is the realm of **Dynamic Analysis**, and its absolute cornerstone, the indispensable tool for direct, hands-on observation, is the **debugger**. As we briefly introduced in Chapter 3, if static analysis is reading the script, dynamic analysis via a debugger is like sitting in the director's chair during a live performance, armed with a universal remote capable of pausing the action, examining every detail under a magnifying glass, and controlling the tempo down to the individual frame. This chapter section delves into **Behavioral Analysis Techniques**, focusing squarely on mastering the debugger to watch the code live and unravel its runtime secrets.

Think of the limitations we encountered in static analysis. We couldn't always be certain about the values of variables derived from user input or network data. We couldn't definitively resolve the target of an indirect function call calculated dynamically. We could only see the *potential* paths; we couldn't know which specific path would be taken under given conditions. The debugger is our primary means of overcoming these limitations. It bridges the gap between potentiality and actuality by allowing us to observe and interact with the program state *as it evolves* during execution. This level of intimate control and observation is simply invaluable for confirming hypotheses, understanding data transformations, pinpointing the root cause of specific behaviors (or bugs), and ultimately gaining a precise understanding of what the code does when it actually matters.

The Debugger's Mechanism: Orchestrating Controlled Execution

Before wielding the tool, it's helpful to understand conceptually how a debugger exerts its control. Debuggers aren't magic; they rely on specific services provided by the **Operating System** and sometimes leverage special **CPU hardware features**. When you attach a debugger to a target process (the "debuggee"), the OS essentially grants the debugger special privileges over that process. On Linux, this interaction is often mediated by the ptrace system call (Process TRACE). On Windows, a set of functions known collectively as the Windows Debug API (DebugActiveProcess, WaitForDebugEvent, ContinueDebugEvent, etc.) facilitates this control. These OS mechanisms allow the debugger process to perform actions like:

Reading and Writing Memory: The debugger can directly inspect and modify the contents of the debuggee's virtual memory space.

Accessing Registers: The debugger can read the current values of the CPU registers (instruction pointer, general-purpose registers, flags, etc.) when the debuggee is paused and can often modify them.

Receiving Notifications: The OS notifies the debugger when certain "debug events" occur in the debuggee. These events are the key to controlled execution. Common events include process/thread creation and exit, module (DLL/SO) loading and unloading, exceptions (including those triggered by software breakpoints or errors like memory access violations), and single-step completions.

Controlling Execution: After receiving a debug event and pausing the debuggee, the debugger can instruct the OS how to resume execution – perhaps continuing normally, executing just one instruction (single-stepping), or terminating the process.

Breakpoints, the most common way to pause execution, are typically implemented using exceptions. A software breakpoint involves replacing an instruction byte with a special INT 3 (interrupt 3, opcode 0xCC on x86) instruction. When the CPU hits this, it generates a breakpoint exception, which the OS passes to the debugger. The debugger then handles the pause, replaces the original byte, and potentially adjusts the instruction pointer back one byte before resuming. Hardware breakpoints use dedicated CPU debug registers to trigger an exception when a specific address is accessed or executed, without modifying the code itself. Understanding this mechanism helps appreciate why debuggers can sometimes be detected (by checking for 0xCC bytes or analyzing exception handling) and why hardware breakpoints are stealthier but limited.

Initiating the Session: Launching vs. Attaching

Your journey into dynamic analysis typically begins in one of two ways:

Launching: You instruct the debugger to start the target program directly. The debugger handles the process creation and immediately gains control *before* the program's primary code begins executing (often pausing at the system loader's entry point or just before the application's official main/WinMain). This is useful for analyzing initialization routines or when you want to observe the program from the very beginning. Many graphical debuggers offer a simple "Open" or "File -> Open Executable" option for this. On the command line with GDB, you'd simply type gdb ./myprogram and then run. With WinDbg, you can use windbg.exe C:\path\to\program.exe.

Attaching: If the target program is already running, you can attach the debugger to the existing process. You'll need the Process ID (PID) of the target, which you can usually find using the OS's task manager (Task Manager, Activity Monitor, ps aux | grep processname) or more detailed tools like Process Explorer/Process Hacker. Once attached, the debugger typically pauses all threads within the target process immediately, allowing you to set breakpoints and inspect state before resuming execution. This is necessary for analyzing services, long-running applications, or specific instances of a program where attaching mid-execution is desired. Graphical debuggers have an "Attach" or "Attach to Process" menu option. With GDB, use gdb attach PID. With WinDbg, use windbg.exe -p PID.

Once launched or attached, the debugger usually presents you with a view showing the code (disassembly, often centered around the current instruction pointer), register values, memory views, and stack information, ready for your first command.

Setting the Stage: Strategic Use of Breakpoints

The power of the debugger lies in its ability to halt execution precisely where you need it to. You don't want to single-step through millions of instructions from the program's entry point. Instead, you leverage findings from your prior **static analysis** to set strategic **breakpoints**. A breakpoint acts as a designated pause point.

Why Breakpoints? To stop execution right before or right at a section of code you want to investigate closely. This allows you to examine the program's state (registers, memory) *immediately preceding* the interesting code, understand the inputs, and then carefully observe the effects as you step through it.

Placing Breakpoints: Where should you set them? This depends heavily on your analysis goals and what you learned statically:

Function Entry Points: If static analysis identified a function likely responsible for a key action (e.g., encrypt_data, send_network_packet, validate_input), set a breakpoint at its very first instruction (address obtained from IDA/Ghidra). This lets you examine the arguments passed to it just before it starts working.

API Calls: Placing breakpoints directly on imported API function calls (like kernel32!CreateFileW or libc!connect) or on the CALL instruction just *before* the API call is extremely common. Breaking *before* the call lets you inspect the arguments being prepared. Breaking *on* the API entry point itself (less common for standard APIs unless debugging library code) or using API hooking frameworks (like Frida) achieves similar results.

Critical Code Sections: If you identified a specific loop, a crucial conditional jump determining success/failure, or a complex calculation, set breakpoints just before or within that section to observe the data flow and control flow decisions live.

After Interesting Operations: Sometimes you want to see the *result* of an operation. You might set a breakpoint *after* a function call suspected of decrypting data to examine the resulting buffer in memory. Or break after a loop finishes to see the final computed value.

Error Handling Paths: Setting breakpoints in error handling routines identified statically can help understand how the program behaves under failure conditions.

Types of Breakpoints in Practice:

Software Breakpoints: Your default choice for most code locations. Easy to set via address (bp 0x401500 in WinDbg/x64dbg, b *0x401500 in GDB) or function name (bp myprogram!myfunction in WinDbg, b myfunction in GDB if symbols are available). Remember their detectability.

Hardware Breakpoints: Use these sparingly but strategically. Excellent for: *Data Breakpoints:* Setting a breakpoint on a specific memory address (e.g., a global variable, a key structure member) that triggers when the memory is **written to** (ba w4 0x40A010 in WinDbg - set write breakpoint of size 4 bytes at address; similar watchpoint commands in GDB/x64dbg) or **read from/written to** (ba r4 ..., ba e4 ...). This is invaluable for tracking how and when critical data changes, without needing to find every instruction that accesses it.

Executing from ROM/Flash: Hardware execution breakpoints (ba e1 ...) are needed if the code resides in memory that cannot be modified (like Read-Only Memory), where software breakpoints cannot be written.

Stealth: Useful when suspecting anti-debugging checks specifically looking for software (0xCC) breakpoints.

Conditional Breakpoints: Extremely useful for reducing noise. Imagine a function called thousands of times within a loop, but you only care about the iteration where ECX holds a specific value. You could set a conditional breakpoint: bp 0x401500 ".if (ecx == 0x1A) {} .else {gc}" (WinDbg syntax: set breakpoint, if ECX is 0x1A stop, otherwise go continue). GDB uses break *0x401500 if $ecx == 0x1a. This prevents countless unnecessary breaks.

Setting breakpoints effectively transforms the debugger from a passive observer into a precise surgical instrument, allowing you to target your investigation exactly where needed.

Controlling the Performance: Step, Run, Inspect, Repeat

Once the program hits a breakpoint and execution pauses, the real interactive analysis begins. The debugger gives you fine-grained control over how execution proceeds, allowing you to dissect the logic instruction by instruction while continuously monitoring the program's state.

Execution Commands: The Debugger's Remote Control Buttons:

Run/Continue (g in WinDbg/GDB, F9 in x64dbg/OllyDbg): Resumes execution of the program normally. It will run freely until it hits another breakpoint, encounters an exception (like a crash), finishes execution, or is interrupted manually.

Step Into (t in WinDbg/GDB, F7 in x64dbg/OllyDbg): Executes *only* the single instruction currently pointed to by the instruction pointer (EIP/RIP). If this instruction is a CALL to another function, the next pause will be at the very first instruction *inside* the called function. This is your tool for maximum detail, allowing you to follow execution into every function call and analyze its internal logic. Use this when you need to understand precisely what a specific function does or trace a value through a complex call chain.

Step Over (p in WinDbg/GDB, F8 in x64dbg/OllyDbg): Also executes the single next instruction. However, if that instruction is a CALL, the debugger executes the *entire* called function (including all instructions within it and any functions it calls) without pausing inside it, and only pauses again on the instruction immediately *after* the CALL instruction returns. This is incredibly useful for efficiency. You use step over when you trust a function (e.g., it's a standard library function like printf or memcpy), you've already analyzed it, or you simply aren't interested in its internal details at this moment and only care about its net effect or return value. Trying to step into every single library function would be incredibly tedious.

Step Out (gu up to frame in WinDbg, finish in GDB, Shift+F8 often): If you have stepped *into* a function and decided you don't need to analyze it further, step out instructs the debugger to continue running until the current function returns to its caller. Execution will then pause at the instruction immediately following the original CALL in the calling function. It's a way to quickly exit the current function's context.

Other Controls: Many debuggers offer commands like "Run to Cursor" (execute until the instruction where the text cursor is placed) or "Run until condition met" or "Run until return," providing further convenience for navigating code without manually stepping hundreds of times.

Inspection: Understanding the Current Scene:
Every time execution pauses (at a breakpoint or after a step), you *must* inspect the program's state to understand the context and the effect of the executed instruction(s). The debugger provides various windows or commands for this:

Registers: Always check the key registers. What is the value in EAX/RAX (often used for return values or calculations)? How did ECX/RCX (often a counter or pointer) change? Crucially, examine the **Flags register** (e.g., EFLAGS/RFLAGS) after comparison (CMP, TEST) or arithmetic instructions. Are the Zero Flag (ZF), Sign Flag (SF), Carry Flag (CF), Overflow Flag (OF) set or cleared? These flags directly determine whether subsequent conditional jumps (JE, JNE, JS, JG, etc.) will be taken or not. Understanding flag status is essential for tracing control flow accurately.

Memory: Use memory dump/view windows to examine specific addresses. If a register (say, RSI) points to a buffer, dump the memory starting at the address contained in RSI. If the code just wrote to [RBP+var_C], examine that stack location. Does the data look like ASCII text? Encrypted data? A valid pointer? Is the buffer being filled as expected? Are heap chunk headers being corrupted? You can often ask the debugger to interpret memory as different data types (bytes, words, dwords, qwords, floats, pointers, strings, even disassembled code).

Stack: Examine the call stack view. Which function called the current function? What arguments were passed (visible on the stack frame below the return address)? What are the values of local variables relative to RBP or RSP? Understanding the stack provides crucial context, especially in nested function calls.

Modification (Interactive Probing):

As mentioned, debuggers usually let you modify register values (r eax=1 in WinDbg, set $eax=1 in GDB) or memory content (eb address value in WinDbg, set {unsigned char}address = value in GDB). This isn't just for fixing things; it's a powerful analytical technique:

Testing Conditionals: Pause just before a critical conditional jump. Examine the flags or register being tested. Manually change the register value or use a debugger command to flip the relevant flag (e.g., toggle the Zero Flag) and then let execution continue. Does forcing the opposite path reveal interesting behavior or bypass a check?

Altering Inputs: Pause after data is loaded into a buffer (e.g., user input). Modify the buffer contents in memory before the processing function is called. How does the function react to unexpected or malicious input you inject?

Simulating Function Results: Pause immediately after a function call returns. Manually change the return value in EAX/RAX (e.g., change an error code to a success code, or vice versa). How does the calling code handle this altered result?

This interactive modification allows you to actively probe the program's logic and resilience in ways static analysis cannot. However, do it judiciously, as random changes will likely just crash the program. Keep track of the modifications you make.

The Iterative Workflow: Where Static Meets Dynamic

The true power of dynamic behavioral analysis using a debugger emerges when it's used in **synergy with static analysis**. It's an iterative loop, a conversation between the static map and the live exploration:

Static Analysis (IDA/Ghidra, etc.):

Identify regions of interest (functions, loops, checks).

Understand the potential control flow (CFG).

Understand potential data flow (register/memory usage patterns).

Identify specific addresses for functions, potential data locations, or critical instructions.

Formulate hypotheses about behavior and purpose (e.g., "I think function 0x401230 calculates a checksum based on the input buffer passed via RSI").

5.2. Monitoring and Instrumentation: Listening to System Interactions

we've mastered the art of microscopic examination with the debugger, stepping through code instruction by instruction. This gives us incredible detail but sometimes fails to show the bigger picture. Imagine trying to understand the traffic flow of an entire city by only watching one car's engine up close. You miss the broader interactions – where does the car go? What roads does it use frequently? Who does it communicate with? In reverse engineering, sometimes we need to zoom out from the instruction-level view and observe how our target program interacts with its surrounding environment – the **Operating System**, the **file system**, the **network**, and potentially **other processes**. This is where **System Monitoring** and **Dynamic Instrumentation** techniques become invaluable complements to debugging. They act as surveillance systems and targeted probes, listening in on the program's external conversations and allowing us to intercept or even modify its behavior at key interaction points, often without the overhead or potential detection issues of a full debugger.

System Monitoring Tools: Passive Surveillance of OS Interactions

The first category involves tools that passively (or near-passively) monitor and log the interactions between running processes and the operating system kernel or core system libraries. They provide a higher-level, event-based view of the program's behavior, focusing on *what* resources it accesses or *what* system services it requests, rather than the intricate details of *how* its internal code achieves this. These tools are fantastic for getting a quick behavioral baseline, identifying key external interactions, and detecting suspicious activity patterns, especially in malware analysis or initial application assessment.

Process Monitor (ProcMon) - The Windows Standard: For anyone doing dynamic analysis on Windows, **Process Monitor (ProcMon)**, part of the venerable Sysinternals suite (created by Mark Russinovich and Bryce Cogswell, now owned by Microsoft and available for free download), is an absolutely essential, indispensable tool. It operates by using a file system filter driver and other low-level techniques to intercept and log, in real-time, a massive amount of system activity. By default, it captures:

File System Activity: Every attempt to open, create, read, write, query information about, rename, or delete a file or directory. It shows the full path, the result (success/failure, specific error codes like "FILE NOT FOUND", "ACCESS DENIED"), and often details like the amount of data read/written or the specific file information queried.

Registry Activity: Every attempt to open, create, query, set, or delete registry keys and values. It shows the full registry path, the value data being read or written (if possible), and the result code.

Network Activity: Captures TCP/UDP connection attempts, sends, receives, and disconnects, showing local and remote IP addresses, ports, and sometimes the amount of data transferred (though not typically the data content itself – for that you usually need a network sniffer like Wireshark).

Process and Thread Activity: Logs process creation, thread creation, process/thread exit events, and often DLL loading.

The sheer volume of data captured by ProcMon can be overwhelming at first – it logs activity from *all* running processes on the system simultaneously.

The key to using it effectively lies in **Filtering**. ProcMon has a powerful filtering engine (Filter -> Filter... or Ctrl+L) that lets you precisely narrow down the displayed events. The most common and crucial filter is by **Process Name** or **Process ID (PID)**. You configure a filter to "Include" events where the "Process Name is myprogram.exe" (or whatever your target is). This immediately cuts through the noise and shows only the system interactions initiated by your target application.

Using ProcMon Effectively:

Start Capture: Launch ProcMon (usually requires administrative privileges) and ensure capturing is enabled (File -> Capture Events, Ctrl+E, or the magnifying glass icon).

Apply Filters: Immediately set up filters. The most basic is Process Name is your_target.exe -> Include. You might add more filters later (e.g., exclude results that are SUCCESS if you're looking for errors, or include only WriteFile operations if you only care about what's being written).

Run Target Application: Launch the program you want to analyze. Perform the actions you want to observe (e.g., saving a file, connecting to a server, installing something).

Stop Capture: Once the activity of interest is complete, stop the ProcMon capture (Ctrl+E again) to prevent the log from growing excessively.

Analyze the Log: Now, examine the filtered events. Scroll through the timeline.

What files did it touch? Look for CreateFile, ReadFile, WriteFile entries. Did it read a configuration file from AppData? Did it write a log file to C:\Logs? Did it drop any suspicious .tmp or .exe files in C:\Windows\Temp (common malware behavior)?

What registry keys did it access? Look for RegOpenKey, RegQueryValue, RegSetValue. Did it read settings from HKCU\Software\Vendor\App? Did it write to HKLM\Software\Microsoft\Windows\CurrentVersion\Run (a standard persistence location)?

Did it make network connections? Look for TCP Connect, UDP Send. What remote IP addresses and ports did it contact? Can you correlate these with known malicious infrastructure or legitimate update servers?

Did it launch other processes? Look for Process Create. Did it launch cmd.exe or powershell.exe (potentially "Living off the Land")? Did it start other instances of itself?

ProcMon gives you a detailed chronological narrative of the program's interactions with the core OS resources, often revealing crucial behavior without needing to set a single breakpoint in a debugger. It's fantastic for understanding installation routines, configuration loading, data saving mechanisms, persistence techniques, and basic network activity.

Code Example: Interpreting ProcMon Output (Conceptual)

Imagine ProcMon shows the following sequence for malware.exe:

Time	Process	PID	Operation	Path	Result	Detail
10:01:01	malware.exe	1234	RegOpenKey	HKCU\Software\Microsoft\Windows\CurrentVersion\Run	SUCCESS	Desired Access: Read/Write
10:01:01	malware.exe	1234	RegSetValueEx	HKCU\Software\Microsoft\Windows\CurrentVersion\Run\UpdaterService	SUCCESS	Type: REG_SZ, Length: 50, Data: C:\Users\Admin\AppData\Local\Temp\updater.exe
10:01:02	malware.exe	1234	CreateFile	C:\Users\Admin\AppData\Local\Temp\updater.exe	SUCCESS	Desired Access: Generic Write, Disposition: OverwriteIf
10:01:02	malware.exe	1234	WriteFile	C:\Users\Admin\AppData\Local\Temp\updater.exe	SUCCESS	Offset: 0, Length: 102400
10:01:02	malware.exe	1234	CloseFile	C:\Users\Admin\AppData\Local\Temp\updater.exe	SUCCESS	
10:01:03	malware.exe	1234	TCP Connect	malware.exe:51234 -> bad.domain.com:80	SUCCESS	
10:01:03	malware.exe	1234	TCP Send	malware.exe:51234 -> bad.domain.com:80	SUCCESS	Length: 128

RE Interpretation: Even without looking at disassembly, this ProcMon log tells a compelling story:

The malware successfully opens the standard user Run key in the registry, indicating an attempt to achieve persistence.

It writes a value named UpdaterService to that key, pointing to an executable file (updater.exe) located in the Temp directory. This ensures updater.exe will run automatically on the next user login.

It then creates and writes a significant amount of data (102 KB) to that exact updater.exe file, strongly suggesting it's dropping a payload or a copy of itself.

Finally, it initiates a TCP connection to a suspicious-sounding domain (bad.domain.com) on port 80 (HTTP) and sends some data.

This high-level behavioral summary immediately flags the malware as persistent, likely dropping files, and communicating with a C&C server, guiding further investigation.

Linux Equivalents (strace, lsof, perf): On Linux, the landscape is slightly more fragmented, but powerful tools exist.

strace: This is the classic utility for tracing **system calls**. It hooks into the kernel's ptrace mechanism and logs every system call made by a process, along with its arguments (interpreted to the best of strace's ability) and return value. Running strace ./myprogram will show you calls like openat(), read(), write(), socket(), connect(), execve(), clone() (for thread creation), brk()/mmap() (for memory allocation), etc. It provides a view very similar in *intent* to ProcMon, focusing on kernel interactions, though its output format is textual and might require more parsing/filtering. You can filter strace output using options like -e trace=file (only file-related syscalls) or -p PID (attach to a running process). It's invaluable for understanding file/network/process interactions on Linux.

lsof (List Open Files): This utility lists all files (including network sockets, pipes, devices) currently opened by processes. Running lsof -p PID shows what files and network connections a specific process has open, which can be useful for quick checks without real-time tracing.

perf: A much more powerful and complex performance analysis and tracing tool built into the Linux kernel. While often used for profiling, perf can also be used for detailed tracing of system calls, kernel functions, userspace function calls (with proper symbols/debug info), hardware events, and more. It offers lower overhead than strace for some tasks but has a steeper learning curve. Tools like **bpftrace** (leveraging **eBPF** - extended Berkeley Packet Filter) provide an even more powerful and flexible modern alternative for sophisticated system-level tracing and monitoring on Linux, allowing users to write safe, custom tracing scripts that run within the kernel.

System monitoring tools give you that essential high-level overview of how the program interacts with the OS environment. They excel at quickly identifying file, registry, and network activity, serving as a perfect starting point or complement to lower-level debugging. Their main limitation is that they typically don't show the *internal* logic or data manipulation *within* the program itself, only its interactions at the OS boundary.

Dynamic Instrumentation Frameworks: Targeted Intervention and Modification

Taking dynamic analysis a significant step further, we arrive at **Dynamic Instrumentation Frameworks**. These tools bridge the gap between passive monitoring (like ProcMon/strace) and full, often heavyweight debugging. Instrumentation allows you to *inject* your own code into a running target process and *programmatically* intercept, monitor, and even **modify** its behavior at specific points, usually focusing on function calls. Think of it as performing highly targeted microsurgery on the live program, allowing you to observe and alter its actions with precision and flexibility, often with less overhead and potentially less chance of detection than a traditional debugger.

Frida: The De Facto Standard: As highlighted previously, **Frida** has become the dominant toolkit in this space due to its power, flexibility, extensive platform support (Windows, macOS, Linux, iOS, Android, QNX), and relatively accessible scripting interface (primarily JavaScript, but with bindings for Python, C#, Swift, etc.).

The Frida Workflow:

Identify Target Function(s): Typically, you use static analysis (IDA/Ghidra) first to identify the specific functions within the target process whose behavior you want to monitor or modify. This could be an exported API function (like kernel32!CreateFileW), an internal application function at a specific address (0x405060), a Java method in an Android app (com.example.app.NetworkManager.sendData), or an Objective-C method in an iOS app (-[LicenseChecker checkLicense]).

Write a Frida Script: You write a script (usually .js) using Frida's JavaScript API. The core operation is typically Interceptor.attach(targetPointer, { onEnter: function(args) { ... }, onLeave: function(retval) { ... } });.

targetPointer: You get this using Frida functions like Module.getExportByName('library.dll', 'FunctionName'), Module.findExportByName(...), ptr("0x405060"), Java.use('com.example.ClassName').methodName.implementation = ..., or ObjC.classes.ClassName['- methodName'].implementation = ...

onEnter(args): This JavaScript function executes *just before* the original target function is called. The args array holds the arguments passed to the function. Inside onEnter, you can:

Log Arguments: Read the values of arguments (args[0], args[1], etc.) using appropriate functions based on type (readPointer(), readUtf8String(), readInt(), readByteArray(), etc.) and print them to the console (console.log(...)).

Modify Arguments: Overwrite argument values (args[0].writeUtf16String("..."), args[1] = ptr("0x...")). This allows you to change the input the target function receives.

Save Context: Store argument values or other state in this context (this.arg1 = args[0]) so you can access it later in the onLeave handler.

onLeave(retval): This JavaScript function executes *just after* the original target function returns but *before* control is given back to the caller. The retval object holds the original return value. Inside onLeave, you can:

Log Return Value: Inspect the return value (console.log("Returned: " + retval)).

Modify Return Value: Change the value that will be returned to the caller (retval.replace(ptr("0x1"))). This is incredibly powerful for bypassing checks (e.g., forcing a license check function to always return "success").

Access Saved Context: Use values saved in onEnter (console.log("Input was: " + this.arg1)).

Inject and Run: Use the Frida command-line tool (or Python bindings) to inject your script into the target process (either by launching it with -f or attaching to it with -p PID or -U for USB devices like Android/iOS). Frida injects its agent and your script, the hooks become active, and your onEnter/onLeave functions will execute whenever the target function is called, printing output to your console or performing modifications.

Code Example: Frida Script to Bypass a Simple License Check (Conceptual)
Imagine a function CheckLicense() at address 0x401000 which returns 1 for a valid license and 0 for invalid. We want to force it to always return 1.

```
// frida_bypass_license.js
```

```
const targetAddress = ptr("0x401000"); // Address of
CheckLicense function

Interceptor.attach(targetAddress, {
    onEnter: function (args) {
        // Optionally log when the function is entered
        console.log("[CheckLicense] Entered. Args: " +
args[0] + ", " + args[1] + " ..."); // Assuming some args
    },
    onLeave: function (retval) {
        // Log the original return value (0 or 1)
        console.log("[CheckLicense] Original return value: "
+ retval.toInt32());

        // Check if the original return value indicates
failure (e.g., 0)
        if (retval.toInt32() == 0) {
            console.log("  -> License check failed! Modifying
return value to 1 (Success).");
            // Replace the return value with 1 (success)
            retval.replace(ptr("0x1"));
        } else {
            console.log("  -> License check already
succeeded.");
        }
    }
});

console.log("Hook installed on CheckLicense at " +
targetAddress + ". Waiting...");
```

Usage: Run frida -l frida_bypass_license.js -p TARGET_PID (attach) or -f target.exe (launch). Now, whenever the target application calls the function at 0x401000, this script will intercept the return. If the original function returned 0 (failure), the script will log this, change the return value to 1 (success) before control goes back to the caller, potentially tricking the rest of the application into thinking the license is valid.

Frida's Versatility: Frida's power extends far beyond simple logging and return value modification. You can use it to:

Bypass SSL Pinning: Intercept certificate validation functions in mobile apps and force them to accept your proxy's certificate, allowing HTTPS traffic decryption.

Extract Dynamic Data: Hook decryption functions and log the plaintext results.

Fuzzing Internal Functions: Hook functions and replace their arguments with randomly generated data to test internal parsing or processing logic.

API Exploration: Enumerate loaded classes and methods in Java/ObjC environments, call methods directly, and observe results.

Anti-Debugging Defeats: Hook functions like IsDebuggerPresent and force them to return false.

Lower-Level Frameworks (Intel Pin, DynamoRIO): For scenarios requiring even finer-grained control, maximum performance, or complex analysis algorithms that are cumbersome to implement in JavaScript, lower-level **Dynamic Binary Instrumentation (DBI)** frameworks exist.

Intel Pin: A popular framework developed by Intel. You write analysis tools ("Pintools") in C/C++. Pin dynamically intercepts the target application's code *before* it executes, recompiles it on the fly (a process called JIT compilation or dynamic translation), and weaves in your analysis code at specific points (e.g., before/after specific instructions, basic blocks, or function calls). This allows for extremely detailed instruction-level tracing, memory access tracking (used for dynamic taint analysis), and building complex custom analyses with minimal performance overhead compared to interpreted hooking like Frida.

DynamoRIO: Another powerful open-source DBI framework supporting multiple platforms. Similar in concept to Pin, you write analysis clients in C/C++. It provides a robust API for instrumenting code at various granularities. Both Pin and DynamoRIO are used extensively in academic research and for building specialized security analysis tools (e.g., for finding memory corruption vulnerabilities dynamically, analyzing obfuscated code, or building complex emulators).

Trade-offs: The major advantage of DBI frameworks is their fine-grained control and potential performance. The disadvantage is complexity – writing Pintools or DynamoRIO clients requires C/C++ expertise and a deep understanding of the framework's intricate API, making them significantly less accessible than Frida for many common tasks.

Instrumentation, whether high-level with Frida or low-level with Pin/DynamoRIO, empowers the reverse engineer to move beyond passive observation. It allows for targeted interception, runtime data extraction, and on-the-fly modification of program behavior, enabling analysis strategies that are simply impossible with traditional debuggers or passive monitoring alone. It's a vital technique for tackling many modern RE challenges, from mobile security assessments to bypassing sophisticated protections.

Conclusion: Layered Observation for Comprehensive Insight

Debugging provides the ultimate microscopic view, allowing instruction-by-instruction control and state inspection. System monitoring tools like ProcMon and strace provide a crucial higher-level view of OS interactions, revealing file, registry, network, and process activities without delving into internal code execution. Dynamic instrumentation frameworks like Frida bridge the gap, enabling targeted interception and modification of runtime behavior with programmatic flexibility.

None of these dynamic analysis techniques entirely replace the need for static analysis (to understand the code structure and identify targets) or sometimes even traditional debugging (for complex state exploration). Instead, they form a layered set of observational tools. A skilled reverse engineer understands the strengths and weaknesses of each – knowing when to reach for ProcMon for a quick behavioral overview, when to fire up Frida to hook a specific function and extract data, and when to attach a full debugger for intricate step-by-step tracing. Using these tools in concert provides a much more comprehensive and efficient path to understanding the true runtime behavior of software than relying on any single technique alone.

5.3. Sandboxing and Virtualization: Running Wild in a Padded Cell

let's delve into the indispensable practices of **Sandboxing and Virtualization** within the context of dynamic analysis. While debugging offers intricate control (Chapter 5.1) and monitoring/instrumentation provides targeted observation (Chapter 5.2), there are scenarios, particularly when dealing with potentially hostile or unknown software like malware, where safety, speed, and automated behavioral overview take precedence over deep, manual dissection. This is the realm where sandboxing and virtualization technologies become absolutely critical components of the reverse engineer's arsenal, acting as protective barriers and automated observation platforms. Think of them as specialized containment facilities – padded cells or controlled laboratories – where potentially dangerous subjects can be observed without risking harm to the wider environment.

Virtualization: The Foundation of Safe Analysis Environments

Before diving into automated sandboxes, it's crucial to understand the underlying technology that enables much of modern dynamic analysis safety: **Virtualization**. Virtualization software, known as a **Hypervisor**, allows you to run multiple, isolated **Virtual Machines (VMs)** on a single physical computer (the host). Each VM functions like a complete, independent computer system with its own virtual hardware (CPU, RAM, disk, network card) and runs its own instance of an operating system (the guest OS, typically Windows, Linux, or macOS for analysis).

Common hypervisors include:

Type 2 Hypervisors (Hosted): These run as applications on top of your existing host operating system. Examples include **VMware Workstation/Player** (Windows/Linux), **VMware Fusion** (macOS), **Oracle VirtualBox** (cross-platform, open-source), and **Parallels Desktop** (macOS). They are generally easier to set up and manage for desktop use.

Type 1 Hypervisors (Bare-Metal): These run directly on the host hardware, acting as the primary operating system themselves. Examples include **VMware ESXi**, **Microsoft Hyper-V** (often integrated into Windows Pro/Enterprise), and **KVM (Kernel-based Virtual Machine)** integrated into the Linux kernel. They typically offer better performance and isolation but are more common in server environments or dedicated analysis setups.

Why Virtualization is Non-Negotiable for Dangerous Code:

The primary benefit of using VMs for analyzing potentially malicious software (or even just unstable or unknown legitimate software) is **Isolation**. The VM creates a strong boundary between the guest OS (where you run the suspect code and your analysis tools) and your host OS (your actual work machine).

Containment: If the malware being analyzed attempts to encrypt files, delete system data, install rootkits, spread across a network, or otherwise cause damage, its actions are confined *entirely* to the guest OS within the VM. Your host machine remains untouched and safe.

Network Isolation: VMs can be configured with virtual network interfaces that can be completely disconnected from the physical network, connected only to other VMs on the host (host-only networking), or connected through a NAT (Network Address Translation) layer that isolates them from the main LAN while potentially allowing controlled internet access (often used with network simulators). This prevents malware from spreading laterally across your real network or immediately communicating with external C&C servers.

Revertibility (Snapshots): This is perhaps the most powerful feature for analysts. Hypervisors allow you to take **snapshots** of a VM's entire state (disk content, memory content, device state) at a particular moment. You can set up a clean analysis VM with all your tools installed, take a snapshot, run the malware, perform your dynamic analysis, and then, regardless of how badly the malware infected or altered the guest OS, you can instantly **revert** the VM back to the clean snapshot state in seconds or minutes. This allows you to analyze sample after sample without the tedious process of completely rebuilding your analysis environment each time. Taking snapshots *before* potentially destructive actions within the analysis itself is also common practice.

Standard Practice: Using dedicated analysis VMs is not just recommended; it is **standard operating procedure** for virtually all professional malware analysts and security researchers performing dynamic analysis. Analyzing unknown binaries directly on a host machine connected to personal or corporate networks is considered extremely reckless. Setting up a stable, clean, well-configured analysis VM (often Windows, sometimes Linux) with necessary tools (debuggers, disassemblers, monitoring tools, network simulators) and maintaining clean snapshots is a fundamental prerequisite.

Configuring Analysis VMs:
Setting up an effective analysis VM involves more than just installing an OS:

Guest OS Choice: Often Windows 7 (less inherent mitigation than Win10/11, potentially allowing older malware to run more easily, but becoming less representative) or Windows 10/11 (more realistic target, but requires understanding modern mitigations). Linux VMs are used for Linux malware.

Guest Additions/Tools: Installing the hypervisor's guest additions (VMware Tools, VirtualBox Guest Additions) improves usability (better graphics, shared clipboard, file sharing), BUT these tools are also primary indicators used by malware for VM detection. A truly stealthy analysis VM might omit these or use techniques to hide their presence.

Installed Software: Include common applications (Office suite, PDF reader, web browser, archive utility) that malware might target or check for to make the environment look more like a real user machine and less like a bare analysis box.

Analysis Tools: Pre-install your preferred debuggers (x64dbg, WinDbg), disassemblers (IDA Free/Pro, Ghidra), monitoring tools (ProcMon, Wireshark), network simulators (FakeNet-NG, INetSim), scripting runtimes (Python), hex editors, etc.

Networking: Configure networking carefully. Often start with "Host-Only" or disconnected. Use network simulators running *on the host* or in a separate dedicated "gateway" VM to intercept and respond to the analysis VM's network traffic safely. Avoid direct bridged access to your primary network unless absolutely necessary and with extreme caution.

Snapshot Strategy: Maintain a pristine "Clean Base" snapshot. Before analyzing a sample, revert to this snapshot. After analysis, revert again to ensure no cross-contamination. You might take intermediate snapshots during analysis if you reach an interesting state you want to return to. Virtualization provides the essential safety net, allowing analysts to handle dangerous code responsibly. While not its primary purpose, the VM environment itself becomes the stage for much of the manual dynamic analysis described previously (running debuggers, ProcMon, etc., *inside* the guest OS).

Automated Sandboxes: High-Throughput Behavioral Analysis

Building directly upon the foundation of virtualization and incorporating automated OS interaction monitoring (similar to ProcMon/strace) and analysis engines, **Automated Sandboxes** aim to provide a rapid, hands-off assessment of a program's behavior, primarily designed for malware triage and initial analysis.

As discussed under monitoring tools (Chapter 5.2's overlap with sandbox technology), the core workflow involves:

Submission: The analyst submits the suspicious file (or URL) to the sandbox system (either a self-hosted instance like Cuckoo or an online service).

Execution: The sandbox automatically selects or provisions an appropriate analysis VM (based on file type or user choice), copies the sample into it, and executes the sample within that isolated guest OS.

Monitoring: While the sample runs (for a predefined time, typically a few minutes), the sandbox's backend monitors its interactions with the guest OS using API hooking or other techniques, logging file, registry, process, and network activity. It often captures network traffic (PCAP) and may take periodic screenshots. Some systems allow basic simulated user interaction.

Analysis & Reporting: After execution completes or times out, the sandbox analyzes the collected logs and artifacts. It might perform additional static analysis on dropped files or memory dumps, run YARA rules, query threat intelligence feeds based on observed indicators (IPs, domains, hashes), and apply behavioral heuristics. It then compiles a comprehensive **report** summarizing the findings – high-level behavior, detailed event logs, extracted network/file IOCs, process trees, screenshots, analysis scores, and potentially links to known malware families.

Benefits of Automated Sandboxing:

Safety: Inherits the isolation benefits of virtualization.

Speed: Provides a behavioral summary much faster than manual analysis, often in just minutes. Indispensable for high-volume environments.

Automation: Requires minimal human interaction for the basic analysis run.

Consistency: Provides standardized reports across different samples.

IOC Extraction: Automatically identifies and extracts actionable indicators (IPs, domains, hashes, registry keys, filenames) critical for immediate defense updates.

Initial Assessment: Quickly answers the question: "Does this exhibit obviously malicious behavior?" allowing analysts to prioritize efforts.

Choosing a Sandbox:

The choice between self-hosted open-source (like **Cuckoo Sandbox**) and online/commercial services involves trade-offs:

Cuckoo: Offers maximum control and customization over the analysis environment and process. No data leaves your infrastructure. Requires significant expertise and resources to set up, maintain, tune, and potentially harden against evasion. Excellent for research or organizations with specific needs and capabilities.

Online Services (Any.Run, Hybrid Analysis, Joe Sandbox, etc.): Offer convenience, zero setup/maintenance overhead, often integrate extensive threat intelligence, and provide features like **Any.Run's interactivity**. The main downsides are cost (for premium features/volume), reliance on the provider's environment configuration (which might be well-known to attackers), and the fact that samples are submitted externally.

Commercial Appliances/Platforms (VMRay, FireEye, etc.): Provide polished, supported, enterprise-focused solutions often boasting superior evasion resistance (e.g., using techniques less reliant on obvious guest OS hooking), deeper analysis capabilities, and integration with broader security ecosystems, but at a premium price.

Practical Example: Interpreting a Sandbox Report Section

A typical sandbox report might include a section summarizing network activity:

```
// Sample JSON snippet from a hypothetical sandbox report
{
  "network": {
    "tcp_connections": [
      {
        "remote_ip": "198.51.100.10",
        "remote_port": 80,
        "local_port": 51234,
        "status": "success",
        "protocol": "HTTP",
        "metadata": {
          "hostname": "suspicious-updates.example.com",
          "url": "/checkin.php?id=ABC123XYZ",
          "method": "GET",
          "user_agent": "Mozilla/4.0 (compatible; MSIE 6.0;
Windows NT 5.1)"
        }
      },
      {
        "remote_ip": "203.0.113.55",
        "remote_port": 6667,
        "local_port": 51235,
        "status": "success",
        "protocol": "IRC",
        "metadata": {} // Less detail perhaps for non-HTTP
      }
    ],
    "dns_requests": [
      {"hostname": "suspicious-updates.example.com",
"resolved_ip": "198.51.100.10", "type": "A"},
      {"hostname": "irc.someotherserver.org", "resolved_ip":
"203.0.113.55", "type": "A"}
    ],
    "extracted_iocs": ["198.51.100.10", "suspicious-
updates.example.com", "203.0.113.55",
"irc.someotherserver.org"]
  }
  // ... other sections for file, registry, process
activity ...
}
```

RE Interpretation: This snippet clearly shows the program made two successful TCP connections. One was an HTTP GET request to a specific URL on suspicious-updates.example.com (likely C&C check-in or download attempt). The other was to a different IP on port 6667, identified as IRC (a protocol sometimes used for botnet C&C). The DNS requests confirm how these hostnames were resolved. The sandbox automatically extracts the IPs and domains as actionable IOCs. This provides immediate, valuable intelligence about the malware's communication channels.

The Cat and Mouse Game: Evasion Techniques

The major Achilles' heel of both general virtualization used for manual analysis and automated sandbox environments is **evasion**. Malware authors *know* analysts use these tools and invest significant effort into detecting and bypassing them. If malware detects it's running in an analysis environment, it might simply refuse to exhibit any malicious behavior, making it appear benign.

Common evasion tactics include:

VM Artifact Checking: Searching for tell-tale signs of the hypervisor.

Virtual Hardware Signatures: Checking MAC address prefixes known to belong to VMware/VirtualBox, specific device names (e.g., VMware SVGA II adapter), or predictable hardware serial numbers.

Guest Tools/Drivers: Looking for specific files, drivers, services, or registry keys installed by VMware Tools or VirtualBox Guest Additions (e.g., VBoxService.exe, vmtoolsd.exe, related registry keys).

I/O Port Checks: Interacting with specific I/O ports used internally by some hypervisors.

CPU Instruction Timing/Features: Certain instructions might execute with slightly different timings inside a VM, or specific CPU features reported by CPUID might indicate virtualization. Red Pill and similar techniques rely on subtle differences in how certain instructions behave on virtual vs. physical hardware.

Analysis Tool Detection: Searching for running processes associated with debuggers (x64dbg.exe), monitoring tools (procmon.exe), or analysis frameworks. Checking for common debugger hooks or known memory modifications.

Environment Profiling: Checking for factors unlikely in a typical user environment but common in analysis VMs: specific usernames (Admin, User, Malware), common analysis directory paths (C:\analysis), default language/keyboard settings, lack of recent documents, minimal uptime, unusual screen resolution, or very low CPU core/memory count.

Timing/Delay Tactics:

Stalling: Inserting long Sleep() calls or performing useless computationally intensive loops to wait out the limited execution time window of automated sandboxes.

Time Bombs: Only activating the malicious payload after a specific date/time, or after the system has been running for a certain duration.

Interaction Required: Waiting for specific mouse movements, clicks within application windows, or complex keyboard input sequences that automated sandboxes often don't simulate realistically. Any.Run's interactivity specifically helps combat this.

Countering Evasion: Effectively analyzing evasion-aware malware often requires moving beyond default sandbox configurations or basic VM setups.

Hardening VMs: Customizing the VM environment to remove common VM artifacts – changing MAC addresses, renaming virtual hardware in the registry, disabling or hiding guest tools services, ensuring realistic username/hostname/system configuration, increasing resource allocations (CPU cores, RAM).

Using Stealthier Tools: Employing debuggers with better anti-anti-debugging features, using hardware breakpoints instead of software ones, leveraging lower-level instrumentation frameworks (Pin/DynamoRIO) that might be harder to detect than higher-level hooking, or even analyzing within kernel mode where user-mode checks are less effective.

Patching Evasion Checks: If static analysis can identify the specific code performing the evasion check, manually patching it out (using a debugger or hex editor on the binary *before* execution) can force the malware down its malicious path even in an analysis environment. Frida scripts are often used to hook and bypass checks dynamically (e.g., force IsDebuggerPresent to return false).

Modifying Sandbox Behavior: Some sandbox systems allow customization, like extending execution time, simulating more realistic user interaction, or modifying the environment to appear less generic.

Conclusion: Isolation and Automation as Essential Pillars

Sandboxing and virtualization are not merely conveniences; they are essential safety mechanisms and powerful analysis accelerators, particularly when dealing with the inherent risks of malware analysis. Virtualization provides the fundamental **isolation** and **revertibility** needed to handle dangerous code without jeopardizing the analyst's primary system. Automated sandboxes build upon this, adding layers of automated **monitoring** and **reporting** to deliver rapid behavioral assessments ideal for high-volume triage and extracting initial intelligence.

However, analysts must remain acutely aware of their limitations, primarily the constant threat of **evasion techniques**. While excellent for initial insights and filtering, sandbox reports cannot always be taken as the definitive truth, especially for sophisticated malware. True understanding often requires progressing beyond automated reports to skilled **manual dynamic analysis** (using debuggers and instrumentation tools, often within carefully hardened VMs designed to resist evasion) integrated tightly with thorough **static analysis**.

Dynamic Analysis: Completing the Picture

Across these three sections – direct behavioral analysis with debuggers (5.1), broader system interaction monitoring and instrumentation (5.2), and safe execution via sandboxing/virtualization (5.3) – we see the multifaceted nature of dynamic analysis. It provides the crucial **ground truth** about runtime behavior, revealing actual data values, resolving dynamic dependencies, confirming control flow paths, and observing environmental interactions that static analysis can only predict or infer.

It's the indispensable counterpart to static analysis. The most effective reverse engineering process almost invariably involves a continuous, fluid **dialogue between static and dynamic techniques**. Static analysis builds the map, identifies points of interest, and generates hypotheses. Dynamic analysis explores those points, verifies the hypotheses with live data, resolves runtime ambiguities, and uncovers new behaviors or data that feed back into refining the static map. One might find an interesting function statically, set a breakpoint to observe its arguments dynamically, discover a decryption key is passed, use that key in static analysis to decrypt data sections, identify new network indicators from the decrypted data, use dynamic instrumentation to log traffic related to those indicators, and so on.

Chapter 6: File Format Analysis

let's venture into a new territory: the files themselves. So far, we've mostly talked about analyzing executable code – the programs that run. But those programs almost always interact with data stored in files: configuration files, saved documents, game states, databases, media assets, network captures, and so much more. Sometimes these files use well-known, documented formats (like .txt, .jpg, .zip), but often, especially with proprietary software or specialized applications (including malware!), you'll encounter custom file formats with no public documentation. **File Format Analysis** is the skill of dissecting these data containers to understand their structure and interpret their contents.

Think of it like being presented with a locked, unlabeled box. You know there's something valuable inside (the data), but you need to figure out how the box is constructed (the structure) before you can reliably open it and understand what's inside. This chapter will guide you through understanding file structures in general, techniques for extracting and interpreting the data within, and strategies for tackling those tricky custom formats.

6.1. Understanding File Structures: Order from Chaos

let's dive into the fundamental challenge of understanding **File Structures**. When you first encounter a file, particularly one without a familiar extension or originating from an unknown source, it might seem like just an opaque stream of digital data. At the most fundamental level, that's exactly what it is: a sequence of bytes stored on a disk or transmitted over a network. However, for that sequence of bytes to hold any usable information, the software that creates and reads the file must impose some form of **structure** upon it. This structure is the hidden blueprint, the organizing principle that transforms raw data into meaningful records, images, settings, or instructions.

Imagine trying to comprehend a dense academic textbook where all the letters were run together without spaces, punctuation, chapter breaks, headings, or page numbers. It would be an exercise in frustration, rendering the valuable information within practically inaccessible. File structures provide the digital equivalents of these organizational elements. They define how the raw bytes are grouped and interpreted to represent different pieces of information – numbers, text strings, images, commands, metadata – and establish the relationships between these pieces. As a reverse engineer tasked with understanding a file format, your primary goal is to uncover and decipher this hidden structure, effectively learning the "grammar" and "syntax" defined by the file's creators.

The Welcoming Committee: File Headers and Magic Numbers

Often, the very beginning of a file serves as an introduction, containing crucial information needed to interpret the rest of the content. This initial section is commonly referred to as the **file header**. Think of it as the combined title page, publisher information, and table of contents for the digital document. Headers typically contain **metadata** – data *about* the main data, rather than the primary content itself.

One of the most common and immediately useful pieces of metadata found in many file headers is the **Magic Number** (also sometimes called a file signature). This isn't related to illusion; it's a specific, predefined sequence of bytes located right at the start of the file (offset 0). Its purpose is to act as a unique identifier, a fingerprint, for the file type. Operating systems and applications can look at these first few bytes to determine the likely format of the file, often regardless of its filename or extension. This is incredibly useful because file extensions can be easily changed, deliberately misleading, or simply missing (especially in data recovery or forensics scenarios).

Recognizing magic numbers is frequently the very first step in analyzing an unknown file. Loading the file into a hex editor and examining the initial bytes can provide an instant identification clue. Many sequences are well-known:

4D 5A (ASCII "MZ"): Identifies a Windows PE (Portable Executable) file, like .exe or .dll. Named after Mark Zbikowski.

7F 45 4C 46 (ASCII .ELF where \x7F is non-printable): Identifies an ELF (Executable and Linkable Format) file, common on Linux and other Unix-like systems.

50 4B 03 04 (ASCII "PK.."): The header for a file entry within a ZIP archive. Since many modern formats are ZIP containers (like .docx, .xlsx, .jar, .apk), seeing this signature is very common. Named after Phil Katz, creator of PKZIP.

25 50 44 46 (ASCII "%PDF"): The start of a Portable Document Format (PDF) file.

89 50 4E 47 0D 0A 1A 0A (ASCII .PNG....): The unique signature for a Portable Network Graphics (PNG) image file.

FF D8 FF (often followed by E0 or E1): Marks the Start Of Image (SOI) for a JPEG image file.

47 49 46 38 37 61 or 47 49 46 38 39 61 (ASCII "GIF87a" or "GIF89a"): Signatures for Graphics Interchange Format (GIF) image files.

CA FE BA BE (Hexspeak "Cafe Babe"): The magic number for Java .class files.

The list goes on and on, covering document types, archives, multimedia formats, executables, disk images, and more. Numerous online databases catalogue these magic numbers (sometimes called file signatures). When faced with an unknown file, loading the first few bytes into a hex editor and searching for the observed sequence online is often the quickest way to get a preliminary identification. Seeing those familiar MZ bytes at the start of a file with a .dat extension immediately tells you you're likely dealing with a disguised executable, drastically changing your analysis approach.

Code Example: Practical File Identification with Python

Let's create a more robust Python script than the conceptual one before to demonstrate identifying files based on their magic numbers. This script will define a dictionary of known signatures, read the beginning of specified files, and report potential matches.

```python
#!/usr/bin/env python3
# -*- coding: utf-8 -*-

import os
import argparse
from typing import Dict, Optional, Tuple

# Define known file signatures (Magic Numbers)
# Structure: { signature_bytes: (description, offset) }
# Offset indicates where the signature starts (usually 0)
FILE_SIGNATURES: Dict[bytes, Tuple[str, int]] = {
    # Executables / Libraries
    b'\x4D\x5A': ("Windows PE Executable (DOS MZ Header)",
0),
    b'\x7F\x45\x4C\x46': ("ELF Executable/Object File", 0),
    b'\xCA\xFE\xBA\xBE': ("Java Class File", 0), # Big Endian
    b'\xFE\xED\xFA\xCE': ("Mach-O Binary (32-bit)", 0), # Big
Endian (classic PowerPC)
```

```
    b'\xFE\xED\xFA\xCF': ("Mach-O Binary (64-bit)", 0), # Big
Endian
    b'\xCE\xFA\xED\xFE': ("Mach-O Binary (32-bit, LE)", 0), #
Little Endian (modern Intel macOS <= Mojave)
    b'\xCF\xFA\xED\xFE': ("Mach-O Binary (64-bit, LE)", 0), #
Little Endian (modern Intel/ARM macOS >= Catalina)

    # Archives
    b'\x50\x4B\x03\x04': ("ZIP Archive Entry / Container
(docx, jar, apk, etc.)", 0),
    b'\x1F\x8B\x08': ("GZIP Archive", 0),
    b'\x42\x5A\x68': ("BZIP2 Archive", 0), # 'BZh'
    b'\xFD\x37\x7A\x58\x5A\x00': ("XZ Archive", 0), # .7zXZ..
    b'\x52\x61\x72\x21\x1A\x07\x00': ("RAR Archive v1.50+",
0), # Rar!...
    b'\x52\x61\x72\x21\x1A\x07\x01\x00': ("RAR Archive
v5.0+", 0), # Rar!....

    # Images
    b'\x89\x50\x4E\x47\x0D\x0A\x1A\x0A': ("PNG Image", 0),
    b'\x47\x49\x46\x38\x37\x61': ("GIF Image (87a)", 0),
    b'\x47\x49\x46\x38\x39\x61': ("GIF Image (89a)", 0),
    b'\xFF\xD8\xFF': ("JPEG Image (SOI Marker)", 0), # Note:
Further bytes needed for confirmation (e.g., E0 for JFIF, E1
for EXIF)
    b'\x42\x4D': ("BMP Image (Windows Bitmap)", 0), # 'BM'
    b'\x49\x49\x2A\x00': ("TIFF Image (Little Endian)", 0), #
'II*'
    b'\x4D\x4D\x00\x2A': ("TIFF Image (Big Endian)", 0), #
'MM.*'

    # Documents
    b'\x25\x50\x44\x46': ("PDF Document", 0), # '%PDF'
    b'\xD0\xCF\x11\xE0\xA1\xB1\x1A\xE1': ("Microsoft Office
Compound File (doc, xls, ppt - pre-OOXML)", 0), # OLE CF

    # Audio / Video
    b'\x49\x44\x33': ("MP3 Audio File (ID3v2 tag)", 0), #
'ID3'
    b'\x52\x49\x46\x46': ("RIFF Container (WAV, AVI)", 0), #
'RIFF'

    # Other
    b'\x3C\x3F\x78\x6D\x6C': ("XML Document (starts with
'<?xml')", 0),
    b'\x7B\x22': ("JSON Data (heuristic - starts with
'{\"')", 0),
    b'\x7B\x0A\x20\x20': ("JSON Data (heuristic - starts with
'{\\n  ')", 0),
```

```python
b'\x53\x51\x4C\x69\x74\x65\x20\x66\x6F\x72\x6D\x61\x74\x20\x3
3\x00': ("SQLite Database File", 0) # "SQLite format 3."
}

# Determine the maximum header length needed for reliable
identification
MAX_HEADER_LEN = max(len(sig) for sig in
FILE_SIGNATURES.keys())

def identify_file_type(filepath: str) -> str:
    """
    Identifies the file type based on its magic number
(header signature).

    Args:
        filepath: Path to the file to analyze.

    Returns:
        A string describing the identified file type or an
error message.
    """
    if not os.path.exists(filepath):
        return f"Error: File not found at '{filepath}'."
    if not os.path.isfile(filepath):
        return f"Error: '{filepath}' is not a regular file."

    try:
        filesize = os.path.getsize(filepath)
        if filesize == 0:
            return f"File '{os.path.basename(filepath)}' is
empty."

        # Determine how many bytes to read (max needed or
file size, whichever is smaller)
        bytes_to_read = min(MAX_HEADER_LEN, filesize)

        with open(filepath, 'rb') as f:
            header = f.read(bytes_to_read)

        # Iterate through known signatures (longest first for
specificity)
        # Sorting by length ensures longer matches take
precedence (e.g., RAR v5 vs RAR general)
        sorted_sigs = sorted(FILE_SIGNATURES.items(),
key=lambda item: len(item[0]), reverse=True)

        for signature_bytes, (description, offset) in
sorted_sigs:
            # Check if the file is large enough for this
signature and offset
```

```python
            if offset + len(signature_bytes) <= len(header):
                # Compare the relevant slice of the header
                if header[offset : offset +
len(signature_bytes)] == signature_bytes:
                    hex_sig = signature_bytes.hex().upper()
                    return f"Detected Type: {description}
(Signature: 0x{hex_sig} at offset {offset})"

        # If no known signature matched
        header_preview = header[:min(16,
len(header))].hex().upper() # Show first 16 bytes hex
        return f"File type unknown based on
{len(FILE_SIGNATURES)} known signatures. Header starts with:
0x{header_preview}..."

    except PermissionError:
        return f"Error: Permission denied reading file
'{filepath}'."
    except Exception as e:
        return f"An unexpected error occurred processing
'{filepath}': {e}"

def main():
    """Main function to parse arguments and process files."""
    parser = argparse.ArgumentParser(
        description="Identify file types based on magic
numbers (header signatures).",
        epilog="Example: python identify_file.py report.pdf
image.bin unknown_data.xyz"
    )
    parser.add_argument(
        'files',
        metavar='FILE',
        nargs='+',  # Require one or more files
        help='Path(s) to the file(s) to analyze.'
    )

    args = parser.parse_args()

    print(f"--- Analyzing {len(args.files)} file(s) ---")
    print(f"Using {len(FILE_SIGNATURES)} known signatures,
checking up to {MAX_HEADER_LEN} bytes.\n")

    for filepath in args.files:
        print(f"Analyzing '{filepath}'...")
        result = identify_file_type(filepath)
        print(f"-> {result}\n")

    print("--- Analysis complete ---")

if __name__ == "__main__":
```

How it Works (Step-by-Step):

Import Libraries: Import os for file system interaction and argparse for command-line argument handling. Import typing for type hints (good practice).

Define Signatures: The FILE_SIGNATURES dictionary stores the core knowledge. Keys are bytes objects representing the magic number sequences. Values are tuples containing a human-readable description and the offset (usually 0) where the signature is expected. Using b'\x...' ensures we are working with raw bytes, not text strings. Note how specific formats might have variations (GIF87a vs GIF89a, different Mach-O variants). Longer signatures are generally more reliable.

Calculate Max Length: Determine the longest signature defined (MAX_HEADER_LEN). We only need to read this many bytes from the start of each file to perform all checks. This optimizes reading for very large files.

identify_file_type Function:

Takes the filepath as input.

Performs basic validation: does the file exist? Is it a file (not a directory)? Is it empty?

Calculates how many bytes to actually read (bytes_to_read).

Opens the file in **binary read mode ('rb')**. This is crucial; opening in text mode ('r') can lead to decoding errors or newline conversions, corrupting the raw byte sequence.

Reads the required number of bytes using f.read(bytes_to_read).

Sorts the known signatures by length, longest first. This prevents a shorter signature (like MZ) from incorrectly matching a file that actually starts with a longer, more specific signature that *also* happens to begin with MZ.

Iterates through the sorted signatures.

For each signature, it checks if the read header is long enough to contain the signature at the specified offset.

It then compares the relevant *slice* of the header (header[offset : offset + len(signature_bytes)]) directly with the signature_bytes. Direct byte comparison is essential.

If a match is found, it formats a descriptive string including the signature hex representation and offset, then immediately returns.

172

If no known signature matches after checking all of them, it returns an "unknown" message, showing a hex preview of the first few bytes read. Includes try...except blocks for robust error handling (file not found, permissions, other read errors).

main Function:

Uses argparse to allow the user to specify one or more filenames on the command line.

Prints some introductory information.

Loops through the list of provided file paths.

Calls identify_file_type for each file.

Prints the result returned by the identification function.

if __name__ == "__main__": block: Standard Python idiom ensures the main() function is called only when the script is executed directly (not when imported as a module).

Running the Example: Save the code (e.g., as identify_file.py). Create some empty or dummy files (or use existing ones like a PDF, a ZIP file, a text file, an executable). Run it from your terminal: python identify_file.py mydocument.pdf myarchive.zip myprogram.exe unknowndata.bin plain.txt. The script will output its analysis for each file. This demonstrates the practical application of magic number analysis, a core RE task.

Beyond Magic Numbers: Other Header Intelligence

While the magic number provides the initial identification, file headers often contain much more valuable metadata that guides further parsing and understanding:

Version Numbers: Many file formats evolve over time. A **version number** (often stored as one or two bytes, or sometimes a four-byte integer) embedded in the header allows software to identify which iteration of the format specification the file adheres to. A program reading the file can check this version number and potentially adjust its parsing logic accordingly, perhaps enabling compatibility with older versions or activating features specific to newer ones. For a reverse engineer, noting the version number is important because different versions might have significantly different internal structures or features, requiring different analysis approaches or structure definitions. Sometimes version information is encoded less directly, perhaps within flags or size fields.

Size Information: Headers frequently contain fields specifying sizes. This could be the **total size of the file** (useful for validating integrity or determining if the file is truncated), the **size of the header itself** (so the parser knows where the actual data begins), or sizes of specific **data chunks** or sections within the file. These size fields are critical for reliable parsing, especially for variable-length data sections. If the header says the image data block is 10240 bytes long, the parser knows exactly how much data to read for that block. Incorrect size information can indicate file corruption.

Offsets/Pointers: For complex formats, the header might contain **offsets** – numerical values that act like pointers, indicating the byte position (relative to the start of the file, or sometimes relative to the end of the header or another landmark) where a specific data structure, table, or section begins. Executable formats like PE and ELF rely heavily on offsets in their headers to locate crucial sections like the code segment, data segments, import/export tables, relocation information, and resource directories. File systems use offsets within directory entries to point to the data blocks belonging to a file. For a reverse engineer, these offsets are like the page numbers in the table of contents – they provide direct navigation routes to important parts of the file, allowing you to jump directly to relevant data structures without sequentially scanning the entire file. Understanding whether an offset is absolute (from file start) or relative is crucial for calculating the correct target location. Successfully parsing the header – extracting the magic number, version, sizes, and offsets – is often the mandatory first step before you can even begin to make sense of the file's main content.

Structuring the Content: Common Data Organization Patterns

Once past the header (or sometimes integral to it), the main data payload of a file needs organization. Several common patterns are employed, each with implications for parsing and analysis:

Fixed-Size Fields: This is perhaps the simplest approach, often used for straightforward records or data structures where the size of each piece of information is known beforehand and constant. The structure is defined as a sequence of fields, each occupying a predetermined number of bytes. For example, a simple customer record might be defined as: 4-byte Customer ID (integer), followed by a 30-byte Name (fixed-length string, perhaps null-padded), followed by a 4-byte Last Purchase Timestamp (integer), followed by a 2-byte Status Code (short integer).

RE Implications: Parsing fixed-size structures is generally straightforward using tools that understand basic data types (integers, floats) and endianness. You simply read the expected number of bytes for each field sequentially. Defining structures in tools like IDA/Ghidra or creating templates for 010 Editor/ImHex is relatively easy. The main downside is potential wasted space if data doesn't always fill the fixed size (like the 30-byte name field if most names are shorter), but the predictability simplifies processing. Examples include simple database table dumps, certain sensor log formats, or entries in bitmap image headers.

Variable-Length Fields: Many types of data, especially text strings or binary blobs, don't have a naturally fixed size. File formats accommodate this using several methods:

Length-Prefixed: This is a very common and robust technique. The variable-length data field is immediately preceded by one or more bytes that explicitly encode the *length* of the upcoming data. The parser reads the length field first, then reads exactly that many bytes for the data field. The length field itself might be a single byte (limiting data length to 255 bytes), two bytes (up to 65535 bytes), or four bytes (up to 4GB). Pascal strings classically use a single length byte prefix. Network protocols frequently use 2- or 4-byte length prefixes (often in big-endian order) for message components.

RE Implications: Parsing requires a two-step read: read length, then read data based on length. It's efficient as there's no wasted space. Understanding the size and endianness of the *length field* itself is crucial.

Null-Terminated: Primarily used for text strings, particularly in C-language contexts. The string consists of a sequence of characters followed by a single null byte (\x00) acting as a delimiter or terminator. The length isn't stored explicitly; the parser reads bytes until it encounters the null byte.

RE Implications: Simple to implement, but requires scanning the data to find the terminator. If the null terminator is missing or corrupted, the parser might read far beyond the intended end of the string, potentially leading to buffer overflows if reading into a fixed-size buffer – a classic security vulnerability. Not suitable for binary data that might naturally contain null bytes.

Other Delimiters: Less common for general file formats but sometimes seen are other character delimiters (like newlines \n for lines in text files) or specific byte sequences marking the end of a variable-length record.

Type-Length-Value (TLV) Encoding: This is a highly flexible and extensible pattern, particularly common in network protocols (like SNMP, some parts of TLS) and certain configuration or data serialization formats (like BER/DER used in X.509 certificates). Each piece of data is represented by a triplet:

Type (Tag): A code (often one or two bytes) identifying the *kind* of data (e.g., integer, string, IP address, custom application type).

Length: Specifies the size (in bytes) of the following Value field. The format of the Length field itself might be fixed or variable.

Value: The actual data bytes, interpreted according to the Type code.

RE Implications: TLV parsing involves reading the Type, then reading the Length, then reading Length bytes for the Value. This structure makes it easy to add new data types later without breaking older parsers (they can simply skip unknown Type codes based on the Length field) and naturally handles optional fields (if a type isn't present, its TLV triplet is simply omitted). Identifying the codes used for different Types is key to understanding the data. Nested TLV structures (where the Value field itself contains more TLV triplets) are also possible, allowing for complex hierarchical data.

Chunk-Based Formats: Some formats are structured as a sequence of independent **chunks** or blocks. Each chunk typically starts with its own header containing a **Chunk Type/ID** (identifying what kind of data the chunk holds, often a 4-byte identifier like 'IHDR', 'PLTE', 'IDAT' in PNG) and a **Chunk Length** field indicating the size of the following chunk data. Optionally, a checksum (like CRC32) might follow the data for integrity validation. Examples include PNG (Portable Network Graphics), RIFF (Resource Interchange File Format, used by WAV audio and AVI video), and IFF (Interchange File Format).

RE Implications: Parsers can navigate these formats by reading the chunk ID and length, deciding whether to process the chunk data (if the ID is recognized) or simply seeking forward by the chunk length plus header size to skip over unknown or irrelevant chunks. This provides robustness and extensibility. Reverse engineering involves identifying the different chunk

IDs used, understanding the structure of the data within each recognized chunk type, and how the chunks relate to form the overall file content.

Code Example: Parsing Diverse Structures with Python struct and Manual Logic

Let's enhance our Python toolkit to parse some of these different structures from a hypothetical binary file.

```python
#!/usr/bin/env python3
# -*- coding: utf-8 -*-

import struct
import os

# Hypothetical file content generation (for demonstration)
def create_test_file(filename="structured_data.bin"):
    """Creates a binary file with mixed structures."""
    try:
        with open(filename, 'wb') as f:
            # --- Header (Magic + Version + Data Offset) ---
            magic = b'STRC'
            version = 1  # uint16, Little Endian
            data_offset = 50 # uint32, Little Endian (where
record data starts)
            # '<4s H I' => Little Endian, 4-char bytes,
unsigned short, unsigned int
            header_fmt = '<4sHI'
            header_data = struct.pack(header_fmt, magic,
version, data_offset)
            f.write(header_data)
            print(f"Wrote Header
({struct.calcsize(header_fmt)} bytes):
{header_data.hex().upper()}")

            # --- Some padding or other header info ---
            padding_len = data_offset -
struct.calcsize(header_fmt)
            f.write(b'\x00' * padding_len)
            print(f"Wrote {padding_len} padding bytes.")

            # --- Data Area ---
            # Record 1: Fixed Size
            rec1_id = 101 # uint32 LE
            rec1_name = b"Alice\0\0\0\0\0\0\0\0\0\0\0" # 16
bytes fixed, null padded
            rec1_val = 500 # uint16 LE
            rec1_flags = 0x0A # uint8
            # '<I 16s H B' => LE, uint32, 16-byte string,
ushort, ubyte
            rec1_fmt = '<I16sHB'
```

```
            rec1_pad_len = 24 - struct.calcsize(rec1_fmt) #
Example record size 24 bytes
            rec1_padding = b'\xDD' * rec1_pad_len # Use non-
zero padding
            rec1_data = struct.pack(rec1_fmt, rec1_id,
rec1_name, rec1_val, rec1_flags) + rec1_padding
            f.write(rec1_data)
            print(f"Wrote Record 1 (Fixed, {len(rec1_data)}
bytes): {rec1_data.hex().upper()}")

            # Record 2: Variable Length (Length-Prefixed
String)
            rec2_id = 102 # uint32 LE
            rec2_string = b"Bob went to the store." #
Variable content
            rec2_strlen = len(rec2_string) # uint16 LE
(length of string)
            # Write ID, then Strlen, then String
            f.write(struct.pack('<I', rec2_id))
            f.write(struct.pack('<H', rec2_strlen))
            f.write(rec2_string)
            rec2_len = 4 + 2 + rec2_strlen
            print(f"Wrote Record 2 (VarStr, {rec2_len}
bytes): ID={rec2_id}, Len={rec2_strlen},
Str='{rec2_string.decode('ascii')}'")

            # Record 3: TLV structure
            rec3_id = 103 # uint32 LE
            f.write(struct.pack('<I', rec3_id))
            # TLV 1: Type=1 (uint16 value), Length=2,
Value=12345
            tlv1_type = 1 # uint8
            tlv1_len = 2  # uint8
            tlv1_val = 12345 # uint16 LE
            f.write(struct.pack('<BBH', tlv1_type, tlv1_len,
tlv1_val))
            # TLV 2: Type=2 (string value), Length=dynamic,
Value="Status: OK"
            tlv2_type = 2 # uint8
            tlv2_val_str = b"Status: OK"
            tlv2_len = len(tlv2_val_str) # uint8
            f.write(struct.pack('<BB', tlv2_type, tlv2_len))
            f.write(tlv2_val_str)
            rec3_len = 4 + (1+1+2) + (1+1+tlv2_len)
            print(f"Wrote Record 3 (TLV, {rec3_len} bytes):
ID={rec3_id}, TLV1(T=1,L=2,V=12345),
TLV2(T=2,L={tlv2_len},V='Status: OK')")

            # Record 4: Chunk Example (Type, Length, Data,
CRC maybe)
            chunk_type = b'DATA' # 4 bytes
```

```
            chunk_payload =
b'\x01\x02\x03\x04\x05\x06\x07\x08\x09\x0A'
            chunk_len = len(chunk_payload) # uint32 BE
(Network Byte Order often for lengths)
            # Example CRC32 - calculation omitted for
brevity, just dummy value
            chunk_crc = 0xDEADBEEF # uint32 BE
            # '>I 4s {chunk_len}s I' - Big Endian uint32 Len,
4-byte Type, Data, BE uint32 CRC
            # Write Type, Length, Payload, CRC separately as
size is dynamic
            f.write(chunk_type)
            f.write(struct.pack('>I', chunk_len)) # Big
Endian Length
            f.write(chunk_payload)
            f.write(struct.pack('>I', chunk_crc)) # Big
Endian CRC
            rec4_len = 4 + 4 + chunk_len + 4
            print(f"Wrote Record 4 (Chunk, {rec4_len} bytes):
Type='DATA', Len={chunk_len},
Payload={chunk_payload.hex().upper()}, CRC=DEADBEEF")

        print(f"\nCreated test file: {filename}")
        return filename
    except Exception as e:
        print(f"Error creating test file: {e}")
        return None

def parse_test_file(filename):
    """Parses the hypothetical structured binary file."""
    if not filename or not os.path.exists(filename):
        print(f"Cannot parse, file not found or not created:
{filename}")
        return

    print(f"\n--- Parsing {filename} ---")
    try:
        with open(filename, 'rb') as f:
            # 1. Read and Unpack Header
            header_fmt = '<4sHI' # LE: 4-byte magic, ushort
version, uint data_offset
            header_size = struct.calcsize(header_fmt)
            header_packed = f.read(header_size)
            if len(header_packed) < header_size: raise
EOFError("Could not read header.")

            magic, version, data_offset =
struct.unpack(header_fmt, header_packed)
            # Decode magic bytes for printing
            try:
                magic_str = magic.decode('ascii')
```

```python
        except UnicodeDecodeError:
            magic_str = magic.hex().upper() # Show hex if
not ASCII

        print(f"Header Parsed: Magic='{magic_str}'
(0x{magic.hex().upper()}), Version={version}, Data
Offset={data_offset}")

        # Validate Magic Number (optional but good
practice)
        if magic != b'STRC':
            print("Warning: Unexpected Magic Number!")

        # Seek to the data offset specified in the header
        current_pos = f.tell()
        if current_pos < data_offset:
            # Read padding if needed, or seek
            f.seek(data_offset)
            print(f"Seeked/Skipped {data_offset -
current_pos} bytes to reach data offset {data_offset}.")
        elif current_pos > data_offset:
            print(f"Warning: Current position
{current_pos} is already past data offset {data_offset}.
Something is wrong.")

        # Check if we can read data (avoid reading past
EOF)
        file_end_pos = os.path.getsize(filename)

        # 2. Parse Record 1 (Fixed Size)
        print("\nParsing Record 1 (Fixed Size):")
        rec1_fmt = '<I16sHB' # Format excluding padding
for easier unpacking
        rec1_read_size = struct.calcsize(rec1_fmt)
        rec1_total_size = 24 # Total expected size
including padding

        if f.tell() + rec1_total_size <= file_end_pos:
            rec1_packed_main = f.read(rec1_read_size)
            rec1_padding_read = f.read(rec1_total_size -
rec1_read_size) # Read padding separately

            rec1_id, rec1_name_bytes, rec1_val,
rec1_flags = struct.unpack(rec1_fmt, rec1_packed_main)
            # Decode name, handling potential null bytes
            rec1_name =
rec1_name_bytes.partition(b'\0')[0].decode('ascii',
errors='replace')

            print(f"  ID    : {rec1_id}")
```

```
                print(f"  Name  : '{rec1_name}' (Raw:
{rec1_name_bytes.hex().upper()})")
                print(f"  Value : {rec1_val}")
                print(f"  Flags : 0x{rec1_flags:02X}")
                print(f"
Padding:{rec1_padding_read.hex().upper()}")
            else: print("  Not enough data remaining for
Record 1.")


            # 3. Parse Record 2 (Variable Length String)
            print("\nParsing Record 2 (Var Length String):")
            id_fmt = '<I' # LE uint32 ID
            len_fmt = '<H' # LE uint16 Length
            id_size = struct.calcsize(id_fmt)
            len_size = struct.calcsize(len_fmt)

            if f.tell() + id_size + len_size <= file_end_pos:
                rec2_id_packed = f.read(id_size)
                rec2_id = struct.unpack(id_fmt,
rec2_id_packed)[0]

                rec2_len_packed = f.read(len_size)
                rec2_strlen = struct.unpack(len_fmt,
rec2_len_packed)[0]
                print(f"  ID    : {rec2_id}")
                print(f"  StrLen: {rec2_strlen}")

                if f.tell() + rec2_strlen <= file_end_pos:
                    rec2_string_bytes = f.read(rec2_strlen)
                    try:
                        rec2_string =
rec2_string_bytes.decode('ascii')
                    except UnicodeDecodeError:
                        rec2_string = f"(Binary Data:
{rec2_string_bytes.hex().upper()})"
                    print(f"  String: '{rec2_string}'")
                else: print(f"  Not enough data remaining for
string of length {rec2_strlen}.")
            else: print("  Not enough data remaining for
Record 2 header (ID/Len).")


            # 4. Parse Record 3 (TLV structure)
            print("\nParsing Record 3 (TLV):")
            if f.tell() + id_size <= file_end_pos:
                rec3_id_packed = f.read(id_size)
                rec3_id = struct.unpack(id_fmt,
rec3_id_packed)[0]
                print(f"  ID    : {rec3_id}")
```

```
                    # Parse TLV 1
                    tlv_header_fmt = '<BB' # uint8 Type, uint8
Length
                    tlv_header_size =
struct.calcsize(tlv_header_fmt)
                    if f.tell() + tlv_header_size <=
file_end_pos:
                        tlv1_header_packed =
f.read(tlv_header_size)
                        tlv1_type, tlv1_len =
struct.unpack(tlv_header_fmt, tlv1_header_packed)
                        print(f"  TLV 1: Type={tlv1_type},
Length={tlv1_len}")
                        if f.tell() + tlv1_len <= file_end_pos:
                            tlv1_value_packed =
f.read(tlv1_len)
                            if tlv1_type == 1 and tlv1_len ==
2:
                                tlv1_val = struct.unpack('<H',
tlv1_value_packed)[0] # uint16 LE
                                print(f"      -> Value (uint16):
{tlv1_val}")
                            else: print(f"      -> Value (raw
hex): {tlv1_value_packed.hex().upper()}")
                        else: print(f"    Not enough data for
TLV 1 value (length {tlv1_1
```

6.2. Extracting and Interpreting Data: Making Sense of the Bytes

we've now grasped the common ways files are structured – the headers, magic numbers, data organization patterns like fixed fields or TLV, and the ever-present concept of endianness (Chapter 6.1). We have a mental framework, a potential blueprint derived from examining the overall layout. The next crucial stage is to move from understanding the *potential* structure to actively **extracting the data** embedded within that structure and, just as importantly, **interpreting its meaning correctly**. This is where the raw sequence of bytes transforms into usable information – numbers, names, coordinates, flags, commands. It involves leveraging the right tools and tackling several common interpretation pitfalls head-on.

The Hex Editor: Your Ground-Level Entry Point

As emphasized before, your initial foray into the data often begins with a **Hex Editor** (like HxD, 010 Editor, ImHex). It's your fundamental tool for viewing the unadulterated bytes that make up the file. Loading the file into a hex editor provides that immediate, unfiltered perspective:

Viewing Raw Data: You see the grid of hexadecimal byte values, alongside their ASCII representation. This lets you visually scan for recognizable patterns, confirm the presence of magic numbers or headers you might expect, and spot obvious text strings embedded within the data.

Manual Navigation: You can easily jump to specific offsets within the file, perhaps offsets derived from values read in the file header, to examine the data located there.

Manual Verification: As you hypothesize about the structure (e.g., "I think this 4-byte sequence at offset 0x20 is a little-endian integer representing the number of records"), the hex editor allows you to select those bytes and use the editor's data inspector tool (if available) to instantly see their interpretation as different integer types (signed/unsigned, LE/BE). This provides immediate feedback on your structural assumptions.

Spotting Patterns: Sometimes, visual patterns emerge in the hex view that suggest structure. Repeating sequences might indicate padding or default values. Blocks of highly random-looking data might suggest compression or encryption (more on this later). Sections with many bytes corresponding to printable ASCII characters clearly indicate text data.

Simple Extraction: For extracting small, isolated pieces of information (like a single key value or an embedded filename) whose location you've determined, selecting the bytes and copying them out (often as a hex string) from the hex editor might be sufficient.

The hex editor is indispensable for this initial exploration, validation, and pattern spotting. It's the ground truth. However, relying *solely* on manual interpretation within a hex editor for analyzing a complex file format quickly becomes incredibly inefficient and highly prone to errors. Imagine manually decoding hundreds of intricate records, each with multiple fields of different types and endianness – keeping track of offsets, converting hex values, and documenting everything by hand is a recipe for exhaustion and mistakes.

Structure Parsing Tools: Automating the Decoding Process

This is where tools designed specifically for defining and parsing binary structures provide a monumental leap in efficiency and accuracy. Instead of manually interpreting bytes based on your deduced structure, you *teach* the tool about the structure, and it automatically decodes the file according to your rules. Two prominent approaches stand out:

Binary Templates (e.g., 010 Editor): Tools like 010 Editor allow you to write "templates" using a C-like scripting language. This template defines the sequence and types of data structures expected within the file. You can define structs, specify basic data types (int, uint, char, float, double, etc.), set endianness (LittleEndian(), BigEndian()), define arrays (fixed or dynamic size), use if statements or switch cases to handle conditional formatting based on previously read values (like version numbers or type flags), and much more. When you run the template on a file, 010 Editor parses the data according to your script and displays the results in a hierarchical tree view, neatly labeling each field with its name and interpreted value. This instantly transforms the raw hex view into a meaningful representation of the file's contents based on your reversed understanding. Changes to the template immediately re-parse the file, making iterative refinement easy.

Code Example: Conceptual 010 Editor Template Enhancement

Building on the previous example template SimpleRecord.bt:

```
// Enhanced Conceptual 010 Editor Template:
SimpleRecord_v2.bt
// Assume Little Endian globally for this format
LittleEndian();

// Define known flag bits using an enum for readability
enum <byte> RecordFlags {
    FLAG_ACTIVE = 0x01,
    FLAG_IMPORTANT = 0x02,
    FLAG_BACKUP = 0x04,
    FLAG_RESERVED = 0x08 // etc.
    // Bit manipulation functions can be used within structs
too
};

// Define the fixed-size record structure
typedef struct {
    uint32 recordID;
    char    name[16];
    uint16 value;
    RecordFlags flags; // Use the enum type here
    byte    _padding <hidden=true, comment="Alignment
padding">;
    // Add a comment directly to the structure definition
} SimpleRecord <read=ReadSimpleRecord>; // Associate a read
function
```

```
// Custom function to read and potentially color based on
flags
string ReadSimpleRecord(SimpleRecord& rec) {
    string s;
    // Format a summary string for the results view
    SPrintf(s, "ID:%u Name:'%s' Val:%u Flags:0x%02X",
            rec.recordID, ReadString(rec.name), rec.value,
rec.flags);

    // Example: Change background color based on flags
    if (rec.flags & FLAG_IMPORTANT) {
        SetBackColor(cLtRed);
    } else if (rec.flags & FLAG_ACTIVE) {
        SetBackColor(cLtGreen);
    } else {
        SetBackColor(cWhite);
    }
    return s; // Return the formatted string
}

// Main parsing logic for a file containing:
// Header, then variable number of records

// --- Header Structure ---
struct FileHeader {
    char    magic[4];
    uint16 version;
    uint16 reserved; // Added a reserved field
    uint32 data_offset;
    uint32 record_count; // Added record count
} header <comment="Main File Header">;

// --- Basic Validation ---
if (header.magic != "STRC") Warning("Magic number
mismatch!");
if (header.version > 1) Printf("Warning: File version %d may
not be fully supported.\n", header.version);

// --- Jump to Data and Parse Records ---
FSeek(header.data_offset);
Printf("Parsing %d records starting at offset 0x%X...\n",
header.record_count, header.data_offset);

local uint i;
for (i = 0; i < header.record_count; ++i) {
    // Use the typedef'd struct to parse each record
    SimpleRecord records_array <comment="Record Index">;
    // Add dynamic comment to template results
    SetComment(records_array, Str("%d", i));
    // ReadSimpleRecord function associated via typedef will
be called
```

```
}

Printf("Parsed %d records successfully.\n", i);

// Check if we are at the end of the file (optional)
if (!FEof()) {
    Warning("Extra data found after parsed records at offset
0x%X", FTell());
}
```

Explanation: This enhanced conceptual template shows more features: defining enums for flags, using typedef with a custom read function (ReadSimpleRecord) for presentation logic (like coloring based on flags or formatting summary strings), adding comments directly into the template results, performing basic validation based on header values, and parsing an array of records based on a count found in the header. This illustrates how templates transform parsing from manual byte-reading into executing a high-level structural definition.

Declarative Format Languages (e.g., Kaitai Struct): An alternative approach is using a declarative language to describe the binary format's structure, independent of any specific programming language. **Kaitai Struct** is a prime example. You create a YAML file (.ksy) describing the sequence of fields, their data types (integer sizes, endianness, floating-point types, strings, custom structures, arrays, etc.), conditional logic (if), and repetitions (repeat). The Kaitai Struct compiler then takes this .ksy file and automatically generates parser code in your choice of various target programming languages (Python, C++, C#, Java, JavaScript, PHP, Ruby, Go, and more).

Benefits: The key advantage is **language independence**. Define the format *once* in the .ksy file, and you can generate parsers for multiple languages, making it ideal for cross-platform tools or libraries. It strongly encourages creating a clean separation between the format definition and the code that uses the parsed data. The declarative nature often leads to concise and readable format definitions.

Process: You create the .ksy file describing the format based on your reverse engineering findings. You then use the Kaitai Struct compiler (ksc) to generate source code (e.g., a Python .py file). Finally, you import and use this generated parser module in your own application code to easily read data from files conforming to the format.

186

Code Example: Kaitai Struct .ksy Definition for SimpleRecord

```
# Kaitai Struct Definition: simple_record_file.ksy
meta:
  id: simple_record_file
  title: Hypothetical File with Header and Simple Records
  file-extension: bin
  endian: le # Specify Little Endian globally

seq:
  # Define the header structure first
  - id: header
    type: file_header
    doc: The main file header.

  # Kaitai automatically handles reading up to an offset if
needed
  # via 'pos' attribute and instance data (`_io.seek()`).
  # Alternatively, define padding explicitly if its size is
known.
  # We'll assume the parser handles seeking using the offset
later.

  # Define an array of records, using the count from the
header
  - id: records
    type: simple_record
    repeat: expr # Repeat based on an expression
    repeat-expr: header.record_count # Read this many records
    doc: Array of fixed-size data records.

# Define the types used in the sequence
types:
  file_header:
    seq:
      - id: magic
        contents: 'STRC' # Validate magic number directly
        doc: File identifier, must be "STRC".
      - id: version
        type: u2 # Unsigned 2-byte integer (uint16)
      - id: reserved
        type: u2
      - id: data_offset
        type: u4 # Unsigned 4-byte integer (uint32)
        doc: Offset from start of file to the first record.
      - id: record_count
        type: u4
        doc: Number of records in the file.

  simple_record:
    seq:
      - id: record_id
```

```
          type: u4
        - id: name_bytes
          size: 16 # Fixed size byte array
          type: bytes
        - id: value
          type: u2
        - id: flags
          type: u1
        - id: padding
          size: 1 # Explicitly define the padding
          # Can mark as unused later in processing if needed
      # Define 'instances' for calculated properties like the
cleaned name
      instances:
        name: # Processed name property
          # Value is a lazily calculated expression
          value: str(name_bytes, 'ascii').split('\x00')[0]
          doc: ASCII name, extracted up to the first null
terminator.
```

Explanation: This .ksy file declaratively defines the structure:

* meta: Provides information about the format. endian: le sets the default.

* seq: Defines the top-level sequence of elements in the file: first a header (of type file_header), then records (an array of type simple_record).

* types: Defines the custom structures (file_header, simple_record).

* Inside file_header, fields (magic, version, etc.) are defined with their Kaitai data type (u2=uint16, u4=uint32) and documentation. The magic field includes contents: 'STRC' which acts as an assertion during parsing – if the bytes don't match, parsing fails.

* Inside simple_record, fields are defined similarly (bytes for raw byte arrays, u1=uint8).

* The records field uses repeat: expr and repeat-expr: header.record_count to tell the parser to read exactly the number of simple_record structures specified in the previously parsed header.record_count field.

* The instances section within simple_record shows how to add calculated, convenient properties – here, name automatically processes the raw name_bytes to give a clean Python string.

Generating and Using the Parser (Python):

Install Kaitai Struct compiler (ksc).

Compile the KSY: ksc -t python simple_record_file.ksy (This creates simple_record_file.py).

Use the generated parser in your Python code:

```
# Python code using the generated parser
from simple_record_file import SimpleRecordFile # Import
generated class
import os

# Assume structured_data.bin was created by the previous
Python example
test_filename = "structured_data.bin"
```

try:

```
    # Parse the file from disk using the generated class
    parsed_data = SimpleRecordFile.from_file(test_filename)

    print("--- Parsing with Kaitai Struct ---")
    print(f"Header Magic    :
{parsed_data.header.magic.decode('ascii')}") # Access magic
via object
    print(f"Header Version  : {parsed_data.header.version}")
    print(f"Header Rec Count:
{parsed_data.header.record_count}")
    print(f"Data Offset     :
{parsed_data.header.data_offset}") # Access offset

    print(f"\nFound {len(parsed_data.records)} records:")
    for i, record in enumerate(parsed_data.records):
        # Access fields directly as attributes of the record
object
        print(f"  Record {i}:")
        print(f"    ID     : {record.record_id}")
        # Access the calculated 'name' instance property
        print(f"    Name   : '{record.name}'")
        print(f"    Value  : {record.value}")
        print(f"    Flags  : 0x{record.flags:02X}")
        print(f"    Padding:{record.padding.hex().upper()}")
```

except Exception as e:

```
    # Kaitai parsers raise specific exceptions on format
errors (like magic mismatch)
    print(f"Error parsing file with Kaitai Struct: {e}")
    # Example: Might raise ValidationNotEqualError if magic
bytes don't match
```

finally:

```
    # Clean up the test file
    if os.path.exists(test_filename):
        print(f"\n--- Cleaning up {test_filename} ---")
        os.remove(test_filename)
```

Result: This Python code cleanly parses the file using the Kaitai-generated SimpleRecordFile class. It accesses the header and record fields as simple object attributes (parsed_data.header.version, record.record_id, record.name), hiding the complexities of byte reading, struct.unpack, and seeking, which are now handled by the generated parser based on the .ksy definition.

Both binary templates and declarative languages like Kaitai Struct represent a massive leap forward from manual hex editing for complex formats. They allow you to codify your understanding of the file structure in a reusable way, automate the extraction process, reduce errors, and provide excellent self-documentation of the format itself. Building such a template or .ksy definition becomes a primary goal during file format reverse engineering.

The Crucial Step: Correct Interpretation

Simply extracting bytes or having a tool parse fields isn't enough. You need to **interpret** that raw data correctly to derive meaningful information. This involves carefully considering several factors:

Endianness (Revisited): As stressed before, correctly identifying whether multi-byte numerical values (like integers, floats, offsets) are stored in **Little-Endian** or **Big-Endian** format is non-negotiable. Using the wrong interpretation results in garbage values. Your parsing tool (Python struct, 010 templates, Kaitai Struct endian key) needs to be configured correctly based on your analysis of the format or its origin.

Data Types: A sequence of, say, 4 bytes can represent many different things. You need to determine the correct **data type**:

Integer Sizes: Is it an 8-bit (int8_t/uint8_t), 16-bit (int16_t/uint16_t), 32-bit (int32_t/uint32_t), or 64-bit (int64_t/uint64_t) integer?

Signed vs. Unsigned: Does the integer represent only non-negative values (unsigned) or can it be negative (signed, typically using two's complement representation)? Interpreting 0xFFFFFFFF as unsigned yields 4,294,967,295, while interpreting it as signed yields -1.

Floating-Point: Are the bytes representing a floating-point number (e.g., 32-bit IEEE 754 float or 64-bit double)? The byte patterns for floats are completely different from integers.

Bitfields / Flags: A single byte or word might not represent a single number but rather a collection of individual **flags**, where each bit signifies a boolean state (on/off). You need to determine the meaning of each bit position, often

through analyzing the code that uses bitwise operations (AND, OR, TEST) on the value.

Pointers/Offsets: Is a 4-byte or 8-byte value an integer, or is it actually an **address** or **offset** pointing to another location within the file or memory? Context (e.g., header fields named "offset", values falling within reasonable file size ranges) is key.

Timestamps: Is an integer (often 32-bit or 64-bit) representing time, perhaps as seconds since the Unix epoch (Jan 1, 1970), or using a Windows FILETIME structure (64-bit count of 100-nanosecond intervals since Jan 1, 1601), or some other custom format?

Custom Enums: Is an integer value actually representing a specific enumerated state (e.g., 0=Idle, 1=Processing, 2=Error)?

Your parsing logic or template needs to specify the correct type for struct.unpack, Kaitai definitions (u4, s4, f4, f8), or template declarations (int, uint, float, struct Bitfield { bool flag1:1; bool flag2:1; ... }). Guessing based on typical usage (e.g., sizes are usually unsigned, flags fit in bytes) or analyzing the code that uses the value is often necessary.

String Representation: How are text strings stored? We covered the main types:

Null-Terminated: Scan bytes until \x00 is found. Common in C-based formats.

Length-Prefixed: Read a length field (1, 2, or 4 bytes, check endianness!), then read that many bytes for the string data. Very common and robust.

Fixed-Length: Read a predetermined number of bytes. The string might be shorter, padded with nulls or spaces. You might need to trim the padding after reading.

Understanding the method used is crucial for extracting the correct text without reading too little or too much data.

Character Encoding: Once you've extracted the bytes representing a string, you need to decode them using the correct **character encoding** to display readable text. Simply assuming ASCII will often fail with modern text containing international characters or symbols. Common encodings include:

ASCII: 7-bit encoding, represents basic English characters, numbers, punctuation. Bytes above 127 are not defined.

Extended ASCII / Codepages: Various 8-bit encodings (like Latin-1/ISO-8859-1, Windows-1252) that assign characters to the upper 128 values. Problematic as different codepages assign different characters.

UTF-8: Variable-length encoding, backward compatible with ASCII for the first 128 characters. Uses 1-4 bytes per character. The dominant encoding on the web and Linux. Handles all Unicode characters.

UTF-16 (LE/BE): Uses 2 bytes (or 4 for rarer characters via surrogate pairs). Common in Windows APIs (wchar_t) and Java internal strings. Requires handling endianness (UTF-16LE vs UTF-16BE). A Byte Order Mark (BOM) sequence (\xFF\xFE for LE, \xFE\xFF for BE) at the start often indicates the encoding and endianness.

UTF-32 (LE/BE): Uses 4 bytes for every character. Less common due to space usage but simpler encoding. Also requires endianness handling.

Other: EBCDIC (mainframe), Shift-JIS (Japanese), GBK (Chinese), etc. Attempting to decode bytes using the wrong encoding results in **mojibake** (garbled text, often with symbols like □) or UnicodeDecodeError exceptions in programming languages. You often need to guess the encoding based on context (Windows origin suggests UTF-16LE or a Windows codepage, web/Linux suggests UTF-8, East Asian origin suggests specific encodings), look for BOMs, or analyze the code that writes/reads the string to see which encoding APIs are used.

Code Example: Python Encoding Demonstration

```python
    # Demonstrate encoding issues
original_utf8 = "Hello, κόσμε! €" # Contains Greek and Euro
symbol
original_utf16le = "Windows API €"

# Encode the strings into bytes
bytes_utf8 = original_utf8.encode('utf-8')
bytes_utf16le = original_utf16le.encode('utf-16le') # Little
Endian

print(f"UTF-8 Bytes       : {bytes_utf8.hex().upper()}")
print(f"UTF-16LE Bytes    : {bytes_utf16le.hex().upper()}")

# --- Attempt to decode using CORRECT encodings ---
try:
    decoded_utf8 = bytes_utf8.decode('utf-8')
    print(f"\nDecoding UTF-8 bytes as UTF-8: '{decoded_utf8}'
(Success!)")
except Exception as e: print(f"Decoding UTF-8 as UTF-8
failed: {e}")
```

```
try:
    decoded_utf16 = bytes_utf16le.decode('utf-16le')
    print(f"Decoding UTF-16LE bytes as UTF-16LE:
'{decoded_utf16}' (Success!)")
except Exception as e: print(f"Decoding UTF-16LE as UTF-16LE
failed: {e}")

# --- Attempt to decode using INCORRECT encodings ---
print("\n--- Incorrect Decoding Attempts ---")
try:
    # Try decoding UTF-8 bytes as Latin-1 (a common mismatch)
    decoded_wrong1 = bytes_utf8.decode('latin-1')
    print(f"Decoding UTF-8 bytes as Latin-1:
'{decoded_wrong1}' (Mojibake!)")
except Exception as e: print(f"Decoding UTF-8 as Latin-1
failed: {e}")

try:
    # Try decoding UTF-16LE bytes as UTF-8
    decoded_wrong2 = bytes_utf16le.decode('utf-8')
    print(f"Decoding UTF-16LE bytes as UTF-8: Causes Error")
except UnicodeDecodeError as e:
    print(f"  -> Error as expected: {e}") # Often errors out
except Exception as e: print(f"Decoding UTF-16LE as UTF-8
failed differently: {e}")

try:
    # Try decoding UTF-16LE as UTF-16 BE (wrong endianness)
    decoded_wrong3 = bytes_utf16le.decode('utf-16be')
    print(f"Decoding UTF-16LE bytes as UTF-16BE:
'{decoded_wrong3}' (Likely wrong chars or error)")
except Exception as e: print(f"Decoding UTF-16LE as UTF-16BE
failed: {e}")
```

Result: Running this code shows how decoding byte sequences with the wrong character encoding leads to either incorrect, garbled output (mojibake) or outright decoding errors, demonstrating the necessity of identifying the correct encoding.

Handling Concealed Data: Compression and Encryption

Finally, be prepared for situations where parts of the file aren't immediately interpretable because the data has been transformed to either save space (**Compression**) or protect confidentiality (**Encryption**). Both often result in sections of the file exhibiting **high entropy** – appearing visually random in a hex editor, lacking the patterns typical of uncompressed text or structured binary data. However, they require different analysis approaches.

Compression: File formats often compress large chunks of data (like image pixel data, document text, or embedded resources) to reduce the overall file size. Common algorithms include **zlib** (based on Deflate, used in PNG, GZIP, ZIP), **bzip2**, **LZMA** (used in 7-Zip), Zstandard (Zstd), or proprietary schemes.

Identification: High entropy is a primary indicator. Sometimes the format specification or surrounding data structures will include a flag indicating compression or identifying the algorithm used. Headers specific to compression formats (like the GZIP header \x1F\x8B\x08) might sometimes be present if a whole compressed stream is embedded. More reliably, **analyzing the code** that reads/writes this section using static or dynamic analysis is key. Look for calls to known decompression libraries (like libz, libbz2) or specific API functions (inflateInit, BZ2_bzDecompress).

Handling: Once you've identified a compressed block and likely the algorithm, you usually need to **extract** that specific sequence of bytes from the file and then use a standard tool or library corresponding to the algorithm to **decompress** it. The result of decompression should then be a stream of bytes representing the original, uncompressed data (e.g., raw pixel data, plain text, another structured format), which you can then analyze further.

Code Example: Decompressing zlib Data with Python

```python
     import zlib
import os

# Assume 'compressed_data.zlib' contains raw Deflate/zlib
compressed bytes
# Create a dummy compressed file first
original_data = b"This is the original data. " * 10 # Some
repetitive data
compressed_data = zlib.compress(original_data, level=9) #
Compress using zlib
filename = "compressed_data.zlib"
```

```python
try:
    with open(filename, 'wb') as f:
        f.write(compressed_data)
    print(f"Created '{filename}' with {len(compressed_data)}
compressed bytes (Original: {len(original_data)} bytes).")

    print(f"\n--- Attempting to decompress '{filename}' ---")
    with open(filename, 'rb') as f:
        compressed_read = f.read()
```

```
    # Attempt decompression using zlib
    try:
        decompressed_data = zlib.decompress(compressed_read)
        print(f"Decompression Successful! Recovered
{len(decompressed_data)} bytes.")
        # Try to decode as text (may fail if binary)
        try:
            print("Decompressed content (as UTF-8):")
            print(decompressed_data.decode('utf-8'))
        except UnicodeDecodeError:
            print(f"Decompressed content (raw
hex):\n{decompressed_data.hex().upper()}")

    except zlib.error as e:
        print(f"zlib Decompression Error: {e}. Is it valid
zlib/deflate data?")
    except Exception as e:
        print(f"An unexpected error occurred during
decompression: {e}")
```

finally:

```
    # Clean up
    if os.path.exists(filename):
        print(f"\n--- Cleaning up {filename} ---")
        os.remove(filename)
```

Explanation: This script first compresses some sample data using Python's built-in zlib library and writes it to a file. It then reads the file back and uses zlib.decompress to recover the original data. This demonstrates the typical workflow: identify the compressed block, extract it, and use the appropriate library/tool to decompress it before further analysis.

Encryption: Data might be encrypted to protect its confidentiality. Like compressed data, encrypted sections usually exhibit high entropy. However, unlike compression (which uses standard algorithms), encryption requires a **secret key** in addition to the algorithm.

Identification: Again, high entropy is a clue, but statically indistinguishable from compression. Context might help (e.g., sections labeled "license," "userdata," "password"). The most reliable method is **code analysis**. Search for calls to cryptographic APIs (CryptEncrypt, BCryptEncrypt, standard libraries like OpenSSL, Botan, etc.) or patterns indicative of well-known encryption algorithms (like distinctive S-boxes or round constants used in AES or DES).

Handling: This is significantly harder than decompression. Even if you identify the encryption algorithm (e.g., AES-256-CBC), you *cannot* decrypt the data without the correct **key** and often the correct **Initialization Vector (IV)**. Finding the key becomes a major reverse engineering challenge in itself. You need to analyze the code to determine:

Where does the key come from? Is it hardcoded (bad!), derived from user input (e.g., a password via a key derivation function like PBKDF2), embedded in another file, received from a server, or stored in secure hardware?

How is the IV generated or obtained?

What specific mode of operation (ECB, CBC, GCM, etc.) is used?

Recovering encryption keys often involves extensive static analysis (tracing data flow related to crypto API calls) and dynamic analysis (setting breakpoints on crypto functions to intercept the key/IV arguments in memory, sometimes requiring bypassing anti-debugging). Successfully recovering encrypted data requires overcoming these significant hurdles to obtain the key material. Simply extracting the encrypted blob is useless without the corresponding key.

Successfully extracting data and, more importantly, correctly interpreting its type, encoding, endianness, and potential transformations like compression or encryption is paramount. It's the process by which raw bytes stored according to a deduced structure are converted back into the meaningful information the software intended to represent.

6.3. Custom File Format Reversing: Navigating the Unknown

let's tackle one of the most challenging and rewarding aspects of reverse engineering: deciphering **Custom File Formats**. We've explored how standard structures like headers, magic numbers, and common data organization patterns bring order to files (Chapter 6.1), and how to extract and correctly interpret data once that structure is known (Chapter 6.2). But what happens when you encounter a file that follows none of the familiar conventions? Perhaps it's a proprietary save game format, a unique configuration file for specialized hardware, a custom data log from industrial equipment, or even how a piece of malware stores its encrypted configuration. There's no public documentation, no obvious magic number, and the internal layout seems entirely alien. This is where true reverse engineering detective work begins, demanding a blend of analytical techniques, creative thinking, and often significant persistence. Unraveling a custom format is like deciphering an unknown language without a Rosetta Stone – you need to find clues, infer rules, and build your understanding piece by piece.

This process rarely relies on a single magic bullet. Instead, it's an interplay between examining the raw data itself and, crucially, analyzing the software that *creates* and *consumes* that data. We'll explore the key strategies employed: leveraging the associated program through static and dynamic analysis, comparing different file versions to isolate changes, hunting for patterns directly within the binary data, forming and testing hypotheses about the structure, and the critical importance of documenting your findings throughout the journey.

The Prime Suspect: Analyzing the Associated Program

Often, your single most powerful weapon when faced with an unknown file format isn't the file itself, but the **program that reads or writes it**. If you have access to this program (e.g., the game executable that loads the save file, the configuration utility that uses the .dat file, or even the malware sample itself), you can apply the static and dynamic analysis techniques we've already covered (Chapters 4 and 5) specifically focusing on how the program interacts with the file data. This provides invaluable, direct insight into the format's structure and meaning, as the code *must* implicitly contain the logic for parsing and interpreting the bytes.

Static Analysis: Following the Code's Interaction with Data

Using your disassembler and decompiler (IDA Pro, Ghidra, etc.), your goal is to pinpoint the code sections responsible for file input/output (I/O). This involves searching for calls to known file handling functions:

Standard C/C++ Libraries: Look for functions like fopen, fclose, fread, fwrite, fseek, ftell, fscanf, fprintf. In C++, also look for interactions with stream objects like ifstream::read, ofstream::write, istream::seekg, ostream::seekp.

OS-Specific APIs:

On Windows: CreateFileW / CreateFileA, ReadFile, WriteFile, SetFilePointer / SetFilePointerEx, CloseHandle.

On Linux/Unix: The underlying system calls often wrapped by libc: open/openat, close, read, write, lseek.

Framework-Specific APIs: If the application uses frameworks like .NET or Java, look for their file handling classes (System.IO.FileStream, System.IO.BinaryReader/Writer in C#; java.io.FileInputStream, java.io.FileOutputStream, java.io.DataInputStream/OutputStream in Java). Once you locate potential file I/O calls (using import table analysis, string searches for filenames, or xrefs to file-related functions), the crucial next step is to analyze the **surrounding code**:

Identify Buffers: Where is the data being read *into*, or where is it being assembled *before* being written? Look at the arguments passed to the read/write functions. The buffer argument (often a pointer passed in a register like RSI or pushed onto the stack) tells you where the data resides in memory just after a read or just before a write. Analyze how this memory buffer is declared (is it a fixed-size stack buffer? A dynamically allocated heap buffer via malloc/new?) and how it's accessed. Observing code accessing [buffer_pointer + 0x4], [buffer_pointer + 0x8], etc., strongly suggests fields within a data structure being read from or written to the file. Apply data flow analysis (Chapter 4.3) backward from the buffer pointer argument in a write call (to see how the structure was populated) or forward from the buffer pointer after a read call (to see how the read data is parsed and used).

Track Sizes: How much data is being read or written in each call? Look at the size and count arguments passed to functions like fread or fwrite, or the nNumberOfBytesToRead/Write argument in ReadFile/WriteFile. Is it a fixed constant size (suggesting fixed-size records or fields)? Is the size read from another variable or calculated just before the call (suggesting length-prefixed variable data or dynamically sized chunks)? Tracing how these size arguments are determined is critical for understanding the structure.

Analyze Offsets: How does the program navigate within the file? Look for calls to seeking functions (fseek, lseek, SetFilePointer). What determines the offset value passed to these functions? Is it a fixed constant? Is it read from a header field or calculated based on previously read sizes? This reveals how the program jumps between different sections or records within the file.

Looping Constructs: Often, files contain multiple records or entries. Look for loops (identified via control flow analysis, Chapter 4.2) that enclose file read or write operations. How does the loop determine when to stop? Does it read a record_count from the header and loop that many times? Does it read until fread returns 0 (End Of File)? Does it check for a specific sentinel value or record type marker? Understanding the looping mechanism reveals how sequences of data entries are handled.

Data Processing Logic: Examine the code immediately *after* a read operation or immediately *before* a write operation. How is the data in the buffer manipulated? Are values endian-swapped? Are fields extracted and stored into program variables or objects? Are values calculated and then formatted before being written? Is data being compressed/decompressed (inflate/deflate) or encrypted/decrypted (CryptEncrypt/CryptDecrypt) before writing or after reading? This code directly reflects the interpretation and encoding rules of the file format.

Conceptual Example: Disassembly Snippet around fread
    ; Assume RDI holds FILE* stream pointer
; Assume RBP-30h is allocated for a Record structure buffer

```
loc_ReadLoopStart:
   lea      rsi, [rbp-30h]     ; RSI = destination buffer
(&record_buffer)
   mov      edx, 18h           ; EDX = size per element (0x18 =
24 bytes)
   mov      ecx, 1             ; ECX = number of elements to read
(1 record)
   ; RDI already holds FILE*
   call     _fread             ; call fread(&record_buffer, 24,
1, stream)
```

; Check return value (number of elements read)
```
   cmp      rax, 1             ; Did fread return 1 (success)?
   jnz      loc_ReadLoopEnd    ; If not 1 (likely 0 for EOF),
exit loop
```

; Process the record read into [rbp-30h]
```
   mov      eax, [rbp-30h+4]   ; Load field at offset +4 from
buffer into EAX
   mov      [rbp-40h], eax     ; Store it somewhere else (e.g., a
local variable)
   movzx    ecx, word ptr [rbp-30h+14h] ; Load word at offset
+0x14 into ECX (zero-extend)
   call     ProcessRecordValue ; Call function, potentially
passing values
```

```
    jmp     loc_ReadLoopStart ; Jump back to read next record
loc_ReadLoopEnd:
    ; ... loop finished ...
```

RE Interpretation: This snippet clearly shows:

* A loop (loc_ReadLoopStart to jmp loc_ReadLoopStart).

* A call to fread attempting to read 1 element of size 24 bytes (0x18) into a buffer located at [rbp-30h] on the stack. This strongly implies a fixed-size record structure of 24 bytes.

* The return value of fread (rax) is checked against 1 to detect the end of the file or an error, controlling the loop exit via jnz.

* Inside the loop (after successful read), specific offsets *within* the buffer are accessed (+4, +14h). [rbp-30h+4] likely reads the second field (assuming the first is at +0), suggesting it's a 4-byte field (since eax is used). [rbp-30h+14h] reads a 2-byte field (word ptr) at offset 20 (0x14).

* This immediately tells the analyst the file contains fixed-size 24-byte records, and reveals the likely size and location of at least two fields within that record structure. Analyzing ProcessRecordValue would reveal how the field at offset 0x14 is used.

Dynamic Analysis: Observing Live File Interactions

Static analysis shows potential interactions; dynamic analysis using a debugger confirms them and reveals runtime data.

Breakpoint on I/O Functions: Set breakpoints on the specific file I/O functions identified statically (fread, WriteFile, ReadFile, etc.).

Examine Buffers on Break: When the breakpoint hits *before* a WriteFile or fwrite, examine the contents of the source memory buffer being passed as an argument. This shows you the exact bytes being written to the file, reflecting the program's serialization logic. When the breakpoint hits *after* a ReadFile or fread, examine the destination buffer; this shows the raw bytes just read from the file before any parsing.

Inspect Sizes and Offsets: Check the values of the arguments specifying the number of bytes to read/write or the file offset for seeking. Are they constants? Are they values loaded from other memory locations (which you can then examine)? This confirms size information and navigation logic.

Check Return Values: After an I/O call returns, examine the return value (usually in EAX/RAX). Did the operation succeed? Did ReadFile/fread return the expected number of bytes? Error codes (retrieved via GetLastError() on Windows or checking errno on Linux) provide specific reasons for failures.

Trace Data Processing: After a successful ReadFile/fread, single-step (step into/step over) through the subsequent instructions. Watch exactly how the data loaded into the buffer is accessed, parsed, converted (endian swap?), and stored into program variables or structures. This provides ground truth on how the program interprets the file data. Similarly, before a WriteFile/fwrite, step *backward* or set earlier breakpoints to see how the data buffer being written was constructed.

Call Stack Context: When a breakpoint on an I/O function hits, always examine the **call stack**. This tells you *which part* of the program initiated the file operation. Is it happening during initialization? In response to a user action (like "Save")? Within a background processing loop? This provides crucial context about *why* the file is being accessed at that moment. Combining static analysis (to find the I/O locations and understand the surrounding code structure) with dynamic analysis (to see the actual data being transferred and processed at runtime) is often the most effective way to definitively reverse engineer a custom file format when the associated program is available. The code *is* the specification, and analyzing its interaction with the file reveals that specification.

Differential Analysis: Finding Meaning in Change

What if static/dynamic analysis of the program is too difficult (heavy obfuscation, complex code), or you don't have the program, only file samples? Another powerful technique, particularly effective for files that represent application state (like configuration files, user profiles, or especially **save game files**), is **Comparison** or **Diffing**. The principle is simple: if you can make a small, known change within the application and observe the resulting changes in the saved file, you can correlate the two and map specific data fields.

The Process:

Establish Baseline: Generate or obtain a starting version of the file (File A). Let's say it's a game save where your character has 100 health points.

Introduce Minimal Change: Perform *one specific, small, quantifiable action* within the application that will alter the saved state. For example, in the game, lose exactly 5 health points, so health is now 95. Make *no other changes* if possible (don't move, don't pick up items).

Generate Second State: Save the game again, creating File B.

Perform Binary Diff: Use a **binary diffing tool** to compare File A and File B. Crucially, use a tool designed for binary files, not text files. Text diff tools assume lines of text and will likely produce useless results for binary formats. Tools like VBinDiff, Meld (which can handle binary comparison), HxD (File -> Compare), 010 Editor (Tools -> Compare Files), or even simple command-line tools like cmp -l fileA fileB (on Linux, shows differing byte offsets and values) are suitable.

Analyze Differences: The diff tool will highlight the exact byte offsets where File A and File B differ. Examine these highlighted bytes.

Correlate: Since the *only* intentional change you made in the application was decreasing health from 100 to 95, the differing bytes *must* somehow represent the character's health value. Look at the highlighted bytes. Do they look like numbers? Perhaps a 4-byte integer? Try interpreting the bytes from File A at that offset as an integer (considering both little- and big-endian). Does it yield 100? Now interpret the bytes from File B at the same offset. Does it yield 95? If yes, you've successfully located the memory location storing the player's health! Note the offset, size (e.g., 4 bytes), type (integer), and endianness.

Repeat and Refine: Now, repeat the process with another minimal change. Increase score by 10 points. Save. Diff. Find the changed bytes and map the score field. Pick up one specific item. Save. Diff. Map the inventory slot or item ID field. Toggle a single configuration setting. Save. Diff. Map the flag byte or setting value. By making small, isolated changes and comparing the resulting files, you can incrementally build up a detailed map of the file format's structure and the meaning of various fields.

Code Example: Simple Python Binary Differ

This script provides a basic byte-level comparison, highlighting differing offsets and values.

```python
#!/usr/bin/env python3
# -*- coding: utf-8 -*-

import argparse
import os

def compare_binary_files(file1_path: str, file2_path: str,
max_diffs: int = 100):
```

Compares two binary files byte-by-byte and reports differences.

```
    Args:
        file1_path: Path to the first file.
        file2_path: Path to the second file.
        max_diffs: Maximum number of differences to report.
Set to 0 for all.
```

Returns:

```
        None. Prints differences to the console.
    """
    if not os.path.exists(file1_path):
        print(f"Error: File not found '{file1_path}'")
        return
    if not os.path.exists(file2_path):
        print(f"Error: File not found '{file2_path}'")
        return
```

try:

```
        size1 = os.path.getsize(file1_path)
        size2 = os.path.getsize(file2_path)
        diff_count = 0
        reported_diff_count = 0

        print(f"Comparing '{os.path.basename(file1_path)}'
({size1} bytes) vs. '{os.path.basename(file2_path)}' ({size2}
bytes)")

        # Handle size differences first
        if size1 != size2:
            print(f"Warning: Files have different sizes
({size1} vs {size2} bytes). Comparison limited to the smaller
size.")
            compare_limit = min(size1, size2)
        else:
            compare_limit = size1
```

Open files and compare byte by byte

```
        with open(file1_path, 'rb') as f1, open(file2_path,
'rb') as f2:
            for offset in range(compare_limit):
                byte1 = f1.read(1)
                byte2 = f2.read(1)

                if byte1 != byte2:
                    diff_count += 1
```

```python
                        if max_diffs == 0 or reported_diff_count
< max_diffs:
                            # Report difference (Offset, File1
byte, File2 byte)
                            print(f"  Offset 0x{offset:08X}:
{byte1.hex().upper()} != {byte2.hex().upper()}")
                            reported_diff_count += 1
                    elif reported_diff_count == max_diffs:
                        print(f"  ... (Reached max
differences to report: {max_diffs})")
                        reported_diff_count += 1 # Prevent
further reports

                # Simple progress indicator (optional, can
slow down for huge files)
                # if (offset + 1) % (1024 * 1024) == 0:
                #     print(f"  Processed { (offset + 1) //
(1024 * 1024)} MB...")

        print(f"\nComparison finished. Found {diff_count}
differing bytes.")
        if size1 != size2:
            print(f"Note: Only compared up to offset
0x{compare_limit-1:X} due to size difference.")
        elif diff_count == 0:
            print("Files are identical.")

    except Exception as e:
        print(f"An error occurred during comparison: {e}")

def main():
    parser = argparse.ArgumentParser(description="Compare two
binary files and show differing bytes.")
    parser.add_argument("file1", help="Path to the first
file.")
    parser.add_argument("file2", help="Path to the second
file.")
    parser.add_argument(
        "-m", "--max-diffs", type=int, default=100,
        help="Maximum number of differences to display (0
for all). Default: 100"
    )
    args = parser.parse_args()
    compare_binary_files(args.file1, args.file2,
args.max_diffs)

if __name__ == "__main__":
    main()
```

Using the Differ: Save as bindiff.py. Run like: python bindiff.py save_game_v1.sav save_game_v2.sav. It will output lines like Offset 0x000001A4: 64 != 5F, indicating that at hex offset 1A4, the byte changed from 0x64 (100 decimal) to 0x5F (95 decimal). Correlating this with your known in-game change (health 100 -> 95) pinpoints this byte (or sequence, if multiple differ) as the health field.

Limitations: Diffing works best with uncompressed, unencrypted data where state changes result in localized modifications. If the file format uses heavy compression, encryption across large blocks, or includes constantly changing values like timestamps or checksums covering large sections, simple binary diffing becomes less effective as small logical changes might result in widespread, complex byte differences that are hard to map back meaningfully. It also requires the ability to controllably generate slightly different file versions using the application.

Direct Pattern Analysis: Reading the Binary Tea Leaves

Sometimes you have neither the program nor the ability to generate diffable file versions. You might only have a single sample file. In these cases, you fall back on meticulous **direct pattern analysis** within the hex editor, combined with statistical analysis – essentially trying to read the "tea leaves" of the raw binary data.

Visual Patterns: Look for visually recognizable patterns:

Repeating Bytes: Long sequences of 0x00 (null padding/empty space), 0xFF (sometimes used as uninitialized markers), ASCII spaces (0x20), or other repeating bytes can indicate alignment padding, delimiters, or unused sections.

ASCII/Unicode Text: Use the character view alongside the hex view. Look for any human-readable strings, even short ones or fragments. These might be labels, identifiers, embedded scripts (JSON, XML), configuration directives, or debug messages. Follow up using your tool's string extraction features.

Regular Structures: Do values seem to align consistently on, say, 4-byte or 8-byte boundaries? This often suggests the data is organized into structures where members are aligned for efficient CPU access.

Incrementing/Decrementing Sequences: Sequences like 00 01 02 03 or related values might indicate counters, IDs, or lookup table indices.

Numerical Patterns: Scrutinize sequences of bytes that *might* represent numbers:

Are there values that, when interpreted as 16-bit, 32-bit, or 64-bit integers (try both LE and BE!), seem plausible for common uses like counts, sizes, or offsets (e.g., falling within the file size)?

Are there sequences that match the distinct bit patterns of **IEEE 754 floating-point** numbers (float or double)? These look quite different from integers. Data inspectors in hex editors are vital here. Such sequences often represent coordinates, measurements, or other real-world values.

Are there many bytes that are either 0x00 or 0x01, potentially suggesting boolean flags?

Entropy Analysis: Analyzing the **information density** or **randomness** (entropy) of different sections of the file can provide crucial clues about data encoding. Entropy is typically measured on a scale (e.g., 0 to 8 bits per byte).

Low Entropy Regions: Sections with low entropy (e.g., below 6 or 7, depending on the measure) usually contain data with repeating patterns or limited character sets. This strongly suggests uncompressed structured binary data, plain text (ASCII/UTF-8, often lower entropy than random binary), or regions filled with padding (like zeros, which have very low entropy).

High Entropy Regions: Sections with high entropy (e.g., approaching 8 bits per byte) indicate the data is very close to random. This is the hallmark of **effectively compressed** data (good compression removes redundancy, making data appear more random) or **strongly encrypted** data (good encryption algorithms produce output statistically indistinguishable from random noise).

Tools: Several tools can visualize entropy. binwalk has an entropy analysis option (-E). ImHex can display entropy graphs directly. Kaitai Struct WebIDE includes entropy calculation. Specialized scripts or tools for plotting entropy across a file are also available. Seeing a sharp transition from a low-entropy header/section to a large high-entropy block strongly suggests the start of compressed or encrypted data, guiding further analysis towards finding decompression or decryption routines in the associated code (if available).

Code Example: Simple Shannon Entropy Calculation in Python

```
import math
import os
from collections import Counter
```

```
def calculate_shannon_entropy(data_bytes: bytes) -> float:
    """
    Calculates the Shannon entropy for a given byte sequence.
    Result is in bits per byte (range 0.0 to 8.0).
    Higher values indicate more randomness / less
predictability.
    """
    if not data_bytes:
        return 0.0

    byte_counts = Counter(data_bytes)
    total_bytes = len(data_bytes)
    entropy = 0.0

    for byte_val, count in byte_counts.items():
        probability = count / total_bytes
        # Shannon entropy formula: - sum(p_i * log2(p_i))
        entropy -= probability * math.log2(probability)

    return entropy

# --- Demonstration ---
# Example Data Blocks
text_data = b"This is some sample text data with predictable
patterns."
compressed_data =
b'\x78\x9c\xcb\x48\xcd\xc9\xc9\x57\x28\xcf\x2f\xca\x49\x51\x0
4\x00\x0c\x8e\x04\x7f' # zlib compressed "hellohello"
encrypted_data = os.urandom(100) # Pseudorandom bytes often
resemble encrypted data
null_padding = b'\x00' * 100

# Calculate and print entropy
print(f"Text Data Entropy          :
{calculate_shannon_entropy(text_data):.4f} bits/byte")
print(f"Compressed Data Entropy  :
{calculate_shannon_entropy(compressed_data):.4f} bits/byte")
# Should be relatively high
print(f"Encrypted (Random) Data:
{calculate_shannon_entropy(encrypted_data):.4f} bits/byte") #
Should be close to 8.0
print(f"Null Padding Entropy       :
{calculate_shannon_entropy(null_padding):.4f} bits/byte") #
Will be 0.0
```

Explanation: This function implements the standard Shannon entropy formula. It counts the frequency of each byte value in the input data, calculates the probability of each byte occurring, and sums the -p*log2(p) term for all byte values. Running this demonstrates how different types of data exhibit different entropy levels: text is somewhat predictable (medium entropy), compressed/encrypted data looks random (high entropy), and padding is completely predictable (zero entropy). Analyzing entropy block-by-block across a file can reveal transitions between these data types.

Direct pattern analysis requires more experience and intuition than the other methods. It often yields initial clues or helps segment the file into regions deserving different kinds of closer inspection, rather than providing a complete structural breakdown on its own. However, in the absence of other leads, it's an essential starting point.

The Scientific Method: Hypothesis and Testing

Regardless of which technique(s) you employ – code analysis, diffing, pattern hunting – reverse engineering a custom format fundamentally follows a scientific method:

Observation: Gather clues using the techniques above (code behavior, diff results, hex patterns, entropy).

Hypothesis: Formulate a specific, testable assumption about the file's structure or the meaning of a field. For example: "Based on the diff, the 4 bytes starting at offset 0x1A4 represent the player's gold count as a little-endian unsigned integer." Or, "The code reads a 2-byte value at offset 0x08, multiplies it by 24, and uses that result as an offset for fseek; therefore, the field at 0x08 likely represents a record index or count, and 24 is the record size."

Testing/Experimentation: Design a way to validate or refute your hypothesis.

Consistency Check: Does the hypothesis fit with other observations? If 0x1A4 is the gold count, do nearby fields plausibly represent other player stats? If 0x08 is the record count, does multiplying it by the assumed record size lead to a plausible end-of-records offset within the file?

Predictive Parsing: Based on your hypothesis, try to parse the *next* field or record. Does it yield sensible data according to the assumed structure? Building a parser/template (like the Python/Kaitai/010 examples) is an excellent way to test structural hypotheses systematically. If the parser reads the entire file without errors and extracts seemingly valid data according to your rules, your hypothesis gains strong support.

Controlled Modification (Use with Caution!): This provides strong evidence but carries risks. If you hypothesize field X controls feature Y, carefully modify *only* the bytes corresponding to field X in the file using a hex editor. Load the modified file back into the *original application* (assuming you have it and potentially have bypassed integrity checks). Does feature Y change in the predicted way? For example, changing the bytes at 0x1A4 – does the gold count display differently in the game? Does changing a hypothesized flag bit toggle the corresponding option in the application's settings? If the application crashes, it strongly suggests the bytes you changed were indeed important, though perhaps not in the way you initially thought – the crash itself provides valuable information. If the application ignores the change completely, your hypothesis about that field's function might be wrong, or maybe the application recalculates/overwrites it. This requires careful execution and interpretation.

Refinement/Iteration: If the test validates your hypothesis, integrate it into your growing model of the file format (e.g., document the field in your template or notes). If the test refutes it, discard or modify the hypothesis based on the new evidence and formulate a new one. Continue this cycle of observe-hypothesize-test-refine, incrementally building up your understanding of the format's structure and semantics, field by field, record by record, section by section.

Documentation: The Indispensable Record

Throughout this entire iterative process, **meticulous documentation** is not an optional extra; it's absolutely crucial for success, especially with complex formats. Your brain can only hold so much detail, and you *will* forget earlier findings or lines of reasoning if you don't write them down. Good documentation prevents redundant work, facilitates collaboration if working in a team, and forms the concrete output of your reverse engineering effort. Effective documentation methods include:

In-Tool Annotations: Leverage the commenting and renaming features of your primary analysis tools. Add comments directly in your disassembler/decompiler explaining how specific code processes file data. Rename variables and functions related to file I/O and parsing with meaningful names derived from your analysis.

Parsing Scripts/Templates: As emphasized before, creating a **Kaitai Struct .ksy file**, a **010 Editor .bt template**, or even just a well-commented **Python**

script using struct.unpack is one of the best forms of documentation. The code itself *is* the specification you've uncovered. It's executable, testable, and directly represents the format structure.

Structure Definitions: Define C-style struct definitions within your RE tool (IDA/Ghidra support this) or in external notes, detailing field names, offsets, data types, endianness, and their inferred meanings.

Diagrams: Visual diagrams (created with tools like Draw.io, PlantUML, Mermaid, or even just whiteboard photos) can be incredibly helpful for visualizing the overall file layout, relationships between sections, complex structure nesting, or state machines if the format involves them.

Textual Notes: Maintain separate text files or notes within your project documenting your analysis process, hypotheses tested (both successful and failed), unresolved questions, assumptions made, relevant offsets, flag bit meanings, discovered algorithms (checksums, simple encryption), and links to related resources or code sections.

Record every finding, no matter how small. Note the **offset**, **size**, **data type**, **endianness**, and **inferred meaning** for each field you identify. Document any conditional logic, variable-length encoding methods, or chunk types discovered. Comprehensive documentation transforms a complex RE task from a confusing jumble into a manageable, traceable investigation.

Conclusion: Bringing Structure to Data Through Integrated Techniques

Reverse engineering custom, undocumented file formats is undoubtedly one of the more challenging applications of the RE skillset. Success rarely comes from a single technique but rather from a synergistic combination of approaches tailored to the specific problem. Analyzing the program that interacts with the file, when possible, provides the most direct link between code logic and data representation. Differential analysis offers a powerful experimental method for mapping state changes to specific byte locations, particularly for configuration or save files. Direct pattern hunting in a hex editor, coupled with statistical analysis like entropy calculation, provides essential clues when other methods are unavailable or insufficient. Throughout the process, the iterative cycle of forming hypotheses, testing them through consistency checks, parsing attempts, or controlled modification, and meticulously documenting findings in reusable formats like parsing templates is paramount.

Whether your goal is to enable interoperability for data exchange, recover information from a legacy system, understand how malware stores its configuration, or modify a game save file, mastering these strategies for navigating the unknown is essential. It's a process that demands technical skill in using analysis tools, logical deduction, pattern recognition, patience, and above all, a methodical approach to transforming an opaque sequence of bytes back into structured, meaningful information. You are, in effect, learning to read the software's private language for recording its state and knowledge, one carefully deciphered byte at a time.

Chapter 7: Malware Reverse Engineering

This area is incredibly dynamic, a constant cat-and-mouse game between malware authors and analysts. What you learn today might need adapting tomorrow. But the fundamental principles remain. Let's explore how to classify malware, the specific techniques for dissecting it, and how that analysis leads to defenses.

7.1. Malware Classification and Characteristics: Knowing Your Enemy

let's pivot into a domain where reverse engineering skills are not just useful, but absolutely essential on a daily basis: the challenging and constantly evolving world of **Malware Analysis**. Up until now, we've discussed general software structures, tools, and analysis techniques that apply broadly. Now, we focus these skills onto targets that are actively malicious, designed specifically to harm systems, steal data, or disrupt operations, and crucially, often built with the explicit intention of resisting analysis. Understanding the nature of these threats is the crucial first step. This section, **Malware Classification and Characteristics**, serves as our foundational intelligence briefing – teaching us how to recognize the different kinds of adversaries we face and the common strategies they employ, effectively helping us "know the enemy" before engaging in the technical deep dive.

The Importance of Triage and Classification

When faced with a suspicious file – perhaps an email attachment flagged by security systems, a strange executable downloaded from the web, or an artifact recovered during an incident response investigation – the immediate impulse might be to jump straight into a disassembler or debugger. However, with the sheer volume of potential threats encountered daily, this deep-dive approach for every sample is impractical and inefficient. A more effective strategy begins with **triage** and **classification**. Before investing hours into meticulously dissecting the code, it's incredibly helpful to form a preliminary assessment: What *kind* of malicious program might this be? What is its likely objective? What common behaviors should I anticipate? Malware isn't a single entity; it's a diverse ecosystem of different "species," each evolved for a particular malicious purpose. Trying to analyze ransomware using the exact same checklist and initial focus as analyzing a simple adware dropper would be inefficient. Knowing the likely category helps you prioritize your analysis efforts, anticipate the kinds of techniques the malware might use, and focus your search on the most relevant indicators and functionalities. It provides context, turning a blind investigation into a more guided inquiry.

A Bestiary of Malware: Common Categories and Their Goals

Let's survey some of the major categories of malware frequently encountered by analysts. Keep in mind that modern threats are often sophisticated **hybrids**, blending techniques and functionalities from multiple categories. A single malware sample might act as a downloader initially, then install spyware components, and finally provide backdoor access. Nonetheless, understanding these primary classifications provides a valuable starting framework:

Ransomware: This category has gained significant notoriety due to its direct and often devastating financial impact. The primary goal of ransomware is **extortion**. Typically, it encrypts the victim's valuable files (documents, databases, backups) using strong cryptography, making them inaccessible. It then demands a ransom payment (usually in cryptocurrency like Bitcoin) in exchange for the decryption key. Modern ransomware often adds further extortion layers, such as **data exfiltration** (stealing sensitive data *before* encryption and threatening to leak it publicly if the ransom isn't paid) or threatening **Denial-of-Service (DoS)** attacks.

RE Focus: When analyzing ransomware, key areas of interest include identifying the specific **encryption algorithms** used (AES, Salsa20, RSA are common), understanding how **cryptographic keys** are generated, managed (are they generated locally? communicated with a C&C server?), and stored (or destroyed). You'll look for file system traversal logic (how it finds files to encrypt), the exclusion logic (files/directories it avoids, like system files), the implementation of the encryption loops themselves, and any **Command and Control (C&C)** communication used to obtain keys, report status, or receive payment instructions. Persistence mechanisms are also analyzed to understand how it might reinfect or maintain presence. Sometimes, flaws in the implementation (weak key generation, improper use of crypto APIs) might allow for decryption without paying, making RE crucial, though increasingly rare for sophisticated variants.

Banking Trojans (Bankers): These are specialized trojans focused specifically on **financial theft**. Their goal is typically to steal online banking credentials, credit card numbers, or directly manipulate financial transactions.

RE Focus: Analysis often involves understanding sophisticated techniques like **web injection**, where the malware dynamically modifies legitimate banking websites as they are rendered in the victim's browser, perhaps adding extra fields to login forms to capture security codes or displaying fake messages to trick the user. You'll look for code that hooks browser processes, monitors network traffic (especially HTTPS, often requiring analysis of how it bypasses certificate validation), targets specific banking URLs, or logs keystrokes specifically within browser forms (**form grabbing**). **Keylogging** capabilities targeting banking sessions are common. Exfiltration of stolen data via C&C channels is a critical component to analyze. These trojans are often highly targeted and frequently updated to bypass bank security measures.

Spyware / Keyloggers: This broad category encompasses malware designed for **covert surveillance and information theft**. While sometimes targeted (corporate espionage, nation-state spying), simpler forms might be bundled with other unwanted software.

Keyloggers: Specifically record every keystroke typed by the user, often logging window titles to capture credentials entered into specific applications or websites.

General Spyware: Might go further, capturing screenshots, recording audio via the microphone, activating the webcam, stealing files from specific directories, accessing browser history and stored passwords, or exfiltrating credentials from specific applications (like email clients or FTP software).

RE Focus: Analysis involves identifying the specific **hooking mechanisms** used to intercept keyboard input (e.g., SetWindowsHookEx on Windows, input event device monitoring on Linux), screenshot APIs (BitBlt, screen capture libraries), audio/video capture APIs, file access routines for data theft, browser interaction code, and the C&C mechanism used to exfiltrate the collected information securely and covertly. Persistence and stealth are paramount for spyware to remain undetected over long periods.

Droppers / Downloaders: These often represent the **first stage** of a more complex infection. Their primary purpose is not direct harm but rather to **install other malicious payloads**.

Downloaders: Contain logic to connect to a C&C server or a hardcoded URL, download one or more additional malware files, and then execute them.

Droppers: Have the secondary payload(s) embedded directly within their own code body (often encrypted or compressed). Upon execution, the dropper extracts and writes the payload(s) to disk, then executes them.

RE Focus: The main focus here is understanding the **payload delivery mechanism**. For downloaders, analyze the network communication code (APIs like URLDownloadToFile, WinHttpRequest, socket calls) and identify the download URLs or C&C logic. For droppers, find the code responsible for locating, possibly decrypting or decompressing, and writing the embedded payload to disk (look for large data blobs, decryption routines, WriteFile calls) and the code that subsequently launches it (CreateProcess, ShellExecute). These initial stage tools are often designed to be small and relatively simple to evade initial detection, relying on the downloaded/dropped payload for the main malicious activity. They might have minimal persistence or C&C features for themselves.

Worms: Worms are defined by their ability to **self-propagate**, spreading from one computer system to another, often autonomously. Unlike viruses, they typically don't require attaching to an existing file to spread.

RE Focus: The critical element to analyze is the **propagation mechanism**. How does it find new targets? Does it scan local networks for vulnerable machines? Does it exploit specific software vulnerabilities (like SMB exploits for WannaCry/NotPetya)? Does it spread via removable media (USB drives)? Does it send copies of itself via email or messaging platforms? Analyzing the network scanning code, exploit payloads (shellcode), and replication logic is paramount. Worms often carry other payloads (like installing a backdoor or ransomware), which also require analysis.

Rootkits: These are designed for **ultimate stealth and persistence**, aiming to hide the presence of other malware (or themselves) from the user and security software by fundamentally subverting the operating system itself.

User-Mode Rootkits: Operate in the less privileged user space but use techniques like **API hooking** within multiple processes (injecting DLLs and intercepting calls to file listing, process listing, or network connection APIs) to filter out results and hide malicious files, processes, or network activity from view by standard tools.

Kernel-Mode Rootkits: These are far more powerful and dangerous, running with the highest OS privileges (Ring 0). They can directly modify core OS data structures and code in memory. Common techniques include hooking the **System Service Dispatch Table (SSDT)** or **Interrupt Descriptor Table (IDT)** to intercept system calls or hardware interrupts, using **Direct Kernel Object Manipulation (DKOM)** to hide processes by removing them from the kernel's internal linked lists, installing malicious filter drivers (for file system, network stack, or keyboard), or patching kernel code directly. UEFI/BIOS rootkits (Bootkits) are even deeper, compromising the system *before* the main OS even loads.

RE Focus: Analyzing rootkits is highly complex. User-mode rootkits require analyzing process injection, extensive API hooking code (identifying detours and filter logic), and inter-process communication. Kernel-mode rootkit analysis requires specialized tools (like WinDbg configured for kernel debugging, often needing a two-machine setup), deep understanding of OS internals specific to the target kernel version, and the ability to analyze kernel-mode assembly code and driver interaction models. Identifying DKOM requires comparing kernel structure data in memory against expected states. Bootkit analysis often involves reversing firmware (BIOS/UEFI) and understanding the secure boot process. The primary goal is to understand *how* the rootkit achieves stealth and identify the modifications it makes so they can be detected and potentially reversed.

Viruses: The classic form of malware, though perhaps less prevalent now than Trojans or ransomware as the primary threat. Viruses are defined by their need to **infect other legitimate files** (executables, scripts, sometimes document macros) by inserting a copy of their own malicious code into the target file. When the infected host file is executed, the virus code runs first, potentially performing a payload action and then attempting to infect other files before (hopefully) transferring control back to the original host code.

RE Focus: Analysis centers on the **infection logic**. How does the virus find target files? What types of files does it infect? How does it insert its code (prepending, appending, finding code caves/cavities, overwriting)? How does it modify the host file's entry point or structure to ensure its own code executes first? Understanding this is key to detecting infected files and potentially disinfecting them (which can be difficult without damaging the host).

Adware / Potentially Unwanted Programs (PUPs): This category occupies a gray area. **Adware** primarily focuses on displaying unwanted advertisements (pop-ups, injected banners) to the user, often by installing browser toolbars, Browser Helper Objects (BHOs), or modifying browser settings. **PUPs** might bundle adware, change browser settings (homepage, search engine), install unnecessary software, or collect user data for marketing purposes, often with dubious consent obtained during installation of other "free" software. While not always strictly "malicious" in the sense of stealing data or destroying files, their behavior is often deceptive, privacy-invasive, and degrades system performance and user experience.

RE Focus: Analysis often involves identifying browser modification techniques, analyzing installer bundles to see what else gets installed, tracing network communication for downloading ad content or configurations, and understanding persistence mechanisms (often less sophisticated than malware but still annoying). Legal considerations can be complex here, as adware/PUP distributors often try to operate within the bounds of vague EULA clauses.

Common Characteristics: The Malware Analyst's Mental Checklist

While the specific payloads and goals differ across these categories, many malware families share common underlying operational requirements and, therefore, exhibit recurring characteristics and behaviors that analysts specifically look for. Recognizing these common patterns helps orient the investigation regardless of the initial classification.

Persistence: Malware rarely wants to be a one-shot affair; it needs to survive system reboots and ensure it continues running long after the initial infection vector (e.g., a malicious email attachment being opened) is gone. Achieving persistence is therefore a primary objective. Analysts constantly hunt for evidence of common persistence techniques:

Registry Run Keys (Windows): Adding entries (paths to the malware executable) under keys like HKCU\Software\Microsoft\Windows\CurrentVersion\Run,

HKLM\Software\Microsoft\Windows\CurrentVersion\Run (and RunOnce variants) is one ofclassName='markdown formatted double-spaced'd persistence mechanisms. Analysis involves checking for RegSetValueEx calls targeting these specific keys.

Scheduled Tasks (Windows/Linux): Creating tasks that automatically launch the malware at specific times (e.g., system startup, user login) using the Task Scheduler service (schtasks.exe, at command) or cron (Linux). Look for APIs related to task scheduling or execution of scheduler commands.

Services (Windows/Linux): Installing the malware as a system service (Systemd unit files, init.d scripts on Linux; CreateService, StartService APIs on Windows) ensures it runs automatically in the background, often with system privileges.

Startup Folders (Windows): Placing shortcuts (.lnk files) or copies of the malware executable in the user's or All Users' Startup folders.

Advanced/Obscure Techniques: Malware increasingly uses less common methods to avoid detection: Windows Management Instrumentation (WMI) event subscriptions that trigger malware execution based on system events, DLL Hijacking (placing a malicious DLL where a legitimate application expects to find one, causing the app to load the malware), COM object hijacking (replacing registry entries for legitimate COM objects to point to malware), Browser Helper Objects (BHOs), boot sector infections (Bootkits), UEFI firmware implants, and many others. Identifying these requires deeper system knowledge and analysis of less common APIs or system modifications.

Analyzing the specific WriteFile, RegSetValueEx, CreateService, CreateProcess calls and their parameters related to these mechanisms is key.

Command and Control (C&C or C2) Communication: Many types of malware, particularly trojans, ransomware (for key exchange/reporting), botnets, and spyware, need to communicate with their operators or infrastructure residing elsewhere on the internet. This C&C channel serves multiple purposes:

Receiving Instructions: Telling a bot what DDoS target to attack, instructing spyware what data to collect, telling ransomware where to send victim IDs.

Exfiltrating Data: Sending stolen credentials, logged keystrokes, sensitive files, or system information back to the attacker.

Downloading Updates/Payloads: Fetching newer versions of the malware or downloading additional malicious modules.

Reporting Status: Confirming successful infection ("beaconing"), reporting system information.

RE Focus: Analyzing C&C communication is paramount. Look for calls to **networking APIs** (socket, connect, send, recv, HttpSendRequest, InternetConnect, etc.). Identify the **remote endpoints** (IP addresses or domain names – hardcoded strings? decrypted dynamically?). Understand the **protocol** used:

HTTP/HTTPS: Very common. Analyze the URLs, HTTP methods (GET/POST), custom headers, user-agent strings, and the format of data sent/received (often URL-encoded, JSON, or custom binary, possibly encrypted/encoded within the HTTP body). HTTPS requires dealing with TLS encryption (often involving bypassing certificate validation dynamically).

DNS Tunneling: Abusing the DNS protocol itself to encode data within lookup requests or responses, often used for stealthy C&C as DNS traffic is less frequently blocked or inspected deeply. Look for unusual DNS query patterns or large/non-standard DNS records.

IRC / Other Protocols: Older botnets often used IRC channels for C&C. Custom TCP or UDP protocols are also common, requiring careful reverse engineering of the message formats and sequences by analyzing network captures alongside the code handling send/recv.

Domain Generation Algorithms (DGAs): Sophisticated malware doesn't rely on hardcoded domains (which are easily blocklisted). Instead, it uses a DGA – an algorithm (often based on the current date/time or other seeds) to generate a large number of potential C&C domain names pseudo-randomly. The attackers only need to register one or a few of these generated domains for the malware to find its C&C server. Reverse engineering the DGA algorithm itself is necessary to predict future C&C domains and proactively block them.

Analyzing network traffic captures (PCAPs) in conjunction with reversing the code responsible for building and parsing the network messages is standard practice.

Stealth (Evasion & Anti-Analysis): Malware authors desperately want their creations to remain undetected by security software (Antivirus, EDR) and to frustrate or prevent analysis by reverse engineers. Therefore, incorporating stealth techniques is almost universal. This directly overlaps with the Software Protection mechanisms discussed in Chapter 8, but employed for malicious ends. Common techniques include:

Packing and Obfuscation: Compressing or encrypting the main payload, using polymorphic/metamorphic engines to change the code's appearance, employing control flow flattening, encrypting strings, inserting junk code – all designed to break static signatures and confuse disassemblers/decompilers. Analysis requires unpacking (often dynamically) and dealing with the obfuscation layers.

Dynamic API Resolution: Avoiding direct imports of suspicious API functions (which AV scanners often look for). Instead, manually loading libraries (LoadLibrary/dlopen) and resolving function addresses at runtime (GetProcAddress/dlsym), often using hashed function names rather than clear text strings.

Anti-VM / Anti-Sandbox: Detecting execution within virtualized or automated sandbox environments and altering behavior (e.g., exiting, running benign code only) to avoid generating a malicious report. Analysis requires hardening the environment or patching the checks.

Anti-Debugging: Detecting the presence of attached debuggers (using APIs like IsDebuggerPresent, timing tricks, exception handling checks) and exiting or crashing if found. Requires using stealthier debugging techniques or patching the checks.

Rootkit Techniques: Employing user-mode or kernel-mode methods to hide processes, files, network connections, or registry keys from standard system tools and potentially even security software.

Living off the Land (LotL): Minimizing the deployment of custom malicious binaries by instead leveraging legitimate tools already present on the system (PowerShell, WMI, certutil, Bitsadmin, rundll32, etc.) via scripts or commands to perform malicious actions. This makes detection based on malicious files harder, shifting focus to anomalous *behavior* of legitimate tools.

Dealing with these stealth techniques is a core part of the malware RE process, often requiring significant effort before the actual core payload logic can even be reached. The specific countermeasures employed by analysts will be explored in later sections.

Payload: Finally, there is the **payload** – the ultimate reason the malware exists, the core malicious action it performs after potentially achieving persistence, establishing C&C, and evading initial detection. The nature of the payload defines the malware's primary category:

Encrypting files (Ransomware)

Stealing credentials/data (Trojans, Spyware, Keyloggers)

Providing remote access (Backdoors, RATs)

Launching DDoS attacks (Bots)

Spreading to other systems (Worms)

Displaying ads (Adware)

Corrupting data or wiping disks (Wipers)

Analyzing the payload involves reverse engineering the specific code sections responsible for these actions – the encryption loops, the input hooking functions, the data exfiltration routines, the network flooding logic, the file infection algorithms, etc. This is often where the deepest and most time-consuming code analysis takes place, requiring the full range of static and dynamic RE techniques.

Conclusion: Context is Key

Understanding malware classification and common characteristics provides crucial context that transforms malware reverse engineering from a potentially random exploration into a more structured, hypothesis-driven investigation. By making an educated guess about the malware's likely category (Ransomware? Trojan? Downloader?) based on initial indicators (delivery method, filenames, strings, preliminary sandbox results) and keeping the common operational characteristics (Persistence, C&C, Stealth, Payload) in mind as a mental checklist, the analyst can:

Focus Efforts: Prioritize looking for specific types of API calls, registry keys, network protocols, or code patterns associated with the suspected category.

Anticipate Behavior: Know what kind of actions to expect during dynamic analysis (e.g., expect network connections for a Trojan, expect file encryption attempts for ransomware).

Interpret Findings: Place observed behaviors or code sections into a meaningful framework related to the malware's likely objectives.

Identify Key IOCs: Know what types of indicators (registry keys for persistence, C&C domains, dropped filenames) are most relevant to extract for defense based on the malware type.

This initial intelligence gathering and contextual understanding phase doesn't replace the need for detailed code-level analysis, but it makes that analysis significantly more efficient and effective. It helps you know *what* you're looking for and *why* certain behaviors are significant in the broader narrative of the malware's operation.

7.2. Dissecting Malicious Code: Peeling Back the Layers of Deception

let's sharpen our focus and delve into the specifics of **Dissecting Malicious Code**. This is where the art of reverse engineering shifts from a potentially neutral analysis of complex systems into a direct confrontation with an adversary. While the fundamental tools and techniques we've discussed – disassemblers, debuggers, system monitors, instrumentation frameworks – remain our primary instruments, the *context* changes dramatically. Unlike typical software development where clarity and maintainability are often goals, malware authors actively strive for the opposite. They build defenses, lay traps, and employ layers of deception specifically designed to hinder, mislead, and ultimately defeat analysis. Therefore, reverse engineering malware becomes less like deciphering a complex but well-intentioned manual and more like carefully navigating a booby-trapped maze, systematically peeling back layers of protection to reveal the dangerous mechanism hidden within.

The Paramount Rule: Analysis Safety and Isolation

Before we even consider loading a suspicious file into a tool, the absolute, non-negotiable first principle is **safety**. Malware is, by definition, designed to be harmful. Accidentally executing it on your primary workstation, a machine connected to your personal or corporate network, or any system containing sensitive data can have catastrophic consequences – data loss, financial theft, network compromise, becoming part of a botnet, and more. Therefore, all malware analysis, especially dynamic analysis involving execution, *must* be conducted within a strictly **controlled and isolated environment**.

Virtual Machines (VMs): The Standard Containment: As established when discussing virtualization fundamentals (Chapter 5.3), using **Virtual Machines** is the cornerstone of safe malware analysis. Software like VMware Workstation/Player, Oracle VirtualBox, or KVM/QEMU allows you to run a guest operating system (typically Windows or Linux, matching the malware's target) completely isolated from your host machine.

Containment: Any actions the malware takes (file deletion, registry changes, encryption) are restricted to the VM's virtual disk and memory.

Snapshots: The ability to take snapshots of the VM's state is critical. Set up a "clean" analysis environment with your tools pre-installed, take a snapshot, analyze the malware, and then simply **revert** to the clean snapshot afterwards. This instantly removes all traces of the malware and prepares the environment for the next sample, saving countless hours compared to manually cleaning or rebuilding. It also allows you to return to specific intermediate states during a complex analysis run if needed.

Network Isolation: VMs offer flexible network configuration. For initial analysis, configure the VM's network adapter to be **disconnected** or set to **"Host-Only"** networking. This prevents the malware from immediately contacting external Command and Control (C&C) servers or spreading laterally across your physical network. For analyses requiring network interaction simulation, tools like **FakeNet-NG** or **INetSim** are essential. These tools run either on the host or in a separate dedicated "gateway" VM and intercept network traffic originating from the analysis VM. They can simulate responses to common protocols like DNS (resolving any domain to a controlled IP), HTTP/S (serving predefined or custom files), SMTP, FTP, IRC, etc. This tricks the malware into thinking it's online, potentially revealing C&C communication patterns, downloaded secondary payloads, or exfiltration attempts, all within a safe, controlled environment. Never connect an analysis VM directly to the internet or your main network unless you have a very specific reason, understand the risks completely, and have implemented appropriate external network security controls.

Dedicated Hardware (Less Common): In some high-security environments or for analyzing malware with extremely sophisticated anti-VM techniques, analysts might use physically separate ("air-gapped") machines dedicated solely to malware analysis. This provides the ultimate level of isolation but is less flexible and more resource-intensive than using VMs.

Treat Every Sample as Loaded: Assume every unknown sample is dangerous until proven otherwise through careful analysis. Handle files carefully, avoid accidental execution outside the isolated environment, and maintain strict separation between your analysis setup and your everyday work systems. There is no room for carelessness when dissecting malicious code.

Challenge 1: Packers and Protectors – Piercing the Outer Shell
Often, the very first obstacle a malware analyst encounters isn't the core malicious logic itself, but rather an outer protective layer known as a **packer**, **crypter**, or **protector**. Malware authors frequently use these tools for several reasons:

Evading Static Signatures: Antivirus scanners often rely on finding specific byte sequences (signatures) associated with known malware. Packing compresses or encrypts the original malware code, replacing it with a different structure (the packer "stub"). This changes the file's signature, allowing it to bypass simple signature-based detection, at least until the specific packed version is analyzed and new signatures are created.

Hindering Static Analysis: Since the actual malicious code isn't directly visible in the packed file's static disassembly, initial static analysis becomes much less effective. Analysts are confronted only with the packer stub's code, which is often relatively small and designed primarily to unpack the real payload.

Adding Anti-Analysis Features: Commercial protectors and even some sophisticated custom packers often incorporate anti-debugging and anti-VM techniques directly into the stub, making even the *unpacking process* difficult to observe.

Identification: How do you know if a file is packed? Several clues can help:
Signature Tools: Utilities like **PEiD** (older but classic), **Detect It Easy (DiE)**, or Exeinfo PE are specifically designed to scan executable files and compare their characteristics against databases of known packers, cryptors, protectors, and compilers. They might report "UPX packed," "Themida/WinLicense," "ASPack," "FSG," etc.

Section Characteristics: Packed executables often have unusual PE section names (e.g., .UPX0, .UPX1, .aspack) or sections with non-standard permissions (e.g., a section marked both Writable and Executable RWX, potentially where the code will be unpacked). The entry point might reside in a section different from the usual .text section.

High Entropy: The section containing the packed/encrypted data will typically exhibit very high entropy (close to 8 bits per byte), appearing random in a hex editor, whereas the small packer stub itself might have normal code entropy. Entropy analysis tools (binwalk -E, visualizers) can highlight this.

Few Imports: The packer stub often has a very small import table, perhaps only importing functions essential for loading, memory management (VirtualAlloc, VirtualProtect), and execution transfer (LoadLibrary, GetProcAddress might be present but less common than in unpacked code). The *real* imports needed by the malicious payload are typically resolved dynamically by the packer or the unpacked code itself.

Unusual Entry Point Code: The code at the entry point might look like a typical packer stub: often pushing all registers onto the stack (PUSHAD/PUSHFD), performing calculations likely related to finding module base addresses or decrypting data, calling memory allocation/protection functions, and ending with a jump or indirect call that transfers control to the unpacked code.

The Unpacking Process: Dynamic Analysis is Key

Since static analysis of the packed file is limited, unpacking almost always requires **dynamic analysis** using a debugger. The general strategy is to allow the packer stub to execute its unpacking routine in memory and then intercept execution just *before* control is transferred to the newly unpacked, original malicious code. This critical location is known as the **Original Entry Point (OEP)**.

The Typical Unpacking Workflow in a Debugger (e.g., x64dbg):

Load the Packed File: Open the packed executable in your debugger (running inside your safe VM!). The debugger will likely pause at the system loader's entry point or just before the packer stub's entry point code.

Set Initial Breakpoints Strategically: Don't just single-step from the beginning (packers can be complex). Set breakpoints on APIs commonly used for allocating executable memory or changing memory permissions, as the packer needs to create a space for the unpacked code and mark it as executable. Key Windows APIs include:

kernel32!VirtualAlloc / ntdll!NtAllocateVirtualMemory: Allocates new memory regions.

kernel32!VirtualProtect / ntdll!NtProtectVirtualMemory: Changes the protection flags (Read/Write/Execute) of existing memory regions. Packers often allocate writable memory, write the unpacked code, then use VirtualProtect to change it to Read/Execute (RX) before jumping to it. Sometimes kernel32!WriteProcessMemory (if unpacking into another process, less common for simple packers).

Run to Breakpoint: Execute the program (F9). It will likely hit one of your memory management breakpoints. Examine the arguments (especially the requested size and protection flags) and the return value (the allocated memory address).

Monitor Memory Writes: Set **memory breakpoints** (often hardware breakpoints for efficiency and stealth) on the newly allocated writable memory region returned by VirtualAlloc or the region targeted by VirtualProtect. Resume execution (F9). The debugger should now break when the packer stub *writes* the unpacked bytes into this memory region. You might hit this breakpoint multiple times as the code is written, possibly in chunks or after decryption loops.

Find the Control Transfer: Once the unpacking *appears* complete (e.g., VirtualProtect has been called to make the section executable, or the write breakpoints stop triggering), the next crucial step is to find the instruction where the packer stub transfers execution *to* the unpacked code (the OEP). This is often achieved via:

A direct JMP to the start address of the unpacked section.

An indirect jump like JMP EAX where EAX holds the OEP address.

A PUSH OEP_Address; RETN sequence (acting like a jump).

A CALL followed immediately by function logic that never returns normally but acts as the entry point.

You need to carefully step through the code *after* the final memory write or VirtualProtect call, watching for these types of control transfers pointing into the newly executable region. Setting an execution hardware breakpoint at the beginning of the unpacked region can also help catch this transition.

Identify the OEP Address: Note the precise memory address where the unpacked code begins execution. This is your OEP.

Dump the Unpacked Code: Once execution is paused *at* or just *before* the OEP, the unpacked malicious code resides in memory. Now you need to dump it to a file for offline static analysis. Use your debugger's memory dumping features or specialized tools like **Scylla** or **PE-sieve**. You need to specify the starting address (the base address of the unpacked module, often the same as the address returned by VirtualAlloc if it allocated a new region) and the size of the memory region to dump (often found in the PE header if the packer reconstructed one in memory, or guessed).

Fix the Dump (Optional but Recommended): The raw memory dump often isn't a perfectly valid executable file. The packer might not have rebuilt the PE headers correctly in memory, or more commonly, the **Import Address Table (IAT)** will be broken. The packer resolved API addresses dynamically during unpacking and filled the IAT in memory, but these resolved addresses are specific to that particular execution instance (due to ASLR) and won't be valid if you load the dumped file later. Tools like **Scylla** excel at **IAT reconstruction**. While attached with a debugger just before the OEP, Scylla can scan memory, analyze the packer's initialized IAT, and rebuild a functional IAT within the dumped file, making static analysis tools like IDA/Ghidra much happier and more effective when analyzing the dump. You'll also typically need to set the OEP address correctly in the dumped file's headers.

Conceptual Code Snippet: Debugger Commands/Actions
Imagine analyzing with x64dbg inside a VM:

```
// 1. Load packed_malware.exe in x64dbg


// 2. Set breakpoints on memory APIs
bp kernel32!VirtualAlloc
bp kernel32!VirtualProtect


// 3. Run (F9). Program breaks at VirtualAlloc.
//   Note arguments (size, protection RW), return value (allocated address,
e.g., 0x6A0000)


// 4. Set memory breakpoint on write to the allocated region
//   (Go to Memory Map tab, find region 0x6A0000, right-click ->
Breakpoint -> Memory, On Write)
```

//   OR use hardware breakpoint: 'bphw RVA_of_allocated_mem, w, 1' (watch 1 byte for write) - syntax varies

// 5. Run (F9). Might break multiple times on memory write. Let it continue.
//   Eventually breaks at VirtualProtect. Note arguments (address=0x6A0000, new_protection=PAGE_EXECUTE_READ)

// 6. Carefully STEP (F8/F7) after VirtualProtect returns. Watch for JMPs/CALLs into 0x6Axxxx region.
//   Suppose we find: JMP 0x6A1234 <<< This is likely the OEP!

// 7. Note OEP = 0x6A1234. Base Address of module seems to be 0x6A0000.

// 8. Use a dumping plugin (Scylla plugin in x64dbg):
//   Launch Scylla, select the process, enter OEP (relative to base = 0x1234), click 'IAT Autosearch', then 'Get Imports', then 'Dump PE' (saving as unpacked.exe), and optionally 'Fix Dump' to apply the rebuilt IAT to unpacked.exe.

// 9. Now load unpacked.exe into IDA/Ghidra for static analysis!

Unpacking is often the necessary first step before meaningful analysis of the core malware logic can even begin. While tools like UPX sometimes have standard command-line unpackers (upx -d), malware authors frequently modify common packers or use custom ones specifically to break these standard unpackers, forcing reliance on manual dynamic analysis.

Challenge 2: Code Obfuscation – Creating a Smokescreen

Once unpacked (or if the malware wasn't packed initially), the next layer of defense encountered is typically **Code Obfuscation**. Malware authors deliberately transform their code to make it significantly harder for humans and automated tools to read, understand, and analyze, without changing its ultimate functionality. The goal is to increase the time and effort required for reverse engineering, hoping analysts will give up or make mistakes. Think of it as writing a clear message, then encrypting parts, rearranging sentences, adding meaningless paragraphs, and using obscure synonyms.

Common obfuscation techniques include:

String Encryption/Encoding: Critical strings like C&C domain names, filenames, registry keys, passwords, API names, or even simple error messages are rarely left in plain text where they can be easily found using a string search tool or grep. Instead, they are encrypted (using simple algorithms like XOR with a hardcoded key, RC4, or sometimes stronger ciphers like AES) or encoded (like Base64, Hex, or custom schemes). The malware contains a small decryption/decoding routine that is called only immediately before the string is needed.

De-obfuscation: Requires identifying the encrypted data blobs and the corresponding decryption routine. Static analysis might reveal loops performing XOR operations or calls to known decoding functions. Analyzing the decryption function itself is key – what algorithm is used? Where does the key come from (hardcoded nearby? calculated dynamically?). Once understood, you can often write a simple script (e.g., in Python) to replicate the decryption algorithm and decrypt all strings offline. Alternatively, dynamic analysis is very effective: set a breakpoint *after* the decryption function returns and simply read the decrypted string directly from memory (e.g., from the buffer pointer returned in EAX or passed as an argument). Frida is also excellent for hooking the decryption function and automatically logging the results.

Dynamic API Resolution (Import Obfuscation): As mentioned under packers, malware avoids listing suspicious API calls (like InternetConnect, CreateRemoteThread, SetWindowsHookEx) in its import table. Instead, it dynamically finds the addresses of these functions at runtime. Common methods:

LoadLibrary / GetProcAddress: Manually load the required DLL (LoadLibrary) and then get the function's address by its name (GetProcAddress). The function name itself might be encrypted/obfuscated within the malware.

PEB Walking / Module Parsing: Manually traversing the kernel's **Process Environment Block (PEB)** structure in memory to find lists of loaded modules (DLLs), then parsing the module's export table directly to find function addresses, often without calling GetProcAddress explicitly (a stealthier technique).

API Hashing: The malware stores pre-calculated hash values for the names of the APIs it needs. At runtime, it iterates through functions exported by loaded DLLs (found via PEB walking), calculates the hash of each exported function name using the same algorithm, and compares it to its stored target hashes. When a match is found, it has the address of the needed API. This avoids storing readable API names anywhere in the binary.

De-obfuscation: Requires identifying the resolution logic. Statically, you might find the hashing algorithm (if used) and the list of stored hashes, allowing you to build a lookup table offline (e.g., hash common API names yourself and see which match). Dynamically, setting breakpoints on the indirect CALL instruction that executes the resolved API allows you to see the target address (which you can look up) in the register just before the call. Hooking GetProcAddress (if used) with Frida reveals resolved functions. Analyzing PEB walking code requires careful stepping in the debugger.

Junk Code Insertion / Dead Code: Adding instructions or entire code blocks that have no actual effect on the program's outcome. This might involve sequences like PUSH EAX; POP EAX, performing calculations whose results are never used, or conditional jumps based on opaque predicates (conditions that always evaluate the same way but are hard for static analyzers to determine). The goal is to increase code size, break simple pattern matching, and confuse analysts navigating the disassembly or CFG. Identifying and ignoring junk code often requires careful manual data flow analysis to see which code actually contributes to meaningful results.

Control Flow Flattening: A particularly disruptive technique aimed squarely at confusing CFG visualization and analysis. As described previously, it transforms the natural structured flow (loops, ifs) into a state machine managed by a central dispatcher block. Execution constantly jumps between small "real logic" blocks and the dispatcher, making it incredibly difficult to follow the intended sequence or identify loops/conditionals from the graph alone. Analyzing flattened code often involves meticulously tracing execution paths dynamically, focusing on how the state variable controlling the dispatcher is modified, or using advanced static analysis techniques like symbolic execution or specialized de-flattening algorithms (if available and effective against the specific flattening implementation).

Instruction Substitution / Encoding: Replacing common instructions with more complex or unusual equivalent sequences (e.g., replacing MOV EAX,

0 with XOR EAX, EAX or SUB EAX, EAX). Sometimes involves simple arithmetic obfuscation (e.g., calculating a constant value through convoluted math instead of loading it directly). In extreme cases, it can involve implementing parts of the program using a custom, interpreted **bytecode** running on an embedded **Virtual Machine (VM)**, a technique borrowed from high-end software protectors (VMProtect, Themida). This forces the analyst to first reverse engineer the custom bytecode language and the VM interpreter itself – a massive undertaking.

Successfully dissecting obfuscated malware requires patience and often a combination of techniques. Dynamic analysis is frequently key to observing decrypted strings or resolved APIs. Static analysis helps identify the decryption/resolution/obfuscation routines themselves. Scripting (Python, Frida) can automate the reversal of simpler obfuscation like XOR encryption once the key and algorithm are known. Tackling heavily obfuscated or VM-protected code remains one of the most challenging areas of malware RE.

Challenge 3: Anti-Analysis Techniques – Detecting the Observer

Beyond simply making the code hard to *read* (obfuscation), malware often includes explicit checks designed to detect whether it's being *analyzed* and to alter its behavior if observation is detected. These **Anti-Analysis** (Anti-RE, Anti-Debugging, Anti-VM, Anti-Sandbox) techniques aim to prevent analysts from easily observing the malware's true malicious behavior in a controlled environment.

Common Detection Methods:

Debugger Detection:

API Checks: Calling kernel32!IsDebuggerPresent() (checks a flag in the PEB), kernel32!CheckRemoteDebuggerPresent() (checks another process), or lower-level checks via ntdll!NtQueryInformationProcess with the ProcessDebugPort or ProcessDebugObjectHandle information classes.

Timing Discrepancies: Using instructions like RDTSC (Read Time Stamp Counter) to measure the time taken to execute a small block of code. Debugger single-stepping or breakpoint handling introduces significant overhead, making the execution time much longer when a debugger is attached compared to running normally.

Exception Handling Tricks: Deliberately causing exceptions (like INT 3 software breakpoints, privileged instructions, or invalid memory accesses) and checking how the system's exception handler behaves. Debuggers often alter the default exception handling flow. Checking for software breakpoint opcodes (0xCC) in memory.

Hardware Breakpoint Detection: Trying to set hardware breakpoints and checking if they trigger exceptions as expected (some anti-debug tricks involve manipulating debug registers).

Self-Debugging: Attempting to attach a debugger to its own process; if it succeeds, another debugger wasn't already attached.

VM/Sandbox Detection:

Hardware/BIOS Artifacts: Querying for virtual hardware names/vendors/serial numbers via WMI, registry (HKLM\HARDWARE\DESCRIPTION\System often contains telling strings), or specific CPUID instruction results. Checking for MAC addresses known to belong to VMware/VirtualBox NICs. Looking for BIOS strings common to VMs.

Guest Tools/Drivers/Processes: Checking for the presence of files, directories, running processes (vmtoolsd.exe, VBoxService.exe), registry keys, or specific drivers associated with VMware Tools or VirtualBox Guest Additions.

I/O Port Communication: Some VMs have specific I/O ports used for communication between guest and host (e.g., VMware's backdoor). Malware might try sending commands to these ports.

Global System Artifacts: Checking for low CPU core count, small RAM size, small disk size, presence of common analysis tool installation paths (C:\Analysis), generic usernames (Admin, User, Sandbox), specific window class names used by sandbox environments, or lack of user activity metrics (e.g., mouse movement, recent document history).

Known Sandbox IPs/Hostnames: Checking if the machine's IP address or resolved external IP address belongs to a known sandbox provider.

Malware Reactions upon Detection:

If the malware believes it's being analyzed, it typically won't proceed with its malicious payload. Common reactions include:

Terminate Silently: Simply calling ExitProcess without performing any harmful actions.

Decoy Behavior: Executing a benign code path that does nothing harmful, perhaps displaying a fake error message or seemingly functioning normally but without activating C&C or payload routines. This is designed to fool automated systems into classifying it as benign.

Infinite Loops/Stalling: Entering a tight loop or long Sleep call to waste analysis time.

Crash/Corrupt: Deliberately causing a crash or attempting to corrupt the analysis environment or tools (less common, but possible).

Countering Anti-Analysis: The Analyst Fights Back:

Overcoming these defensive measures is crucial for observing the malware's true behavior. Strategies include:

Patching the Checks: The most direct approach. Use static analysis to locate the specific code performing the anti-analysis check (e.g., the call to IsDebuggerPresent and the subsequent conditional jump based on its return value). Then, use a debugger's memory patching capabilities (while paused) or a hex editor (on the file) to modify the check. This might involve:

Replacing the anti-analysis function call with NOP instructions.

Changing the conditional jump after the check to always take the "non-detected" path (e.g., changing JNZ to JZ or JMP, or NOPping it out).

Patching the anti-analysis function itself (if feasible) to always return the "benign" result (e.g., making IsDebuggerPresent always return 0).

Conceptual Example: Patching IsDebuggerPresent Check (x86 Assembly)

```
            ; Original Code
CALL IsDebuggerPresent ; Returns non-zero in EAX if debugger
detected
TEST EAX, EAX          ; Sets Zero Flag if EAX is 0
JNZ  loc_DebuggerDetected ; Jump if EAX was non-zero
(debugger present)
; ... continue normal execution ...
loc_DebuggerDetected:
CALL ExitProcess       ; Exit if debugger found

; Patched Code (Method 1: Force non-detected path)
CALL IsDebuggerPresent
TEST EAX, EAX
JZ   loc_DebuggerDetected ; CHANGE JNZ to JZ. Now jumps if
EAX *is* zero. Since EAX!=0 when debugged, jump won't happen.
                       ; Alternatively: NOP out the JNZ
instruction entirely (replace with 0x90 bytes)
                       ; Alternatively: JMP
loc_ContinueNormal (if feasible)
; ... continue normal execution ...
loc_DebuggerDetected:
CALL ExitProcess
```

```
; Patched Code (Method 2: NOP out the check)
NOP                         ; Replace CALL byte(s)
NOP                         ; ...
XOR EAX, EAX                ; Ensure EAX is 0 for the TEST
TEST EAX, EAX
JNZ  loc_DebuggerDetected ; JNZ will now never be taken
; ... continue normal execution ...
```

Environment Hardening (Anti-Anti-VM): Modify the analysis VM environment to remove or disguise common VM artifacts. Change MAC addresses, rename devices in the registry, use tools to patch guest drivers to report differently, customize usernames/hostnames/system specs to look more realistic. This is an ongoing battle as malware authors find new detection methods. Projects like Pafish or al-khaser can be run inside a VM to test how effectively it hides virtualization artifacts.

Using Stealthier Tools: Employ debugging or instrumentation techniques less likely to be detected:

Rely more on **Hardware Breakpoints** than easily detectable software breakpoints.

Use **Kernel-Mode Debugging** (WinDbg) for user-mode malware, as user-mode detection tricks are often ineffective against a kernel debugger.

Utilize **Dynamic Instrumentation Frameworks** like Frida carefully. While powerful, the injected Frida agent (frida-agent.so/.dll) can sometimes be detected if malware specifically looks for it in memory or hooks relevant functions. Careful scripting might be needed to bypass checks *before* attaching main hooks. Lower-level DBI might be stealthier in some cases.

Dynamic Modification: Use debugger scripting or Frida to hook the anti-analysis functions (IsDebuggerPresent, specific registry query functions, etc.) *as they are called* and dynamically modify their return values on the fly to always indicate a "clean" environment, regardless of the actual state.

Conceptual Code Example: Frida Bypassing IsDebuggerPresent

```
// frida_bypass_IsDebuggerPresent.js
const isDebuggerPresentPtr =
Module.getExportByName('kernel32.dll', 'IsDebuggerPresent');

Interceptor.replace(isDebuggerPresentPtr, new
NativeCallback(() => {
  console.log("[IsDebuggerPresent] Called! Forcing return
value to 0 (False).");
  return 0; // Always return FALSE (0)
```

```
}, 'int', [])); // 'int' is return type, [] is arg types
(none)

console.log("IsDebuggerPresent hook installed. Any calls will
return 0.");
```

Usage: Run frida -l frida_bypass_IsDebuggerPresent.js -f malware.exe. Any time the malware calls IsDebuggerPresent, this hook intercepts it, prints a message, and returns 0, effectively blinding the malware to the debugger's presence via this specific check.

Defeating anti-analysis techniques often requires creativity, platform-specific knowledge, and a willingness to combine patching, environment modification, and dynamic interception.

The Integrated Workflow: Synergy in Action

Successfully dissecting complex, layered malware is rarely achieved through a single technique. It demands an integrated approach, constantly cycling between different tools and analysis modes:

Initial Assessment (Automation Focus): Submit to a **sandbox** for a quick behavioral overview and IOC extraction. Run **static scanners** (YARA, packer detectors) for initial classification and known threat detection.

Guided Static Analysis (Manual): If the sample is potentially interesting or unknown, load it (or the sandbox memory dump) into **IDA/Ghidra**. Use the sandbox report to focus on functions related to observed behaviors (e.g., the registry write for persistence, the network connection loop). Start identifying packer stubs, potential decryption routines, or anti-analysis checks. Begin renaming and commenting.

Unpacking/De-obfuscation (Dynamic Focus): Use a **debugger** (inside a safe, potentially hardened VM) to dynamically unpack the code if necessary, dumping the OEP memory. Use the debugger or **Frida** to bypass initial anti-analysis checks or observe the results of string/API decryption routines identified statically. Extract the unpacked/de-obfuscated code/data.

Deep Payload Analysis (Static + Dynamic Iteration): Load the cleaned-up code back into **IDA/Ghidra**. Perform in-depth static analysis (control flow, data flow) of the core malicious logic (the payload). Use the **debugger** or **Frida** frequently to verify hypotheses, resolve dynamic values, trace complex algorithms step-by-step, and understand interactions with runtime data or OS state. Use **ProcMon/strace/Wireshark** alongside the debugger to correlate internal code execution with external system interactions.

Documentation and Reporting: Continuously document findings: recovered algorithms, decrypted strings, C&C protocols, persistence mechanisms, IOCs, evasion techniques used, and overall functionality. Build **YARA rules** to detect specific features found.

This iterative feedback loop – where static findings guide dynamic investigation, and dynamic observations refine static understanding – is the key to unraveling the layers of deception employed by malware authors. It requires patience, persistence, a diverse toolkit, and a constant awareness of the adversarial nature of the target.

7.3. Developing Countermeasures: Turning Analysis into Protection

we've braved the intricate defenses, peeled back the layers of obfuscation, and meticulously dissected the core logic of malicious code (Chapter 7.2). But the journey of malware reverse engineering doesn't end simply with understanding *how* the threat operates. The crucial, practical culmination of this intense analytical effort lies in **Developing Countermeasures** – translating the hard-won knowledge gleaned from analysis into actionable intelligence and concrete tools that help **detect, block, mitigate, and ultimately defend** against the very malware we just took apart. Reverse engineering malware isn't just an intellectual puzzle; it's a vital component of the cybersecurity ecosystem, directly informing and strengthening our collective defenses. This section explores how the insights gained during dissection become the building blocks for effective security measures.

From Analysis Findings to Actionable Intelligence: Indicators of Compromise (IOCs)

Perhaps the most immediate and tangible output of any malware analysis effort is the extraction of **Indicators of Compromise (IOCs)**. These are specific, observable artifacts or pieces of forensic data that reliably indicate the presence of a particular piece of malware on a system or network. Think of them as the unique fingerprints or calling cards left behind by the malicious software. Identifying and extracting these IOCs is a primary goal during analysis because they provide concrete, often easily shareable data points that security tools and analysts can use to detect infections.

Common types of IOCs derived directly from reverse engineering include:

Cryptographic File Hashes: Calculating cryptographic hashes (typically **MD5**, **SHA-1**, and **SHA-256**) of the original malware executable file(s), any files it drops onto the system (like secondary payloads, configuration files, or decoy documents), and potentially even specific malicious code sections dumped from memory. If a file on a user's system matches a known malicious hash, it's a very high-confidence indicator of infection by that specific malware sample or a close variant (if the hash covers a core component). These are fundamental for basic file scanning in antivirus (AV) engines and endpoint security tools. They are easy to generate and share but also brittle – any minor change to the malware file (even a single byte) will completely change its hash, allowing attackers to easily evade hash-based detection through polymorphism or simple recompilation.

Network Indicators: These relate to the malware's communication activities, crucial for detecting C&C traffic or download attempts:

IP Addresses: Specific IPv4 or IPv6 addresses that the malware attempts to connect to for C&C servers, drop zones (where stolen data is uploaded), or download locations for secondary payloads. These are often extracted from configuration sections (after decryption), string analysis, or observed dynamically during network traffic analysis (via sandbox reports, Wireshark, etc.). IP-based blocking on firewalls and intrusion detection systems (IDS/IPS) is a common defense. However, attackers frequently rotate IPs or use compromised legitimate infrastructure, making IP IOCs relatively short-lived sometimes.

Domain Names: Fully Qualified Domain Names (FQDNs) used for the same purposes as IP addresses (C&C, drop zones, download). These are often preferred by attackers as they can more easily repoint a domain name to a new IP address if the old one gets blocked. Domains might be hardcoded, decrypted, or generated dynamically via Domain Generation Algorithms (DGAs). Identifying malicious domains allows for blocking at the DNS level or within web proxies and firewalls. Extracting DGA seeds and algorithms (via RE) allows predicting and pre-emptively blocking future C&C domains.

URLs: Specific URLs (including paths and query parameters) contacted by the malware, often over HTTP/S. These can indicate specific C&C endpoints, files being downloaded, or data exfiltration points. URL filtering is a standard feature of web security gateways.

Network Protocols/Ports: While less specific, observing communication over unusual ports or using non-standard protocols might serve as a weaker indicator or contribute to behavioral rules.

Host-Based Indicators: These are artifacts left on the infected machine itself:

Specific Filenames/Paths: Full paths to files created or dropped by the malware (e.g., C:\Users\Admin\AppData\Local\Temp\updater.exe, /tmp/.x11d, %APPDATA%\Microsoft\Kernel\syshost.exe). Endpoint security tools can monitor for the creation or presence of files at these specific locations. Attackers often try to randomize filenames to evade this.

Registry Keys/Values (Windows): Specific keys or values created or modified by the malware, especially those used for **persistence** (e.g., values under HKCU\...\Run, HKLM\...\Run, keys related to new services or scheduled tasks) or configuration storage. Monitoring critical registry locations for suspicious changes is a common EDR technique.

Mutex Names: Malware often creates named **mutexes** (synchronization objects) using APIs like CreateMutex to ensure only one instance of itself runs on the system at a time. These mutex names are often unique to a specific malware family or campaign (e.g., \\Sessions\\BaseNamedObjects\\Global_MyApp_Mutex_XYZ123). Searching for the existence of these named mutexes can be a reliable host-based detection method. These are often found by analyzing synchronization API calls or strings within the binary.

Unique Strings/Code Patterns: Sometimes, even after de-obfuscation, specific code sequences, unique debug messages left by the authors, custom cryptographic constants, or particular string artifacts within the malware binary are distinctive enough to serve as reliable indicators, especially when used in **YARA rules**.

Code Example: YARA Rule incorporating various IOCs

Let's expand the previous YARA concept to include multiple IOC types identified during analysis of a hypothetical trojan:

```
        import "pe"      // For PE specific features like
Imphash
import "math"   // For entropy calculation (optional example)


rule Trojan_Example_Family_Combo {
    meta:
        description = "Detects Example Trojan Family based on
multiple indicators"
```

```
        author = "RE Team"
        date = "2023-10-28"
        reference = "Internal Analysis Report #12345"
        hash1 = "sha256_of_main_component_unpack"
        hash2 = "sha256_of_dropped_dll"

    strings:
        // Host-based Artifacts
        $reg_persist =
"Software\\Microsoft\\Windows\\CurrentVersion\\Run\\GraphicsU
til" wide ascii nocase // Persistence key value name
        $mutex_name = "Global\\{E1A3B7C4-FF28-40ab-91F5-
DEADBEEFC0DE}" wide ascii // Unique mutex observed
        $dropped_dll = "sysperf.dll" wide ascii nocase //
Name of a dropped component
        $config_file = "%APPDATA%\\sysconfig\\settings.dat"
wide ascii nocase // Config file path

        // Network Indicator (Decrypted C&C domain)
        $cnc_domain = "secure-updates.support-service.net"
ascii

        // Code/Data Artifact (e.g., part of custom protocol
header)
        $protocol_header = { 5A A5 FF 01 ?? ?? 00 00 } // Hex
signature, ?? are wildcards

    condition:
        // --- Basic file checks ---
        ( uint16(0) == 0x5A4D ) and // Must be MZ header
        ( filesize > 50KB and filesize < 500KB ) and // Size
heuristic

        // --- Core Indicator Logic (require multiple hits
for confidence) ---
        (
            // Combination 1: Persistence and Network
            ( $reg_persist or $mutex_name ) and $cnc_domain
        ) or (
            // Combination 2: Dropped file and protocol
snippet
            $dropped_dll and $protocol_header at
100..pe.sections[0].virtual_address +
pe.sections[0].virtual_size // search in first code section
after header
        ) or (
            // Combination 3: Specific Imphash often seen
with this family (use value from analysis)
            pe.imphash() ==
"f3a4a1b0d6a8f3e4e1c3e5a2a0d9f8b7" and ($mutex_name or
$cnc_domain)
```

```
        ) or (
            // Combination 4: High count of multiple
indicators (higher confidence)
            3 of ($reg_persist, $mutex_name, $dropped_dll,
$config_file, $cnc_domain, $protocol_header)
        )
        // Optional Entropy Check (if indicative for this
family)
        // and math.entropy(pe.sections[1].raw_data_start,
pe.sections[1].raw_data_size) > 7.2
}
```

Explanation: This more realistic YARA rule demonstrates combining multiple IOCs identified through RE. It requires the presence of certain combinations (or) of host-based artifacts ($reg_persist, $mutex_name, $dropped_dll), network indicators ($cnc_domain), and potentially code patterns ($protocol_header) or file characteristics (pe.imphash(), filesize, entropy - commented out). Requiring multiple indicators (#strings > N or boolean logic) significantly reduces false positives compared to relying on a single artifact. Creating such effective rules requires careful analysis to identify indicators that are both *specific* to the malware family and reasonably *stable* across minor variants.

Sharing and Utilizing IOCs: These extracted IOCs are critical operational intelligence. They are fed into various security platforms:

Antivirus/EDR: File hashes, YARA rules, mutex names, registry keys.

Firewalls/IPS: IP addresses, domain names.

Web Proxies/Gateways: Domain names, URLs.

SIEM Systems: Correlating logs based on file hashes, IPs, domains, registry changes across the environment.

Threat Intelligence Platforms (TIPs): Aggregating IOCs from various sources (including RE labs) to provide a broader picture of ongoing threats and campaigns. Sharing IOCs (often via standardized formats like STIX/TAXII) within the cybersecurity community is crucial for collective defense.

Creating good, high-fidelity IOCs – those that are specific enough to avoid flagging legitimate software (low false positives) yet broad enough to catch minor variants (good coverage) – is a key skill derived directly from thorough reverse engineering.

Beyond Static Artifacts: Behavioral Detection Rules

While IOCs based on static artifacts (hashes, strings, IPs) are valuable, sophisticated malware often employs techniques to change these indicators frequently (polymorphism changes hashes, DGAs change domains, randomization changes filenames). Relying solely on static IOCs leads to a reactive defense that's always one step behind the attackers. Malware reverse engineering enables a more proactive and resilient defense strategy by informing the creation of **Behavioral Detection Rules**.

Instead of looking for *what* the malware *is* (a specific file hash), behavioral rules focus on *what* the malware *does*. These rules define sequences or combinations of actions that are highly indicative of malicious intent, even if the specific executable file involved is unknown or constantly changing. These rules are often implemented in advanced security solutions like Endpoint Detection and Response (EDR) platforms, which have deeper visibility into process behavior and OS interactions than traditional AV. Developing effective behavioral rules requires a deep understanding of the malware's **Tactics, Techniques, and Procedures (TTPs)**, knowledge gained directly through reverse engineering its code and observing its execution:

Example Scenario: Through static and dynamic analysis, you determine that a specific ransomware variant typically performs the following sequence:

Starts execution from an unusual location (e.g., %APPDATA%\Temp).

Injects code into a legitimate system process like explorer.exe using CreateRemoteThread and WriteProcessMemory.

The injected code in explorer.exe makes an outbound network connection to one of several known C&C IP ranges.

The injected code then begins rapidly enumerating files on disk using FindFirstFile/FindNextFile.

Shortly after, the same explorer.exe process begins opening numerous user document files (.doc, .xls, .pdf) with write access using CreateFile.

Calls to cryptographic APIs like CryptEncrypt or BCryptEncrypt are observed originating from within the compromised explorer.exe process, targeting the opened file handles.

Finally, original files might be deleted or overwritten using DeleteFile or WriteFile with encrypted data.

Crafting the Behavioral Rule: Based on these RE observations, an EDR engineer could create a rule that triggers an alert or blocking action if *most* or *all* of the following conditions are met within a short time window for a single originating process lineage:

Process Origin: Process launched from a non-standard or temporary path.

Code Injection: Detected process injection into a common target like explorer.exe or svchost.exe.

Network Connection: Outbound connection from the injected process to IP addresses within known malicious ranges or using suspicious ports/protocols.

File Enumeration: High rate of file system enumeration calls.

Mass File Write Access: Numerous files with common document extensions opened with write privileges by the injected process.

Suspicious Crypto API Calls: Use of encryption APIs originating from an unexpected process context (like explorer.exe encrypting user files).

File Deletion/Overwriting: Subsequent deletion or heavy writing activity related to the files accessed earlier.

Code Example: Conceptual EDR Rule Logic (Pseudo-code)

Conceptual EDR rule logic inspired by RE findings

```
# This is highly simplified pseudo-code

function on_process_event(event):
  pid = event.process_id
  process_path = event.process_path
  parent_pid = event.parent_process_id

  if event.type == 'Process Create' and
is_suspicious_path(process_path):
    mark_process_as_potentially_suspicious(pid)

  if event.type == 'API Call' and event.api_name in
['CreateRemoteThread', 'WriteProcessMemory']:
    target_pid = event.arguments['target_pid']
    if
is_common_injection_target(get_process_name(target_pid)) and
is_process_potentially_suspicious(pid):
        mark_process_as_injector(pid)
        mark_process_as_potentially_compromised(target_pid)

  if event.type == 'Network Connect':
    if is_process_potentially_compromised(pid) and
is_suspicious_ip_range(event.remote_ip):
        increase_suspicion_score(pid, weight=2)

  if event.type == 'File Access' and event.operation ==
'Open' and event.access_mode == 'Write':
```

```
    if is_process_potentially_compromised(pid) and
is_common_document_extension(event.file_path):
        increment_suspicious_file_write_count(pid,
event.file_path)
        if get_suspicious_file_write_count(pid) > 50: #
Threshold
            increase_suspicion_score(pid, weight=3)

  if event.type == 'API Call' and event.api_name in
['CryptEncrypt', 'BCryptEncrypt']:
      if is_process_potentially_compromised(pid):
          increase_suspicion_score(pid, weight=2)

  # Combine scores or check for sequence patterns
  if get_total_suspicion_score(pid) > 10 or
check_for_ransomware_sequence(get_events_for_pid(pid)):
      trigger_alert('High confidence ransomware behavior
detected', process_path, pid)
      block_process(pid) # Take remediation action
      # ... further actions ...
```

Explanation: This pseudo-code illustrates how multiple behavioral indicators derived from RE (suspicious path, injection, network connection, file access patterns, crypto API use) could be combined within an EDR rule. Instead of relying on a single artifact, it looks for a *constellation* of suspicious activities occurring together, making it much harder for malware to evade simply by changing its hash or C&C domain. Creating such robust behavioral rules requires a deep, RE-driven understanding of *how* malware achieves its objectives, not just *what* artifacts it leaves behind.

Informing Vulnerability Management and Patching

Malware analysis doesn't just reveal information about the malware itself; it often sheds light on the **vulnerabilities** in legitimate software or operating systems that the malware **exploits** to gain initial access or escalate privileges. When analyzing the infection vector or privilege escalation modules of a malware sample, reverse engineers might identify the specific Common Vulnerabilities and Exposures (CVE) identifier being targeted, or even discover a **zero-day vulnerability** (one previously unknown to the vendor or public).

This information is critical for effective **Vulnerability Management**:

Patch Development: Findings are shared (often under responsible disclosure policies) with the software vendor, providing them with the technical details needed to develop and release security patches to fix the exploited vulnerability.

Patch Prioritization: For organizations managing large fleets of systems, knowing that a *specific* vulnerability is being actively exploited *in the wild* by malware (information often derived from RE reports) significantly increases the urgency of deploying the relevant patch compared to dealing with vulnerabilities that are only theoretical risks.

Workarounds and Mitigation: Even before a patch is available, understanding the exploit mechanism might allow security teams to implement temporary mitigations or workarounds (e.g., disabling a specific service, configuring firewall rules to block exploit traffic, enabling specific OS exploit mitigations like DEP or ASLR if they hinder the exploit). Reverse engineering malware thus plays a vital role in the broader security ecosystem by directly informing the patching and mitigation process, helping to close the security gaps exploited by attackers.

Fueling Threat Intelligence and Strategic Defense

Beyond immediate detection and patching, the aggregated results of analyzing thousands of malware samples over time build a crucial body of **Threat Intelligence**. Reverse engineering contributes significantly to this strategic understanding:

Tracking Threat Actors: Identifying shared code, infrastructure, tools, or TTPs across different malware samples helps researchers cluster activity, attribute campaigns to specific known attacker groups (whether cybercriminal or nation-state), and understand their evolving capabilities, motivations, and targets.

Understanding the Malware Ecosystem: Analyzing droppers, downloaders, C&C panels, exploit kits, and crypter services helps map out the complex underground economy and infrastructure supporting malware distribution and operation.

Identifying Trends: Recognizing shifts in common persistence mechanisms, preferred C&C protocols, new obfuscation techniques, or targeted vulnerabilities allows the security industry to anticipate future threats and adapt defenses accordingly. For example, the shift towards fileless malware and LotL techniques was identified through analysis and necessitated changes in EDR detection strategies.

Improving Remediation: Detailed analysis reports inform incident responders on exactly how to clean an infected system – which files to delete, which registry keys to remove, which services to disable, and what other changes need to be reverted to ensure complete eradication of the malware and any backdoors it may have installed.

Reverse engineering provides the ground truth necessary to build this intelligence, moving beyond simple alerts to a deeper, strategic understanding of the threat landscape, enabling more proactive and effective long-term security postures.

The Ongoing Battle: An Enduring Need for RE

Dissecting malware is undoubtedly one of the most challenging and dynamic areas of reverse engineering. It requires a robust technical foundation, a deep understanding of OS internals and networking, familiarity with cryptographic concepts, mastery of specialized tools, and crucially, a security mindset attuned to the adversarial nature of the target. Malware authors are constantly innovating, employing new techniques to evade detection and hinder analysis. This necessitates continuous learning, adaptation, and tool development on the part of the defenders.

However, the effort is profoundly rewarding. Each piece of malware successfully dissected contributes directly to the collective defense. By extracting IOCs, informing behavioral rules, identifying exploited vulnerabilities, and contributing to threat intelligence, malware reverse engineering empowers individuals and organizations to better protect themselves and their data. It turns understanding the adversary's weapons into the building blocks of our own shields. As long as malicious actors seek to exploit software, the need for skilled reverse engineers to take apart their creations and expose their secrets will remain paramount in the ongoing battle for cybersecurity. Now, having explored the techniques used to analyze malware, we can turn our attention to the other side of the coin – the mechanisms legitimate developers use to *protect* their own software from analysis and unauthorized use.

Chapter 8: Software Protection Mechanisms

let's switch hats. In the last chapter, we delved into the mind of the malware author, analyzing code designed to attack. Now, we're looking at the flip side: the techniques legitimate software developers use to *defend* their creations. **Software Protection Mechanisms** are designed to safeguard intellectual property, prevent unauthorized use or copying, and hinder analysis that could lead to cracking, cheating, or vulnerability discovery. Understanding these defenses is crucial for a reverse engineer, whether your goal is legitimate security testing, interoperability work, or simply curiosity. Knowing how software protects itself helps you anticipate the challenges you'll face and guides your analysis strategy. We'll look at controlling usage (copy protection/DRM), making the code itself harder to understand (obfuscation), and actively fighting back against analysis tools (anti-RE).

8.1. Copy Protection and Digital Rights Management: Controlling the Gates

let's transition from discussing how to analyze *malicious* software to understanding the mechanisms legitimate developers employ to *protect* their own creations. While malware authors use defenses primarily for evasion and hindering analysis, legitimate developers implement **Software Protection Mechanisms** for fundamentally different, though sometimes overlapping, reasons: safeguarding their intellectual property, ensuring users are properly licensed, preventing unauthorized copying and distribution, and sometimes protecting sensitive algorithms or data embedded within the application.

This broad field encompasses everything from simple serial number checks to incredibly complex, multi-layered systems. The oldest and most fundamental goal is controlling *who* can use the software and under *what conditions*, aiming to protect the developer's revenue stream in a world where digital copies are trivially easy to make. This falls under the general umbrellas of **Copy Protection** and its more modern, sophisticated incarnation, **Digital Rights Management (DRM)**. The core objective, however complex the implementation, boils down to verifying that the running instance of the software is legitimate and authorized according to the terms set by the developer or publisher.

The Early Days: From Paper Manuals to Disk Tricks

In the nascent years of personal computing software distribution (late 1970s, early 1980s), the methods used to prevent unauthorized copying were often charmingly low-tech, reflecting the physical media (primarily floppy disks) and the computing environment of the time. These early attempts were frequently more about creating minor hurdles than robust barriers, often prioritizing simplicity over effectiveness.

Many will recall the era of **manual-based copy protection**. You'd launch the game or application, and it would prompt you with something like: "Please enter the 7th word on page 12, line 5 of the user manual." The software itself contained the question and the expected answer. Since photocopying entire manuals was significantly harder and more expensive than copying a floppy disk, this provided a basic level of deterrence against casual copying. Variations included using physical **code wheels** – multi-layered cardboard or plastic discs that needed to be rotated to align symbols based on an on-screen prompt to reveal a required code. Other creative physical items bundled with the software (known affectionately as "feelies" in the game industry) sometimes served a similar purpose. The clear weakness was that once someone shared the required codes or words online or through bulletin board systems (BBS), the protection was entirely circumvented.

More technically interesting were the protections tied directly to the physical characteristics of the **floppy disk media**. Standard disk copying utilities (like COPY in MS-DOS or dedicated tools) worked by reading sectors sequentially based on the operating system's understanding of the disk format (e.g., track number, sector number, sector size). Protection schemes deliberately violated these standards:

Non-Standard Formatting: Data might be written using unusual sector sizes, different gaps between sectors, or tracks containing more or fewer sectors than the OS expected. Standard copy tools would fail to read or replicate this non-standard structure. The protected program contained custom low-level code (often bypassing the OS disk routines entirely and talking directly to the floppy drive controller hardware) to read these specifically formatted "key" sectors.

Intentional Errors: Developers might deliberately write data with incorrect Cyclic Redundancy Check (CRC) values or format sectors with deliberate physical flaws (e.g., weak bits). Standard copy programs, designed to ensure data integrity, would often try to "correct" these errors during the copy process or simply fail. The protected program, however, would specifically *look* for these expected errors using custom read routines; if the errors were absent (because the disk was a "corrected" copy), the check failed.

Physical Alterations: Some ambitious schemes even involved physically modifying the disk media itself, such as burning tiny holes with a laser ("laser-locks") at specific track locations. The drive's read head could potentially detect these physical alterations, which standard duplication equipment obviously couldn't replicate.

While ingenious, these early floppy disk protections were often brittle, incompatible with some hardware variations, and still susceptible to specialized disk copying software ("nibble copiers") that attempted to replicate the disk bit-by-bit, including timing and formatting irregularities, rather than relying on the OS file system structure. They also offered no protection once software moved beyond physical distribution. The inconvenience and relative ineffectiveness of these early methods drove the need for more software-centric approaches as PCs became more powerful and networking emerged.

License Keys (Serial Numbers): The Basic Gatekeeper

As software distribution evolved and disk-based tricks became less feasible or desirable, the **License Key** (often called a serial number or product key) became the standard, ubiquitous method for basic copy protection. The concept is straightforward:

A user purchases a legitimate copy of the software.

They receive a unique (or sometimes batch-unique) alphanumeric key. During installation or first run, the software prompts the user to enter this key.

The software contains embedded **validation logic** that checks if the entered key is mathematically valid according to some predetermined algorithm. If the key validates, the software proceeds; otherwise, it refuses to run or operates in a limited trial mode.

The strength of this system depends entirely on the sophistication of the **key validation algorithm**.

Simple Algorithms: Early implementations often used relatively simple checksums or mathematical relationships. For example, the key might need to have specific digits sum to a certain value, or different parts of the key might be related through basic arithmetic or logical operations (XOR, shifts). Sometimes, parts of the key might encode allowed features or expiration dates.

Cryptographic Validation: More robust implementations incorporate cryptographic principles. A common approach involves asymmetric cryptography (public-key crypto). The developer generates a public/private key pair. The validation code embedded in the software contains the *public* key. The developer uses the *private* key (kept secret) to generate and digitally sign valid license keys or activation data containing user information and permissions. The software uses the embedded public key to verify the digital signature on the entered license key/data. Since only the developer possesses the private key, only they can generate licenses with valid signatures. Other variations might involve symmetric algorithms where the key is somehow derived or embedded securely.

Storage: The entered key, or a flag indicating successful validation, typically needs to be stored somewhere persistently, often in the Windows Registry, a configuration file (.ini, .xml, JSON), or a dedicated license file in the application's data directory or user profile.

Reverse Engineering Challenges & Bypasses: Basic license key schemes are often notoriously vulnerable to reverse engineering:

Finding the Validation Code: Analysts use static analysis to search for strings associated with license entry prompts ("Enter your license key:", "Invalid Serial Number:") or error messages. They trace backward from these points in the disassembly/decompilation to find the function(s) responsible for accepting the key and performing the check. Common indicators are loops iterating through key characters, mathematical operations performed on key segments, comparisons against hardcoded values or calculated checksums, or calls to string comparison or cryptographic verification functions.

Analyzing the Algorithm: Once located, the validation logic is meticulously analyzed using both static techniques (understanding the assembly/pseudo-code) and dynamic analysis (debugging). The analyst steps through the validation function in a debugger, providing a known invalid or valid key, and observes precisely how the input key is processed, what comparisons are made, and which specific instruction or conditional jump determines success or failure.

Patching: If the validation logic ultimately culminates in a single conditional jump (e.g., JE jumps to success if the key is valid, JNE jumps to failure), the simplest bypass is often to **patch** this jump. Using a hex editor or debugger memory modification, the conditional jump can be changed to an unconditional jump (JMP) that always goes to the success path, or simply replaced with NOP instructions, effectively removing the check entirely. Sometimes, patching involves changing the instruction immediately *before* the jump, perhaps forcing a comparison result that guarantees the desired path (e.g., changing a register value or modifying a flag). This requires identifying the exact bytes of the instruction(s) to modify. (Care must be taken not to break alignment or other code, and checksums might need addressing).

Key Generation ("Keygen"): If the validation algorithm itself is simple enough (e.g., based on reversible math or checksums rather than strong cryptography), a more sophisticated bypass is to reverse engineer the algorithm completely and then write a separate small program – a **keygen** – that implements the *key generation* logic (or finds inputs that satisfy the validation logic). This keygen can then produce an unlimited number of valid-looking license keys that the original software will accept. Reversing cryptographically strong validation (like signature checks) to create a true keygen is generally infeasible without access to the developer's private key; however, attackers might still find flaws in *how* the crypto is used or checked, allowing for bypasses even without breaking the underlying cryptography.

Simple license keys provide a basic barrier but are easily shared and highly susceptible to reverse engineering and patching or keygenning if the validation algorithm is weak or implemented insecurely within the client software itself. This inherent vulnerability led developers to seek methods involving external validation.

Online Activation: Calling Home for Permission

To combat the ease of key sharing and offline cracking, **Online Activation** became a widespread standard, especially for commercially valuable software. The core idea is to move the critical validation step from the local machine to a secure server controlled by the developer.

The Typical Flow:

The user installs the software and enters their purchased license key (which might now just be a unique identifier or entitlement token).

The software contacts a dedicated **activation server** over the internet, sending the license key along with potentially some **machine-specific identifiers** (like hardware hashes or a generated unique machine ID).

The activation server maintains a database of valid keys and their activation status. It checks if the submitted key is valid, hasn't been activated too many times (or on too many different machines, based on the stored hardware IDs), and potentially verifies other license terms (like subscription status).

The server sends back a **response** to the client software. This might be a simple success/failure message, or more commonly, a digitally signed **activation blob** or **token** containing authorization information, possibly tied to the submitted machine identifiers.

The client software receives the response. If successful, it stores the activation blob/token locally (registry, file) as proof of activation. Subsequently, when the software runs, it performs a **local check** for the presence and validity of this stored activation data. Some systems might also require periodic **re-activation checks** ("phoning home") with the server to ensure the license remains valid (e.g., subscription hasn't lapsed).

Hardware Binding (Integration with Activation): Online activation is often tightly coupled with **Hardware Binding**. The goal is to tie a specific license activation to a particular machine, preventing the user from simply copying an activated installation (along with its stored activation token) to another computer. During the activation process, the client generates a unique fingerprint or hash based on various stable hardware components:

CPU serial number (if available and accessible)

Motherboard UUID or serial number

Primary hard drive serial number

MAC address of the primary network interface

Sometimes properties of the OS installation (like a Windows SID) or even BIOS information.

The choice of *which* IDs to use involves a trade-off between stability (IDs that rarely change, like motherboard UUID) and uniqueness/availability. Relying on IDs that change frequently (like MAC addresses on USB network adapters or removable drive serials) can cause legitimate activation failures after minor hardware changes. This generated machine hash is sent to the activation server along with the license key. The server might store this hash, associate it with the activated key, and potentially incorporate it into the signed activation token it returns. On subsequent launches, the software regenerates the *current* machine hash and verifies it against the hash stored in the activation token or performs a local check dependent on this binding.

Advantages: Online activation significantly hinders casual key sharing and simple offline patching/keygenning of the primary validation logic (since the critical check happens server-side). It allows developers central control over licensing, enabling features like limited activation counts, subscription enforcement, easier license revocation for fraud, and potentially usage tracking (raising privacy concerns). Hardware binding adds another layer, preventing activated copies from being trivially moved between machines.

Reverse Engineering Challenges & Bypasses: While stronger than offline keys, online activation is not impervious:

Client-Side Analysis: The core challenge shifts to analyzing the *client software's* communication and local checking logic. Static analysis involves finding the code responsible for contacting the activation server (look for networking APIs like WinHttpRequest, HttpClient, curl library calls, or lower-level socket functions) and the code responsible for handling the server's response and performing subsequent local checks. What URL does it contact? What data format is used for requests/responses (JSON, XML, custom binary)? Is the communication encrypted using TLS/SSL? How is the returned activation token stored locally? Where is the code that checks this token on startup?

Network Traffic Interception: Use network sniffing tools (Wireshark) and web proxies capable of intercepting and potentially decrypting HTTPS traffic (**Burp Suite, OWASP ZAP, mitmproxy**) to directly observe the activation requests and responses exchanged between the client and server. This requires configuring the analysis environment to route traffic through the proxy and often involves bypassing **certificate pinning** implemented in the client (where the client specifically checks if the server's TLS certificate is the expected one, preventing standard MITM proxy interception). Bypassing pinning often requires dynamic instrumentation (e.g., using Frida to hook the certificate validation functions). Analyzing the captured traffic reveals the exact API calls, parameters, and response formats.

Patching the Local Check: If the software stores an activation token locally and performs a check on this token at startup, the most common bypass strategy is often to reverse engineer and **patch out this local check**. Even if the initial online activation fails or is skipped, patching the subsequent check within the client binary might allow the software to run as if activated. This requires finding the code performing the local validation (often near program startup) and modifying the conditional jumps determining success/failure.

Server Emulation: A much more complex approach involves completely reverse engineering the client-server activation protocol. By analyzing captured valid activation traffic, an attacker could build a **fake activation server**. This emulator runs locally or on a controlled network and intercepts the client's activation requests. It mimics the real server's expected responses, always returning a "successful activation" message or a valid-looking (though perhaps generically generated) activation token. This tricks the client software into believing it has been successfully activated without ever contacting the real server. This requires significant effort to fully replicate the server's behavior and potentially its cryptographic signing mechanisms if activation tokens are signed.

Bypassing Hardware Binding: If hardware binding is employed, techniques focus on either fooling the ID generation or patching the check. This might involve hooking the OS API calls used to retrieve hardware IDs (like WMI queries or registry reads for serial numbers) using Frida or a debugger to always return consistent, fake values. Alternatively, analysts might try to patch the code that compares the current machine hash against the stored activation hash.

Limitations: Online activation's primary drawbacks are user-facing: it requires an internet connection for activation (and possibly for periodic checks), relies on the vendor maintaining the activation servers indefinitely (raising concerns about long-term usability if the vendor disappears or shuts down servers for older products – a major issue for **software preservation**), and hardware binding can cause significant hassle for users who upgrade their computers or need to reinstall frequently, often requiring manual support intervention to reset activations.

Hardware Dongles: Physical Keys to the Kingdom

For applications demanding a very high level of protection, particularly expensive specialized software (CAD, scientific modeling, professional audio/video production), developers often turn to **Hardware Dongles** (also known somewhat archaically as "security keys" or "HASPs" after an early prominent brand). These are typically small USB devices that must be physically plugged into the computer for the protected software to run.

Beyond Simple Storage: Crucially, modern dongles are *not* just simple USB flash drives containing a license file. They are sophisticated **secure microcontrollers** with their own CPU, secure non-volatile memory (where licenses and keys can be stored safely), and often hardware-accelerated cryptographic engines.

The Mechanism: The protected software is specifically designed to communicate with the dongle via a vendor-provided **driver** and **runtime API**. This communication typically involves:

Presence Check: The software first checks if the correct dongle is physically present and if its driver is functioning.

Authentication/Challenge-Response: The software often engages in a cryptographic **challenge-response** protocol with the dongle. The software sends a random challenge (a nonce) to the dongle. The dongle, using a secret key stored securely within its chip (inaccessible to the software on the host PC), performs a cryptographic calculation (like signing the challenge or encrypting it) and sends the response back. The software verifies this response using a corresponding public key or shared secret. This proves the presence of the authentic hardware dongle.

License/Feature Checks: The software can query the dongle for specific license information stored within its secure memory (e.g., "Is feature X enabled?", "What's the expiration date?", "How many concurrent users are allowed?").

Remote Execution/Decryption: For maximum security, parts of the software's critical code or sensitive data (like decryption keys for core assets) might be encrypted. The software might send this encrypted data *to the dongle*, have the dongle perform the decryption using a key stored securely on the chip, and receive the plaintext result back. Alternatively, performance-critical algorithms might even be executed *partially on the dongle's microcontroller*.

Why Dongles Offer Strong Protection: The key security advantage is that critical secrets (cryptographic keys) and potentially sensitive verification or execution logic reside *within the secure hardware chip* of the dongle itself.

Standard software reverse engineering techniques (disassembly, debugging on the host PC) cannot directly access or extract information from the dongle's secure internal memory or observe the code executing *on* the dongle's microcontroller. This makes replicating the dongle's functionality purely in software (emulation) extremely difficult, bordering on impossible without sophisticated hardware attacks.

Reverse Engineering Challenges & Bypasses: Bypassing dongle protection is generally considered very hard compared to purely software-based schemes:

Analyzing Software Interaction: RE efforts typically focus on the **host-side software** components: the application code that *calls* the dongle vendor's API, and the vendor-provided driver itself. Analysts might statically analyze these components to understand the sequence of API calls, the data formats used in communication, and how the results are interpreted by the application. Dynamic analysis involves setting breakpoints on the vendor API calls within the application or driver, or using USB monitoring tools (like Wireshark with USBPcap on Windows/Linux, or hardware USB analyzers) to sniff the low-level communication between the host driver and the USB device, attempting to reverse engineer the underlying protocol (which is often encrypted or obfuscated).

API Hooking/Patching: Sometimes, vulnerabilities are found not in the dongle itself, but in how the application *uses* the dongle API. For instance, the application might call CheckLicense() but fail to correctly handle the error code if the dongle isn't present or the license is invalid, potentially allowing a patch to bypass the check's consequence. Hooking the API calls with Frida might allow forcing success return codes, though robust protections often have secondary checks or rely on crypto responses that are hard to fake.

Dongle Emulation: The "holy grail" for bypassers is creating a software emulator that perfectly mimics the behavior of the physical dongle, tricking the host software into thinking the real dongle is present. This is extraordinarily difficult due to the need to replicate the dongle's internal secure logic and cryptographic keys. It often requires successfully extracting firmware and keys from the dongle's chip via invasive hardware attacks (like decapsulation, microprobing, side-channel analysis) – skills far beyond typical software RE. Simple USB traffic replays usually fail because of the challenge-response mechanisms.

Dongle Cloning: Physically duplicating the dongle is sometimes possible but usually requires specialized hardware knowledge and equipment and may be defeated by internal serialization or pairing mechanisms.

Limitations: While providing strong technical protection, dongles have significant practical drawbacks: they add cost to the software, require users to manage a physical device (which can be lost, stolen, or damaged), rely on driver installations which can cause compatibility issues or require updates, and occupy a physical port on the computer.

Digital Rights Management (DRM): The Multi-Layered Fortress

The term **Digital Rights Management (DRM)** represents a broader, more encompassing philosophy and implementation of access control, moving beyond simple copy protection or license validation towards continuous, pervasive control over how digital content or software is used. DRM is particularly prevalent for high-value digital media (movies, music, ebooks) and especially in the **PC gaming industry** where piracy and cheating are major concerns.

DRM systems are typically not single techniques but rather **complex, multi-layered frameworks** that integrate various protection strategies, often including:

Strong Encryption: The core executable code, critical game assets, or the media stream itself are usually heavily encrypted. Decryption often occurs dynamically, "just-in-time" (JIT), only for the parts of the code or data needed at that moment, making it much harder to dump a fully decrypted version from memory.

Controlled Execution Environment: The DRM system often creates a kind of sandbox or virtualized layer around the protected application. It monitors and controls the application's interactions with the operating system, hooking API calls, managing memory access, and potentially running parts of the DRM logic in a highly privileged context (sometimes even involving kernel-mode components).

Active Anti-RE Measures: Modern DRM systems are explicitly designed to resist reverse engineering. They incorporate sophisticated **anti-debugging** techniques (often multiple layers, detecting both user-mode and kernel-mode debuggers), **anti-virtual machine** detection, **anti-tampering** checks (using checksums, code hashing, and potentially polymorphic code to detect modifications), and defenses against **memory dumping** and **instrumentation** tools like Frida. These checks are often performed continuously throughout the application's runtime.

Online Checks and Binding: Frequent communication with authentication servers might be required, not just for initial activation but potentially periodically during gameplay or media playback, verifying licenses, downloading time-limited decryption keys, or updating DRM components. Binding to specific hardware configurations is also common.

Code Obfuscation/Virtualization: Critical parts of the DRM's own code, as well as potentially sections of the protected application's code (particularly license checks or critical game logic vulnerable to cheating), are often heavily obfuscated using techniques like control flow flattening or even translated into a custom bytecode format executed on an embedded virtual machine (a hallmark of protectors like VMProtect, often used in conjunction with or as part of DRM solutions).

Prominent Examples: Well-known examples include **Denuvo Anti-Tamper** (widely used in PC games, focuses heavily on code virtualization, integrity checks, and online activation tied to hardware, making static patching extremely difficult), **Widevine**, **PlayReady**, **FairPlay** (used for streaming video/audio services, often leveraging hardware-backed Trusted Execution Environments - TEEs on devices for secure key management and decryption), and older systems like SecuROM or SafeDisc.

The Continuous Arms Race: The world of high-end DRM is characterized by a relentless **arms race** between the DRM vendors and skilled reverse engineers often operating within the game cracking scene ("the scene") or security research community.

DRM vendor releases a new version with novel techniques.

RE groups acquire the protected software (e.g., a new game).

An intensive, often collaborative, reverse engineering effort begins, focusing on understanding the DRM layers, finding weaknesses in the implementation (logic flaws, timing attacks, information leaks, ways to bypass specific checks), and developing methods to circumvent the protection (e.g., emulating license server responses, patching checks in memory dynamically, finding ways to extract decryption keys). This can take days, weeks, or even months of expert effort.

If successful, a bypass method or "crack" is released.

The DRM vendor analyzes the bypass, identifies the weakness exploited, develops countermeasures, and incorporates them into the next version of their DRM.

The cycle repeats.

Reverse Engineering Challenges: Analyzing modern DRM systems represents the pinnacle of RE difficulty:

Extreme Complexity: Multiple interlocking layers of protection.

Heavy Obfuscation/Virtualization: Requires specialized techniques and immense effort to understand the protected code sections.

Active Anti-Analysis: Constant checks for debuggers, VMs, hooks, making dynamic analysis incredibly challenging and requiring stealthy tools or patching the anti-RE code first.

Kernel-Mode Components: Some DRMs install drivers or filter file system/network access at the kernel level, requiring kernel debugging expertise.

Trusted Execution Environments (TEEs): Media DRM often relies on hardware security features (like Intel SGX, ARM TrustZone) where decryption keys and processes are isolated even from the main OS kernel, making software-only analysis extremely difficult or impossible.

User Impact: While often effective initially against piracy or cheating, aggressive DRM systems are frequently criticized by legitimate users for causing significant **performance overhead** (due to constant checks, encryption/decryption), introducing **instability or crashes**, creating **compatibility issues** with certain hardware or software configurations, requiring persistent **online connections**, and raising concerns about **intrusiveness and privacy**. The balance between effective protection and positive user experience is a constant challenge for developers employing DRM.

The Reverse Engineer's Perspective: Targeting the Gatekeeper

When confronting any of these copy protection or DRM mechanisms, the reverse engineer's initial focus fundamentally shifts. Before delving into the application's core features or algorithms, the **protection system itself becomes the primary target**. Understanding *how* the gatekeeper works is the prerequisite to potentially getting past it (whether for legitimate analysis, security testing, or, in illegitimate cases, circumvention).

The analyst must identify the *type* of protection employed (simple key check? online activation? dongle? complex DRM?) as this dictates the most likely avenues of approach. Is the critical check local and potentially patchable? Does it rely on a server that could perhaps be emulated or whose response could be spoofed? Does it depend on secure hardware (dongle, TEE) that is likely resistant to software-only attacks? Is the code heavily obfuscated or virtualized, requiring specialized de-obfuscation efforts? Are anti-debugging or anti-VM checks present that need to be bypassed before effective dynamic analysis can even begin?

Analyzing software protection mechanisms requires the full spectrum of reverse engineering skills – static analysis to find checks and understand logic, dynamic analysis to observe behavior and capture runtime data, network analysis to understand online components, potentially hardware analysis for dongles or TEEs, and a deep understanding of obfuscation and anti-RE techniques. It's a challenging field that directly confronts deliberate attempts to prevent the very understanding the reverse engineer seeks.

8.2. Code Obfuscation Techniques: Muddying the Waters

let's shift our focus from mechanisms designed primarily to control *access* (like copy protection and DRM discussed in 8.1) to techniques aimed squarely at hindering *understanding* – the realm of **Code Obfuscation**. While copy protection erects gates and demands keys, obfuscation acts more like a smokescreen or a camouflage pattern applied directly to the software's inner workings. Its goal is to make the compiled code, even if readily accessible in an executable file, incredibly difficult, time-consuming, and confusing for a reverse engineer to analyze and comprehend.

Imagine being given the architectural blueprints for a complex building, but instead of clear lines and standard symbols, the plans are deliberately scrambled. Lines are replaced with convoluted squiggles, labels are written in a nonsensical code, extra misleading diagrams are inserted, and entire sections seem unnecessarily complex. The building *can* still be constructed correctly following these obfuscated plans (the software still *functions*), but anyone trying to understand the *design* from the blueprints faces a monumental challenge. This is the essence of code obfuscation. Its primary objective isn't necessarily to make reverse engineering theoretically *impossible*, but rather to dramatically increase the **cost** – measured in time, effort, required expertise, and sheer frustration – hopefully deterring all but the most skilled, well-resourced, and persistent analysts.

The motivations behind employing obfuscation are varied. Legitimate developers might use it to:

Protect Intellectual Property: Shielding valuable, proprietary algorithms or unique implementation techniques from competitors who might try to reverse engineer and copy them.

Hinder Cheating/Tampering: In games, obfuscating critical logic related to game rules, player stats, or anti-cheat mechanisms makes it harder for players to develop cheats or modifications.

Complement Licensing: Making the license verification code itself harder to locate and analyze increases the difficulty of creating simple patches or bypasses.

Obscure Vulnerabilities ("Security Through Obscurity"): While highly controversial and generally considered a poor security practice on its own, some developers might mistakenly believe that hiding flaws through obfuscation makes them less likely to be discovered by attackers. However, dedicated attackers are often unfazed, and relying on obscurity instead of fixing the underlying bug is dangerous.

Of course, as we saw vividly in the malware analysis chapter, **malware authors** are arguably the most prolific users of obfuscation. For them, it serves purely defensive purposes: evading signature-based detection by antivirus software and making analysis by security researchers as difficult and time-consuming as possible to delay the development of defenses and attribution efforts.

The techniques employed range from relatively simple transformations easily applied by automated tools to incredibly sophisticated, multi-layered approaches requiring deep compiler and systems knowledge to implement effectively. Let's dissect some of the most common categories.

Identifier Renaming: Stripping Away Meaning

This is often the simplest and most universally applied form of obfuscation, frequently performed to some extent even by standard compilers during optimization (to save space in symbol tables, if they are kept at all). However, dedicated obfuscation tools take this much further. While original source code uses meaningful names for variables (customerName, networkBuffer), functions (CalculateInterest, SendPacket), and classes (UserProfile, DatabaseConnection), these names are high-level semantic anchors invaluable to human understanding. Compilers typically discard local variable names entirely when generating machine code. Obfuscators can ensure that *all* internal symbols (function names, global variables, class/method names where possible depending on the language runtime) that *could* potentially remain in the binary or be easily recovered by decompilers are systematically **renamed** to meaningless, short, or deliberately confusing identifiers.

Common renaming strategies include:

Sequential/Short Names: Renaming everything to a, b, c, aa, ab, etc., or Class1, MethodA, FieldX.

Unprintable/Confusing Characters: Using characters that are visually similar (like l and I) or technically valid but hard to type or visually parse in symbol names (where permitted by the binary format or language runtime).

Hashing: Renaming based on a hash of the original name or content, resulting in seemingly random alphanumeric strings.

Impact on RE: While stripped binaries already lack most original names, aggressive identifier renaming primarily impacts the **readability of decompiled pseudo-code**. A decompiler might reconstruct the logic perfectly, but if every function is sub_ABC123 and every variable is v4 or field_8, understanding the high-level purpose and data flow becomes significantly harder. It forces the analyst to rely much more heavily on meticulous **manual renaming** during the reverse engineering process, deducing the purpose of functions and variables based purely on their usage context (data flow, control flow, API calls) – a core RE skill we've already emphasized, but made much more crucial and pervasive by obfuscation. This technique doesn't significantly hinder analysis of the *assembly* itself (which rarely uses names directly), but it acts as a substantial barrier to quick understanding via decompilation.

String Encryption and Encoding: Hiding the Signposts

Readable text strings embedded within a binary are often among the first things an analyst looks for, providing immediate clues about functionality, targets, or potential errors (as discussed in Chapter 4.1). Obfuscators know this and routinely employ **string encryption** or **encoding** to hide these valuable signposts. Instead of embedding "Error: Invalid License" or "connect_to_server_api_v2" directly in the .data or .rodata sections, the obfuscator stores these strings in an encrypted or encoded form. The program then includes a small **decryption/decoding routine**. Only immediately before the string is actually needed (e.g., passed to printf or used in an API call), this routine is called to transform the obfuscated data back into the original plaintext string, usually in temporary memory (like a stack buffer). The plaintext string exists in memory only fleetingly, making it much harder to discover through static file analysis or simple memory dumping.

Common Techniques:

XOR Encryption: Extremely common due to its simplicity and speed. Each byte of the plaintext string is XORed with a single byte or a repeating multi-byte key. The encrypted string and the key (or logic to derive the key) are stored in the binary. The decryption routine simply performs the same XOR operation again to recover the plaintext.

Other Simple Ciphers: Sometimes slightly more complex but still relatively weak symmetric ciphers like RC4 might be used.

Base64/Hex Encoding: Strings might be encoded using standard schemes like Base64 or simple hexadecimal representation and then decoded at runtime. This isn't encryption but does prevent direct reading via simple string tools.

Custom Schemes: Obfuscators might implement their own simple substitution or transposition ciphers, or combinations of encoding and encryption.

Stack Strings: Sometimes strings aren't stored in data sections at all but constructed dynamically on the stack at runtime, character by character or chunk by chunk, making static discovery impossible.

Reverse Engineering Strategy: Tackling encrypted/encoded strings is a standard RE workflow:

Identification: Locate the obfuscated data blobs (often appearing as seemingly random bytes in data sections) and identify the decryption/decoding function that uses them. Strings view might show garbage, but xrefs to the data might lead to the function. Or, you might see a pattern where data is loaded, a specific function is called, and the result is then immediately used by an API like printf or CreateFile. That middle function is your decryption routine target.

Static Analysis of Routine: Disassemble/decompile the decryption function. Understand its algorithm. Is it a simple byte-wise XOR loop? What is the key? Is the key hardcoded nearby, passed as an argument, or calculated? Is it a standard decoding function like Base64Decode?

Offline Decryption: Once the algorithm and key are known (especially for simple schemes like XOR), it's often easiest to write a small **script** (e.g., in Python) to replicate the logic and decrypt *all* encrypted strings found in the binary offline. This populates your analysis notes or tool comments with the real string values.

Dynamic Analysis: If static analysis of the routine is difficult, dynamic analysis is highly effective. Set a breakpoint *just after* the decryption function returns. Examine the memory location where the decrypted string is stored (often pointed to by the return register EAX/RAX or an output buffer argument). The plaintext string will be directly visible in the debugger's memory view or character representation.

Instrumentation (Frida): This is often the most efficient dynamic approach. Write a Frida script to **hook** the decryption function. In the onLeave handler, read the return value (the pointer to the decrypted string) or the output buffer argument and use readUtf8String() or readUtf16String() to log the plaintext directly to your console. This automatically reveals every decrypted string as the program runs without needing manual breakpoints.

Code Example: Simple Python XOR Decryption

Imagine static analysis reveals a function that loops through a byte array (encrypted_bytes), XORing each byte with a repeating key (0xAB, 0xCD, 0xEF).

```python
# Python script to decrypt strings based on RE findings

def xor_decrypt(encrypted_bytes: bytes, key: bytes) -> bytes:
    """Decrypts data using repeating multi-byte XOR key."""
    decrypted = bytearray()
    key_len = len(key)
    for i, enc_byte in enumerate(encrypted_bytes):
        key_byte = key[i % key_len] # Cycle through key bytes
        decrypted.append(enc_byte ^ key_byte)
    return bytes(decrypted)

# Example data discovered during RE
encrypted_string_blob = \
bytes.fromhex('E1C8ECE6C8FAAFDEC6EEADDEEFDACAFB') # Hex
representation from disassembler
```

```
decryption_key = b'\xAB\xCD\xEF' # Key identified from
analysis

# Perform decryption
decrypted_bytes = xor_decrypt(encrypted_string_blob,
decryption_key)

# Attempt to print as text (assuming it was originally text)
try:
    # Determine potential encoding (guess or based on
context)
    # Often need to try utf-8, utf-16le, latin-1 etc.
    plaintext = decrypted_bytes.decode('utf-8')
    print(f"Encrypted Hex:
{encrypted_string_blob.hex().upper()}")
    print(f"Key Hex       : {decryption_key.hex().upper()}")
    print(f"Decrypted     : '{plaintext}'")
except UnicodeDecodeError:
    print(f"Decrypted bytes (not valid UTF-8):
{decrypted_bytes.hex().upper()}")
except Exception as e:
    print(f"An error occurred: {e}")
```

Example Usage within RE workflow:
1. Identify blob and key in IDA/Ghidra.
2. Copy hex bytes for blob and key into this script.
3. Run script -> get plaintext string.
4. Go back to IDA/Ghidra and add a comment/rename data label with the plaintext.

Explanation: This script implements the common repeating XOR decryption. The analyst plugs in the hex bytes of the encrypted data and the key discovered through RE, and the script outputs the likely plaintext. This simple automation drastically speeds up dealing with common string obfuscation.

Control Flow Obfuscation: Tangling the Execution Paths

This category of techniques directly attacks the analyst's ability to understand the program's logical flow by deliberately making the **Control Flow Graph (CFG)** confusing, complex, or misleading. The goal is to obscure loops, conditional branches, and the overall sequence of execution.

Control Flow Flattening: This is a powerful and prevalent technique. The obfuscator restructures a function, breaking its original logic into numerous small **basic blocks**. A central **dispatcher block** (or pre-dispatcher and post-dispatcher) is introduced, along with a **state variable**. Each original logic block is modified to end by updating the state variable (indicating which block should execute next) and then unconditionally jumping *back* to the dispatcher. The dispatcher block contains complex conditional logic (often using nested if/else or a computed goto/switch) that examines the current value of the state variable and then jumps to the corresponding next logic block.

Impact: The resulting CFG looks like a "spaghetti graph" or "windmill" – dozens or hundreds of small nodes all seemingly connecting only to and from the central dispatcher node(s). The original if/else structures, loops, and sequential flow are completely obscured. Decompilers, which rely heavily on analyzing CFG structure, often fail badly on flattened code, producing massive, unreadable switch statements or deeply nested, incomprehensible goto-laden pseudo-code. Following the logic manually by tracing jumps back and forth through the dispatcher is extremely tedious and error-prone.

RE Strategy: Analyzing flattened control flow is challenging.

Focus on the Dispatcher: The key is understanding the logic within the dispatcher block. How does it use the state variable to choose the next target? What values can the state variable take?

State Variable Tracking: Meticulously track how the state variable is modified at the *end* of each logic block and how that value determines the *next* block chosen by the dispatcher. Dynamic analysis (debugging, tracing) is often essential here to observe the sequence of state variable values and the resulting jumps for a given execution path.

Manual Reconstruction: Sometimes possible for simpler cases to manually reconstruct the original CFG by mapping out the state transitions.

Symbolic Execution: Advanced techniques like symbolic execution (using frameworks like angr) can sometimes automatically explore the state transitions and potentially simplify or "de-flatten" the graph, but this is computationally intensive and not always successful.

Specialized Tools/Scripts: For specific flattening patterns used by known obfuscators, dedicated scripts or plugins might exist within the RE community to help automate the reconstruction process.

Conceptual CFG Before/After Flattening (Mermaid Syntax)

```
    %% --- Original Simple If/Else ---
graph TD
    A[Check Condition] -->|True| B[Then Block];
```

```
    A -->|False| C[Else Block];
    B --> D[Merge Point];
    C --> D;
```

%% --- After Flattening (Conceptual) ---

graph TD
```
    Start --> Dispatcher{Dispatcher};
    Dispatcher -- state == 1 --> BlockA[Block A: Orig. Cond
Check; set state = (true ? 2 : 3)];
    Dispatcher -- state == 2 --> BlockB[Block B: Orig. Then
Block; set state = 4];
    Dispatcher -- state == 3 --> BlockC[Block C: Orig. Else
Block; set state = 4];
    Dispatcher -- state == 4 --> BlockD[Block D: Orig. Merge;
set state = 5];
    BlockA --> Dispatcher;
    BlockB --> Dispatcher;
    BlockC --> Dispatcher;
    BlockD --> End; // Or back to dispatcher if part of
larger func
```

Explanation: The simple diamond shape of the if/else is transformed into multiple blocks that always jump back to the central Dispatcher, making the original structure completely non-obvious from the graph alone.

Opaque Predicates: An opaque predicate is a conditional branch (if P then A else B) where the condition P *always* evaluates to either true or false at runtime, but it's constructed in such a way that it is computationally difficult or impossible for a **static analysis** tool (like a disassembler or decompiler) to determine this outcome definitively.

Examples:

Mathematical Identities: if $(x * x < 0)$ (always false for real integer x). if $((y+1)*(y-1) == y*y - 1)$ (always true).

Pointer Aliasing Tricks: if (ptr1 == ptr2) where static analysis cannot easily prove if ptr1 and ptr2 might point to the same object under certain conditions (but the programmer knows they never will in the intended execution).

Concurrency/Timing: Using conditions based on thread scheduling or precise timing that are predictable in the real runtime but look non-deterministic to static analysis.

Environment Checks: Predicates based on complex interactions with the environment that the obfuscator assumes will always yield a certain result on typical user machines but might differ in analysis environments.

266

Purpose: Opaque predicates are primarily used to **mislead static analysis tools**. An always-false predicate can be used to insert a conditional jump to a block of **dead/garbage code**. The static analyzer or decompiler, unable to prove the predicate is always false, will analyze this dead path as if it were reachable, wasting analysis time and potentially generating confusing or incorrect output that includes the dead code logic. An always-true predicate can be used to obscure an unconditional jump or make simple sequential code appear branched. They can also be used to embed **anti-debugging** or **anti-VM checks**, where the "normally unreachable" path (from the static analyzer's perspective) contains the detection logic and termination code, making it harder to find and patch statically.

RE Strategy: The key to defeating opaque predicates is usually **dynamic analysis**. Running the code in a debugger and observing the predicate's condition being evaluated will quickly reveal that it always resolves the same way (e.g., the JNZ after if ($x*x < 0$) is *never* taken). Once identified, the analyst can manually patch out the conditional jump (e.g., change it to a NOP or an unconditional JMP) in their static analysis database (or sometimes dynamically) to force the analysis tools to ignore the dead path. Symbolic execution can sometimes automatically prove the invariance of simpler opaque predicates. Recognizing common mathematical identities or pointer comparison patterns statically can also raise suspicion.

Instruction-Level Obfuscations: Minor Roadblocks

These techniques operate at a lower level, manipulating individual instructions or short sequences.

Instruction Substitution: Replacing a single, simple machine instruction with a sequence of other instructions that achieve the exact same functional result but are perhaps longer, less common, or slightly harder to read immediately.

Examples: Replacing MOV EAX, 0 (move zero into EAX) with XOR EAX, EAX (XOR register with itself always yields zero) or SUB EAX, EAX. Replacing a simple INC ECX (increment ECX) with ADD ECX, 1 or LEA ECX, [ECX+1]. Replacing TEST EAX, EAX (test if EAX is zero) with CMP EAX, 0 or OR EAX, EAX.

Impact: Primarily increases code size slightly and can momentarily confuse analysts relying on exact instruction patterns. It slightly hinders automated signature matching based on exact byte sequences.

RE Strategy: Usually only a minor annoyance. Experienced analysts quickly recognize these equivalent sequences. Good decompilers often simplify these back into the most common high-level equivalent (e.g., x = 0; regardless of whether MOV or XOR was used).

Dead Code Insertion: Interspersing blocks of instructions, or even entire functions, that are provably **never executed** (e.g., code reachable only via an always-false opaque predicate) or whose execution has **no effect** on the program's meaningful state (e.g., performing calculations whose results are immediately overwritten or never used – identified via data flow analysis).

Impact: Primarily increases the sheer volume of code the analyst must potentially examine, slowing down analysis. Can break simple checksums or pattern matching if inserted cleverly. Can significantly confuse decompilers if they mistakenly incorporate dead code logic into the generated pseudo-code.

RE Strategy: Requires careful **control flow analysis** (identifying unreachable code blocks) and **data flow analysis** (identifying calculations whose results are unused – "dead stores"). Setting breakpoints dynamically and observing that certain code sections are never hit can confirm unreachability. Code coverage tools (often based on instrumentation) can also highlight executed vs. unexecuted code during a dynamic run. Identifying and mentally (or via tool annotations) filtering out dead code is crucial for focusing on the relevant logic.

Virtualization-Based Obfuscation: The Ultimate Fortress?

Arguably the most formidable category of obfuscation currently in widespread use, particularly by high-end software protectors like **VMProtect** and **Themida**, is **Virtualization-based Obfuscation**. This technique fundamentally alters the way the protected code executes.

The Concept: Instead of compiling critical parts of the original application directly to native machine code (like x86 or ARM), the obfuscator performs these steps:

Translation: It translates the original native instructions into a completely **custom, proprietary bytecode language** designed specifically by the obfuscator's creators. Each bytecode instruction might correspond to one or several original native instructions, or perform higher-level operations.

Virtual Machine (VM) Embedding: It embeds a **VM Interpreter** – a complex piece of native code – directly within the protected application. This interpreter's sole job is to fetch, decode, and execute the custom bytecode.

Replacement: The original native code sections are replaced with calls into this VM interpreter, passing it a pointer to the start of the corresponding custom bytecode sequence.

Execution Flow: When the protected application runs and reaches a virtualized section:

Control is transferred to the embedded VM interpreter.

The VM interpreter fetches the first custom bytecode instruction.

It decodes the bytecode, determining the operation to perform.

It executes the operation, potentially manipulating a virtual CPU state (virtual registers, simulated stack) maintained by the interpreter in memory.

It fetches the next bytecode instruction, and the cycle repeats.

Eventually, a special bytecode or condition might transfer control back out of the VM interpreter to regular native code.

Why It's So Effective: VM-based obfuscation presents multiple daunting layers for the reverse engineer:

Unknown Architecture: Standard disassemblers (IDA, Ghidra) cannot understand the custom bytecode; they just see the native code of the *VM interpreter* itself.

Hidden Logic: The original program logic is no longer present as native instructions but is encoded in the opaque bytecode format. Static analysis tools are largely ineffective on the bytecode itself without understanding the VM.

Interpreter Complexity: The VM interpreter itself is often large, complex, and may employ its *own* layers of obfuscation (flattening, anti-debugging) to make analyzing *it* difficult.

Multiple VMs: Some protectors use multiple different VM architectures within the same binary for different code sections, each requiring separate analysis.

Reverse Engineering Strategy: Tackling VM-based protection is considered an advanced RE task, often requiring significant expertise and dedicated effort:

Identify VM Entry/Exit: First, locate the points where native code calls into the VM interpreter ("VM Entry") and where the interpreter returns

control ("VM Exit" or calls back to native code). This often involves looking for characteristic function calls or "markers" inserted by the protector.
Analyze the VM Interpreter: This is the core task. You need to reverse engineer the native code of the VM interpreter itself. This involves: Understanding its main execution loop (fetch-decode-execute). Identifying the "VM context" structure in memory w

8.3. Anti-Reverse Engineering Strategies: Fighting the Analyst

let's explore the final category of defensive measures often encountered in protected software and, perhaps even more frequently, in sophisticated malware: **Anti-Reverse Engineering (Anti-RE)** strategies. While Code Obfuscation (Chapter 8.2) aims to make the code itself confusing and hard to read, Anti-RE techniques take a more active, confrontational approach. They are specifically designed to **detect** the *process* of reverse engineering itself – identifying when analysis tools like debuggers, virtual machines, sandboxes, or monitoring frameworks are being used – and then **react** in ways intended to thwart the analysis, mislead the analyst, or simply shut down the operation.

Think of obfuscation as camouflaging your base, making it hard to see what's inside. Anti-RE is like setting up motion detectors, infrared sensors, guard dogs, and tripwires around the perimeter. It actively looks for intruders (the analyst and their tools) and triggers alarms or countermeasures when they are detected. These techniques turn the reverse engineering process from a passive puzzle-solving exercise into a direct engagement where the software actively fights back against being observed or manipulated. Understanding these strategies is crucial because encountering them often requires adapting your analysis environment, using stealthier techniques, or directly identifying and neutralizing the detection mechanisms before meaningful analysis can proceed. Unsurprisingly, these techniques overlap heavily with the anti-analysis methods employed by malware authors (as seen in Chapter 7.2), as both groups share the goal of hindering external examination.
Detecting the Observer: Common Anti-Analysis Techniques

Anti-RE strategies first need a way to sense the presence of an analyst or their tools. Numerous techniques have been developed, targeting different aspects of common analysis environments and tools.

Debugger Detection: Spotting the "Man in the Middle"

Detecting if the program is running under the control of a debugger is perhaps the most common form of Anti-RE. Debuggers fundamentally alter the execution environment, and these alterations can often be detected:

Explicit API Checks: Operating systems provide direct ways to check for debugger attachment.

Windows: kernel32!IsDebuggerPresent() is the simplest; it checks a specific flag (BeingDebugged) within the Process Environment Block (PEB), a kernel data structure accessible from user space. kernel32!CheckRemoteDebuggerPresent() checks the same flag for another process (or the current one). ntdll!NtQueryInformationProcess using the ProcessDebugPort (returns non-zero if debugged), ProcessDebugObjectHandle, or ProcessBasicInformation (which includes the PEB address containing the flag) are lower-level alternatives.

Linux: Uses the ptrace system call. A common check involves trying to ptrace its own process (ptrace(PTRACE_TRACEME, 0, NULL, NULL)). If this call fails with specific error codes (like EPERM), it often indicates another process (the debugger) is already tracing it. Checking the /proc/[pid]/status file for the TracerPid field (which shows the PID of the attaching debugger, or 0 if none) is another method.

Timing Discrepancies: Debuggers introduce significant overhead. Executing code step-by-step, handling breakpoint exceptions, and communicating with the debugger process takes vastly more time than native execution. Anti-debug code can exploit this by:

Measuring the time taken to execute a small block of known code using high-resolution timers (like the RDTSC - Read Time Stamp Counter instruction on x86, or OS-level high-precision timers). If the elapsed time exceeds a certain threshold, it assumes a debugger is attached due to single-stepping or breakpoint latency.

Comparing the results of different timers that might progress differently under debugging conditions.

Exception Handling Tricks: Debuggers intercept and handle exceptions differently than the OS normally would. Malware/protectors can exploit this:

Breakpoint Scanning: Checking their own code memory for the INT 3 opcode (0xCC) used by software breakpoints.

Deliberate Exceptions: Triggering specific exceptions (e.g., INT 3, INT 1 for single-stepping traps, privileged instructions, deliberate division by zero, or invalid memory access) and carefully analyzing how the exception handler (SEH on Windows, signal handlers on Linux) behaves. Differences in the handler's execution flow or context when a debugger is present can reveal it. For instance, trying to handle INT 3 directly might indicate no debugger is intercepting it first.

Unhandled Exception Filter Manipulation: Interacting with the SetUnhandledExceptionFilter API on Windows. Debuggers often interfere with this filter chain.

Hardware Breakpoint Artifacts: While stealthier, hardware breakpoints utilize specific debug registers (DR0-DR7 on x86). Anti-debug code can attempt to read or write to these registers directly (though this is often privileged). If the access behavior differs from expected (e.g., an exception occurs where none should), it might indicate debugger manipulation. Some techniques involve setting hardware breakpoints themselves and checking if expected debug exceptions occur.

Structural Anomalies: Debuggers might slightly alter process memory layouts or data structures. Checking for these subtle differences (e.g., PEB flag locations relative to other structures, specific handle values).

Thread Hiding: Using ntdll!NtSetInformationThread with ThreadHideFromDebugger on Windows can make a specific thread largely invisible to user-mode debuggers.

Code Example: Simple IsDebuggerPresent Check (Windows C++)

```cpp
// SimpleDebuggerCheck.cpp
#include <windows.h>
#include <stdio.h>

int main() {
    printf("Checking for debugger...\n");

    if (IsDebuggerPresent()) {
        printf("Debugger DETECTED! Taking evasive action (or
just exiting).\n");
        // In real malware/protection: exit, crash, run decoy
code, etc.
        MessageBoxW(NULL, L"Debugger Detected!", L"Anti-RE",
MB_OK | MB_ICONWARNING);
        return 1; // Indicate failure or detection
```

```
    } else {
        printf("No debugger detected. Proceeding with normal
execution.\n");
        // ... application's real logic would go here ...
        MessageBoxW(NULL, L"No Debugger Found.", L"Anti-RE",
MB_OK | MB_ICONINFORMATION);
        return 0;
    }
}
```

RE Perspective:

* *Static Analysis:* Seeing the explicit call to IsDebuggerPresent followed by a conditional check (e.g., TEST EAX, EAX then JNZ DebuggerFoundLabel) immediately signals an anti-debugging measure.

* *Bypass (Patching):* Locate the JNZ instruction after the TEST. Patch it to JZ (Jump if Zero - i.e., jump if *no* debugger) or NOP it out. Now, even if IsDebuggerPresent returns non-zero (true), the jump to the detection handler won't occur.

* *Bypass (Dynamic Hooking - Frida):* Use the Frida script shown previously to intercept IsDebuggerPresent and force it to always return 0, making the check ineffective.

Virtual Machine / Sandbox Detection: Identifying execution within a virtualized or automated analysis environment is crucial for evasion, as described under sandboxing (Chapter 5.3). Techniques focus on detecting artifacts unique to these environments:

Hardware/BIOS Strings: Searching for specific strings in simulated hardware names reported by WMI/registry (e.g., "VMware", "VirtualBox", "QEMU Virtual CPU"), or specific BIOS vendor strings.

File System Artifacts: Checking for the existence of guest tools installation directories (C:\Program Files\VMware\VMware Tools), driver files (vmmouse.sys, vboxguest.sys), or known sandbox directories (C:\analysis).

Registry Keys: Querying for keys associated with VM software (HKLM\SOFTWARE\VMware, Inc.\VMware Tools).

MAC Addresses: Checking the network adapter's MAC address against known prefixes assigned to VMware (00:0C:29, 00:50:56, 00:05:69) or VirtualBox (08:00:27).

Running Processes/Services: Enumerating running processes or services and looking for names associated with guest tools (vmtoolsd.exe, VBoxService.exe) or common analysis tools.

I/O Port Communication: Attempting to communicate via hypervisor-specific I/O ports.

Instruction/Timing Quirks: Exploiting subtle differences in how certain instructions execute or timing discrepancies specific to VMs ("Red Pill" type checks).

Generic Environment Checks: Looking for low screen resolutions, lack of user activity (no recent files), minimal system uptime, low CPU/RAM resources, or generic usernames/computer names that often characterize analysis VMs.

Analysis Tool Detection (Beyond Debuggers): Malware might also explicitly look for other common analysis tools running concurrently:

Process Enumeration: Calling APIs like CreateToolhelp32Snapshot/Process32First/Process32Next (Windows) or reading the /proc filesystem (Linux) to get a list of running processes. It then compares process names against a blacklist of known RE tools (idaq.exe, ghidra.exe, x64dbg.exe, ollydbg.exe, Procmon.exe, ProcessHacker.exe, Wireshark.exe, etc.).

Window Enumeration: Searching for specific window class names or window titles associated with these tools using APIs like FindWindow or EnumWindows.

Driver/Service Checks: Looking for drivers or services associated with certain tools (e.g., ProcMon's driver).

Code Integrity Checks / Anti-Tampering: These techniques aim to detect if the program's own code has been modified in memory, often targeting software breakpoints or patches applied by analysts.

Checksums: Calculating a simple checksum (like sum-of-bytes or CRC32) over critical code sections at runtime and comparing it against a stored expected value. If a breakpoint (0xCC) or patch has modified the code, the checksum will mismatch.

Cryptographic Hashing: Using stronger cryptographic hash functions (MD5, SHA-1, SHA-256) for the same purpose. More robust against intentional collisions than simple checksums.

Self-Modification Verification: Sometimes used in conjunction with self-modifying code; the code might check if its modifications have occurred correctly, potentially detecting debugger interference.

Code Relocation Checks: Ensuring code sections haven't been moved in memory unexpectedly.

API Hooking Detection: As monitoring and instrumentation tools like Frida or ProcMon often work by hooking APIs (redirecting calls through their own analysis code), some protectors attempt to detect this.

Checking Prologue Bytes: The most common hooking method involves overwriting the first few bytes of the target API function with a JMP instruction redirecting to the hook handler. Anti-RE code can read the first few bytes of critical APIs (e.g., kernel32!CreateFileW, ntdll!NtMapViewOfSection) and compare them against the expected original bytes or look for specific JMP opcodes (E9, EB, FF 25).

Verifying System Call Numbers: For APIs that directly wrap system calls, it might retrieve the expected system call number and compare it against the value actually used when the function is invoked, potentially detecting interception layers.

Stack Tracing: Examining the call stack during execution of a potentially hooked function. If unexpected modules or function frames appear in the stack trace before the expected system library frame, it might indicate a hook.

Reaction Strategies: How the Software Fights Back

If any of the detection techniques above indicate the presence of analysis, the Anti-RE mechanism triggers a predefined **reaction strategy**. The goal is usually to prevent successful analysis or mislead the analyst.

Terminate Execution (Crash / Exit / Loop): The simplest reaction is to simply stop running.

ExitProcess/TerminateProcess: Call functions to immediately exit.

Stealth Exit: Exit cleanly without error messages, perhaps making the analyst think the program just finished normally or had an unrelated configuration issue.

Intentional Crash: Dereference a null pointer, divide by zero, execute an invalid instruction, or call a termination API to cause an immediate crash, preventing further debugging or observation.

Infinite Loop: Enter a tight while(1) loop to hang the analysis process. This stops analysis in its tracks but provides a clear signal *that* an anti-RE check was triggered (if the analyst observes the exit/crash occurs right after a suspected check).

Decoy Behavior (Misdirection): More insidious reactions involve altering the program's behavior subtly without terminating, aiming to waste the analyst's time or lead them to incorrect conclusions.

Disable Functionality: The program might detect the debugger/VM but continue running, *however*, it silently disables the specific functionality the analyst is likely interested in. For example, if a debugger is detected, the license check routine might be skipped entirely, or the code responsible for connecting to the C&C server or decrypting the final payload might simply never be executed. The analyst observes the program "running" but doesn't see the critical malicious behavior.

Fake Data/Actions: The program might proceed but perform *decoy* actions. It could connect to benign websites instead of the real C&C server, "decrypt" data using a dummy key resulting in garbage output, or write harmless files to disk while skipping the real payload deployment. This is especially common in response to sandbox detection, aiming to generate a "clean" automated report.

Altered Timing: Introducing random or significantly longer delays only when analysis is detected, making debugging tedious or triggering sandbox timeouts.

"Phoning Home" / Alerting: In some cases, particularly with commercial software protection or potentially targeted malware, the Anti-RE mechanism might attempt to send a message back to a developer/attacker server indicating that an analysis attempt (perhaps with details about the detected environment) has occurred. This has obvious privacy implications and is less common due to the risk of revealing C&C infrastructure.

Attacking the Tools (Rare/Risky): Extremely aggressive Anti-RE might try to exploit known vulnerabilities *within* the analysis tools themselves (debuggers, disassemblers, emulators) to crash them, corrupt their state, or even potentially gain execution control within the analyst's environment. This is highly risky for the protector/malware author (exploits are hard, might fail, reveal intent) and legally dubious.

The reaction strategy chosen often depends on the context – malware trying to be stealthy might prefer silent exits or decoy behavior, while software protection might simply crash or refuse to run if tampered with.

Countering Anti-Reverse Engineering: The Analyst's Countermoves

Successfully analyzing software employing Anti-RE techniques requires recognizing the checks and actively bypassing or neutralizing them. The countermeasure depends heavily on the specific detection method being used.

Patching the Checks (Most Common): As illustrated with the IsDebuggerPresent example, the most direct approach is often to **identify** the specific code performing the anti-RE check using static analysis (searching for known APIs, suspicious logic patterns) or dynamic analysis (observing crashes/exits after certain instructions) and then **patch** it.

Locate the Check: Find the call to IsDebuggerPresent, the RDTSC timing loop, the VM artifact query, the checksum calculation, the hook detection code, etc.

Identify the Consequence: Find the conditional jump (JZ, JNZ, JE, etc.) that branches to the "detection occurred" reaction path based on the check's result.

Apply the Patch:

Modify the Jump: Change the conditional jump to force the "clean environment" path (e.g., JNZ -> JZ, JE -> JNE, or replace with JMP to the clean path, or replace with NOPs).

Modify the Result: Patch the instruction(s) just before the conditional jump to force the desired outcome (e.g., ensure EAX is zero before TEST EAX, EAX; JNZ Detected).

NOP out the Check: Replace the entire check sequence (e.g., the call to IsDebuggerPresent and the following TEST/JNZ) with NOP instructions.

How to Patch: Use a debugger's memory modification capabilities while paused *before* the check executes, or use a hex editor to modify the executable file on disk *before* running it (requires understanding instruction byte encodings and handling potential file integrity checks). Saving patched executables allows repeated analysis without reapplying dynamic patches.

Code Example: Conceptual Patching Workflow

Let's say IDA/Ghidra shows this anti-debug check:

```
      0x401050  CALL   CheckTimingDifference ; Returns 1 in
EAX if timing suggests debugger
0x401055  TEST   EAX, EAX
0x401057  JNZ    0x401080              ; Jump to crash routine
if EAX is non-zero
0x401059  ; ... continue normal code ...
...
0x401080  MOV    ECX, 0               ; Crash routine
```

```
0x401085  MOV     EAX, [ECX]              ; Read from NULL ->
crash
```

Analysis: The JNZ at 0x401057 jumps to the crash routine if CheckTimingDifference returns non-zero (debugger detected).

Patch Strategy (using hypothetical debugger commands or hex editing):

* *Option 1 (Modify Jump):* Find the bytes for the JNZ instruction at 0x401057 (e.g., 75 27 which means JNZ relative +0x27 bytes). Change the 75 opcode to 74 (opcode for JZ) while keeping the offset byte 27. Now it only jumps to crash if EAX *is* zero (no debugger), effectively bypassing the anti-debug. Or replace 75 27 with two NOP bytes (90 90).

* *Option 2 (Modify Result):* Set a breakpoint at 0x401055. When hit, manually set EAX to 0 (set $eax=0 in GDB). Then continue. The TEST EAX, EAX will set ZF, and the JNZ will not be taken. (Requires dynamic intervention each time).

* *Option 3 (NOP Check):* Replace the CALL at 0x401050 (e.g., 5 bytes E8 ?? ?? ?? ??) and the TEST (e.g., 2 bytes 85 C0) with NOPs (7 bytes of 90), ensuring the JNZ's condition is never met appropriately.

Environment Modification (Anti-Anti-VM): As detailed in the Sandboxing/Virtualization section, actively modify your analysis VM to remove or disguise the artifacts that anti-VM checks look for (changing hardware IDs in registry/WMI, removing guest tools traces, using realistic configurations). This is often a continuous effort as new detection methods emerge. Dedicated tools or scripts sometimes assist in "hardening" VMs against common checks.

Using Stealthier Analysis Techniques: Choose tools and methods less likely to trigger common detections:

Prioritize **Hardware Breakpoints** over software breakpoints when tampering is suspected.

Employ **Kernel-Mode Debugging** (e.g., WinDbg over KDNET/serial) which bypasses most user-mode detection checks.

Use **Dynamic Instrumentation Frameworks (Frida, Pin)** carefully. They can sometimes be detected, but they also offer the flexibility to *hook and modify the anti-RE checks themselves* dynamically, often more easily than patching. For instance, a Frida script can replace IsDebuggerPresent, VM check functions, or timing functions with versions that always return "clean" results.

Perform more analysis **statically** if dynamic detection is proving too difficult to bypass, focusing on understanding logic without execution.

Analyze on **bare-metal hardware** (using a dedicated, isolated machine) if VM detection is insurmountable, though this increases risk and reduces flexibility.

Automated De-obfuscation/Unpacking Tools: If the Anti-RE checks are embedded within layers of obfuscation or packing, dealing with those layers first (using techniques from Chapter 8.2 and section 7.2) is often necessary before the checks can even be located and patched. Tools that automate unpacking or specific de-obfuscation techniques can indirectly help bypass embedded Anti-RE.

Understanding the Reaction: Sometimes, simply understanding *how* the software reacts to detection is enough. If it just exits silently, you know you triggered something and need to find the check. If it enters decoy mode, recognizing this requires comparing behavior with and without the suspected analysis tool present, often involving careful analysis of both code paths revealed statically.

Conclusion: The Analyst vs. The Defenses

Anti-Reverse Engineering techniques represent a direct challenge, turning the analysis process into an interactive contest. Developers and malware authors deploy these checks as tripwires to detect and deter investigation. For the reverse engineer, encountering these techniques requires a shift in strategy. It's no longer enough to simply read the code; one must also anticipate, detect, and neutralize the software's own attempts to observe and react to the analysis process itself.

The primary countermeasures involve either modifying the **environment** to appear benign (hardening VMs) or directly modifying the **target software** (patching checks statically or dynamically). Patching checks, either by altering conditional logic or NOPping out detection routines, is often the most direct and effective approach once the checks are located. Dynamic instrumentation frameworks like Frida provide powerful capabilities for bypassing checks on-the-fly by hooking relevant functions. Choosing the right countermeasure depends on the specific detection method used and the analyst's tools and expertise. Successfully overcoming Anti-RE barriers often requires creativity, persistence, and a deep understanding of both the target software and the analysis tools being used.

The Shield Wall

Together, Copy Protection/DRM (controlling access), Code Obfuscation (hindering understanding), and Anti-Reverse Engineering (detecting/reacting to analysis) form the **"Shield Wall"** – the developer's or malware author's arsenal for defending their software against external examination and unauthorized use. These techniques range from trivial obstacles easily bypassed to highly sophisticated, multi-layered systems representing state-of-the-art challenges.

For the reverse engineer, whether performing malware analysis, security research, interoperability work, or pursuing knowledge, this shield wall represents the set of hurdles that must be systematically understood and overcome. Recognizing the *type* of protection is the first step. Knowing *how* copy protection verifies licenses informs bypass strategies. Understanding *how* code is obfuscated guides de-obfuscation efforts. Recognizing *how* anti-RE checks detect analysts allows for targeted countermeasures. Learning to systematically analyze and, when necessary and legally/ethically permissible, bypass these diverse protection mechanisms is the subject of the next logical step in our journey (as originally intended for Chapter 9 in your outline), moving from understanding the defenses to actively dismantling them.

Chapter 9: Bypassing Protections

let's navigate some potentially treacherous waters. We've explored how software protects itself (Chapter 8). Now, we delve into the methods used to analyze and potentially *circumvent* those protections. This chapter discusses identifying weaknesses, the common techniques used in "cracking," and, crucially, the ethical tightrope one walks when engaging in these activities. **Important Disclaimer:** This chapter describes techniques often associated with software cracking (bypassing copyright protection). While understanding these methods is vital for security professionals (to test defenses, perform penetration testing) and reverse engineers (for legitimate purposes like interoperability or data recovery), applying them to circumvent licenses you haven't legally acquired constitutes software piracy, which is illegal and unethical. Our purpose here is educational – to understand the *how* so we can build better defenses or operate within legitimate bounds, **not** to encourage illegal activity.

9.1. Identifying Vulnerabilities: Finding the Cracks in the Armor

let's embark on the crucial first phase of potentially circumventing software protections: **Identifying Vulnerabilities**. Before you can even think about bypassing a gate, disabling a trap, or navigating around an obstacle course (as explored in Chapter 9.2), you must first meticulously survey the defenses, understand their construction, and probe for weaknesses. Think of it as the reconnaissance phase in a complex operation. Software protection mechanisms, ranging from simple license checks to intricate Digital Rights Management (DRM) systems, layered obfuscation, and active anti-reverse engineering traps (as detailed in Chapter 8), can seem daunting. Yet, it's essential to remember that these systems, no matter how complex, are ultimately designed and implemented by humans. They are software and logic constructs, and like all software, they are susceptible to design flaws, implementation bugs, incorrect assumptions, and oversights. Finding these "cracks in the armor" is the primary objective of this initial stage, and it relies heavily on the systematic application of the static and dynamic analysis skills we have cultivated throughout this book.

"Vulnerability" in this context doesn't *only* refer to classic security exploits that lead to code execution (though such flaws might certainly exist within protection code). It more broadly encompasses *any* weakness, design flaw, or implementation shortcut that allows the protection's intended function to be circumvented, disabled, or bypassed. It could be a single instruction that can be easily patched, a poorly chosen algorithm, an insecure way of storing state, a naive check for analysis tools, or a logical oversight in error handling. Our task is to become expert fault-finders, meticulously examining the structure and behavior of the protection mechanism itself.

Leveraging Static Analysis: Mapping the Defense Grid

Static analysis – examining the code without executing it using tools like IDA Pro, Ghidra, radare2, or Hopper – forms the bedrock of our initial reconnaissance. The goal is to build a comprehensive map of the protection mechanism's implementation within the software, identify its key components, understand its logic flow, and pinpoint potential weak points based purely on its structure and code patterns. This involves several targeted approaches:

Locating the Protection Code: Zeroing In on the Target

Before analyzing the *how*, we need to find the *where*. Sophisticated protections are often deliberately interwoven with the main application logic to make them harder to isolate, but there are common starting points and techniques for locating the relevant code sections:

String Searches: This remains one of the most fruitful initial steps. Use your disassembler's string analysis features or standalone string tools to search the binary for keywords related to protection, licensing, activation, or anti-analysis. Look for terms like: "license", "serial", "key", "register", "activate", "trial", "expired", "invalid", "protection", "tamper", "debug", "trace", "VMware", "VirtualBox", "integrity", "checksum", or specific vendor names associated with known protection libraries (e.g., "Sentinel", "HASP", "CodeMeter", "Armadillo", "Themida", "VMProtect"). Pay close attention to error messages displayed when protection checks fail (e.g., "Invalid Serial Number Entered.", "Activation Failed. Please contact support.", "Debugger detected - unloading."). These strings are often located near the code that performs the check or handles the failure condition.

API Call Analysis: Examine the program's import table or search the code for calls to APIs commonly associated with protection mechanisms. The presence of certain calls strongly suggests relevant code sections:

Licensing/Configuration: APIs for reading registry keys (RegOpenKeyExW, RegQueryValueExW), reading files (CreateFileW, ReadFile targeting .lic, .dat, or config files), getting system time (GetSystemTimeAsFileTime) for trial period checks.

Online Activation/Networking: Winsock (socket, connect, send), WinINet (InternetOpenW, HttpSendRequestW), or higher-level HTTP client libraries often indicate communication with activation servers.

Hardware Identification: APIs querying hardware specifics used for binding (WMI queries via COM, GetAdaptersInfo, specific registry hardware keys, CPUID instruction).

Anti-Debugging: Direct calls like IsDebuggerPresent, CheckRemoteDebuggerPresent, NtQueryInformationProcess, or indirect methods involving exception handling (SetUnhandledExceptionFilter) or timing (QueryPerformanceCounter, RDTSC).

Anti-VM: Specific WMI queries, registry checks, or direct I/O port interactions.

Cryptography: Calls to Windows CryptoAPI/CNG (Crypt*, BCrypt*, NCrypt*), OpenSSL functions, or other known crypto libraries might be involved in key validation, license decryption, or integrity checking. Finding where these potentially relevant APIs are called provides excellent starting points for deeper investigation.

Tracing Backwards from Outcomes: Identify code responsible for observable outcomes related to the protection. For example, locate the code that displays the "Registration Successful!" message box or the "Trial Period Expired" dialog. Once you find the function call responsible for this UI feedback (e.g., MessageBoxW, printf), use your disassembler's cross-reference (xref) capabilities to see where *that* function call is made. Trace backward up the call stack and through the preceding control flow. You'll likely traverse through conditional jumps (JE, JNZ) that branched based on the outcome of the actual protection check performed earlier in the execution flow. This "follow the breadcrumbs backward" approach is highly effective for pinpointing the core decision-making logic.

Analyzing Initialization/Startup Code: Protection checks often occur early in the program's execution lifecycle – during initialization, before the main window appears, or when a protected feature is first accessed. Carefully analyzing the code near the program's entry point (main, WinMain, DllMain, or constructor functions for global objects) might reveal initialization calls for protection libraries or early license status checks.

Identifying Known Library Patterns: If the software uses a known third-party protection library (like Sentinel LDK, Flexera FlexNet, Wibu CodeMeter, or even commercial obfuscators/protectors like Themida/VMProtect), experienced analysts might recognize specific code patterns, function names (if not stripped), API calling conventions, or structural artifacts associated with that particular vendor's system. Identifying the specific protection system used significantly narrows the scope and allows leveraging existing public research or knowledge about common weaknesses or analysis techniques for that system. Tools like DiE or PEiD can help with initial identification.

Conceptual Example: Searching for License Strings with Python & Regex
While disassemblers have built-in string views, sometimes a quick external scan can be useful. This script conceptually searches a binary file for common license-related keywords.

```python
#!/usr/bin/env python3
# -*- coding: utf-8 -*-

import re
import argparse
import os

def find_interesting_strings(filepath: str, min_len: int =
6):
    """
    Searches a binary file for potentially interesting
strings (ASCII/UTF-16LE)
    related to licensing, activation, debug, vm etc. (Case-
insensitive)

    Args:
        filepath: Path to the binary file.
        min_len: Minimum length of contiguous printable chars
to consider a "string".

    Returns:
        A list of tuples: (offset, string_type, found_string)
    """
```

```python
    results = []
    # Regex for printable ASCII sequences (adjust min_len as
needed)
    # Printable ASCII range: 0x20 (space) to 0x7E (~)
    ascii_regex = re.compile(b"([\\x20-\\x7E]{" +
str(min_len).encode('ascii') + b",})")

    # Regex for potential UTF-16 LE sequences (Printable
ASCII followed by null)
    # Looks for (AsciiChar \x00){min_len,}
    utf16le_regex = re.compile(b"((?:[\\x20-\\x7E]\\x00){" +
str(min_len).encode('ascii') + b",})")

    # Keywords to search for (case-insensitive)
    keywords = [
        b'license', b'serial', b'key', b'register',
b'activate', b'trial',
        b'expire', b'invalid', b'tamper', b'protect',
b'debugger', b'trace',
        b'vmware', b'virtualbox', b'vbox', b'qemu',
b'sandbox', b'checksum',
        b'integrity', b'patch'
        # Add more domain-specific keywords if needed
    ]
    keywords_regex = re.compile(b'|'.join(keywords),
re.IGNORECASE)

    try:
        with open(filepath, 'rb') as f:
            file_content = f.read()

        # Find all potential ASCII strings
        for match in ascii_regex.finditer(file_content):
            offset = match.start()
            ascii_string = match.group(1)
            # Check if this string contains any keywords
            if keywords_regex.search(ascii_string):
                try:
                    results.append((offset, "ASCII",
ascii_string.decode('ascii')))
                except UnicodeDecodeError:
                    pass # Ignore potential non-ascii within
the range

        # Find all potential UTF-16 LE strings
        for match in utf16le_regex.finditer(file_content):
            offset = match.start()
            utf16le_bytes = match.group(1)
            # Attempt to decode the full UTF-16 sequence
            try:
```

```python
                    # Need to ensure byte length is even for
UTF-16 decode
                    # The regex ensures pairs, but add a check
just in case
                    if len(utf16le_bytes) % 2 == 0:
                        potential_utf16_str =
utf16le_bytes.decode('utf-16le')
                        # Check decoded string for keywords
(need bytes comparison still)
                        if
keywords_regex.search(potential_utf16_str.encode('utf-
16le')):
                            results.append((offset, "UTF-16LE",
potential_utf16_str))
                except UnicodeDecodeError:
                    pass # Skip if not valid UTF-16

        # Sort results by offset for readability
        results.sort(key=lambda x: x[0])

    except FileNotFoundError:
        print(f"Error: File not found: {filepath}")
    except PermissionError:
        print(f"Error: Permission denied for file:
{filepath}")
    except Exception as e:
        print(f"Error processing file {filepath}: {e}")

    return results

def main():
    parser = argparse.ArgumentParser(description="Find
potentially interesting strings in binary files.")
    parser.add_argument("file", help="Path to the binary file
to scan.")
    parser.add_argument("-l", "--min-len", type=int,
default=6, help="Minimum string length (default: 6)")
    args = parser.parse_args()

    found_strings = find_interesting_strings(args.file,
args.min_len)

    if found_strings:
        print(f"Found {len(found_strings)} potential matches
in '{args.file}':")
        for offset, stype, text in found_strings:
            # Simple context preview (optional)
            # context_start = max(0, offset - 8)
            # context_end = min(len(file_content), offset +
len(text.encode(stype.lower())) + 8)
```

```
        # hex_context =
file_content[context_start:context_end].hex().upper()
            print(f"   [+] Offset 0x{offset:08X} ({stype}):
\"{text}\"")
    else:
        print(f"No matching strings found in '{args.file}'.")

if __name__ == "__main__":
    main()
```

Explanation: This script reads a binary file, uses regular expressions to find sequences of printable ASCII characters and potential UTF-16LE characters (ASCII followed by null), and then filters these sequences to report only those containing predefined keywords often associated with protection mechanisms. It prints the offset, detected type (ASCII/UTF-16LE), and the found string. While basic (it might miss obfuscated strings or other encodings), running such a script can quickly highlight promising areas in the binary for further investigation with a disassembler (using the reported offsets).

Static Analysis of the Protection Logic:

Once you've located candidate code sections related to the protection, the deep dive begins. What specific types of vulnerabilities or weaknesses are you looking for within this code?

Simplistic Checks / Easily Identifiable Decision Points: The "Holy Grail" for bypassing protection is often finding that the entire complex validation process boils down to a single, simple check near the end. For example, a function IsLicenseValid() might perform numerous complex operations but ultimately return a boolean value (e.g., 1 for valid, 0 for invalid in EAX). The calling code then simply does TEST EAX, EAX followed by JNZ FailureLabel. No matter how complex IsLicenseValid was, bypassing the protection only requires patching that single JNZ instruction. Static analysis involves carefully tracing the control flow (Chapter 4.2) backward from the failure/success outcomes to pinpoint these final decision points and assess their simplicity. Examine the CFG – does the "good path" and "bad path" diverge at only one easily identifiable conditional jump?

Flawed Algorithms (Less Common Now): For license key checks, especially in older software, the validation algorithm itself might be weak. Can you understand the mathematical or logical operations performed on the input key? Is it a simple checksum? A reversible calculation? Can you

287

determine the constraints required for the algorithm to return "true" and potentially write a keygen based on reversing this logic? This usually requires detailed data flow analysis (Chapter 4.3) within the validation function. Modern systems using strong cryptographic signatures for keys are generally immune to this unless there's a flaw in the signature *verification* process itself.

Insecure Cryptography Implementation: Even if standard cryptographic algorithms are used, their *implementation* might be flawed:

Hardcoded Keys/Data: Search the code and nearby data sections vigorously for anything that looks like a hardcoded cryptographic key (e.g., long hexadecimal strings, base64 encoded data, sometimes even ASCII keys directly) or embedded certificate/public key data needed for verification. If keys are embedded directly in the client binary, they can often be extracted statically.

Weak Key Derivation: If keys are derived from user input (like a password or username), examine the key derivation function (KDF). Is it cryptographically strong (like PBKDF2, Argon2, scrypt) with a proper salt, or is it a weak, custom algorithm easily reversed or brute-forced?

Incorrect Algorithm Usage: Does the code correctly use Initialization Vectors (IVs) for block cipher modes like CBC (are they unique and unpredictable)? Does it use deprecated or insecure algorithms or modes (like ECB mode, DES, MD5 for signatures)? Does it fail to properly authenticate encrypted data (leading to padding oracle attacks in some cases)? Static analysis of calls to crypto APIs and the setup of their parameters can reveal these implementation flaws.

Logic Flaws: Beyond crypto, general programming errors can create vulnerabilities:

Error Handling Bypass: Does the code handle errors (e.g., file not found, network timeout during activation) correctly? Sometimes, an error path might accidentally skip the actual license check or set a "valid" flag incorrectly. Explore all error handling branches visible in the CFG.

Uninitialized Data: Does a check rely on a variable that might not always be initialized correctly, potentially defaulting to a state that bypasses the check? Track data flow to ensure variables used in checks have defined origins.

Race Conditions (Harder Statically): If the protection involves multiple threads or interaction with external events, are there potential race conditions where timing differences could lead to an inconsistent state that bypasses a check? Static identification is difficult, but awareness is needed.

Integer Overflows: If checks involve sizes, counts, or time calculations, could providing extremely large inputs cause an integer to wrap around (overflow/underflow), potentially leading to bypasses of size checks or logical errors? Look for arithmetic operations on values derived from external input that are then used in comparisons or memory operations.

Naive Anti-RE Implementations: As discussed in Chapter 8.3, anti-analysis checks themselves can be vulnerable points if implemented simplistically. Finding direct calls to IsDebuggerPresent or simple timing loops makes them easy targets for patching. Complex checks require more effort but still represent potentially bypassable logic.

Insecure State Storage: How and where is the activation status or license data stored persistently (registry, file)? What permissions are set on these locations? Can a non-privileged user modify or delete the license file/registry key to reset a trial period or bypass a check? Is the stored data itself encrypted? If so, where does the key come from? Analyzing the code that reads/writes this state can reveal weaknesses in storage security.

Static analysis allows you to build a detailed understanding of the protection's logic, identify these potential weak points, and formulate targeted hypotheses *before* ever needing to run the code.

Conceptual Disassembly: The Critical Jump

```
        ; ... code performs complex license validation, result
maybe in EBX (1=OK, 0=Fail) ...
0x4050A0  MOV    EAX, EBX          ; Move result to EAX for
testing
0x4050A2  TEST   EAX, EAX          ; Check if EAX is zero
(license failed?)
0x4050A4  JZ     loc_LicenseFailed ; <<< CRITICAL JUMP: Jump
if Zero Flag set (EAX was 0)
; --- Success Path ---
0x4050A6  MOV    [g_IsLicensed], 1 ; Set global licensed flag
0x4050AC  JMP    loc_ContinueExecution
; --- Failure Path ---
loc_LicenseFailed:
0x4050B1  PUSH   OFFSET ErrorMsg_InvalidLicense
0x4050B6  CALL   DisplayErrorMessage
0x4050BB  CALL   ExitApplication
```

```
loc_ContinueExecution:
; ... rest of program ...
```

RE Interpretation: Regardless of the complexity leading up to address 0x4050A0, this static snippet reveals the pivotal decision point is the JZ instruction at 0x4050A4. The entire protection scheme hinges on whether EAX is zero at that moment. This becomes the primary target for analysis and potential patching.

Probing with Dynamic Analysis: Validating and Discovering

While static analysis builds the map and identifies likely weak spots, **dynamic analysis** using debuggers, monitors, and instrumentation frameworks provides the ground truth and allows for interactive probing to confirm hypotheses and uncover runtime-dependent behaviors or vulnerabilities.

Debugging the Protection: Attaching a debugger (x64dbg, WinDbg, GDB) inside your isolated VM is essential:

Confirming Control Flow: Set breakpoints at key locations identified statically (validation function entries, critical conditional jumps, API calls like IsDebuggerPresent). Run the program and verify that execution reaches these points as expected. Step through the logic (t, p / F7, F8) and watch which paths are taken by conditional jumps based on the actual **runtime values** in registers and flags. Does the JZ loc_LicenseFailed get taken when you provide an invalid key? Does it fall through when you (perhaps later) provide a valid one? This validates your understanding of the control flow logic.

Inspecting Runtime Data: When paused at a breakpoint before a check, examine the actual data being used. What value is *really* in the register being compared? What are the exact bytes read from the license file into memory? What does the data structure populated before being sent to the activation server look like? This provides concrete values static analysis can only guess at. Debugger memory views and register windows are crucial here.

Analyzing Dynamic Behavior: Observe how the program behaves in response to actions. Trigger the online activation – what network requests are *actually* sent? Step through the IsDebuggerPresent function – what value does it return in EAX? Run through a timing check loop – what are the start and end timer values? This reveals the concrete results of dynamic operations.

Testing Bypasses Interactively: The debugger is your laboratory for testing bypass hypotheses *before* committing to a file patch:

Forcing Control Flow: Pause just before the critical conditional jump (like the JZ at 0x4050A4 above). Manually modify the Zero Flag in the flags register (most debuggers have a command/UI for this) to the opposite of its current state. Then continue execution (g/F9). Did forcing the "wrong" path bypass the failure condition?

Altering Check Results: Pause just *after* the function performing the core check returns its result (e.g., after IsLicenseValid returns 0 in EAX). Manually change the value in EAX to 1 (set $eax=1). Then continue execution. Does the program now proceed as if licensed?

Modifying Input Data: Pause *before* the validation function is called. Modify the license key data in the memory buffer that will be passed as an argument. Can specific changes satisfy the check?

Disabling Anti-RE Temporarily: Set a breakpoint at the *start* of a suspected anti-debug routine. When hit, use the "Set Instruction Pointer" command (available in most debuggers) to manually jump the execution point *past* the entire anti-debug check, effectively skipping it for this run. Does the program now run further without crashing/exiting?

This dynamic manipulation allows you to quickly test the impact of potential patches without modifying the original file.

Monitoring System Interactions: Use tools like **Process Monitor (ProcMon)** on Windows or **strace** on Linux while running the protected application (ideally performing actions like attempting activation or triggering checks). Filter the output for your target process. This can reveal:

License File Access: Which specific files are read when checking the license? Are there any failed attempts due to permissions?

Registry Access: Which registry keys are queried or written to store license status or activation tokens?

Network Connections: Exactly which IPs/domains and ports are contacted during online activation? This information is vital for potential server emulation or identifying C&C infrastructure if the "protection" is actually malware.

Hardware ID Queries: Which system APIs or registry locations are accessed when the program likely generates a hardware fingerprint for binding?

Network Traffic Analysis: For online activation or checks, intercepting the network traffic with tools like **Wireshark** (for raw packet capture) or web proxies like **Burp Suite/mitmproxy/ZAP** (for HTTP/S traffic) is critical. This involves setting up the proxy in your analysis environment and potentially bypassing TLS/SSL certificate pinning (often requiring Frida):

Observe Protocol: What data is sent in the activation request? What is the format (URL parameters, JSON, XML, custom binary)? What headers are included (Authorization tokens, User-Agent)? What does a success response look like compared to a failure response?

Replay/Modify: Can you capture a valid activation request/response and replay it? Can you modify requests (e.g., change the license key being sent) to probe the server's validation logic?

Instrumentation (Frida for Targeted Observation/Modification): Frida scripts provide a powerful, often stealthier alternative to full debugging for certain tasks:

Hooking Check Functions: Intercept calls to IsLicenseValid, IsDebuggerPresent, specific hardware ID query functions, or crypto verification routines. Log the inputs and outputs, or directly modify the return value to force a desired outcome (like returning true from IsLicenseValid).

Extracting Dynamic Data: Hook functions responsible for decrypting license keys stored in files or received from servers, logging the decrypted key material.

Bypassing Certificate Pinning: Hook the SSL/TLS library functions responsible for certificate validation and force them to always succeed, enabling HTTPS traffic interception via proxies.

Code Example: Conceptual Frida Script to Monitor Hardware ID Queries
Suppose we suspect the program uses GetAdaptersInfo on Windows to get MAC addresses for hardware binding.

```
// frida_monitor_GetAdaptersInfo.js

// Get pointer to the function
const GetAdaptersInfoPtr =
Module.getExportByName('iphlpapi.dll', 'GetAdaptersInfo');
var pIpAdapterInfo = NULL; // Variable to hold buffer pointer
```

```
Interceptor.attach(GetAdaptersInfoPtr, {
    onEnter: function (args) {
        // args[0] is PIP_ADAPTER_INFO pAdapterInfo (output
buffer)
        // args[1] is PULONG pOutBufLen (input/output size)
        console.log("\n[GetAdaptersInfo] Called!");
        console.log("  Input Buffer Length Pointer: " +
args[1]);
        let initialLen = args[1].readULong(); // Read the
initial size provided by caller
        console.log("  Input Buffer Length Value : " +
initialLen);
        // Store the buffer pointer for use in onLeave
        // Note: If called with NULL buffer initially to get
size, this will be NULL
        this.adapterInfoBuffer = args[0];
        this.bufferLenPtr = args[1];
    },
    onLeave: function (retval) {
        // retval is the return code (DWORD)
        console.log("[GetAdaptersInfo] Returned: " +
retval.toInt32() + (retval.toInt32() == 0 ? "
(ERROR_SUCCESS)" : ""));

        // If call succeeded AND buffer pointer was valid,
try to parse/read results
        if (retval.toInt32() == 0 /* ERROR_SUCCESS */
&& !this.adapterInfoBuffer.isNull()) {
            // Read the potentially updated output buffer
length
            let finalLen = this.bufferLenPtr.readULong();
            console.log("  Output Buffer Length Value: " +
finalLen);

            // Try reading some data from the buffer
(structure definition needed for full parsing)
            // IP_ADAPTER_INFO structure is complex (a linked
list)
            // Here, just show the first few bytes including
the MAC address (at offset ~392?)
            // This offset is approximate and depends on
struct definition!
            const macOffset = 392; // Highly approximate
offset to Address member
            if (finalLen >= macOffset + 6) { // Check if
buffer is large enough
                let macBytes =
this.adapterInfoBuffer.add(macOffset).readByteArray(6); //
Read 6 bytes
```

```
            console.log("  Potential MAC Address @
~offset " + macOffset + ": " +
                          Array.from(new
Uint8Array(macBytes)).map(b => b.toString(16).padStart(2,
'0')).join(':').toUpperCase());
          } else {
              console.log("  Buffer too small to read
potential MAC address at offset " + macOffset);
          }
          // Proper parsing would involve iterating the
linked list described by 'Next' pointer
          // using structure definitions from Windows
headers via Frida's NativeFunction/Memory access.
      } else if (retval.toInt32() != 0) {
          console.log("  -> Call failed, cannot read
adapter info.");
      }
    }
});

console.log("Interceptor attached to GetAdaptersInfo.
Waiting...");
```

Explanation: This Frida script hooks GetAdaptersInfo. In onEnter, it logs the input buffer details. In onLeave, it logs the return code. If successful, it attempts to read the first MAC address from the complex IP_ADAPTER_INFO structure returned in the buffer (using an *approximate* offset for demonstration – proper parsing needs the actual struct definition). Running this while the protected program initializes could reveal if and how it retrieves network adapter hardware IDs, providing clues about the hardware binding mechanism.

Fuzzing: While less common for targeted protection bypass, **fuzzing** the input channels related to protection mechanisms (e.g., the license key entry field, the license file parser, the activation response handler) with malformed, oversized, or unexpected data can sometimes trigger crashes or errors that reveal underlying implementation flaws (like buffer overflows) or cause the program to enter an unprotected state due to faulty error handling. This requires identifying the input vector and using appropriate fuzzing tools (like AFL++, honggfuzz) or techniques.

Putting it Together: Synthesis and Hypothesis Testing

Identifying vulnerabilities in protections rarely stems from a single observation. It's typically a process of **synthesis**, combining clues from multiple sources:

Static analysis suggests a simple JZ controls license failure.

Dynamic analysis confirms this jump is taken when an invalid key is entered.

Dynamic modification shows that flipping the Zero Flag before the jump bypasses the failure.

Conclusion: The JZ at that specific address is a key vulnerability, likely patchable.

Or perhaps:

ProcMon shows the program reads license.dat.

Hex editor analysis shows the file is mostly high entropy except for a small header.

Static analysis reveals calls to CryptDecrypt shortly after ReadFile using license.dat.

Debugging intercepts the call to CryptDecrypt and reveals the key is hardcoded nearby in memory.

Conclusion: The license file is encrypted, but the key is embedded in the binary, making decryption and potential modification feasible if the format of the decrypted data can be understood.

This interplay reinforces the **hypothesis-driven** nature of the analysis. You observe, you form a guess ("I think this jump is the check"), you test it (dynamically force the other path or patch it), and you refine your understanding based on the result. Finding that "crack in the armor" – that logic flaw, weak check, exposed key, or naive anti-RE routine – requires methodical exploration using both static and dynamic lenses, constantly looking for inconsistencies, shortcuts, or violations of security best practices within the protection code itself. It is this successful identification of one or more vulnerabilities that paves the way for the specific bypass techniques we'll discuss next.

9.2. Techniques for Cracking Software: Dismantling the Defenses

having successfully navigated the reconnaissance phase and identified one or more vulnerabilities or weak points in the software's protection mechanism (Chapter 9.1), we now move to the stage of actively **bypassing** those defenses. This section delves into the common **Techniques for Cracking**

Software – the practical methods used to circumvent copy protection, license checks, DRM, or other restrictions.

Disclaimer Revisited: It is absolutely crucial to reiterate the statement from the beginning of this chapter. The techniques described here are presented for **educational purposes only**, primarily for security professionals learning offensive/defensive tactics, legitimate reverse engineers performing authorized analysis (like interoperability research under legal exemptions), or malware analysts bypassing anti-analysis layers. Using these techniques to pirate software, bypass licenses you haven't paid for, cheat in games against their terms of service, or distribute cracked software is **illegal and unethical**. This guide aims to provide understanding, not endorsement or encouragement, of these methods. Always operate within legal and ethical boundaries.

Once a vulnerability is understood, the goal is typically to implement a persistent or easily repeatable way to exploit that weakness, effectively neutralizing the protection. The methods vary significantly depending on the nature of the protection and the specific vulnerability found.

Binary Patching: Directly Modifying the Blueprint

Perhaps the most straightforward and historically common technique is **Binary Patching**. This involves making **permanent modifications directly to the executable file(s)** (e.g., .exe, .dll, .so) on disk. The core idea is to alter the specific machine code instructions responsible for the protection check or its consequence, effectively changing the program's logic at that point.

The Process:

Vulnerability Identification (Prerequisite): You must have already pinpointed the exact byte(s) in the file that need to be changed through meticulous static and dynamic analysis (as covered in 9.1). This usually involves identifying a critical conditional jump, a specific comparison value, a call to an anti-RE function, or similar bottleneck. You need the precise **offset** within the file where these bytes reside.

Tool Selection: A **Hex Editor** (HxD, 010 Editor, ImHex, etc.) is the fundamental tool, allowing direct byte manipulation at specific offsets. For more complex patches involving multiple byte changes or calculations, specialized **binary patching tools** or **diffing tools** (like bspatch or xdelta which apply pre-calculated binary differences) might be used, especially for distributing patches rather than performing the edit manually.

Making the Change: The most common patch targets protection logic:
Altering Conditional Jumps: This is the classic bypass. Locate the bytes corresponding to the conditional jump that decides between the "licensed/allowed" path and the "unlicensed/disallowed" path. The goal is typically to force the "allowed" path.

Example: Change a JNE (Jump if Not Equal/Not Zero - often leads to failure) to a JMP (Unconditional Jump - forces the fall-through success path) or a JE (Jump if Equal/Zero - often jumps to success). On x86, JNE rel8 is opcode 75 followed by an 8-bit relative offset; JE rel8 is 74 offset; Short JMP rel8 is EB offset. Changing just the opcode byte (75 to 74 or EB, assuming the destination is reachable by a short jump) might suffice.

Example: Replace the conditional jump instruction entirely with NOP (No Operation - opcode 90 on x86) instructions. If the "allowed" path immediately follows the jump, NOPping out the conditional branch effectively makes execution always fall through to the success case. This requires overwriting the correct number of bytes (e.g., a 2-byte JNZ short needs two 90s).

Changing Comparisons/Values: Sometimes it's easier to modify the comparison that *precedes* the jump. If code checks CMP EAX, 1 followed by JE Licensed, you could potentially patch the 1 to a 0 if EAX is typically 0 in the unlicensed state. Or you might patch the instruction loading EAX to ensure it always holds the value 1 before the comparison.

NOPing Out Calls: If an entire function call performs an unwanted check (e.g., CALL CheckHardwareDongle), you might overwrite the bytes of the CALL instruction with NOPs, effectively removing the call. You must be careful, however, as the calling code might rely on the function to return a specific value in EAX or modify memory; simply NOPing the call might crash the program later if the expected side effects don't occur. Sometimes additional patching (like setting EAX manually after the NOPped call) is needed.

Modifying Strings/Data: Less common for bypassing core logic, but patching might involve changing embedded text strings (e.g., changing "Trial Version" to "Registered Version"), ensuring care is taken with string lengths and null terminators. Changing embedded configuration flags or hardcoded keys (if found) might also be done via patching.

Saving the Modified File: After making the byte changes in the hex editor, save the file, typically under a new name to preserve the original.

Testing: Run the patched executable. Does it now behave as if licensed? Does it bypass the previously observed check? Does it remain stable, or did the patch introduce unexpected crashes?

Handling Integrity Checks: A major complication with binary patching, especially in modern software, is the presence of **internal integrity checks** (checksums, cryptographic hashes calculated over code sections) or **external digital signatures** designed specifically to detect tampering. If the software checksums itself at runtime and finds the patched bytes, it will likely crash, refuse to run, or trigger other defenses. Circumventing these integrity checks often requires *additional* reverse engineering to locate the checking code and patch *that* out as well, significantly increasing the complexity beyond modifying the primary protection check. Patching files protected by strong external DRM that relies on cryptographic signatures verified by the OS or secure loaders is often infeasible without compromising the signing keys.

Advantages: Creates a permanently modified executable that runs without restrictions and doesn't require extra tools or steps at runtime (once patched). Easy to distribute the patched file (though highly illegal in most cases).

Disadvantages: Modifies the original program files, which can be detected by integrity checks. Patching requires precise knowledge of byte offsets and instruction encodings. Mistakes can easily corrupt the executable. Less flexible than memory patching if the protection logic changes slightly across different program versions (the patch offsets might become invalid). Legally problematic for distribution.

Code Example: Conceptual Binary Patching Workflow (Hypothetical)

Imagine our check_value example where JZ loc_LicenseFailed at 0x4050A4 is the critical check. The JZ rel8 instruction on x86 might be encoded as 74 offset_byte.

Identify: Static/dynamic analysis reveals the instruction at file offset (let's say) 0x10A4 is 74 0B (JZ +11 bytes relative). The success path starts at 0x4050A6.

Load: Open the executable in HxD. Go to offset 0x10A4.

Analyze: Observe the bytes 74 0B. We want to *always* take the path *after* this jump (the success path starting 2 bytes later at file offset 0x10A6).

Patch Strategy: Replace the 2-byte JZ instruction with two NOP (90) bytes.

Modify: Overwrite the byte 74 at offset 0x10A4 with 90. Overwrite the byte 0B at offset 0x10A5 with 90.

Save: Save the modified file as program_patched.exe.

Test: Run program_patched.exe. The CPU will now execute NOP; NOP; at the original check location, causing execution to always fall through to the success code at 0x4050A6.

Memory Patching: Runtime Modifications Without File Changes

An alternative to altering the file on disk is **Memory Patching**. Here, the modifications are applied directly to the program's code or data sections **in memory** *after* the program has been loaded by the OS but *before* the critical protection checks execute. The original executable file on disk remains untouched.

How it's Done:

Debugger Analysis: This is often how memory patches are developed and tested initially. Using a debugger (like x64dbg), you set a breakpoint just before the target instruction(s). When hit, you use the debugger's memory modification commands (fill or directly editing in the disassembler/dump views) to overwrite the target bytes in memory with the desired patch (e.g., changing JZ to NOP NOP). Then you let the program continue. The CPU executes the modified instructions in memory.

Automated Loaders/Wrappers: For a persistent bypass without needing the debugger each time, a separate small utility called a **Loader**, **Wrapper**, or **Patcher** is created. This utility:

Starts the target application (target.exe) in a **suspended state** using OS APIs like CreateProcess with the CREATE_SUSPENDED flag (Windows) or fork/exec combined with ptrace (Linux).

Attaches to the suspended process or uses process memory manipulation APIs (WriteProcessMemory on Windows, ptrace's PTRACE_POKEDATA on Linux).

Writes the necessary patch bytes directly into the target process's memory space at the correct virtual addresses (these addresses might need to be adjusted based on ASLR if the target is relocatable). This requires the loader to know the target process's base address.

Optionally, might perform more complex operations like injecting a DLL ("DLL Injection") containing the patching logic, which then executes within the target's address space.

Finally, resumes the main thread of the target application (ResumeThread on Windows, PTRACE_DETACH or PTRACE_CONT on Linux).

The target application then starts executing normally, but when it reaches the patched memory locations, it executes the modified instructions.

Advantages: Does not modify the original executable files on disk, which bypasses simple file-based integrity checks (though more advanced checks might monitor memory). Can be more resilient to minor updates in the target application if the patch logic targets relative offsets or function patterns rather than fixed file offsets. Can sometimes perform more complex runtime patches than feasible with static file modification.

Disadvantages: Requires running the loader/wrapper utility *each time* the target application needs to be started with the protection bypassed. The loader itself might be detected by anti-cheats or security software.

Calculating the correct virtual memory addresses for patching can be complicated by Address Space Layout Randomization (ASLR) if the target executable or DLLs are dynamically relocated; the loader needs logic to find the actual base address and apply patches relative to that. Creating a robust loader requires programming skills and knowledge of process manipulation APIs.

Conceptual Code Example: Windows Loader using WriteProcessMemory (Simplified)

```cpp
// ConceptualLoader.cpp - Highly Simplified Example
#include <windows.h>
#include <stdio.h>
#include <tlhelp32.h> // For process/thread enumeration
(optional)

int main() {
    LPCWSTR targetPath = L"C:\\Path\\To\\TargetApp.exe"; //
Path to the protected app
    LPCWSTR targetCmdLine = NULL; // Optional command line
arguments

    // --- Patch details determined via RE ---
    // Assume TargetApp.exe base address will be 0x400000
(Need ASLR handling in real code)
    DWORD patchOffset = 0x50A4; // Relative offset of the JZ
instruction from base
    BYTE patchBytes[] = { 0x90, 0x90 }; // Replace the 2-byte
JZ with NOP NOP
    SIZE_T patchSize = sizeof(patchBytes);
    // --- End Patch details ---
```

```
    STARTUPINFOW si;
    PROCESS_INFORMATION pi;

    ZeroMemory(&si, sizeof(si));
    si.cb = sizeof(si);
    ZeroMemory(&pi, sizeof(pi));

    printf("Attempting to launch target: %ws\n", targetPath);

    // 1. Create the process in a suspended state
    if (!CreateProcessW(
            targetPath,              // Application path
            (LPWSTR)targetCmdLine,   // Command line (mutable
needed by API)
            NULL,                    // Process handle not
inheritable
            NULL,                    // Thread handle not
inheritable
            FALSE,                   // Set handle inheritance
to FALSE
            CREATE_SUSPENDED,        // <<--- Create
suspended!
            NULL,                    // Use parent's
environment block
            NULL,                    // Use parent's starting
directory
            &si,                     // Pointer to STARTUPINFO
structure
            &pi)                     // Pointer to
PROCESS_INFORMATION structure
        )
    {
        printf("CreateProcess failed (%d).\n",
GetLastError());
        return 1;
    }

    printf("Process created suspended. PID: %d,
Handle: %p\n", pi.dwProcessId, pi.hProcess);

    // --- Apply Memory Patch ---
    // IMPORTANT: In real code, need to handle ASLR!
    // Get actual base address using ReadProcessMemory on PEB
or other techniques.
    // For simplicity, assume base is 0x400000 here.
    LPVOID targetBaseAddress = (LPVOID)0x400000;
    LPVOID patchAddress =
(LPVOID)((DWORD_PTR)targetBaseAddress + patchOffset);

    printf("Attempting to write patch at virtual
address: %p\n", patchAddress);
```

```
    SIZE_T bytesWritten = 0;
    // 2. Write the patch bytes into the target process's
memory
    if (!WriteProcessMemory(pi.hProcess, patchAddress,
patchBytes, patchSize, &bytesWritten)) {
        printf("WriteProcessMemory failed (%d).\n",
GetLastError());
        TerminateProcess(pi.hProcess, 1); // Kill target if
patch failed
        CloseHandle(pi.hProcess);
        CloseHandle(pi.hThread);
        return 1;
    }

    if (bytesWritten != patchSize) {
        printf("Error: Only wrote %zd bytes out of %zd
requested.\n", bytesWritten, patchSize);
        TerminateProcess(pi.hProcess, 1); // Kill target
        CloseHandle(pi.hProcess);
        CloseHandle(pi.hThread);
        return 1;
    }

    printf("Memory patch applied successfully (%zd
bytes).\n", bytesWritten);

    // 3. Resume the main thread of the target application
    printf("Resuming target process main thread...\n");
    if (ResumeThread(pi.hThread) == (DWORD)-1) {
        printf("ResumeThread failed (%d).\n",
GetLastError());
        // Process might already be running, but this is an
error state generally
    } else {
        printf("Target process resumed.\n");
    }

    // 4. Close process and thread handles (we don't need
them anymore)
    CloseHandle(pi.hProcess);
    CloseHandle(pi.hThread);

    return 0;
}
```

Explanation: This simplified C++ code demonstrates the loader concept on Windows. It uses CreateProcess with CREATE_SUSPENDED to launch the target but pause it immediately. It then calculates the target memory address (crucially, hardcoded base address here, needs proper ASLR handling in real world) and uses WriteProcessMemory to overwrite the bytes at that address with the predefined patch (NOP bytes). Finally, it calls ResumeThread to let the target application run with the patch applied in memory. Running this loader effectively starts the target application with the license check already neutralized.

Key Generation ("Keygens"): Replicating the Locksmith's Key

If the software protection relies on validating a user-provided license key using an algorithm embedded *within the client software itself* (rather than purely online validation), a more elegant, though often significantly harder, bypass involves creating a **Key Generator** or **Keygen**. This approach doesn't patch the target software at all; instead, it provides users with an unlimited supply of keys that the *original, unmodified* software will accept as valid.

The Prerequisite: Creating a keygen requires achieving a deep and complete understanding of the **exact key validation algorithm** used by the target software. This is typically the most challenging part.

Locate Validation Logic: Use static/dynamic analysis (as in 9.1) to pinpoint the function(s) responsible for taking the user-entered key and deciding if it's valid.

Reverse Engineer the Algorithm: Meticulously analyze the disassembly/decompilation of the validation routine(s). Trace the data flow of the input key. Identify all mathematical operations (addition, multiplication, XOR, shifts), logical comparisons, checksum calculations, table lookups, string manipulations, and potentially cryptographic operations (though often simpler custom schemes are used if keygenning is feasible) performed on the key or data derived from it (like a username).

Identify Constraints: Determine the exact conditions the input key must satisfy for the validation to return "true". Is it a specific checksum result? Does a transformation of the key need to match an embedded value? Does it involve satisfying multiple independent checks? Does the key format itself (length, character set) matter?

Implementing the Keygen: Once the algorithm and constraints are fully understood, the cracker writes a **separate, standalone program** (the keygen) that either:

Generates Keys: Implements the *reverse* of the validation or directly implements the *generation* algorithm (if deducible) to produce new strings that meet the required validity constraints. Often takes some input (like a desired username) and generates a corresponding valid key.

Searches for Keys: If the keyspace is small enough or the constraints simple, the keygen might simply iterate through possibilities until it finds a key that satisfies the validation checks derived from the RE process.

Complexity: Creating keygens for simple checksums or basic mathematical algorithms can be relatively straightforward once the logic is reversed. However, if the validation uses standard cryptographic hash functions (like comparing the hash of a key + username against a stored value) or especially asymmetric cryptography (verifying a digital signature on the key data using an embedded public key), creating a true keygen is generally considered **infeasible** without breaking the underlying cryptography (highly unlikely) or obtaining the developer's private key (impossible without a major security breach on the vendor's side). Attackers might still find *implementation flaws* around the crypto checks that allow bypass via patching, but generating valid, cryptographically signed keys from scratch is typically off the table.

Emulation and Server Simulation: Faking the External Dependency

When protection relies on external factors like **online activation servers** or physical **hardware dongles**, patching the client-side check is often the primary bypass method. However, a more sophisticated (and often much harder) approach involves **emulating** the required external component, tricking the client software into believing it's interacting with the genuine article.

Activation Server Simulation:

Protocol Analysis: Use network monitoring tools (Wireshark, Burp Suite, potentially with TLS decryption enabled via Frida/patching) to capture and meticulously analyze the communication between the legitimate client software and the real activation server during a successful (if possible) and failed activation attempt. Understand the request URLs/IPs/ports, headers, message formats (JSON, XML, custom binary), parameters sent, and the exact content of success/failure responses. If encryption is used beyond TLS, try to reverse engineer it.

Develop Fake Server: Create a local server application (e.g., using Python with Flask/Http.server, Node.js, etc.) that listens for incoming connections from the client application (you'll need to redirect the client's network requests to your local server, often by modifying the system's hosts file or using DNS poisoning within your analysis network).

Mimic Behavior: Implement logic in your fake server to parse the incoming activation requests from the client and, regardless of the validity of the submitted key or machine ID, always send back a response that perfectly mimics the structure and content of a **successful activation response** observed during your protocol analysis. This might involve sending back specific success codes, generating plausible-looking (but maybe not cryptographically valid, if signatures aren't checked client-side) activation tokens, or simply sending the expected "OK" message.

Result: The client software communicates with your emulator, receives the fake success response, and proceeds as if successfully activated, storing whatever token your emulator provided.

Challenges: Requires thorough protocol RE. If the server response includes digitally signed data and the client properly verifies that signature using an embedded public key, simply faking the response structure isn't enough; you'd need to somehow bypass the signature check in the client as well (patching). Handling different request types or states in the activation protocol can also be complex.

Hardware Dongle Emulation: This aims to create a software-only simulation of the physical dongle's behavior, allowing the protected application to run without the physical device plugged in.

Low-Level Communication Analysis: Requires capturing and reverse engineering the communication protocol between the host driver/API and the physical USB dongle itself. This often involves USB sniffing (Wireshark/USBPcap, hardware USB analyzers) and reverse engineering the vendor's driver (.sys on Windows, kernel module on Linux) and runtime library (.dll/.so) using static/dynamic analysis. This level of analysis is significantly more complex than typical application RE.

Replicating Dongle Logic: Understand the challenge-response mechanisms, license checking commands, and potentially any data decryption or code execution functions handled by the dongle.

Develop Emulator: Create a software component (perhaps a virtual device driver or a hooked API library) that intercepts calls intended for the real dongle driver/API. This emulator needs to perfectly replicate the responses the real dongle would give, including correctly performing any required cryptographic operations based on the challenge-response protocol (which usually requires having somehow extracted the secret keys from the dongle via hardware attacks – the hardest part).

Challenges: As mentioned under dongles (Chapter 8.1), this is extremely difficult due to the secure nature of modern dongle hardware. Extracting the necessary internal keys or firmware usually requires sophisticated invasive hardware attacks. Successfully emulating a secure dongle in software is rare and represents a very high level of RE expertise across both software and hardware domains.

Prerequisite: Addressing Obfuscation and Anti-RE

It's vital to reiterate that *before* applying most of these bypass techniques (especially patching or developing keygens/emulators based on algorithm analysis), you often first need to **deal with any obfuscation or anti-RE layers** employed by the protection system. You can't patch a jump if its location is obscured by virtualization or control flow flattening. You can't easily reverse engineer a validation algorithm if its code is filled with junk instructions and opaque predicates. You can't reliably use a debugger to observe runtime values if sophisticated anti-debugging checks crash the application immediately.

Therefore, a significant portion of the effort in cracking modern, well-protected software is often consumed simply by **neutralizing these preliminary defenses**:

Unpacking: Dynamically running packed code to the OEP and dumping/fixing the unpacked image.

De-obfuscation: Analyzing and reversing string encryption, dynamic API resolution, control flow flattening (often requiring dynamic tracing or specialized tools), or other obfuscation layers to make the core protection logic accessible and understandable.

Bypassing Anti-RE: Finding and patching anti-debugging checks, hardening the VM environment against detection, or using stealthier analysis tools/techniques.

Only once these defensive layers have been peeled back can the analyst effectively target the underlying vulnerabilities in the core protection mechanism using techniques like patching, keygenning, or emulation. The complexity of modern protectors often lies more in these defensive layers than in the fundamental protection concept itself.

Conclusion: The Art of Dismantling

The techniques for bypassing software protections are diverse, reflecting the variety of defensive strategies employed by developers. Binary patching offers a direct, permanent modification by altering code on disk. Memory patching provides a non-persistent runtime modification via loaders. Key generation requires deep algorithmic understanding to replicate valid license keys. Server or dongle emulation involves mimicking external dependencies through sophisticated protocol analysis and replication.

Executing any of these techniques effectively hinges on the success of the preceding vulnerability identification phase. You must know *where* and *how* the protection is weak before you can target it. Furthermore, particularly with modern software, successfully bypassing protection almost always requires first neutralizing underlying obfuscation and anti-RE layers, which often constitutes the bulk of the reverse engineering challenge. While the technical details are fascinating, it is imperative to remember the legal and ethical framework surrounding these activities. Understanding how defenses are dismantled is crucial for building better ones and for performing authorized security assessments, but applying these techniques illicitly carries severe consequences.

9.3. Ethical Considerations in Cracking: The Responsibility of Knowledge

we've journeyed through the technical intricacies of identifying weaknesses in software defenses (Chapter 9.1) and the practical methods employed to bypass them (Chapter 9.2). Now, however, we must pause and address what is arguably the most critical aspect of this entire discussion: the **Ethical Considerations** surrounding these techniques. This isn't just a footnote or a formality; it is the very foundation upon which responsible practice in reverse engineering, security research, and software development must be built. Understanding *how* to dismantle protections is purely a technical skill; knowing *if, when,* and *why* (or explicitly, why *not*) to do so involves navigating a complex landscape of ethics, legality, and professional responsibility. Possessing the knowledge and ability to bypass digital locks confers a significant power, and like all forms of power, it demands careful consideration and constraint. Simply because you *can* pick a lock doesn't grant you the inherent right to open any door you encounter.

The Weight of Knowledge: Responsibility in Reverse Engineering

The ability to reverse engineer software, especially to the point of bypassing intentional protections, is a sophisticated skill set. It requires dedication, analytical thinking, and a deep understanding of computer systems.

However, this technical capability is inherently **dual-use**. The exact same skills and tools that allow a security professional to uncover a critical vulnerability before it's exploited, or enable a developer to achieve legitimate interoperability between systems, can also be employed by individuals with malicious intent to pirate software, steal intellectual property, cheat in online environments, or facilitate other illegal activities.

This inherent duality places a significant burden of responsibility on anyone who cultivates these skills. It's not enough to simply master the technical "how"; one must also grapple constantly with the "should I?" The potential consequences of misusing these skills are not abstract; they can translate into tangible harm – financial losses for developers and businesses, compromised security for users, erosion of trust in digital systems, and significant legal liabilities for the individual involved. Therefore, a rigorous ethical framework and a clear understanding of the legal boundaries are not optional accessories for the reverse engineer; they are essential components of professional and responsible practice. Technical prowess without ethical grounding is, at best, reckless, and at worst, dangerous.

The Legal Landscape: Copyright, Contracts, and Anti-Circumvention

The primary legal structures governing the use and analysis of software, particularly concerning protection mechanisms, are centered around intellectual property rights and contractual agreements, reinforced by specific anti-circumvention legislation in many parts of the world.

First and foremost is **Copyright Law**. Software, in both its source code and compiled binary forms, is typically protected by copyright as a literary or expressive work. This grants the copyright holder (usually the developer or publisher) exclusive rights over reproduction, distribution, adaptation (creating derivative works), and public display/performance. Reverse engineering activities inherently involve making copies (loading into memory, saving decompiled output) and potentially creating derivative works (patching files, producing heavily annotated disassembly listings).

While some limited copying incidental to analysis might fall under exceptions like fair use in certain contexts (a highly complex and jurisdiction-specific legal doctrine), systematically reverse engineering for the purpose of enabling copyright infringement (like piracy) is clearly illegal. The expression of the code is protected, even if the underlying ideas or algorithms might not be.

Second, almost all commercially distributed software (and much freeware or shareware) is accompanied by an **End User License Agreement (EULA) or Terms of Service (ToS)**. When you install or use the software, you typically must agree to these terms, forming a legally binding contract between you and the provider. It is extremely common, almost universal, for EULAs to contain clauses that explicitly **prohibit reverse engineering, decompilation, disassembly, modification, or circumvention of protection mechanisms**. By agreeing to the EULA, you contractually waive certain rights you might otherwise have had under general copyright principles (like fair use for certain analytical purposes). Violating these explicit contractual prohibitions, even if your ultimate goal isn't direct piracy, can constitute a breach of contract, potentially leading to civil liability. While the enforceability of every EULA clause has occasionally been challenged in court under specific circumstances (e.g., related to unconscionability or conflicting public policy), ignoring clear prohibitions against reverse engineering in a legally accepted agreement is a significant legal risk. Always read and understand the license terms of the software you intend to analyze.

Third, adding another layer of legal complexity, particularly in the United States, is the **Digital Millennium Copyright Act (DMCA)**, enacted in 1998. Section 1201 of the DMCA specifically addresses the **circumvention of technological measures** that effectively control access to copyrighted works. This is distinct from direct copyright infringement. The DMCA makes it illegal to bypass technical protections (like encryption, copy protection systems, activation mechanisms, or DRM) *even if the subsequent use of the accessed work would not itself be infringing*. The mere *act* of circumvention is prohibited, subject only to a set of very specific, narrow, and highly conditional statutory exemptions. Similar anti-circumvention laws exist in many other jurisdictions, often stemming from international treaties like the WIPO Copyright Treaty.

These exemptions under the DMCA (and similar laws) are critical to understand because they outline some of the *only* legally sanctioned paths for bypassing protections. These typically include provisions for:

Security Testing: Allowing circumvention for the sole purpose of testing, investigating, or correcting a security flaw or vulnerability, provided it's done with authorization (either explicit permission from the owner or fitting within specific definitions of legitimate security research) and primarily for improving the security of the system or network involved. Responsible disclosure practices are often implicitly or explicitly required. This exemption does *not* provide a license to crack software for personal use under the guise of "security testing."

Interoperability: Allowing circumvention of access controls necessary to identify and analyze elements of a program required to achieve interoperability between independently created computer programs, but only if specific conditions are met (e.g., the information wasn't readily available elsewhere, the resulting compatible program is non-infringing). This exemption is narrowly construed and based on specific court interpretations like *Sega v. Accolade*.

Encryption Research: Allowing circumvention for identifying flaws in encryption technologies, provided the research is legitimate, necessary, and certain other conditions are met.

Law Enforcement and Intelligence: Exemptions for government activities.

Archival Purposes (Limited): Exemptions allowing libraries, archives, and educational institutions to circumvent protections on obsolete works under specific conditions for preservation.

Crucially, none of these exemptions provides a general right to bypass copy protection simply because one possesses the technical means or disagrees with the protection. Furthermore, the DMCA also prohibits the **trafficking** (manufacturing, importing, offering to the public, providing, or otherwise dealing in) tools or services primarily designed or marketed for the purpose of circumventing these technological measures. This is why creating and distributing keygens or patches specifically designed to bypass copy protection is illegal under the DMCA, separate from any underlying copyright infringement claim.

The combined effect of copyright law, restrictive EULAs, and anti-circumvention statutes like the DMCA creates a legal environment where reverse engineering software *specifically for the purpose of bypassing access controls or copy protection mechanisms* is generally prohibited and carries significant legal risks. Engaging in software piracy – using the techniques described in the previous section to gain unauthorized access to software features or capabilities without a valid license, or distributing tools that enable others to do so – exposes individuals to potentially severe consequences. These can include **civil lawsuits** initiated by the copyright holders seeking substantial monetary damages (actual damages or statutory damages, which can be very high), injunctions to stop the activity, and potentially recovery of legal fees. In cases of large-scale commercial piracy or significant willful infringement, **criminal charges** carrying penalties of hefty fines and imprisonment are also possible under copyright law and potentially related statutes like the Computer Fraud and Abuse Act (CFAA) if server access was involved without authorization.

The Ethical Dimension: Beyond Legal Compliance

While the legal framework sets clear boundaries against piracy and unauthorized circumvention, the ethical considerations surrounding reverse engineering often involve more nuance, particularly when motivations other than simple piracy are involved. Ethics compels us to consider the broader impact of our actions beyond just what is strictly legal or illegal.

The core ethical argument against software piracy is straightforward: it involves taking something of value (the result of the developers' time, skill, creativity, and financial investment) without providing the agreed-upon compensation. This directly harms developers and publishers by depriving them of revenue needed to continue funding software development, maintenance, support, and innovation. Widespread piracy can undermine the economic viability of creating certain types of software, ultimately harming all users by reducing the availability and quality of software products. Beyond the financial aspect, it disrespects the creative work and intellectual property rights of the creators. Therefore, using RE skills to facilitate or engage in piracy is widely considered unethical within the professional software development and security communities.

However, ethical questions become more complex when considering the potential legitimate contexts mentioned earlier:

Security Research: Ethically, finding and responsibly disclosing vulnerabilities is generally seen as a positive contribution to the ecosystem,

improving safety for all users. The key ethical component here is
responsible disclosure. Disclosing vulnerabilities privately to the vendor
first allows them to fix the issue before attackers can exploit it widely.
Publicly dropping zero-day exploits without prior vendor notification, or
selling vulnerabilities on the black market, is typically considered unethical
because it prioritizes personal gain or notoriety over user safety. Bypassing
protections *as necessary* to perform authorized security testing falls within
ethical boundaries, but using discovered vulnerabilities for personal gain or
harm does not.

Interoperability: The ethics here are closely tied to the legal justifications.
If achieving interoperability is necessary for fair competition, user choice, or
enabling innovative complementary products, and if the required interface
information is genuinely unavailable through legitimate means, then
carefully limited reverse engineering undertaken *solely* for this purpose
might be considered ethically justifiable by some, especially if it aligns with
legal precedent in the relevant jurisdiction. However, using "interoperability"
as a pretext to simply copy features or steal trade secrets crosses ethical lines.
Transparency about the purpose and methods is important.

Malware Analysis: This is perhaps the clearest ethical justification for
bypassing protections. Malware inherently uses obfuscation and anti-analysis
techniques for harmful purposes. Bypassing these defenses is ethically
imperative to understand the threat, protect potential victims, and develop
countermeasures. The ethical obligation here is to contain the threat and use
the knowledge defensively.

Data Recovery / Legacy Systems / Abandonware: This presents a genuine
ethical gray area. Imagine owning a legitimate license for specialized
software crucial for accessing your own past work or data. Years later, the
software requires online activation, but the company has gone out of
business, and the activation servers are permanently offline. The software
you legally own is now unusable due to an inaccessible protection
mechanism. Or consider historically significant "abandonware" where the
copyright status is unclear or the rights holder shows no interest in
maintaining or distributing the software. In such cases, using reverse
engineering techniques to bypass the defunct activation or protection solely
to regain access to your *own legally acquired software or data,* or for the
purpose of **digital preservation** of culturally significant abandonware, might

feel ethically justifiable to the individual involved. However, it's crucial to recognize that even in these compelling scenarios, the *legality* might still be questionable under broad anti-circumvention laws like the DMCA, which often lack clear exceptions for defunct activation servers or preservation by individuals. Acting ethically here requires careful consideration of the specific circumstances, minimizing harm, and acknowledging the potential legal ambiguity. It does *not* provide justification for pirating currently available software just because activation is inconvenient.

Navigating the Gray: Intent, Curiosity, and Best Practices

The line between legitimate research or learning and illegitimate cracking can sometimes seem thin, particularly when driven by technical curiosity. Many individuals are drawn to reverse engineering simply to understand how things work or to overcome a technical challenge. While **curiosity** is a powerful motivator for learning, it does not, in itself, override legal restrictions or ethical responsibilities. Applying RE skills to commercially protected software just "to see if you can" typically violates EULA terms and potentially anti-circumvention laws. The technical challenge might be intriguing, but channeling that energy towards legitimate targets – open-source software, deliberately designed challenges like CTFs and CrackMes, personal projects, or authorized security research – is the responsible path.

Intent is often cited as a key factor, but it's not a perfect guide. While malicious intent clearly makes actions unethical and illegal, having a "good" intent (like learning or accessing personally owned but technically defunct software) does not automatically make circumventing protections legal under laws like the DMCA. The law often focuses on the *act* of circumvention itself, regardless of the subsequent use, unless a specific statutory exemption applies.

Given these complexities, how should a responsible individual navigate this landscape?

Prioritize Legality: Always operate within the known bounds of the law in your jurisdiction. Be aware of Copyright Law, the DMCA or similar local anti-circumvention statutes, and crucially, the **EULA/ToS** of the specific software you are considering analyzing. If the license explicitly prohibits reverse engineering and you lack a clear, legally recognized exemption (like authorized security testing or fitting squarely within the narrow interoperability guidelines), refrain from attempting to bypass protections on that software.

Clarify Your Purpose: Before starting any analysis that might involve bypassing protections, ask yourself pointed questions: *Why* am I doing this? What is my specific, legitimate goal? Is it security research for a client who authorized me? Is it essential for understanding malware for defense? Am I trying to achieve interoperability for a demonstrably legitimate purpose with no alternative source of information? Is this purely for personal education on a permissive target? Clearly defining your purpose helps align your actions with ethical and legal justifications.

Assess the Risks: What are the potential consequences if my actions are discovered or challenged? Consider legal risks (civil suits, criminal charges), professional reputational damage, and potential technical risks (destabilizing systems if patching goes wrong).

Use Skills Constructively: Strive to apply reverse engineering skills in ways that build up rather than tear down – contributing to security, enabling interoperability where appropriate, preserving digital history, recovering data, analyzing threats, or simply furthering personal technical understanding through legitimate channels.

Seek Professional Advice When Unsure: Legal interpretations, especially concerning fair use, interoperability exemptions, and the DMCA, are complex and fact-specific. Relying on internet forum opinions is unwise. If engaging in activities with potential legal implications (especially in a commercial context), consulting with a qualified lawyer specializing in intellectual property, software law, and cybersecurity is highly recommended.

Defensive Value: Understanding the Attack to Strengthen the Defense
Finally, it's crucial to recognize the immense **defensive value** in understanding the very techniques used to bypass protections. Security professionals, software developers building protections, and penetration testers need to understand the attacker's mindset and methods to be effective. Knowing how common patching techniques work, how keygens are developed for weak algorithms, how server emulators can defeat online checks, or how anti-RE measures are typically bypassed allows defenders to:

Design Stronger Protections: Avoid common pitfalls like simple final check jumps, insecure key storage, weak algorithms, or easily detectable anti-RE checks. Implement multiple, overlapping layers of defense. Incorporate robust integrity checking. Design server-side validation logic more carefully.

Perform Realistic Security Testing: Authorized penetration testers can simulate realistic cracking attempts to evaluate the actual resilience of implemented protections, identifying weaknesses before malicious actors do.

Develop Better Detection: Understanding bypass techniques helps inform the creation of security tools (EDR, anti-cheat) that can better detect memory patching attempts, suspicious debugging activity, or signs of specific bypass tools being used.

In this sense, studying bypass techniques, even without employing them illicitly, is essential defensive knowledge for anyone serious about software security.

Conclusion: Wielding Knowledge Wisely

The technical ability to bypass software protections represents a significant level of reverse engineering skill. However, this chapter underscores that technical capability must be tempered by a deep understanding and respect for the intricate legal frameworks and ethical considerations involved. Software piracy harms creators and the ecosystem. Anti-circumvention laws like the DMCA impose strict legal limits. While narrow exemptions and ethically ambiguous situations exist, the default stance must be one of caution and compliance.

The knowledge of how protections are identified and dismantled is powerful – primarily as a tool for defenders to build stronger systems and for security professionals to test those systems responsibly. It illuminates the constant arms race between protection and circumvention. Wield this knowledge wisely, ethically, and always within the clear boundaries of the law. With this critical foundation of responsibility firmly established, we can proceed to explore the application of reverse engineering principles to the unique challenges presented by modern computing platforms.

Chapter 10: Reverse Engineering Modern Platforms

The techniques we've discussed so far apply widely, but the digital landscape is constantly evolving. Desktop applications are just one piece of the puzzle. Today, we interact constantly with mobile apps, dynamic web applications, and services running entirely in the cloud. Reverse engineering these modern platforms presents unique challenges and often requires adapting our approaches and toolsets. Think of it as moving from analyzing a single, self-contained machine to understanding components within a vast, interconnected ecosystem.

10.1. Mobile Application Analysis: Unpacking the App Stores

Okay, let's transition our reverse engineering focus from the traditional desktop environment to the dynamic and ubiquitous world of **Mobile Applications**. In today's digital landscape, smartphones are central hubs of activity, containing vast amounts of personal and sensitive data, controlling connected devices, and acting as gateways to countless online services. Consequently, the applications running on these devices have become prime targets for analysis, driven by diverse motivations: **security researchers** probing for vulnerabilities, **malware analysts** dissecting mobile threats, **developers** seeking interoperability or understanding competitor features, and even **hobbyists** exploring how their favorite apps function internally. Analyzing mobile apps introduces unique challenges and requires specific tools and techniques tailored to the dominant platforms: **Google's Android** and **Apple's iOS**. While they share the common goal of running applications on mobile hardware, their underlying architectures, programming languages, execution models, security philosophies, and distribution mechanisms differ significantly, leading to distinct reverse engineering workflows for each. Mastering mobile RE necessitates understanding the intricacies of both ecosystems.

Android Application Analysis: Diving into APKs and DEX Bytecode
Android holds the largest global market share, making Android application analysis a critical skill. Apps are typically distributed as **APK (Android**

Package Kit) files, downloadable from the Google Play Store or other sources. Understanding the nature of an APK is the first step.

APK Structure: More Than Just an App

At its core, an APK file is simply a specialized **ZIP archive**. You can actually rename an .apk file to .zip and open it with standard archive tools to inspect its contents. Inside, you'll find several key components:

AndroidManifest.xml: This is the blueprint or manifest file for the application. It's a crucial starting point for static analysis, containing essential metadata about the app's identity, requirements, and components. Written in binary XML format within the APK, it needs to be decoded (tools like apktool do this automatically).

classes.dex (or multiple classesN.dex files): This is the heart of the application's logic. It contains the compiled code in the **DEX (Dalvik Executable)** format. DEX bytecode is executed by the **Android Runtime (ART)** (or its predecessor, Dalvik). It's conceptually similar to Java bytecode but optimized for mobile devices (e.g., it's register-based rather than stack-based like JVM bytecode). If the app exceeds a certain method count limit, it might be split into multiple DEX files (classes2.dex, classes3.dex, etc.). This is the primary target for code analysis.

resources.arsc: Contains precompiled application resources, such as strings, dimensions, and styles referenced by the code. Tools are needed to decode this binary format back into more readable resource values.

res/ directory: Holds uncompiled resources like layouts (XML files defining the UI structure), images (drawables), menus, raw assets, etc. These can provide context about the app's UI and appearance.

assets/ directory: Contains raw asset files that the application can bundle and access directly by filename (e.g., configuration files, databases, bundled scripts).

lib/ directory: This directory is critical as it contains compiled **native code** libraries (.so files, Shared Objects) organized by CPU architecture (e.g., armeabi-v7a, arm64-v8a, x86, x86_64). Applications use native code via the **Java Native Interface (JNI)** for performance-critical tasks (graphics, signal processing), to reuse existing C/C++ codebases, or sometimes deliberately to make reverse engineering harder. Analyzing these .so files requires standard native code RE tools.

META-INF/ directory: Contains application signing information (certificates, manifest signature). This verifies the app's origin and ensures its integrity hasn't been tampered with since signing. Modifying an APK usually requires re-signing it (often with a self-signed development key for analysis purposes).

Analyzing the Blueprint: AndroidManifest.xml

Before diving into the code, always examine the decoded AndroidManifest.xml. It provides a high-level overview of the application's capabilities and potential attack surface:

Package Name: The unique identifier for the app (e.g., com.example.myapp).

Permissions: A crucial section (<uses-permission>). What permissions does the app request? Access to contacts (READ_CONTACTS), SMS (READ_SMS), location (ACCESS_FINE_LOCATION), camera (CAMERA), internet (INTERNET), external storage (WRITE_EXTERNAL_STORAGE), ability to run at startup (RECEIVE_BOOT_COMPLETED)? Unnecessary or excessive permissions are a major red flag for privacy risks or potential malware functionality.

Components: Declares the app's core building blocks:

Activities: Represent individual screens or UI flows.

Services: Perform background operations without a UI.

Broadcast Receivers: Respond to system-wide broadcasts or custom intents (e.g., listen for boot completion, SMS received).

Content Providers: Manage access to shared application data (less common for direct RE focus usually).

Exported Components: Crucially, check if any Activities, Services, or Receivers are marked as android:exported="true". Exported components can potentially be launched or interacted with by *other* applications on the device, representing a potential attack surface if not properly secured with permissions. Implicitly exported components (those with intent filters without explicit export status prior to Android 12) should also be scrutinized.

Application Metadata: May contain API keys, configuration flags, or other relevant info (though sensitive data *shouldn't* be here).

Hardware Features: (<uses-feature>) Declares hardware dependencies (e.g., requiring Bluetooth, NFC, specific sensors).

Understanding the manifest sets the stage, highlighting what the app *claims* it can do and what entry points might be accessible.

Static Analysis of DEX Bytecode: Smali vs. Decompilation

The core logic resides in the classes.dex file(s). Analyzing this DEX bytecode is central to Android RE. There are two primary approaches:

Smali Disassembly: Tools like **apktool** (apktool d myapp.apk) can decompile the APK, decode resources, and disassemble the DEX bytecode into a human-readable assembly language called **Smali**. Smali syntax reflects the underlying register-based DEX instruction set (e.g., move-object, invoke-virtual, iget-object, if-eqz). Analyzing Smali directly provides the most accurate representation of the executed code but requires learning its syntax and is often more tedious than working with decompiled code. It becomes necessary when decompilers fail, produce incorrect output (often due to obfuscation or unusual bytecode), or when you need to understand fine-grained low-level details or make precise patches at the bytecode level (using apktool b to reassemble).

Conceptual Smali Snippet:

```
    # Sample Smali for a simple method
.method public static isLicenseValid(Ljava/lang/String;)Z #
Method signature (takes String, returns boolean Z)
    .registers 4 # Number of registers used by this method
    .param p0, "licenseKey"    # Parameter name (annotation)

    const/4 v0, 0x0 # Assign constant 0 to register v0
(false)
    const-string v1, "VALID_KEY_123" # Assign constant string
to register v1

    # Call string comparison (e.g., String.equals)
    invoke-virtual {p0, v1},
Ljava/lang/String;->equals(Ljava/lang/Object;)Z
    move-result v2 # Move boolean result of call into
register v2

    if-eqz v2, :cond_false # If result (v2) is zero (false),
jump to :cond_false

    # If condition was true (key matched)
    const/4 v0, 0x1 # Assign constant 1 to register v0 (true)

:cond_false
    return v0 # Return value in v0
.end method
```

Interpretation: Even without deep Smali knowledge, we see: parameters (p0), local registers (v0, v1, v2), constants being loaded (const/4, const-string), a method call (invoke-virtual), the result being moved (move-result), a conditional jump based on the result (if-eqz), and finally a return (return v0). Analyzing this directly confirms the logic: compare input key (p0) with "VALID_KEY_123" and return true (1) if equal, false (0) otherwise.

Java/Kotlin Decompilation: For faster understanding of higher-level logic, using **decompilers** is usually preferred. The common workflow involves:

dex2jar: Convert the classes.dex file(s) into a standard Java Archive (.jar) file containing equivalent Java bytecode.

Java Decompiler: Use tools like **JD-GUI** (graphical), **Luyten** (graphical fork of Procyon), **CFR** (command-line), or **Fernflower/Quiltflower** (often integrated into IDEs/other tools) to decompile the Java bytecode within the JAR file back into Java source code. Many modern Android apps are written in **Kotlin**, which also compiles to DEX via Java bytecode; decompilers often handle Kotlin reasonably well, producing Java code that reflects the Kotlin logic, although some Kotlin-specific features might decompile less elegantly.

Integrated Tools: Powerful commercial tools like **JEB Decompiler** or the open-source **Ghidra** can directly disassemble and decompile DEX bytecode into pseudo-code (often Java-like) within a single integrated environment, streamlining the process significantly compared to the dex2jar+JD-GUI route.

Decompilation provides a much more intuitive view of the application's logic, algorithms, and class structure, making static analysis significantly faster than reading Smali. However, accuracy depends heavily on the next point: obfuscation.

Dealing with Obfuscation (ProGuard/R8): Android developers almost universally use tools like **ProGuard** (older) or **R8** (newer, integrated with the Android build system) to **optimize** and **obfuscate** their code before release. These tools perform several crucial actions:

Code Shrinking: Remove unused classes, methods, and fields to reduce the APK size.

Optimization: Apply various bytecode optimizations for potentially better performance.

Identifier Renaming (Obfuscation): This is the most impactful for RE. ProGuard/R8 renames classes, methods, and fields that are not entry points or required by reflection to short, meaningless names (like a, b, c, a.a, a.b). *Impact on RE:* When you decompile an obfuscated app, the resulting Java/Kotlin code will be littered with these meaningless names (e.g., class a { public void b(com.example.pkg.c cVar) {...} }). This strips away the semantic context provided by meaningful names, making it much harder to understand the code's purpose simply by reading the decompilation. Static analysis becomes much more reliant on understanding control flow, analyzing data flow (tracking how renamed variables are used), identifying calls to known Android SDK or standard Java APIs, and meticulously renaming variables and methods *yourself* within the RE tool based on your deduced understanding. The presence of a mapping.txt file alongside an APK (sometimes accidentally included or obtained separately) is invaluable, as it contains the mapping between the original names and the obfuscated names, allowing RE tools to automatically apply the original names during analysis. Malware authors might also employ *additional*, more sophisticated obfuscation techniques beyond ProGuard/R8, such as string encryption, control flow flattening, reflection abuse, or hiding logic within native code, requiring the advanced de-obfuscation techniques discussed previously.

Analyzing Native Libraries (JNI): If the APK includes .so files in the lib/ directory, a portion of the app's logic resides in native code (usually C/C++). The Java/Kotlin code interacts with this native code via the **Java Native Interface (JNI)**. Calls from Java/Kotlin to native functions look like standard method calls but are marked with the native keyword. Calls *from* native code *back to* Java/Kotlin use specific JNI functions provided by the Android environment (env->FindClass, env->GetMethodID, env->CallVoidMethod, etc.).

RE Strategy: Analyzing the Java/Kotlin side involves identifying the native method declarations. Analyzing the .so file itself requires using standard native code reverse engineering tools (**IDA Pro, Ghidra, radare2**) capable of handling the specific CPU architecture (usually **ARM** or **ARM64** for modern Android, sometimes x86/x86_64 for emulators or specific devices). You'll look for exported functions with names matching a specific JNI convention (e.g., Java_com_example_myapp_MyClass_myNativeMethod). Inside these native functions, you'll analyze the ARM or x86 assembly, paying attention to how function arguments (passed from Java, including the JNI environment pointer env and object/class pointers) are accessed and how JNI functions are used to interact back with the Java/Kotlin side (calling methods, accessing fields). Analyzing native code is generally harder than decompiling DEX bytecode, which is precisely why developers sometimes place sensitive logic (license checks, cryptographic routines) there.

Dynamic Analysis on Android: The Runtime Perspective

Static analysis reveals the code's potential, but dynamic analysis shows what it *actually* does at runtime. Given Android's complex lifecycle, interactions between components, reliance on system services, and the prevalence of obfuscation, dynamic analysis is often where the most crucial insights are gained.

Setting Up the Environment: You need a controlled environment for execution:

Emulators: The **Android Emulator** included with Android Studio, or third-party emulators like **Genymotion**, provide virtualized Android environments running on your computer. They are convenient and easily revertible.

Physical Devices (Rooted Recommended): Using a real Android phone or tablet provides the most realistic environment. However, for deep analysis and tool usage (especially Frida), the device typically needs to be **rooted**. Rooting grants privileged access (like su), allowing you to bypass standard security restrictions, install low-level tools, access any application's data directory, and modify the system freely. Use dedicated test devices for r

10.2. Web Application Deconstruction: Beyond the Browser Window

let's shift our reverse engineering lens away from compiled native binaries and mobile apps towards another ubiquitous platform: the **Web Application**. When we talk about "reverse engineering" a web application, our approach and focus change significantly compared to traditional software analysis. This is because a web application fundamentally consists of two distinct parts: the **server-side** code (running on a remote web server, often written in languages like Python, Java, Node.js, PHP, Ruby, C#, etc.) which processes requests and manages data, and the **client-side** code (primarily HTML, CSS, and especially JavaScript) which is delivered to and executed within the user's web browser.

Crucially, as external analysts, we almost never have direct access to the server-side source code or the server environment itself (barring source code leaks or significant security breaches). Therefore, traditional static analysis of backend logic using disassemblers like IDA Pro or Ghidra is simply impossible. Instead, **Web Application Deconstruction**, from a reverse engineering perspective, predominantly focuses on analyzing the **client-side** components that *are* delivered to our browser. Our goal is typically twofold: to understand the logic embedded within the client-side code (how the user interface behaves, how data is manipulated locally) and, more importantly, to decipher how the client-side code **interacts with the hidden server-side backend** by meticulously analyzing the network communication between them, particularly the Application Programming Interface (API) calls. We're essentially examining the visible tip of the iceberg (the client-side) to infer as much as possible about its structure, behavior, and its connection to the submerged, inaccessible mass (the server-side).

The Indispensable Toolkit: Your Browser's Developer Tools

Forget about IDA Pro or Ghidra for a moment; when dissecting the client-side of a web application, your single most powerful and essential tool is already built directly into your modern web browser (Chrome, Firefox, Edge, Safari). These are the **Developer Tools**, often accessible simply by pressing the F12 key or right-clicking on a webpage element and selecting "Inspect" or "Inspect Element". These integrated suites provide a wealth of information and control over how the browser renders pages and executes client-side code, making them the primary workbench for web RE. While external tools certainly have their place (especially network proxies), mastering the browser's built-in tools is the non-negotiable starting point. Let's explore the key components relevant to our analysis:

The Elements (or Inspector) Tab: Deconstructing the Structure

This tab provides a live, interactive view of the **Document Object Model (DOM)** – the structured, tree-like representation of the currently rendered HTML page that the browser builds in memory. It's not just the raw HTML source code; it's the *live* result after HTML parsing, CSS styling, and any JavaScript manipulations have occurred.

Examining HTML Structure: You can navigate the hierarchical tree of HTML elements (tags like <div>, <p>, <input>, <script>), inspect their attributes (id, class, src, href), and see how they are nested. This helps understand the page layout and identify key UI components.

Analyzing CSS Styling: The 'Styles' or 'Computed' sub-pane within the Elements tab shows exactly which CSS rules are being applied to a selected element, revealing how the page achieves its visual appearance and sometimes hinting at hidden elements or state-dependent styling.

Finding Embedded/Linked Scripts: By inspecting <script> tags within the HTML, you can see where JavaScript code is loaded from (src attribute linking to external .js files) or sometimes find snippets of JavaScript embedded directly within the HTML (less common practice for complex code). This helps identify the relevant script files for later analysis.

Locating Event Listeners: Modern web applications are highly interactive. User actions like clicking buttons, submitting forms, hovering over elements, or typing into fields trigger JavaScript functions via **event listeners**. The Developer Tools often provide a way to inspect an element and see exactly which event listeners (like click, mouseover, submit, keydown) are attached to it and which JavaScript functions or code snippets will be executed when those events fire. This is crucial for finding the entry points into the JavaScript logic associated with specific user interactions. Examining the event listeners attached to a "Login" button, for example, will lead you directly to the JavaScript code that handles the login process (collecting credentials, making an API call).

Live DOM Manipulation: You can often directly edit the HTML attributes or content within the Elements tab and see the changes reflected live on the page. This can be useful for testing how the application reacts to unexpected structures, bypassing simple client-side validation that relies on specific element attributes, or unhiding diagnostic elements.

The Elements tab provides the structural context, showing the rendered state of the UI and providing starting points (scripts, event listeners) for diving into the underlying JavaScript logic.

The Network Tab: Monitoring the Conversation with the Server

This is arguably the **most critical tab** for reverse engineering the interaction between the client and the backend server. The Network tab meticulously records **every single HTTP/HTTPS request** made by the browser as it loads and interacts with the web page. This includes requests for:

The main HTML document itself.

CSS stylesheets (.css files).

JavaScript code (.js files).

Images, fonts, and other static assets.

And most importantly for RE: **Asynchronous data requests** made by JavaScript *after* the initial page load, typically using **XMLHttpRequest (XHR)** or the newer **Fetch API**. These requests are how modern Single Page Applications (SPAs) dynamically load data, submit forms, and interact with backend APIs without requiring a full page reload.

For each recorded request, the Network tab provides a wealth of information crucial for analysis:

URL: The full Uniform Resource Locator being requested. This reveals the endpoints of backend APIs (e.g., https://api.example.com/v2/users/123/profile) or the location of static resources.

Method: The HTTP verb used (e.g., GET for retrieving data, POST for submitting data, PUT for updating, DELETE for removing).

Status Code: The HTTP status code returned by the server (e.g., 200 OK, 201 Created, 404 Not Found, 403 Forbidden, 401 Unauthorized, 500 Internal Server Error). Essential for understanding the outcome of the request.

Timing Information: How long different phases of the request took (waiting, receiving, etc.), useful for performance analysis but less often a primary RE focus.

Request Headers: The full set of HTTP headers sent by the browser with the request. Critically important headers to examine include:

Host: Target server hostname.

User-Agent: Identifies the browser.

Content-Type: Specifies the format of the request body (e.g., application/json, application/x-www-form-urlencoded).

Accept: Tells the server what content types the client prefers in the response.

Cookie: Contains session cookies or other relevant cookies being sent to the server, often used for session management and authentication state.

Authorization: Often contains credentials or tokens (e.g., Bearer <JWT_token>, Basic <base64_encoded_credentials>) used for API authentication. Analyzing these is vital for understanding security mechanisms.

Custom Headers (X-...): Applications often use custom headers for specific purposes (e.g., X-API-Key, X-CSRF-Token, X-Request-ID).

Request Payload/Body: The data sent *to* the server with POST, PUT, or PATCH requests. This is where you'll see submitted form data, JSON objects representing data to be created or updated, etc. Understanding the structure and format of this payload is key to understanding the API's input requirements.

Response Headers: The full set of headers sent *back* by the server. Important ones include:

Content-Type: Specifies the format of the response body (e.g., application/json, text/html, image/png).

Content-Length: Size of the response body.

Set-Cookie: Instructs the browser to set or update cookies, crucial for session management.

Location: Used for redirects (e.g., after login).

Cache-Control, Expires, ETag: Related to caching.

Security Headers: Content-Security-Policy, Strict-Transport-Security, X-Frame-Options, etc.

Response Body: The actual content returned by the server. For API calls, this is frequently **JSON (JavaScript Object Notation)** data, but could also be XML, HTML fragments, or other formats. Examining the structure and content of the response body reveals what data the API provides.

Using the Network Tab Effectively:

Filtering: The sheer number of requests can be large. Use the built-in filters (e.g., filter by "Fetch/XHR") to focus specifically on the dynamic API calls made by JavaScript, which are usually the most interesting for understanding client-server interaction. You can also filter by domain or keywords in the URL.

Correlation with Actions: Perform an action in the UI (e.g., click "Load More Posts," submit a form, add an item to cart) and immediately observe the new requests that appear in the Network tab. This directly links user actions to specific backend API calls.

Inspecting Payloads: Carefully examine the structure of JSON or other data sent in request bodies and received in response bodies. This reverse engineers the data models used by the API.

Authentication Flow: Track requests related to login. How are credentials sent? What headers or cookies (Set-Cookie) are returned upon successful login? How are subsequent requests authenticated (e.g., sending back the session cookie or an Authorization: Bearer token)?

Understanding the conversation happening over the network via API calls is often the single most important outcome of client-side web application RE. It reveals the interface to the hidden server-side logic.

Conceptual Example: Interpreting Network Log for API Call

Imagine clicking a "Get User Profile" button triggers the following in the Network Tab (simplified):

Request:

URL: https://api.example.com/v1/users/me/profile

Method: GET

Request Headers:

Accept: application/json

Authorization: Bearer
eyJhbGciOiJIUzI1NiIsIn...[snip]...a_very_long_jwt_token

X-Request-ID: abc-123

Response:

Status Code: 200 OK

Response Headers:

Content-Type: application/json; charset=utf-8

Content-Length: 150

Response Body (JSON):

```json
{
  "userId": "user-987",
  "username": "alice_dev",
  "email": "alice@example.com",
  "fullName": "Alice Developer",
  "accountStatus": "active",
  "preferences": {
    "theme": "dark",
    "notifications": true
  }
}
```

RE Interpretation: This reveals:

* An API endpoint exists at /v1/users/me/profile to fetch the current user's profile.
* It uses the GET method.
* Authentication is performed using a **Bearer Token** (likely a JSON Web Token - JWT) sent in the Authorization header. Obtaining and potentially analyzing this token would be a next step.
* The server responds with JSON data containing specific fields (userId, username, email, nested preferences, etc.). This defines the structure of the user profile data model used by the API.

The Sources (or Debugger) Tab: Executing and Inspecting JavaScript

This tab is where you interact directly with the client-side **JavaScript** code. It acts as a full-fledged JavaScript debugger integrated into the browser.

Viewing Loaded Scripts: You can navigate through all the JavaScript files loaded by the page (whether linked via <script src="..."> or embedded inline). This allows you to read the source code directly. However, as we'll discuss, this code is often not in its original, human-friendly form due to minification/transpilation.

Setting Breakpoints: Just like a native code debugger, you can click in the gutter next to a line number in the JavaScript code to set a **breakpoint**. Execution will pause whenever the browser's JavaScript engine reaches that line. Breakpoints are essential for stopping execution at critical points, such as:

The start of an event handler function triggered by a user action.

Just before an API call (XHR/Fetch) is made, allowing you to inspect the data being sent.

Inside the callback function that processes the response received from an API call, allowing you to see the raw data and how it's handled.

Within complex calculation or validation logic.

Stepping Through Execution: Once paused at a breakpoint, you have standard stepping controls:

Step Over (F10): Executes the current line; if it's a function call, executes the entire function and pauses after it returns.

Step Into (F11): Executes the current line; if it's a function call, pauses at the first line *inside* the called function.

Step Out (Shift+F11): Continues execution until the current function returns, then pauses.

Resume (F8): Continues normal execution until the next breakpoint or event.

Inspecting State: While paused, you can examine the current state of the JavaScript environment:

Call Stack: Shows the sequence of nested function calls leading to the current pause point.

Scope Pane: Displays the values of local variables within the current function's scope, variables in closure scopes, and global variables. This is crucial for understanding the data being manipulated.

Watch Pane: Allows you to enter specific JavaScript expressions (e.g., myVariable, this.currentUser.id, calculateValue(x)) and have the debugger continuously evaluate and display their values whenever execution is paused.

10.3. Cloud-Based Systems Challenges: Peering Through the Fog

Alright, let's explore the final frontier we'll cover in our platform-specific discussions: reverse engineering **Cloud-Based Systems**. This represents a significant paradigm shift compared to analyzing self-contained desktop applications or even mobile apps running locally on a device. In the cloud era, applications are increasingly architected such that the vast majority of the core logic, data processing, and state management resides not on the user's machine, but distributed across potentially numerous servers running within massive data centers managed by cloud providers like Amazon Web Services (AWS), Microsoft Azure, or Google Cloud Platform (GCP). This fundamentally alters the landscape for the reverse engineer.

What often happens is that the client application – whether it's a desktop executable, a mobile app, or the JavaScript running in a web browser – becomes significantly "thinner." Its primary responsibilities might shrink to handling user interface rendering, collecting user input, and acting essentially as an interactive terminal that makes **Application Programming Interface (API)** calls over the network to the powerful backend services hosted in the cloud. The complex business logic, database interactions, heavy computations, and coordination between different functional modules all occur remotely, hidden behind the veil of the cloud infrastructure.

The Invisibility Cloak: Why Server-Side RE is Usually Off-Limits

The most immediate and defining challenge when approaching cloud-based systems is the **fundamental lack of access to the server-side code**. As an external analyst (unless you're performing an internal audit with explicit authorization, or analyzing leaked source code), you simply don't possess the executables, bytecode, scripts, or container images running on the provider's cloud servers. You cannot attach a debugger to a process running deep within AWS EC2 or Azure App Service, nor can you load the backend microservice binary into IDA Pro or Ghidra. The traditional static and dynamic code analysis techniques that are the bedrock of reversing local software become largely inapplicable to the core backend logic.

Therefore, reverse engineering cloud systems necessitates a radical shift in focus: away from dissecting internal code algorithms and towards meticulously analyzing **interfaces and interactions**. The primary target becomes the **API** – the public or private contract defining how the client application (which you *can* often analyze) communicates with the inaccessible cloud backend. Your goal is to understand this API's structure, behavior, security mechanisms, and data formats purely from the outside, treating the backend as an opaque "black box."

Black-Box Analysis: Probing the API Interface

Since we cannot see inside the cloud backend, our analysis relies entirely on observing how it interacts with the outside world (primarily through its APIs) and experimenting with those interactions. This involves two main activities:

Observation (Passive Analysis): The first step is to carefully observe the communication generated by a **legitimate client application** as it interacts normally with the cloud backend. This tells you how the API is *intended* to be used.

Tools: This requires network monitoring tools positioned between the client and the cloud endpoint.

Browser Developer Tools (Network Tab): Essential for web applications, as discussed in 10.2. It logs all HTTP/S requests, including XHR/Fetch calls made by JavaScript to backend APIs.

Intercepting Proxies (Burp Suite, OWASP ZAP, mitmproxy): More powerful than browser tools, these run as intermediaries on your analysis machine. You configure the client application (desktop, mobile, sometimes even browser system settings) to route its network traffic through the proxy. These tools can intercept, log, and importantly, allow you to inspect and even modify *all* HTTP/S traffic in transit. Analyzing HTTPS requires setting up the proxy's Root CA certificate on the client device/system and often involves bypassing **certificate pinning** (using techniques described in mobile RE, like Frida) if the client employs it.

Packet Sniffers (Wireshark): For protocols *other* than HTTP/S, or for lower-level analysis, Wireshark (with appropriate capture drivers like Npcap/USBPcap/tcpdump) captures raw network packets, allowing dissection of any TCP/UDP-based custom protocol. However, analyzing encrypted traffic (like standard TLS/SSL) requires having the session keys, which is usually only possible if you control the client and can extract the keys (e.g., via browser logging or specific system settings) or if you're successfully performing TLS interception with a proxy.

What to Look For: Meticulously examine the captured requests and responses. Pay attention to:

The exact **URLs/Endpoints** being accessed.

The **HTTP Methods** (GET, POST, PUT, DELETE, etc.) used for each endpoint.

Headers sent by the client (especially Authorization, Cookie, Content-Type, User-Agent, custom X- headers).

Request Body content and format (JSON, XML, form data, custom binary).

Response Status Codes (2xx, 4xx, 5xx).

Response Headers (especially Set-Cookie, Content-Type, security headers).

Response Body content and structure (often JSON).

Sequence of Calls: How do different API calls relate to achieve a specific user action (e.g., login flow, data retrieval workflow)?

Experimentation (Active Analysis): Once you have observed how the legitimate client uses the API, you can start actively probing the API yourself by sending crafted requests. This allows you to test assumptions, explore undocumented parameters or endpoints, and assess security.

Tools:

API Clients (Postman, Insomnia): Graphical tools designed specifically for crafting and sending HTTP/S requests. They make it easy to set methods, URLs, headers, request bodies, manage authentication, and view responses in a structured way. Ideal for manual exploration and testing of discovered API endpoints.

Command-Line Tools (curl): A powerful and ubiquitous command-line utility for making HTTP/S requests. Highly scriptable and excellent for quick tests or integrating API calls into automated scripts.

Custom Scripts (Python requests, Node.js axios, etc.): For complex interaction sequences, automated testing, or fuzzing, writing custom scripts using HTTP client libraries in your preferred programming language provides maximum flexibility.

Code Example: Conceptual Probing with Python requests

Suppose observation revealed a GET request to /api/v1/items/{item_id} requires an API key in a header. We can write a script to test different item IDs:

```python
#!/usr/bin/env python3
# -*- coding: utf-8 -*-

import requests # Popular HTTP library for Python
import json
import os
import time

# Configuration (Replace with actual values discovered via
observation)
BASE_URL = "https://api.example-cloud-service.com/api/v1"
# API key obtained through legitimate client analysis or
documentation (if available)
# WARNING: Hardcoding secrets like this is bad practice for
real applications!
# Use environment variables or secure config management in
production.
API_KEY = os.environ.get("MY_APP_API_KEY", "dummy-key-if-not-
set-env")

HEADERS = {
    'Authorization': f'ApiKey {API_KEY}', # Common way to
send API keys
    'Accept': 'application/json',
    'User-Agent': 'MyREAnalysisClient/1.0'
}

def get_item_details(item_id: int) -> Optional[Dict]:
```

```python
    """Attempts to fetch details for a specific item ID from
the cloud API."""
    endpoint = f"{BASE_URL}/items/{item_id}"
    print(f"[*] Probing endpoint: {endpoint}")
    try:
        # Make the GET request with specified headers and
timeout
        response = requests.get(endpoint, headers=HEADERS,
timeout=10) # 10 second timeout

        print(f"  [+] Status Code: {response.status_code}")
        # Print response headers for inspection (optional)
        # print("  [+] Response Headers:")
        # for key, value in response.headers.items():
        #     print(f"      {key}: {value}")

        # Attempt to parse response as JSON if successful
(status code 2xx)
        if response.ok: # Checks if status code is < 400
            try:
                data = response.json()
                print(f"  [+] Success! Received JSON data:")
                # Pretty print the JSON response
                print(json.dumps(data, indent=2))
                return data
            except json.JSONDecodeError:
                print("  [!] Success status code, but failed
to decode JSON response.")
                print(f"  Raw Response Text:
{response.text[:200]}...") # Show start of text
                return None
        else:
            # Handle common error codes explicitly
            if response.status_code == 401:
                print("  [-] Error: Unauthorized (Check API
Key?)")
            elif response.status_code == 403:
                print("  [-] Error: Forbidden (Permission
denied for this ID?)")
            elif response.status_code == 404:
                print(f"  [-] Error: Item ID {item_id} Not
Found.")
            else:
                print(f"  [-] Error: Received unexpected
status code {response.status_code}.")
                print(f"  Response Text:
{response.text[:200]}...")
            return None

    except requests.exceptions.RequestException as e:
        print(f"  [!] Network or Request Error: {e}")
```

```
        return None

# --- Main Execution ---
if __name__ == "__main__":
    if API_KEY == "dummy-key-if-not-set-env":
        print("Warning: MY_APP_API_KEY environment variable
not set. Using dummy key.")

    # Test a sequence of Item IDs
    test_ids = [101, 102, 999, 103, -1] # Include existing
and potentially non-existing IDs

    for an_id in test_ids:
        get_item_details(an_id)
        time.sleep(1) # Brief pause between requests
        print("-" * 20)
```

Explanation: This script uses the popular requests library in Python.

1. It defines the base URL and the API key (retrieved securely from an environment variable if set, otherwise using a placeholder – **never hardcode real keys in scripts shared publicly!**).

2. It sets up the necessary HTTP headers identified during observation (Authorization, Accept).

3. The get_item_details function takes an item_id, constructs the full endpoint URL, and makes a GET request using requests.get().

4. It then checks the response status_code. If it's successful (response.ok), it attempts to parse the response body as JSON using response.json() and prints the structured data.

5. If the status code indicates an error (4xx, 5xx), it prints an informative error message based on common codes (401, 403, 404) or shows the raw text for unexpected errors.

6. Network exceptions (timeouts, connection errors) are caught and reported.

7. The main block demonstrates iterating through a list of test IDs, calling the function for each, allowing the analyst to probe the API for different items and observe the responses, thereby learning about valid ID ranges, data structures, and error handling. This type of experimentation is central to black-box API RE.

Authentication and Authorization: Guarding the Cloud Gates

Understanding *how* the API controls access is paramount. Simply knowing the endpoints and data formats is useless if you cannot make authenticated requests. Analyzing the authentication (proving identity) and authorization (proving identity) and authorization (determining permissions) mechanisms is often the most critical and security-relevant part of cloud API RE.

Common Mechanisms:

API Keys: Static, pre-shared secrets (long strings). Often sent in a custom request header (e.g., X-API-Key: <key>), the Authorization header (e.g., Authorization: ApiKey <key>), or sometimes as a query parameter (less secure). Reverse engineering involves finding where the client obtains or stores this key (is it hardcoded in client code? Stored in a config file? Entered by the user?). Keys grant broad access, and if compromised, are a major security risk.

Session Cookies: After a successful web-based login (often via username/password submitted to a specific login endpoint), the server responds with a Set-Cookie header containing a unique session ID. The browser automatically stores this cookie and sends it back in the Cookie header on all subsequent requests to the same domain. The server uses this session ID to look up the user's authenticated state. RE involves analyzing the login request/response, identifying the session cookie, and ensuring subsequent API requests (using tools like Postman or requests, which need explicit cookie handling) include it.

Token-Based Authentication (OAuth 2.0 / OpenID Connect, JWT): Very common for modern APIs, especially for third-party integrations or mobile apps.

Flow: Often involves complex redirect flows (OAuth). The client first obtains an **access token** (and potentially a **refresh token**) from an authorization server (often after user login/consent). The client then includes the access token in the Authorization: Bearer <token> header of requests to the resource server (the actual API).

JWT (JSON Web Tokens): Access tokens are frequently JWTs. A JWT is a structured string containing encoded JSON data (header, payload with user info and claims/permissions, signature). RE involves capturing these tokens, decoding the header and payload (which are usually just Base64 encoded, *not* encrypted) to see the included information (user ID, roles, expiration time exp, scope scp), and crucially, **validating the signature**. The signature ensures the token hasn't been tampered with. Attempting to modify the payload claims and use the altered token will fail if the server properly validates the signature against the correct public key or shared secret.

However, vulnerabilities can arise if the server accepts tokens signed with weak algorithms (alg: none), uses known weak secrets, or fails to validate the signature correctly.

Analysis Focus:

Identify the mechanism being used (API Key, Cookie, Bearer Token?). Analyze the flow for obtaining the credential (login request, OAuth redirects).

Examine the structure and content of tokens (decode JWTs).

Test authorization: Can a token for User A access User B's data (IDOR/BAC)? Can a token with limited scope access privileged endpoints? Can expired tokens still work? Can signature validation be bypassed?

Inferring Backend Details: Reading Between the Lines

While direct code analysis is out, careful observation of the API's behavior and structure can sometimes provide indirect clues about the underlying backend architecture or technologies, although these are inferences, not certainties.

API Structure & Naming: Does the API design suggest a large, monolithic backend handling all requests, or do distinct URL paths (/auth/, /users/, /products/, /orders/) hint at underlying **microservices**, each responsible for a specific domain? Are naming conventions consistent across endpoints?

Domain Names & Response Headers: Do API requests resolve to generic load balancer URLs, or do they hit specific subdomains or paths that might suggest particular cloud services (e.g., *.execute-api.<region>.amazonaws.com for AWS API Gateway/Lambda, *.azurewebsites.net for Azure App Service)? Do Server headers (nginx, Apache, Kestrel) or custom X-Powered-By headers give clues about the web server or framework used? Do headers reveal use of CDNs or specific cloud load balancers?

Performance Patterns: Are there noticeable "cold start" delays (first request to an endpoint is significantly slower than subsequent ones)? This *might* indicate the use of **serverless functions** (AWS Lambda, Azure Functions, Google Cloud Functions) that need time to initialize on the first invocation after a period of inactivity. Consistently fast responses might suggest continuously running server instances or containers.

Error Message Verbosity: Overly detailed error messages during failures (especially 5xx server errors) can sometimes leak internal function names, file paths, stack traces, database query fragments, or underlying library names, providing unintended glimpses into the backend technology stack. These are just hints, but they can sometimes help build a tentative mental model of the backend architecture, which might guide further security testing or analysis.

Security Analysis in the Cloud Context: Focusing on the Interface
Security testing of cloud-based systems shifts heavily towards analyzing the exposed **API interface** and potential **cloud platform misconfigurations**.

Standard API Vulnerabilities: The OWASP API Security Top 10 provides a good checklist. Testing focuses on:

Broken Object Level Authorization (BOLA) / Insecure Direct Object Reference (IDOR): The #1 API vulnerability. Can User A access/modify User B's data by manipulating IDs in the URL path or request body? Test rigorously by changing IDs (/users/123 to /users/456).

Broken Authentication: Weak login processes, insecure token handling (e.g., JWTs with weak secrets or alg: none), session management flaws.

Broken Function Level Authorization: Can a low-privileged user access API endpoints intended only for administrators by directly calling the endpoint URL?

Improper Assets Management / Mass Assignment: Can attackers modify sensitive object properties (like isAdmin=true) by simply including them in JSON request bodies, even if the UI doesn't expose them?

Security Misconfiguration: Incorrect CORS policies, sensitive information in HTTP headers, verbose error messages leaking internal details.

Injection Flaws (SQLi, NoSQLi, Command Inj.): Send crafted payloads within API parameters or JSON fields and look for error messages or behavioral changes suggesting successful injection. Harder to confirm without code access.

Lack of Resources & Rate Limiting: Can APIs be overwhelmed by excessive requests (DoS)? Is sensitive data like password reset tokens susceptible to brute-forcing?

API Fuzzing: Use automated tools (like Burp Intruder, ZAP Fuzzer, custom scripts, dedicated API fuzzers like FFUF) to send large volumes of unexpected, malformed, boundary-value, or type-confused data to API parameters and headers. Monitor responses for crashes (5xx errors), unexpected success codes (2xx), revealing error messages, or potential security bypasses.

Cloud Configuration Review: Security extends beyond the API code itself to the underlying cloud infrastructure configuration. While direct RE isn't usually possible, analysis might involve searching for related misconfigurations using other means:

Are cloud storage buckets (like AWS S3) accidentally configured for public read/write access, exposing sensitive data?

Are database instances or management interfaces exposed directly to the internet with weak credentials?

Are serverless function permissions overly broad?

Are API Gateway authentication/authorization settings correctly implemented?

Checking for these often involves using specialized cloud security posture management (CSPM) tools or OSINT techniques, blending traditional RE with cloud infrastructure security knowledge.

Leveraging Leaked Information and Client-Side Clues

While direct backend access is unavailable, sometimes information *about* the backend leaks through other channels:

Client-Side Code Analysis: Thoroughly analyze the client application's code (JavaScript, mobile app binary). Developers sometimes leave behind comments, old/internal API endpoint URLs, hardcoded (though they shouldn't!) internal keys or credentials, or logic that hints at backend data structures or assumptions. Decompiled mobile apps might reveal clues about the libraries used for backend communication or data serialization.

Public Repositories / OSINT: Search platforms like GitHub, GitLab, or public Pastebin dumps for the company name, product name, or known developer aliases. You might find accidentally committed source code snippets, configuration files, deployment scripts, or Infrastructure-as-Code (IaC) templates (Terraform, CloudFormation, ARM templates). Analyzing these IaC templates can provide detailed insights into the cloud services used, network configurations, security group rules, and overall backend architecture setup. This moves towards infrastructure analysis but is often triggered by findings during client-side RE.

Conclusion: The Art of Interface Exploration

Reverse engineering cloud-based systems represents a distinct discipline within the broader RE field. With the core logic hidden behind the impenetrable walls of cloud provider infrastructure, the focus shifts decisively from analyzing executable code to meticulously exploring and analyzing the **API interfaces** exposed to the client. It's a process dominated by **black-box interaction analysis**, relying heavily on network monitoring tools (proxies, sniffers) to observe legitimate communication and API testing tools (Postman, curl, scripts) to actively probe and experiment with the API's behavior. Mastering authentication and authorization flows is critical. While direct architectural insights are limited, inferences can sometimes be drawn from API structure, naming, performance, and leaked information. Security analysis concentrates on common API vulnerabilities detectable through input/output testing and understanding potential cloud misconfigurations. Success in this domain demands strong foundations in networking protocols (especially HTTP/S), API design principles, authentication mechanisms (OAuth, JWT), security testing methodologies, and increasingly, familiarity with cloud platform architectures and security models. It's a different kind of puzzle, focused less on deciphering algorithms within assembly and more on understanding the intricate rules of communication and access control governing the interaction between the visible client and the hidden cloud backend.